Winning Behavior:

What the Smartest, Most Successful Companies Do Differently

Terry R. Bacon
and
David G. Pugh

AMACOM
American Management Association

New York • Atlanta • Brussels • Chicago • Mexico City • San Francisco
Shanghai • Tokyo • Toronto • Washington, D.C.

This publication is designed to provide accurate and authoritative information in regard to the subject matter covered. It is sold with the understanding that the publisher is not engaged in rendering legal, accounting, or other professional service. If legal advice or other expert assistance is required, the services of a competent professional person should be sought.

Library of Congress Cataloging-in-Publication Data

Bacon, Terry R.
   Winning behavior : what the smartest, most successful companies do differently / Terry R. Bacon and David G. Pugh.
      p. cm.
Includes index.
ISBN 0-8144-7163-3
   1. Organizational behavior. 2. Organizational effectiveness. I. Pugh, David G. (David George), 1944- II. Title.

   HD58.7.B3423 2003
   658—dc21   2003009902

Printing number

10   9   8   7   6   5   4   3   2   1

Contents

Preface

In a tough market, how do you win more than your share of business? How do you outperform competitors who are as capable as you are and who sell essentially the same products you do, the same way you do, to the same set of customers? How do you differentiate your company and products when your rivals copy your innovations nearly as fast as you can innovate? How, in the toughest global market the world has ever seen, do you build and sustain enough distinctive value to avoid brutal price competition?

These are the questions our clients have been asking us. For the past twenty-five years, we have helped companies develop competitive strategies, improve their business development systems and skills, and create winning proposals and presentations. During that period, we've seen the rise of the global village Marshall McLuhan predicted in 1967, and for many of our clients it has looked like something out of a Stephen King novel. The globalization of markets, the rise of foreign competition, the rapid spread of technology, and the growth of the Internet have made it increasingly tough to compete, especially if you sell higher-priced, value-added products and services. Unless you can offer something so unique that no one else can copy it, you face a barrage of competitors who also have state-of-the-art offerings and customers who demand more and negotiate harder because *everyone* wants their business.

Customers today have a bewildering array of choices. If you can't differentiate yourself in their eyes, you are condemned to market purgatory, where your products are essentially commodities and where lowest price rules. How long can you stay there and remain viable as a business enterprise? You lower your prices to remain competitive, which reduces your margins. Then you have to cut your R&D budget, trim your staff, hammer your suppliers, and reduce quality. At some point, it all falls apart, as it has for Packard Bell, Montgomery Ward, Commodore, Digital Equipment Corporation, Eastern Airlines, TWA, Grand Union Supermarkets, Sperry-Rand, Kmart, and a host of other once-proud companies that have either been absorbed by stronger rivals or have vanished.

Throughout the business world today, barriers are falling and walls are becoming more permeable. The boundaryless organization Jack Welch envisioned at GE has become the paradigm of the new age. Information, technology, knowledge, and people are flowing among companies and across boundaries so rapidly that it is next to impossible to maintain a technological or service edge long enough to sustain real competitive advantage. So it's become more difficult for companies to differentiate themselves from their rivals—at least with traditional forms of differentiation. Nonetheless, some companies consistently outperform their competitors, and we sought to understand why. Certainly, they have excellent business models. They offer state-of-the-art products and excellent services—but so do their less-successful rivals. The primary difference, we discovered, was not that the most successful firms were outperforming their rivals—they were *outbehaving* them.

This is a book about winning more business through behavioral differentiation. We believe it represents an enormous untapped opportunity for many organizations and professionals. Today, the question customers usually ask isn't, *Who can do the work?* They have no trouble finding many qualified providers. The question is, *Whom do we want to work with?* Business development in the new age is increasingly a chemistry test, and the chemistry between the buyer and the seller is shaped by the seller's behaviors. We believe that behavioral differentiation (BD)* is emerging as the final frontier in competitive strategy. It is the one domain of differentiation where you can still achieve and sustain significant gains. To be sure, it's not a substitute for product quality, price competitiveness, or customer satisfaction. Among excellent companies today, these are requisites. Without

---

*"Behavioral differentiation" is the right expression for the concept we are describing in this book, but it is a mouthful, so we will use the acronym "BD" throughout the book to represent this expression as well as the variation "behavioral differentiators."

them, you will not even be in the game. But when you and your rivals all have met these criteria, behavioral differentiation can turn the tide in your favor. It can make the difference when your customers are unable to tell you and your competitors apart on technical capability, product quality, price, and other traditional differentiators.

The masters of BD consistently *outbehave* their rivals. To illustrate this point, we will discuss the behavioral differentiators of such organizations as Nordstrom, Marshall Field's, Enterprise Rent-A-Car, Wal-Mart, Southwest Airlines, EMC, Ritz-Carlton, Harley-Davidson, Hall Kinion, Heidrick & Struggles, Volvo, and Men's Wearhouse. These organizations excel, year after year, because they understand BD and they have the right *leadership, culture,* and *processes* to create and sustain clear behavioral differentiators.

Remarkably, they excel even though their competitors know what they are doing! By any measure, Wal-Mart has been far more successful than Kmart, for instance, although Wal-Mart's business model and management practices are well known. Why hasn't Kmart been able to match Wal-Mart's success? One reason is that Wal-Mart outbehaves Kmart. Likewise, Enterprise Rent-A-Car surpassed its much more established rivals and became number one—largely because it created a strong behavioral differentiator that Hertz, Avis, National, Dollar, Alamo, and Budget are aware of but have not copied. Southwest Airlines has been one of *Fortune* magazine's most admired companies year after year—and has been profitable when its major rivals were losing money. Why? Because they outbehaved their rivals in ways the other airlines were unwilling or unable to replicate. One of the key lessons you will learn about BD is that it is difficult to imitate. Knowing what to do is not the same as doing it.

You will also discover how BD can work for you or against you. *Positive* behavioral differentiators occur when you exceed your customers' behavioral expectations. Like a magnet, they attract customers to you. If you are an acceptable choice in other ways, these customers will *prefer* to work with you, and you will win more business. Furthermore, when you behaviorally differentiate yourself with customers, you raise the bar on your competitors, often without their being aware of it. Conversely, *negative* behavioral differentiators repel customers—they drive a wedge between you and them and can even cause them to actively oppose you. There is no faster way to lose business than to alienate your customers—yet these negative behavioral differentiators are very common.

To help us understand BD, we studied a number of companies that use it successfully. We also conducted research on how consumers viewed behavioral differences among lawyers, physicians, nurses, salespeople, waiters/waitresses, managers, and religious leaders. Our hypothesis was that behavioral differentiation applied to professions as well as to companies, and the research confirmed it. The results will surprise you—but they will also look familiar. If you or others in your organization behave in the ways described, you'll understand why you are winning or losing more business than you should.

As we began this study, we asked ourselves whether positive BD was synonymous with excellent customer service. A lot has been written about customer service, and we felt that writing more about that subject would not be valuable. We concluded that good customer service *can* be a behavioral differentiator, but it often isn't. If your customer service practices are no different from your competitors' customer service practices, then you aren't differentiated at all. Besides, BD goes well beyond customer service. It encompasses your advertising and packaging, your policies toward customers, your systems for interacting with customers, your business development practices, the attitudes and behaviors of your leaders, and the interpersonal skills of all your people who interact with customers. To sustain behavioral differentiation, you must weave it into the fabric of your organization. It starts with the leadership of your company, is driven by the culture and values of your organization, is sustained by the day-to-day processes for getting work done, and reflects both your organization's skills and the skills of your people. Mostly, it must be a genuine expression of your values and mission as an enterprise.

In today's hypercompetitive markets, you must exploit every potential source of differentiation—including how you and your people behave toward your customers. To make this book most useful, we have focused on *practical* steps you can take to understand your customers' behavioral expectations and to develop and enact the kinds of behaviors that will positively differentiate you from your competitors. We've also included numerous case studies and examples of BD—both positive and negative. Finally, we've included a number of suggestions for how you can identify your potential behavioral differentiators and how you can implement those differentiators throughout your organization.

What are the implications for your business? If BD improved your business by only 10 percent, what impact would it have on your top and bottom lines? Alternatively, what would be the impact if your competitors increased their behavioral differentiation and you did nothing? The world has become a more competitive place. The stakes are getting higher. The race will not be won by the swiftest or the strongest. It will be won by the smartest, and being smart in business today means knowing how your behavior, across the spectrum of your people and in every interaction with your customers, can differentiate you from your competitors and help you capture more than your fair share of the business.

Acknowledgments

We would like to thank the numerous people who have contributed to our research and to this book. A project of this magnitude cannot be undertaken without the considerable assistance, cooperation, and goodwill of many people. First, we would like to thank the many professionals in Lore International Institute who contributed ideas, assisted in our research, or otherwise supported us: Allison Andersen, Andrea Seid, Anna Pool, Barb Singer, Brian Schoff, Brooke Lawson, Bruce Spining, Chesney Frazier, Dan Osby, Darnell Place-Wise, DeNeil Peterson, Don Scott, Greg Elkins, Howard Armstrong, Jennifer Vosper, Joey Maceyak, Kathy Uroda, Lat Epps, Linda Simmons, Mark Arnold, Martin Moller, Nancy Atwood, Phyllis Lea, Sean Darnall, Sharon Hubbs, Terryl Leroux, Trish Gyland, Val Evensen, Vickie Petren, and Wendy Ludgewait.

We offer special thanks to the following people:

- ⚑ Jeremy Silman, a chess master whose books taught us a lot about chess—and even more about business and behavioral differentiation. He was gracious enough to give us permission to quote liberally from his books.
- ⚑ Meredith Ashby and Stephen Miles of Heidrick & Struggles (H&S). They provided extraordinary assistance to us by interviewing the following H&S consultants, whom we would also like to thank for their insights and information: Andy Talkington, Bernard Zen Ruffinen, Bonnie Gwin, Caroline Ballantine, Daan de Roos, Denise Studi, Detlef Pries, Dominique Einhorn, Emeric Lepoutre, Gerry Roche, Ignacio Perez, John Gardner,

Joie Gregor, Kyung Yoon, Lee Hanson, Lisa Maibach, Michael Flagg, Nuno Vasconcellos, Thord Thorstensson, Wes Richards, Wolfgang Walter, and Piers Marmion.

▲ Laurie Voss and Pamela Wise. These researchers from the Lore Research Institute did much of the legwork for us. They researched the companies we profile in this book and conducted many of the interviews. They also read the draft and offered numerous suggestions. We could not have completed the project without their invaluable help.

▲ Karen Spear, who read much of the manuscript and offered countless suggestions that have improved the quality and completeness of the book. She is a very perceptive reader, thought partner, and critic.

Of course, no book like this is possible without the cooperation and support of the people in the companies we profiled and other business people who contributed ideas and inspiration. We are profoundly grateful that they agreed to speak to us and share so much about what they do and how they do it. We would especially like to thank the following people who consented to interviews and gave of their time to help us with this book:

▲ From Ritz-Carlton: Patrick Mene, Leonardo Inghelleri, Carter Donovan, Mario Dones, and Robert George.

▲ From EMC: Joseph Walton, Leo Colborne, Walter Rietz, Al Lanzetta, Al Coarusso, Cynthia Curtis, and Don Potter.

▲ From Volvo: Hans-Olov Olsson, Charlotta Källbäck, Nerissa Morris Hampton, and Sven Eckerstein.

▲ From Men's Wearhouse: George Zimmer, Charles Bresler, Dean Sperranza, and Francesca Sterling.

▲ From Southwest Airlines: Herb Kelleher, Jim Parker, Colleen Barrett, Donna Conover, Ginger Hardage, Beverly K. Carmichael, and Joyce Rogge.

▲ From Hall Kinion: Brenda Rhodes, Jeffrey Neal, Rita Hazell, Von Goesling, Catie Fitzgerald, and Jeff Glickman. Also, Craig Silverman, formerly of Hall Kinion.

Special thanks as well to Tom Farmer and Shane Atchison of ZAAZ, Inc. They gave us permission to reprint their PowerPoint complaint to a hotel chain that made history on the Internet. We would also like to thank Michael Abrashoff, a former Navy ship captain whose remarkable story is chronicled in Chapter 6; Paul Krauss, a retired director of a worldwide management consulting firm who offered some keen insights into behavioral differentiation; Lynette Demarest, formerly of GE, who provided insight on GE's Work-Out process; Bill Hardin of Technip, who gave us a great story about interpersonal BD; Louise Powers Ackley, who told us her personal story of buying a Volvo; Joanne Kincer of Encompass, who told us numerous stories of BD and also reviewed portions of the draft; Don Traywick and Deke Lincoln of BE&K, who shared their experiences with BD; and John Tarpey and Bob Moss of Centex Construction Company, both of whom told us of innovative ways to behaviorally differentiate.

A number of Lore professionals were especially helpful in producing this book. Tom Fuhrmark created much of the artwork. He is an outstanding graphic artist and a fine softball coach. Our copyeditor was Marci Braddock. With the *Chicago Manual of Style* in one hand and a red pen in the other, she helped us follow the rules and offered many suggestions that improved the readability of the text. Donna Williams did much of the work to secure permissions, track down quotations, and proofread the drafts. She also did much of the research for Chapter 6. Thanks to all of them for their invaluable assistance.

We also want to express our loving thanks to Karen and Marcy, as well as our children and our families. They have reminded us through the years what different and better are all about. Finally, we would like to thank our acquisitions editor, Ellen Kadin, of AMACOM Books. Ellen has been extraordinarily supportive throughout our project and has been helpful to us in many ways. She's also a New York Mets fan, which speaks well of her.

This book was completed in a compartment on the train to Paris. The lush French countryside outside the window reminded us that some long journeys are worth taking. Yet as pleasant as any journey may be, it's also a blessing when it ends.

TERRY R. BACON
DAVID G. PUGH

THE FINAL FRONTIER

When you survive by reinventing yourself every other day, it's tough to differentiate on a product difference alone.
—Jack Trout, *Differentiate or Die: Survival in Our Era of Killer Competition*

It is very important to ALWAYS expect the best move from your opponent!
—Jeremy Silman, *The Complete Book of Chess Strategy*

Ralph Waldo Emerson wrote that if you can write a better book, preach a better sermon, or build a better mousetrap, though you build your house in the woods, the world will make a beaten path to your door. He wrote that in the early nineteenth century, an era of optimism, progressiveness, and boundless possibility fueled by a vast and largely uncharted frontier. It's not that simple anymore. Differentiating yourself through superior products and services confers only a fleeting advantage in the hypercompetitive, global markets we now face. Following us into the twenty-first century is a tidal wave of concepts, tools, practices, and consultants that drives companies inadvertently but relentlessly toward a crushing sameness. Total quality management (TQM), statistical process control, process mapping, continuous process improvement, benchmarking, best practices, six sigma, balanced scorecard, supply chain management, learning organizations—these are the magic wands waved by W. Edwards Deming; Joseph Juran; Philip Crosby; Peter Drucker, Peter Senge; a host of management consulting firms; and Jack Welch (arguably the finest CEO in the latter half of the twentieth century), who proclaimed in so many words that copying others' best practices is in fact *good*.

In writing about Welch and General Electric, author Robert Slater said, "The ultimate competitive advantage lies in an organization's ability to learn and to rapidly transform that learning into action."[1] More and more, that learning is not simply research, problem solving, and innovating within your own company but is also learning and adopting the best practices, product features, and service innovations of your competitors. In the mid-1990s, benchmarking became a widespread tool for studying your competitors' best practices (as well as best practices in other industries) and adapting their practices to improve your operational effectiveness and margins. Advocates of benchmarking argue that it is smart business—and they're right. If your competitors are working smarter than you are and you can re-create their innovations, you'd be a fool not to. In the course of his remarkable career, Jack Welch was the leading slayer of the "not invented here" syndrome. He said it didn't matter where it was invented; if it's good, if it will help improve GE's business, we will adopt it. It's hard to argue with success, and Welch's Herculean drive to improve quality, operational efficiency, and leadership at GE grew the market cap of that corporation enormously through his tenure and left in its wake legions of delighted investors and envious competitors.

According to a 1995 American Productivity & Quality Center study of corporations using benchmarking, "More than 30 organizations reported an average $76 million first-year payback from their most successful benchmarking project. Among the most experienced benchmarkers, the average payback soared to $189 million."[2] Those are compelling reasons to use benchmarking. In the end, however, the batteries of consultants, process control managers, and TQM experts will lead industries and the companies within them toward a position of near-total entropy in their markets, where there are few distinguishing features between competitors or their products. In his book, *Differentiate or Die,* marketing guru Jack Trout identifies the central issue facing any company today that tries to differentiate itself from its competitors by introducing new and innovative products or services: "The number one competitive response is usually me-tooism. Competing products are becoming more and more alike. Technology enables competitors to tear apart, reverse engineer, and knock off product features even before you have the chance to establish your uniqueness."[3] Service companies, introducing innovative programs for customers, find that competitors have matched those innovations almost before the ink is dry on their brochures. E-business innovators learn that whatever creative business model they put on the Web today will appear in a dozen other sites tomorrow.

It's not that innovation is dead—quite the contrary. In 1999 the U.S. Patent Office received over 270,000 patent applications and granted more than 150,000 of them. Innovation is increasingly crucial—but it won't be enough. Innovations have an increasingly shorter half-life, even with patent protection, as Guy Kawasaki observed in *Harvard Business Review:* "Unless you're a biotech or medical-device company, it's hard to support [the claim that your patents make your business defensible]. If an idea's worth copying, there's a will and a way to get around the patent. File all the patents you like, but investors believe that what makes a company defensible is the ability to out-implement, not out-litigate."[4] At best, product differentiation offers a momentary advantage, which may be enough to capture more market share, charge premium prices, or build an established base of your products (which may increase switching costs for customers). But these advantages are increasingly tenuous and ephemeral, largely because there is a glut of capacity in nearly every industry, and buyers have become less loyal. Perhaps no words better describe today's buyers than *free* and *fickle*. They have more freedom because the world of competitors is beating a path to their door (rather than the reverse), and they have considerably more options than they've had in previous decades. As Jack Trout observes, there were 140 motor vehicle models available in the early 1970s; there are 260 today. He calls it "the tyranny of choice."[5]

Our central theme at this point is that numerous market forces have made it increasingly difficult for companies to create and sustain the traditional sources of differentiation in their products and services. This is true in part because globalization has heightened competition in virtually every industry and market. It's also true because the relentless drive among companies to improve product quality and operating efficiency has tended to level the playing field. At the same time, the Internet has vastly increased the amount of information buyers have and greatly increased their choices, giving buyers a new-found freedom that could scarcely have been imagined only a few years ago. Terry's new watch is an example. When his old watch quit, he went to a local jewelry store to look for a replacement. On display were a dozen men's watches. The salesman drove hard for a buying decision, but Terry was dissatisfied with the choices, so he went to the Internet site LuxurySquare.com, where he could choose from over 3,000 men's watches from numerous manufacturers. He searched for the watch that had exactly the features and design he wanted, and he purchased one for nearly $200 below the manufacturer's listed retail price, which made the local jeweler a victim of the tyranny of choice available to today's e-buyers.

A firm differentiates itself from its competitors when it provides something unique that is valuable to buyers beyond simply offering low price. Differentiation allows the firm to command a premium price, to sell more of its product at a given price, or to gain equivalent benefits such as greater buyer loyalty during cyclical or seasonal downturns.

—Michael Porter, *Competitive Advantage:*
Creating and Sustaining Superior Performance

Internet auctions are having a similar effect—and they are taking their toll on margins, too. One of the earliest B2B innovators was FreeMarkets Online. They identify industrial products and materials that their clients need to buy in large quantities, create exact specifications for those products, find numerous potential suppliers, and then host online auctions where competing bidders bid in real time for the contract. FreeMarkets claims it has created one of the world's most efficient markets; online bidders, watching their margins shrink to new lows, would have to agree. The problem with FreeMarkets, from the seller's perspective, is that it virtually eliminates the competitive advantages gained by product innovation, value-added differentiation, relationship marketing, customer service, and consultative selling. Despite Theodore Levitt's proclamation that "there is no such thing as a commodity,"[6] online B2B auctions are highly effective at commoditizing whatever is being bought and sold. For airlines and hotels that would lose revenue if empty seats and beds aren't filled, Priceline.com's ticket auctions offer a way to capture what would otherwise be lost revenue. But for manufacturers whose margins are already paper-thin, online auctions pose a Darwinian threat—and only the leanest and most efficient will survive.

Harley-Davidson's Journey

Even in less-cutthroat arenas, the crushing sameness we spoke of earlier is growing. Harley-Davidson's journey and the current competitive landscape for heavy cruisers is an example. In the early 1960s, Harley-Davidson had an outlaw image and produced such poor-quality motorcycles that it was not unusual to see cardboard under the kickstands of the display bikes so the oil leaking from the engines wouldn't foul the showroom floor. Only retro geeks and dedicated gearheads who knew how to take apart the bikes and repair them were impressed with the Harley name. By the 1970s, the market was being flooded with Hondas, Kawasakis, Yamahas, and Suzukis, which, in typical Japanese fashion, offered more product features, higher quality, and an informed and more professional army of dealers. In the 1980s, a group of Harley officers bought the company from AMF and, facing bankruptcy for the second time in twenty years, embarked on a quality crusade. Some went to Japan and studied Japanese methods of manufacturing, quality control, and inventory management, and they later instituted much of what they learned in their own factories back home. Today, Harley-Davidson motorcycles meet the highest quality standards. There is virtually no difference in terms of product quality between a Harley, a Honda, and a BMW—no matter what a dealer might tell you.

The traditional and still-rich source of competitive differentiation for Harley-Davidson is the look and sound of their motorcycles. Harleys are known for their retro designs, pioneered by Willie G. Davidson, grandson of one of the company's founders, and for the deep, guttural roar of their pipes. The Harley look evokes a carefree, American nostalgia (see Figure 1-1). The bold curves, black leather, teardrop gas tanks, and miles of chrome lead some of the older owners to reminisce about bobby socks, bellhops, and drive-ins, while others yearn to recapture the rebellious spirit of Marlon Brando in *The Wild Ones.* Whether their idol is Elvis singing "Jailhouse Rock" or Steppenwolf booming "Born to be Wild," Harley owners thrive on an image that projects the irreverent part of themselves that they don't want to let go of.

Figure 1-1. A 1994 Harley Davidson FXSTS Softail Springer. Harley's rivals are working hard to copy this classic retro look. Photo courtesy of Brooke Lawson. Used with permission.

In contrast, Japanese motorcycles have always had a more modern, utilitarian look—cold and soulless—and they sound like dentists' drills. Until recently, when you saw a Harley on the road you could instantly distinguish it from its Japanese rivals. But Japanese and German manufacturers have caught on. The Yamaha V Star 1100 Classic, for example, has the classic Harley retro look. So does the Honda Shadow Sabre. Except for the brand names and logos on the gas tanks, the V Star Classic and Shadow Sabre could easily pass for a Harley Dyna FXD or a Road King Classic—at least to the casual observer. Twenty years ago, Harley executives copied Japanese methods to close the quality gap between their products and Japanese motorcycles. In time, Japanese and German manufacturers will try to copy everything that makes a Harley-Davidson motorcycle distinctive—and Harley's product differentiation will erode.

This endless cycle of innovation and imitation causes competitors to erase each others' competitive advantages virtually as fast as they can be created, and we see this cycle in every industry: automobiles, personal computers, broadband services, retail, fashion, cosmetics, banking and financial services, engineering and construction, and entertainment. Whatever you produce and however you strive to differentiate yourself from your competitors, you are subject to market forces that will inevitably propel you into a market stew where your ingredients are no different from your competitors' and where fickle buyers can pick and choose, seemingly at random.

Business has two central challenges: to create differentiated goods and services customers want, and to do that in such a way that revenue exceeds costs. We are going to focus on the former of these challenges. In the markets of today, filled with entropic forces that continually erode your differentiation, how do you find new ways to differentiate yourself? How do you answer the single most important question in marketing, "Why should customers choose us instead of our rivals?" Companies spend billions of dollars every year trying to answer this question. It is the fundamental question behind all business, and it's becoming increasingly difficult to answer because you and your competitors offer roughly the same things. When one company innovates, its rivals rapidly assimilate those innovations or create functional equivalents and level the playing field again.

Differentiating Yourself Through Behavior

One area of differentiation, however, is difficult to copy, even when competitors have benchmarked your company and learned your best practices. That area is behavior. Behavioral differentiation is difficult to copy because it requires more skill and will than many companies possess—even when they know what you're doing! As we will show in this book, there is a huge gap between knowing how to behave and behaving that way consistently. Most other areas of differentiation can be identified and then copied or matched, but BD is a tough act to follow. When all else is equal, it can make the difference between winning and losing customers and critical contracts. When there is little difference between what you can offer customers and what your competitors can offer them, you can still behave differently toward your customers and gain (or lose) crucial advantage. In the landscape of differentiation, behavior is the final frontier.

Behaviors stem from attitudes, which are, in turn, formed by many things, including friends, family, society, experience and learning. Attitudes can also be affected by what the company communicates to position itself favorably in the minds of its audiences. Attitudes drive the behaviors that lead to a purchase and the opportunity to work together to develop yet more value for one another. This is a relationship, and relationships are the most valuable of all intangibles.
—Ian Gordon, *Relationship Marketing*

BD has the same characteristics that other forms of competitive differentiation have:

▲ *The behaviors must be unique to you.* Your competitors either do not behave the same way or are not as skilled as you are at these behaviors, and customers perceive the difference.
▲ *The customer must value these behaviors.* Your differentiated behaviors must somehow enhance the customer's experience with you.
▲ *The behaviors must reflect your value proposition.* They should be related to what you are selling or otherwise be emblematic of the customer's experience of you and your products or services.

Differentiating behaviors can be simple gestures reflecting good customer service (such as Wal-Mart's practice of having an employee greet all customers as they enter a store) or they can be bolder and more dramatic (as when the CEO of a bidding company demonstrates the company's commitment to a customer and desire to win the contract by appearing at their bid presentation to the customer). Sometimes you win by making a small impression at the right time. Other times you win through an accumulation of differentiating behaviors that occur over a longer period. Remarkably, even when your behavioral practices are well known, a number of your competitors will fail to learn the lesson. Kmart and Montgomery Ward have been examples. In general, neither retailer's frontline employees have been as customer-oriented, friendly, and helpful as those at Wal-Mart. Although they are surely aware of Wal-Mart's customer greeters and the training Wal-Mart employees receive on how to treat customers, neither Kmart nor Ward (which has recently closed its doors forever) learned from Wal-Mart's customer service practices. In August 2000, Kmart's CEO announced three strategic initiatives designed to improve Kmart's financial performance and competitive position, including creating "a customer-centric culture to ensure that the day-to-day activities in every Kmart department are inherently linked to better satisfying and serving Kmart customers."[7] This is certainly the right direction because the fundamental malaise at Kmart is behavioral, but it remains to be seen whether Kmart's executives can truly change the frontline behaviors of every Kmart employee who comes in contact with customers. They've known for years what Wal-Mart does but so far have failed to emulate Wal-Mart–like behaviors.

The opportunity for BD occurs during every interaction with customers—through every stage in the selling and buying process. In this, it is like parenting. You are a parent during every moment with your children. There are no time-outs. Your behavior, good or bad, defines you as a person and a parent. Whether you like it or not, you are a role model for your children 24 hours a day, 7 days a week. Likewise with your customers, your behavior is always on display and is always an indicator of what it will be like to work with you. Behavior is a powerful differentiator because it is—simultaneously—immediate, personal, real, and emblematic. It is real because customers experience it real time, unlike your guarantees and claims, which are promises of future benefit and are therefore "unreal" at the time they are made. Your behavior is emblematic because it represents what they will sooner or later receive (or fail to receive) from your products and services. You are on stage all the time with your customers. Like it or not, you are always either showing them that there is no difference between you and your rivals or you are behaving in ways that positively (or negatively) differentiate you from the other companies that want their business. Here are some cases where companies failed at BD:

▲ The bidder was one of the world's largest engineering and construction firms. The brand and worldwide scope were well established. The customer had no doubt that they could do the work. After they were placed on the shortlist, the bidder was asked to have their proposed project team present their offer. However, they failed to bring their team together until the very last moment, and their presentation appeared disjointed and uncoordinated.

Although this bidder had gone into the presentations ranked number one, they lost the contract because, as the customer said during the debriefing, "We weren't confident that your team could work together effectively."
Lesson: If you are proposing a team to a customer, ensure that your team looks and behaves like a team.

⋏ The bidder was an advertising agency that claimed to be expert in project management, but their presentation to the potential client ran 20 minutes over the schedule and, as a result, the client's CEO missed an important telephone call.
Lesson: Walk your talk. If you claim to be expert in something, then demonstrate it in every interaction with your clients.

⋏ The supplier was one of the world's most well-known consumer camera manufacturers with a strong, universally recognizable brand. However, it shipped its cameras without double boxing, and when a consumer received his shipment, the camera was broken right out of the box. Initially, the consumer was not aware of the malfunction because the instructions sent with the camera were confusing and poorly written. When the consumer later sent the camera in for repair, he was required to submit the original warranty card, which was not supposed to be copied. When the camera was returned, the original warranty card was not returned. As a result of this sequence of problems, the consumer submitted a lengthy complaint to an Internet site devoted to dissing this manufacturer, and warned other potential buyers of this product to avoid it.
Lesson: The packaging, delivery, and servicing of your products is a form of behavior. If your packaging and after-sales service show a lack of care, consumers will assume that all you really care about is moving inventory, and you will lose their trust and confidence.

⋏ The bidder was a large government agency that is perceived to be arrogant and self-focused. They claimed that they had changed and were now very customer-focused. However, they began all their customer presentations with 30 minutes of slides and a videotape on their heritage going back to George Washington.
Lesson: If you claim to be customer-focused, then behave like it and start your presentations with the customer's goals, key issues, and needs—not with your history, the location of your offices, or your extensive capabilities.

In today's highly competitive marketplaces, business development is largely a chemistry test. By the time customers are seriously considering you, they know you can do the work. That's rarely the issue anymore. The question for them isn't, "Who can do the work?" The question is, "Whom do we want to work with?" You make the difference (or fail to) in the myriad of interactions, choices, and behaviors you exhibit when you are pursuing business development opportunities or interacting with customers. When there is a glut of capability in the marketplace, capability becomes commodity, and competition becomes communication—and there is no more real, immediate, or believable form of communication than your behavior. It can make all the difference.

> Relationships are important and will become more important, for, in the end, when all means of production is fully automated, and when the knowledge of man is in databases, this is all there will be. Value will be created by relationships. People will exist in a world of networks.
>
> —Ian Gordon, *Relationship Marketing*

Challenges for Readers

1. TQM, statistical process control, process mapping, continuous process improvement, benchmarking, best practices, six sigma, balanced scorecard, supply chain management—has your company used any of these methods to achieve greater efficiency and productivity? If so, have these improvements given you a competitive advantage? Or have you found that your competitors have done the same and that you are just managing to stay even with them? How much more operational improvement is possible for your company?
2. How competitive are the players in your industry? Are you seeing the "endless cycle of innovation and imitation" that we described in this chapter? How long can you or any other competitor in your industry sustain an advantage based on product innovation?
3. Despite the dot.com collapse in 2000, e-commerce remains a formidable "new kid on the block" for many industries. What impact has the Internet had on your business? What kinds of new choices do your customers have now? And what newer choices are they likely to have in the future as e-commerce continues to evolve?
4. Why should customers choose you instead of your rivals? Do an honest appraisal of the advantages and benefits that you offer but that your competitors don't or can't. How lasting are any advantages you have?
5. As we noted in this chapter, there are no time-outs with behavior. Your behavior toward customers, especially when you are trying to sell them something, communicates what it will be like to work with you. Think

about everyone in your company who interacts with your customers. What message does their behavior send?

Endnotes

1. Robert Slater, *The GE Way Fieldbook* (New York: McGraw-Hill, 2000), p. 93.
2. American Productivity & Quality Center, "Benchmarking: Leveraging Best-Practice Strategies," apqc.org.
3. Jack Trout, with Steve Rivkin, *Differentiate or Die: Survival in Our Era of Killer Competition* (New York: John Wiley & Sons, 2000), p. 20.
4. Guy Kawasaki, "The Top Ten Lies of Entrepreneurs," *Harvard Business Review,* January 2001, p. 23.
5. Jack Trout, with Steve Rivkin, *Differentiate or Die: Survival in Our Era of Killer Competition* (New York: John Wiley & Sons, 2000), p. 1.
6. Theodore Levitt, *The Marketing Imagination,* New, Expanded Edition (New York: The Free Press, 1986), p. 72.
7. Kmart Press Release, August 10, 2000. Since we initially wrote this chapter, Kmart has declared bankruptcy and is reorganizing under new leadership.

2

WE WILL ASSIMILATE YOU

While similarities abound, the differences are crucial.
—Theodore Levitt, *The Marketing Imagination*

Quality is a given these days, not a difference. Knowing and loving your customer is a given, not a difference.
—Jack Trout, *Differentiate or Die: Survival in Our Era of Killer Competition*

To successfully penetrate into the mysteries of the chess board you have to be aware of the magic word of chess: IMBAL-ANCE. An imbalance in chess denotes any difference in the two respective positions.
—Jeremy Silman, *How to Reassess Your Chess*

In Star Trek: The Next Generation, humankind is threatened by the Borg, a soulless and invincible enemy whose threat conveys a chilling finality: "We will assimilate you." The Borg is a race of indistinguishable and inter-changeable bionic beings. Partly flesh and partly machine, they are the grim consequence of their absorption into the collective. The Borg is the ultimate architect of destruction in the *Next Generation* cosmos. As the Federation prepares to fight them, the Borg warns that "resistance is futile." In the psy-chological landscape of *Star Trek: The Next Generation,* the Borg represents our subconscious fear that there may be nothing unique about us after all, that our presence is immaterial because we are like everyone else. Furthermore, the forces pushing us toward this numbing similarity are relentless.

The Entropic Action of Markets

The Borg assimilates whole civilizations and planets in their insatiable drive to conquer all intelligent life in the universe—in essence, to commoditize all intelligent beings by making them uniform. In this, the Borg is the science fiction equivalent of entropy, which is the degree of disorder or uncertainty in a system. Entropy is derived from the Second Law of Thermodynamics, which states that although the amount or *quantity* of energy in the universe is conserved, it may lose *quality*. As James Gleick explains in his landmark book on chaos, entropy is "the inexorable tendency of the universe, and any isolated system in it, to slide toward a state of increasing disorder."[1] The natural state of matter and energy in the universe is uniformity or maximum entropy. If you bring a hot cup of coffee into a cold room, for instance, over time the heat of the coffee will dissipate into the room. The coffee becomes colder and the room slightly warmer as heat of the coffee dissipates into the colder air of the room. Eventually, the coffee and the room reach a uniform temperature. Where previously there was order (in the difference of temperature between the hot coffee and the cold room), there is now disorder or uniformity, because there are no differences in temperature. According to Jeremy Campbell, "Chaos is the easiest, most predictable, most probable state, and it lasts indefinitely. Order is improbable and hard to create. Time is its enemy, because entropy tends to increase with time."[2]

It should be clear that markets are inherently entropic. Over time, market forces tend to make companies and their products more uniform. There is a dissipation of difference as competing companies learn of and assimilate their competitors' advantages—incorporating and absorbing not only each others' product features, service strategies, distribution methods, and advertising practices, but also each other's ideas, best practices, learnings, and people. In a perfectly orderly market—with zero entropy—the differences between competing firms would be perfectly evident to everyone. Customers would have the maximum amount of information about their choices and could see clearly the differences between firms. Because differentiation would be maximized, customers would always make well-informed decisions. There would be no subtlety in the system, and selling would be reduced to ensuring that customers have the information they need to discern the differences between competing firms and their products. What makes this perfectly orderly market impossible are rampant assimilation and noise—another form of entropy (see Figure 2-1).

Noise enters the market in several ways. First, for obvious reasons, companies are not content to allow their competitors' product advantages to remain. When one company gains a technical advantage, others try to copy it.

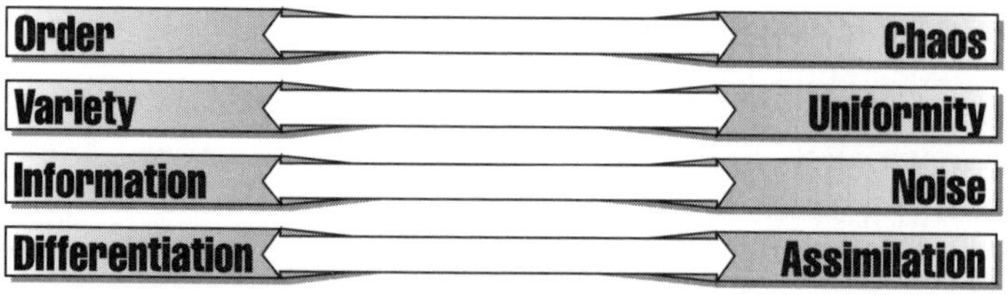

Order	⟨⟩	Chaos
Variety	⟨⟩	Uniformity
Information	⟨⟩	Noise
Differentiation	⟨⟩	Assimilation

Figure 2-1. Market Entropy. Markets are inherently entropic. Over time, market forces assimilate the differences between companies and their products, reducing differentiation and increasing noise, which makes it more difficult for customers to distinguish between the choices available to them.

The feature race in automobiles, home appliances, airplanes, banking services, and electronic components such as televisions and VCRs is an example. Virtually as fast as one company can introduce a new feature, its rivals copy it, and vice versa. This innovation/imitation cycle blurs the distinction between competing products and makes it more difficult for customers to differentiate one product from the next. The result is noise. Second, companies seek to eliminate their rivals' advantages in the language they use to communicate with the market. The phrases "doctor recommended," "scientifically proven," "absolutely guaranteed," "the finest available," "unmatched quality," and the like proliferate through advertising, brochures, labels, and slogans to the point where the distinctions between products are lost in the cacophony of me-tooism that marketers are reduced to because no unused words remain. When their language is depleted from overuse, marketers are confined to slogans, gimmicks, and promises that have been made a thousand times before in the same or similar ways. The result is noise.

Ironically, customers have *less* discernible choice—not more—even though there are more products on the market, because in today's highly entropic markets it is increasingly difficult to tell the competitors apart. For a while, the PalmPilot was the only game in town if you wanted a handheld electronic organizer and computer. Today, it's difficult to tell the Palm™ handhelds from their many rivals. Are Palm's products any better than the Compaq iPAQ Pocket PCs, the Toshiba Pocket PCs, or the VTech Helio Handheld PDAs? Not by outward appearances, and they're offered through the same channels and at about the same price. On the surface, it appears that buyers of handheld computers have more choices today, but where there are no discernible differences between products, there is no choice. It's like choosing between identical oranges on display in a supermarket. As the distinctions between companies and their products blur, market entropy increases—and the challenge marketers confront in creating meaningful differentiation for their companies and products leaves them breathless.

> A differentiated product remains a differentiated product only until the emergence of the first follower. After that it begins to behave as a commodity. Over time, all products tend to become commodities. With the evolution of the market, pioneering companies face the choice of becoming limited-volume, high-priced, high-cost specialty producers or high-volume, low-cost producers of standard products.
>
> —Seymour Tilles, "Segmentation and Strategy," in
> *Perspectives on Strategy from the Boston Consulting Group*

The Dynamics of Differentiation

Harvard's Theodore Levitt argues that there are no true commodities, that everything—including raw materials and other products that would seem to have no distinctions—can be differentiated, and is: "In the marketplace, differentiation is everywhere. Everybody—producer, fabricator, seller, broker, agent, merchant—tries constantly to distinguish his or her offering from all others. This is true even of those who produce, deal in, or buy primary metals, grains, chemicals, plastics, and money."[3] His argument is based on the fact that to some extent all products are intangible. The "product" that customers purchase includes more than just the thing itself; the "product" includes a cluster of expectations that may include safety, reliability, convenience, ease of delivery and installation, and ease of use. Moreover, customers have expectations about dealing with the seller—how knowledgeable the seller is, how informative, outgoing, easy to work with, dependable, responsive, and so on. This cluster of expectations usually extends beyond the person doing the selling and includes the company he or she represents.

In his book, *The Marketing Imagination*, Levitt uses Figure 2-2 to illustrate how buyers and sellers view the product being bought and sold—and how the market dynamically impacts differentiation over time. At the center of the circle is the *generic product*—the thing itself—the laptop computer, cup of coffee, front loader, financial advice, iron ore, or hotel room. No matter whether it is a tangible product or an intangible service, the generic product is the core of what the customer expects you to deliver. Unless you can provide this, you won't be in the market at all. As Levitt notes, this is the "table stake" that al-

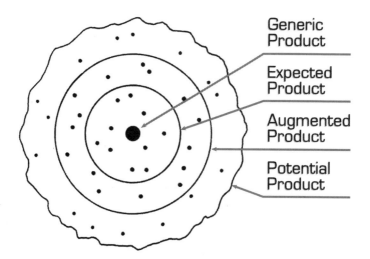

Generic
Product

Expected
Product

Augmented
Product

Potential
Product

Figure 2-2. Levitt's Total Product Concept. In Theodore Levitt's total product concept, the generic product is the thing actually being sold. Differentiation occurs with the augmented product, which shrinks over time as customers' expectations grow. Illustration used with permission.

lows you to play in the game. In and of itself, the generic product is never what a customer buys; it merely allows you to participate in the market.

What customers buy is the *expected product,* which includes all those expectations surrounding the product itself and its delivery and use. When customers buy a laptop computer, for instance, they expect the product to be durable and reliable; to run for a reasonable length of time on its batteries; to be portable and functional—reasonably fast, with sufficient memory capacity and a bright enough color screen to be visible in poor ambient light conditions; and to come with preloaded software (usually Microsoft Office). Moreover, customers expect the laptop buying process to be smooth, helpful, and efficient. They expect a convenient and informative Web site, knowledgeable salespeople (if they buy it at a retail outlet), speedy delivery, easy setup and use, some amount of free telephone support, and a reasonable warranty on the computer. Unless laptop manufacturers and retailers can meet these expectations, they will not be competitive.* In fact, if you ask cus-

---

*As we write this, we could be more specific about laptop buyers' expectations, but those expectations are changing so quickly that we would be out of date well before this book is published. Such is the speed of change and rapid obsolescence of product features in today's markets.

tomers what they are buying, they will mention not only the core or generic product but at least some of the expectations listed above.

It should be apparent that expectations differ by market segment. Even within the laptop market, there are high-end business travel users, high-end graphics users, high-end IT users and programmers, low-end business users, home users, gamers, and educational users, to name just a few ways this market can be segmented. Each of these segments will have different expectations about the expected product, and laptop manufacturers typically target the different segments by offering a range of products with different features and service and support options. What may not be so apparent is that for each segment the *expected product* is essentially a commodity—and this commodity is a moving target. As Levitt notes, the expected product "represents the customer's minimal expectations. Though these vary by customers, conditions, industries, and the like, every customer has minimal purchase conditions that exceed the generic product itself."[4] Over time, as products evolve and more bells and whistles are added, customers learn to raise their expectations. This year's breakthrough product will be next year's has-been—like the inexorable march of time, the bar keeps being raised year after year (and sometimes month after month). To remain minimally competitive, sellers must continually advance the state of their products and services to keep pace with advances in their customers' expectations—but this does not guarantee a competitive advantage. It merely keeps them in the game.

The frontiers of differentiation become visible in what Levitt calls the *augmented product,* which is the expected product plus the innovations companies offer to try to differentiate themselves from their competitors. The augmented product is a cauldron of creation—the new features and functions, the extended services, the longer guarantees, the better selection, the greater availability, and so on. Together, product augmentations form the added value companies try to project as they appeal to customers. This is the battleground for the customers' share of mind (and pocketbook). The evolution in business hotels illustrates the point. For the upscale (but not luxury) business hotel chains, the generic product is the room itself and the services available in the hotel, such as the gift shop, restaurant, lounge, and parking lot. Arguably, these are the price of admission. The expected product could include valet parking service, quick check-in for elite guests, bell and concierge services, health club, room service, dry cleaning, personal amenities such as soap and shampoo, a television, in-room movies, and so on. In recent years, this range of hotel has been offering various augmentations: mini-bars; business centers; in-room fax machines; desks wired for computers; multiline telephones; separate sitting areas; rest areas for travelers who arrive before check-in time; additional personal amenities (bubble bath, coffee makers, hair dryers); adapters for foreign plugs, etc. One could argue which of these value-added augmentations have come to be expected and which are still unique enough to be augmentations. The point is that every augmentation one chain adds puts competitive pressure on the others, who sooner or later adopt it themselves; so the bar keeps being raised and it becomes increasingly difficult for hotel chains to generate new value-added augmentations, particularly within the price range of their target market segments.

In Levitt's scheme, the *potential product* includes all the value-added augmentations that are possible but haven't been thought of yet. It's difficult to cite examples because these value-added features and benefits either have not yet been created or have been created but aren't being offered because they're too expensive (they would move the product beyond the currently acceptable price point) or because the market is not yet demanding them and companies don't currently have an incentive to provide them. Potential products are sometimes born of necessity but often arise through normal innovation. Companies may become desperate to innovate because they are losing position in the marketplace, or customers may begin demanding more product features or services, or technological advances may suddenly make these potential products feasible. Increases in computer network bandwidth, for instance, will drive the introduction of new products to take advance of increased bandwidth.

Levitt's scheme is one of many that describe the dynamic nature of markets and the entropic forces that drive the endless cycle of innovation and imitation that we spoke of earlier. In the long run, companies find it difficult to sustain the differentiation they work so hard to create, yet some manage to do so year after year. Moreover, as we'll discuss next, they do it in different ways.

The Nine Domains of Differentiation

Notwithstanding the fact that differentiation is difficult to achieve and tends to be ephemeral, companies have found a number of ways to distinguish themselves in the marketplace. They do it in one or more of the nine domains of differentiation:

1. Product Uniqueness

The most common form of differentiation is based on unique product features and innovations or on the suite of product features being offered. Generally, this is the most fleeting form of differentiation because it is easiest to copy unless the product has some form of copyright, trademark, or patent protection or unless the product is truly uncopyable. Products that exemplify this form of differentiation include Microsoft Windows, the *Wall Street Journal,* Intel Pentium chips, CIPRO®, and Julia Roberts (see Figure 2-3). Each "product" is unique in some way. Though Windows has competitors, this product has a tremendous "first-mover advantage" and an installed base so dominant that it imposes significant switching costs for consumers. Microsoft's real or virtual monopoly in operating system software gives it commanding differentiation.

The *Wall Street Journal* is differentiated not only by its unique position as the preferred "product" offering financial news and analysis but also by its strong brand. While *Investor's Business Daily* and *Financial Times* are potent rivals, the *Wall Street Journal* has a commanding lead because of the strength, recognition, and vitality of the product. Intel's Pentium chips give them considerable product differentiation, but the product must be reinvented and improved constantly because competitors quickly match the performance of each new Intel chip. CIPRO's unique position is protected by patents—no competitor can copy the formula for CIPRO, but they can develop similar drugs and are racing to do so. Still, until a competitor can create an even better drug for treating anthrax infections, CIPRO will give Bayer a strong, well-differentiated product—and CIPRO has a first-mover advantage that will continue

Figure 2-3. Julia Roberts. Like all actors, models, musicians, artists, and other public figures, *she is the product.* No one can copy the unique qualities that differentiate her from other actors, but her star may fade, as it has for other actors who were once on Hollywood's "A" list.© Jeffrey Markowitz/Corbis Sygma. Photo used with permission.

to give it a commanding lead, at least for a while. We included Julia Roberts in our list to illustrate that some *products* are truly unique. Because she *is* the product, no one can copy her. Nonetheless, the strength of her product will erode over time. New actors will emerge who will capture Hollywood's and filmgoers' imaginations, and Julia Roberts will start losing some film roles to them. As she grows older, there may be less demand for her (alas, it happens to everyone), and if she appears in a series of unsuccessful films, her star will tarnish more quickly—as it has for Sylvester Stallone, Arnold Schwarzenegger, and other previous Hollywood "A" list actors whose luminescence has dimmed in recent years. Product differentiation is tenuous.*

2. Distribution

For a number of companies, the primary form of differentiation is farther down the value chain—in the means or channels of distribution. Exemplars in this domain are Amazon.com, Dell Computer, Mary Kay, and Snap-On. These companies have chosen to reach their target markets in ways that confer an advantage not shared by their rivals who have chosen more traditional channels. The books Amazon.com sells are the same books sold by other bookstores. However, Amazon has several differentiating features. Its Internet-based virtual showroom enables it to display hundreds of thousands of books to the customer. Amazon also maintains a sophisticated product database and customer relationship management systems and uses unique distribution channels and alliances that e-commerce makes possible—and these in turn allow Amazon to provide a host of other services, including used book sales from a network of used book sellers connected to Amazon's network, lists of book recommendations for repeat buyers, and lists of books related to the one a buyer is considering. No bricks-and-mortar bookseller can offer these services as conveniently, readily, and easily as Amazon.com—unless they imitate Amazon on the Web, as Barnes & Noble, Borders, and others have recently done. One advantage the bricks-and-mortar booksellers did have was the consumer's ability to page through books, see the contents, and

---

*On August 26, 2001, Hollywood.com observed that, "Evergreens like Arnold Schwarzenegger and Sylvester Stallone used to be on the A-list, but not anymore. Our longtime action heroes have gotten old, and it seems that newcomers are ready to take their place." (http://www.hollywood.com/news/detail/article/770607). Age may be one factor in the decline in value, but actors, models, and others *who are the product* can also suffer from overexposure. *Premiere* magazine's Sean M. Smith noted that, "No matter how big a movie star you've been, the sad truth is, sometimes the American public just gets sick of seeing your face." (www.premiere.com/PREMIERE/Features/202/wrap/animated.html)

read sample pages. However, in 2001, Amazon introduced sample pages onto its Web site, so the browsers no longer have to go to a bookstore to sample a book's content. Dell's approach is similar in that they ignored the traditional retail store model and sold directly to consumers. Though rivaled now by Compaq, Gateway, and others, Dell's Internet-direct channel remains the champion of built-to-order products sold directly to consumers, because of their award-winning after-sales service; high-quality, state of the art products; and the industry's most successful advertising campaign.

Although Mary Kay has an online presence, its strength comes not from Internet sales but from a distribution channel that rivals traditional department stores, which have a "pull" distribution system for cosmetics. Department stores such as Saks Fifth Avenue and Marshall Field's create a place where people can buy cosmetics and then attract people to these locations through advertising, special services (such as beauty consultants), and the convenience of one-stop shopping. Mary Kay, like Avon and Tupperware, has a "push" form of distribution in which the product is distributed right in consumers' homes. These companies rely on vast networks of independent sales representatives who go to individual consumers (or parties of consumers) and sell the product door-to-door. At last count, Mary Kay had more than 750,000 independent sales associates in 35 countries. Avon, which has been in business for more than 100 years, claims to have 3 million sales reps in 139 countries.

Like Mary Kay and Avon, Snap-On, which sells a variety of hand and power tools, has an army of franchisees who tour their territories in Snap-On vans carrying much of the inventory with them. They call upon auto mechanics and garages and, in many cases, sell the product right from the truck. All of these "push" distribution system companies rely on their franchisees or independent sales reps developing relationships with individual consumers, and it differentiates them from the "pull" distribution systems where individual consumers have to travel to the seller and are less likely to develop personal relationships with the people behind the counter.

Although each of these companies has been able to differentiate itself through its primary distribution channel, nothing in their business model protects them from rivals who choose to copy them. Indeed, Mary Kay's door-to-door sales associates are a knock-off of Avon's and Tupperware's systems. Amazon.com's successful Internet model was quickly copied by Barnes & Noble, Borders, and other bricks-and-mortar booksellers. As we publish this, Amazon.com is just reaching profitability and has been trying to broaden its appeal and utility to consumers by opening other types of specialty "stores," including toys, consumer electronics, apparel, and music. Amazon's future is still uncertain, though Jeff Bezos and company are still predicting profitable times ahead. Had its rivals not been able to emulate Amazon's online distribution channel, however, Amazon might have captured more of the online market for books, and we might be telling a different story.

3. Product Market Segmentation

Some companies differentiate themselves through product market segmentation—focusing on a narrow niche of a broader market. Also known as "category killers," these companies create a store around one retailing segment normally carried by traditional department stores or supermarkets. By specializing in a particular segment, the category killers can offer a greater selection of products, more knowledgeable salespeople, focused service, and cheaper prices than their multidepartment cousins. Examples of successful category killers are PETsMART (pet supplies), Staples and Office Depot (office supplies), REI (camping gear and clothing), Williams-Sonoma (kitchen supplies), Starbucks (coffee), and Toys-R-Us (toys). Category killers like these have been among the fastest growing retailers in the past two decades. Their success breeds imitators, however, so the advantages gained by the first movers in a category tend to be short-lived, and they are often attacked by mass merchandising discounters like Wal-Mart, which can offer super sizes and lower costs. Wal-Mart's own brand of pet food, for example, has seen even higher market share growth than PETsMART—and the success of both of these giants has been at the expense of traditional supermarkets.

Enterprise Rent-A-Car exemplifies another type of product market segmentation—focusing on segments ignored by rivals. The major rental car companies—Hertz, Avis, National, Budget, Alamo, Thrifty, and Dollar—have targeted the frequent business traveler, so they located the majority of their rental facilities at airports. Some, like Hertz, have allied themselves with frequent flyer programs, thus rewarding the frequent business traveler. Their target segment is the 10 percent of the population that accounts for over half of the air travel in the U.S. These frequent flyers typically make five or more business trips per year. Enterprise chose to target the remaining segment— the 90 percent of the population that does the other half of the annual air travel in the U.S. This segment travels by air less frequently (often only one or two trips per year). However, they do rent vehicles for purposes other than business travel to and from an airport:

▲ As a replacement vehicle while their car or truck is being repaired
▲ As a luxury car for special occasions
▲ As a new model car to test drive

▲ As an extra car when they have out-of-town guests

▲ As a vacation vehicle where they drive from home rather than fly to their destination

To serve these customers, Enterprise chose to locate its major facilities in towns and cities where people work and live, rather than at airports, which are typically a greater distance from people's homes. By 2001, Enterprise had more than 4,400 offices and claimed that their rental facilities were no more than 15 miles from 90 percent of the U.S. population. This segmentation strategy has paid off for Enterprise. In 1985, they were still a small, regional car rental company. By 1997, they had surpassed Hertz in annual rentals and are now the largest car rental company in the U.S.

> Uniqueness does not lead to differentiation unless it is valuable to the buyer. A successful differentiator finds ways of creating value for buyers that yield a price premium in excess of the extra cost. The starting point for understanding what is valuable to the buyer is the buyer's value chain.
>
> —Michael Porter, *Competitive Advantage: Creating and Sustaining Superior Performance*

4. Customer Service/After-Sales Service

Farther down the value chain are the companies that differentiate themselves through superior customer service or after-sales service, and this is another way Enterprise Rent-A-Car differentiates itself from its rivals. The greatest single distinction is that Enterprise picks up its customers at no extra cost. This added convenience, especially for infrequent travelers, is another huge differentiator for Enterprise—and it has paid off. In 2002, the company was ranked highest in J.D. Powers and Associates' *Domestic Airport Rental Car Customer Satisfaction Study*—the third year in a row Enterprise has been number one. The company scored highest in four of the five factors that J.D. Powers used to measure customer satisfaction: customer pick-up, rates/value, vehicle return, and reservations.

Other companies that differentiate themselves through customer or after-sales service are Nordstrom, Wal-Mart, Men's Wearhouse, Ritz-Carlton, ServiceMaster, SAS, Southwest Airlines, and Lands' End. These firms excel at making customers feel valued. Through prompt attention, timely response to questions and complaints, the courtesy and friendliness of the staff, and the degree to which they provide expert assistance, these firms differentiate themselves from their rivals. Moreover, they do it at every point of contact with customers—all the points that Jan Carlzon, former CEO of SAS Airlines, referred to as "moments of truth". We call it *high touch/high care,* which means that customers feel a high degree of "touch" in the attention they receive from everyone associated with the company, and a high degree of caring about whether customers' experiences are commensurate with their expectations.

> Last year, each of our 10 million customers came in contact with approximately five SAS employees, and this contact lasted an average of 15 seconds each time. Thus, SAS is "created" 50 million times a year, 15 seconds at a time. These 50 million "moments of truth" are the moments that ultimately determine whether SAS will succeed or fail as a company. They are the moments we must prove to our customers that SAS is the best alternative.
>
> —Jan Carlzon, *Moments of Truth*

In her book *Fabled Service,* Betsy Sanders, a former vice president with Nordstrom, describes what differentiates that premier retailer from many of its rivals: "Nordstrom is a company that has become fabled in the eyes of its customers. What that means, very simply, is that Nordstrom employees provide a level of service that their customers talk about. Because so many customers talk about Nordstrom's service, it has become a benchmark of service in the retail industry. The level of service customers experience at Nordstrom becomes what they expect to find in other stores."[5] The success of firms like Nordstrom in creating differentiation through superior customer service—through high touch/high care—has sparked a virtual flood of copycats, many of whom are embracing customer relationship management system software as their path toward achieving "customer intimacy." Ironically, the attempt to institutionalize customer intimacy through high-tech systems may make customers feel even more distant. It's like those letters we've all received that are obviously written by a computer but open by addressing us by our first name and then list our street address somewhere below. The "fake intimacy" these tools create is no better than telemarketers who call people at home and use personal information to establish a quick "bond." The dead giveaway is that the telemarketer mispronounces our name, sounds like she's reading from a script, and the personal information is obviously inserted at the appropriate points. Fake intimacy is not intimacy; it's dehumanizing and offensive. As we'll discuss later, the way to achieve *real* customer intimacy is to be genuine about it and to get to know your customers well.

5. Breadth of Offerings

One-stop shopping, single point of contact, soup to nuts, full service—these are the appeals of yet another group of companies who seek to distinguish themselves through the breadth of their offerings. Instead of going to a hardware store, a lumberyard, a plumbing supply outlet, and a paint store, homeowners can get everything they need at The Home Depot. One-stop companies offer convenience and confidence to customers. They are more convenient because customers can find most of what they need in one location or from one supplier. They inspire more confidence when knowledgeable employees can answer a variety of consumers' questions or offer advice in a range of product areas.

In the engineering and construction industry, one-stop assumes the form of full-service contractors like Fluor and Bechtel. Known as EPC firms, these companies provide a full range of services: engineering, procurement, and construction. Bechtel, for instance, says that it "provides premier technical, management, and directly-related services to develop, manage, engineer, build, and operate installations for our customers worldwide."[6] Firms like Bechtel often do "green field, turnkey" plant projects, meaning that they start with a green field and end by giving the owner the keys to the fully completed plant. Most of these firms now also offer operations and maintenance services. They do everything their customers need—from soup to nuts. Full-service EPC firms argue that their one-stop approach benefits owners in a number of ways:

⋏ It can reduce cost because they eliminate redundancy.
⋏ It improves communication among designers, draftsmen, engineers, and builders.
⋏ It can reduce the schedule, improve coordination, and simplify the interfaces between the owner's representatives and the contractor.

According to GE Capital Consumer Finance, Citicorp, and other large financial institutions, there are similar benefits to having a full-service financial services provider. Once you have an account or customer service representative you trust, that person can help you take care of all of your insurance, banking, lending, leasing, and credit needs. The one-stop shopping appeal has been great enough in recent years to fuel a number of mergers and acquisitions, including the megamerger of Citicorp with Travelers Group, parent of Travelers Insurance Company, Salomon Brothers, and Smith Barney.

Even small, specialty retailers find one-stop shopping to be a point of differentiation. The Gluten-Free Pantry, an Internet-based gourmet-cooking retailer, opens its Web site by announcing: "We offer convenient one-stop shopping for all your special dietary needs."[7] Of course, one-stop shopping is a differentiator only to the extent that it is unique. When your rivals also offer one-stop shopping, the distinction fades, as has happened to Office Depot. Once unique in the category of large office supply retailers, it is now virtually indistinguishable from Office Max and Staples.

6. Brand

Perhaps the most powerful form of product differentiation occurs when the product becomes a recognizable and valued brand. Brands are powerful because their recognition is a substitute for trust by many buyers in the marketplace. They confer a bias in buying because people tend to trust brand names and symbols. For many people, the brand is a sign of stability, quality, and confidence. Today, the world's hottest brand-name companies include Coca-Cola, Starbucks, Microsoft, Chanel, Mercedes-Benz, Gillette, Harley Davidson, Heineken, Versace, Sony, NIKE, Black & Decker, Talbots, Porsche, Goldman Sachs, McKinsey & Company and Disney, to name a few. In many cases, individual products are more strongly branded than the companies producing them, such as Uncle Ben's Rice, Tampax, Vaseline, Aquafresh, Tabasco sauce, Oil of Olay, and Schweppes. Do you know who produces these products? (The answers are MARS Incorporated, Procter & Gamble, Lever Fabergé, GlaxoSmithKline, McIlhenny Company, Procter & Gamble, and Cadbury Schweppes, respectively.)

Brands can take decades to build, and they offer strong differentiation once they are established in the minds of customers. The billions of dollars spent every year on brand advertising is compelling evidence that strong brands offer significant advantages in the marketplace. Yet they can be eclipsed if aggressive rivals outperform a brand in the hearts and minds of consumers. Sony's Betamax is an example. It was the original videotape format. Early adopters of videotape machines were routinely using the word "betamax" to refer to videotaping equipment. When consumers use the product name or format to refer to the thing itself (as "xeroxing" is routinely used to signify photocopying), the brand is often invulnerable. But Sony's aggressive rivals were not content to allow the Betamax format to dominate videotapes, and they outpromoted and outsold Sony with the VHS format, which was in fact of lower quality than Sony's product. The result? Although Sony claims that Betamax still lives, it has in fact died a marketplace death.

Branding is a powerful differentiator, but it takes considerable effort and investment in advertising to establish and maintain a brand—and even very strong brands can be diluted by aggressive rivals.

7. Size/Market Dominance

Some companies achieve marketplace distinction through their size and dominance of the market. Their advantage accrues through a combination of brand-name recognition, accessibility, capacity, broad expertise, and the ability to create advantage through sheer marketplace muscle. Two of the most muscle-bound firms today are Microsoft and Wal-Mart. Anyone who was conscious during the 1990s will, of course, know of Microsoft's battles with the Justice Department over the massive power it exercised with suppliers, partners, and consumers. Microsoft's size enables it to do more research, develop more products, do more advertising, reach more consumers, attract more partners, and exert more influence over distributors and suppliers than its rivals. Consequently, it has a broader share of the consumers' minds and is able to differentiate itself and its products in ways its rivals cannot match.

Wal-Mart grew on the strength of a superior business model based on having a broad mix of in-stock merchandise, providing excellent customer service, and rewarding employees to minimize pilferage. As it grew, Wal-Mart created outstanding business processes that enabled it to remain the "everyday low price" retailer by controlling costs and by building efficiencies into its operations. It was also able to form special partnerships with suppliers like Procter & Gamble and to obtain brand-name products in larger package sizes, which gave Wal-Mart a lower price-per-ounce for these products than its rivals could offer. Today, Wal-Mart is the largest retailer in the U.S., with a market cap more than five times greater than its nearest rival. Manufacturers who want to place their products with Wal-Mart will go to great lengths to meet Wal-Mart's demands, like offering packages in special sizes, such as bulk, and engaging in joint promotions—greater lengths than they will go to for smaller, less powerful, less pervasive retailers.

Companies that dominate markets and can differentiate themselves through sheer muscle often have a first-mover advantage as well. As the pioneers in a product or market segment, like Microsoft and McDonald's, they typically have a large installed base of their products or numerous facilities in key locations. Customers have become comfortable with their products and may depend on their services. They have strong name recognition; the loyalty of a large segment of customers; and the ability to meet a variety of customer needs because of the sheer size, diversity, and expertise of their workforce. Dell Computer's first-mover advantage came through its innovative, online, direct-to-consumer marketing system. IBM and Cisco Systems achieved it by dominating key product lines (mainframe computers and networking hardware) at a time when demand for those products was growing exponentially. McDonald's did it by inventing and franchising fast food. First movers do not always sustain their advantage, of course, but if they can achieve market dominance by inventing new products, markets, or channels, and if they can sustain their business model through sound business practices, they will continue to differentiate themselves from their also-ran rivals because their size and market dominance enable them to do more, offer more, and invest more than the second-tier players in the market.

8. Low Price

Low price does not differentiate a company's products, but it does offer a differentiating strategy that, when most successful, will drive less-efficient rivals from the market. Low-price leaders like Wal-Mart and Charles Schwab strive to provide goods and services at a lower price than their rivals and to sustain their low-price position by selling to mass markets, maximizing operational efficiency, and managing their logistics and supply chains rigorously. As Michael Porter notes in his book, *Competitive Strategy*, "Cost leadership requires aggressive construction of efficient-scale facilities, vigorous pursuit of cost reductions from experience, tight cost and overhead control, avoidance of marginal customer accounts, and cost minimization in areas like R&D, service, sales force, advertising, and so on."[8]

In the mass retailing markets, low-price leaders can be as devastating as the Mongol hordes sweeping across the steppes of Asia. In the Northeast, for instance, retailing giants like Grand Union, Bradlees, and Montgomery Ward were under attack by such low-price invaders as Kohl's, Target, Best Buy, and the ubiquitous Wal-Mart and Kmart. Unable to match their prices and their operational efficiencies, Grand Union, once a proud retailing giant, has joined Lloyd's, Caldor, Bradlee's, and Montgomery Ward in the retail graveyard.

Occasionally, low-price leaders fall victim to their own strategies. In 1995, NEC's Packard Bell was the leading retail personal computer company in the U.S. It had a 15 percent market share and was being sold in such mainstream outlets as Sears. Packard Bell's principal differentiator was the low price of its PCs. Then those low prices were matched by Compaq, Hewlett-Packard, Gateway, Dell, and other more efficient producers. By late 1996, Packard Bell's market share had dropped 40 percent—a decline the company was unable to arrest. In late 1999, Packard Bell's parent company, NEC, announced massive layoffs and the termination of its U.S.-based consumer business. Packard Bell's demise as a U.S. PC manufacturer is an object lesson for low-price leaders. Its slim margins prevented the company from investing sufficiently in quality control and customer service, and it was done in as much by a poor quality reputation and notoriously bad customer service, which drove buyers into the arms of its competitors, who could differentiate themselves from Packard Bell by higher-quality products, convenient Web-based shopping, and excellent after-sales service.

To this point, we have taken an extended and somewhat unconventional view of the means by which companies strive to differentiate themselves and their products or services from their rivals. It is a shifting landscape as companies try to emulate their competitors' successes while developing more differentiators of their own, and the problem for many companies is that the race is becoming increasingly frantic. Most of the differentiators companies cite as their unique advantages do not actually differentiate them. When those differentiators are put to the test, they either fail the test of uniqueness (because their rivals' products are so similar) or the test of significance (because customers do not care). We wrote this book because there is a ninth alternative: to differentiate yourself based on your behavior. We discovered some companies that do use behavior to differentiate themselves, but most do not, so they have a rich opportunity to build their competitive position, as will those who learn to do so.

9. Behavior

Finally, many companies differentiate themselves behaviorally: through the ways they treat their customers, conduct their business, attract and lead their people, and convey themselves to their markets. Customer service that positively distinguishes a company from its competitors is perhaps the most obvious form of behavioral differentiation, but there are many others. Southwest Airlines does it through the spirit of fun they bring to their company and their passengers—a spirit embodied in their hiring practices (they hire for attitude and train for skills); human resource management (they call it their People Department); slogans ("We smile because we want to, not because we have to"); and their CEO-as-wild-and-crazy-guy (Herb Kelleher, who retired in 2001, was known to arrive for work dressed as Elvis). Not everyone at Southwest Airlines is a comedian, but those who have the urge are encouraged to cut loose. After his plane was delayed on the ground, one captain is said to have announced, "We're sorry for the delay. It seems the machine that smashes your luggage is broken, so we have to smash it by hand and that's taking a little longer."[9]

It should be clear that what Southwest Airlines does to differentiate itself behaviorally goes well beyond traditional customer service. Merely meeting passengers' customer service expectations would not differentiate them from other major airlines—whose pilots, flight attendants, and service reps are all taught the "normal" customer service behaviors. Being polite, smiling, answering passengers' questions, caring for their comfort, helping passengers who need some extra help—these behaviors are rarely positive differentiators because the employees of most airlines do them routinely. But the lightheartedness common on Southwest Airlines flights is differentiating because it is so distinct from the unremarkable experience passengers usually have with other carriers.

Other companies that excel at behavioral differentiation include Men's Wearhouse, Harley Davidson, SAS, Nordstrom, Marshall Field's, Hall Kinion, Heidrick & Struggles, and Centex Construction Group. The people in each of these firms tend to behave in ways that differentiate them from their competitors. Throughout the rest of this book we will explore how each of them does it.

To return to our theme at the beginning of this chapter, market leaders excel at reducing chaos in the marketplace. They resist assimilation by building and sustaining positive differentiation, by giving their customers clear choices. The most successful firms, like Wal-Mart, create differentiation in multiple domains. Wal-Mart combines its low-price leadership strategy with superior customer service and a dominant market position that enables it to outperform its smaller rivals. Southwest Airlines and Enterprise Rent-A-Car combine a product market segmentation strategy (serving markets that their major rivals don't serve) with excellent customer service and behavioral differentiation. Retailers like Nordstrom, Marshall Field's, and Neiman Marcus combine high-quality products, brand image, and outstanding customer service. A smart firm differentiates itself from its rivals in as many ways as it reasonably can because it knows that virtually all of these domains of differentiation can be copied. Over time, the marketplace tends to assimilate difference, so smart firms defend themselves against numbing sameness through multiple forms of differentiation.

Behavioral differentiation is unique in several important respects. Although it can give any company added advantage, it is not a substitute for the other forms of differentiation. *Behavioral differentiation is insufficient by itself to create a sustainable advantage.* If a company doesn't have core products and services its customers value as much as those being offered by its competitors, then behavior alone will not sustain its business. People continue to fly Southwest Airlines because, first and foremost, Southwest gets people where they want to go—safely and on time.

Behavioral differentiation is also unique in that, of all the forms of differentiation, it is the most difficult to copy and the hardest to sustain. It requires the kind of leadership that Herb Kelleher brought to Southwest Airlines and Sam Walton brought to Wal-Mart. It demands an uncommon institutional commitment to exceptional customer service and other behaviors that are truly differentiating. It takes a significant amount of skill and will throughout a company's workforce to create more-than-occasional behavioral differentiation. A lot of companies talk a good game, but in the end only a few have been able to grasp the fundamental insight about behavioral differentiation: *You are how you behave.*

Challenges for Readers

1. In your industry, how rapidly are the differences among competitors assimilated? One characteristic of entropic markets is noise, particularly in how companies communicate why customers should choose them. How much noise do you see in the market communications from you and your competitors? Does it all sound the same? Are any company's communications truly distinctive? Any fresh messages?
2. Using Levitt's market model, analyze your industry. What is the generic product? The expected product (that cluster of value satisfactions that customers expect from the product, no matter whom they buy it from)? What do various competing players offer as their augmented products? What are the potential products?
3. We identified nine domains of differentiation: product uniqueness, distribution, product market segmentation, customer service/after-sales service, breadth of offerings, brand, size/market dominance, low price, and behavior. In which of these domains does your company attempt to differentiate itself from competitors and gain competitive advantage? How successful are you? How lasting or fleeting are your differentiators?

Endnotes

1. James Gleick, *Chaos: Making a New Science* (New York: Viking Penguin Inc., 1987), p. 257.
2. Jeremy Campbell, *Grammatical Man: Information, Entropy, Language, and Life* (New York: Simon and Schuster, 1982), p. 42.
3. Theodore Levitt, "Marketing Success Through Differentiation—of Anything," *Harvard Business Review* (January/February 1980), p. 2.
4. Theodore Levitt, *The Marketing Imagination,* New, Expanded Edition (New York: The Free Press, 1986), pp. 79–80.

5. Betsy Sanders, *Fabled Service* (San Francisco: Jossey-Bass Publishers, 1995), pp. xi–xii.
6. Bechtel Corporation Web site, April 30, 2001.
7. The Gluten-Free Pantry Web site, April 30, 2001.
8. Michael Porter, *Competitive Strategy* (New York: The Free Press, 1980), p. 35.
9. "Southwest's 'Crazy' People First Policy," *Customer Service Management* (May/June 1999), pp. 15–17.

3

YOU ARE HOW YOU BEHAVE

What a product is in its customer-getting and customer-satisfying entirety can be managed. But it seldom is. Things just happen, often entirely too serendipitously.

—Theodore Levitt, *The Marketing Imagination*

A perfect game will end in a draw and is apt to be dull. Yet few games are perfect. Chess is fraught with mistakes. Nobody can win unless somebody makes a mistake. It's been said many times that the victor is he who makes the next-to-the-last mistake.

—Larry Evans, *The 10 Most Common Chess Mistakes*

Behavior is a mirror in which everyone shows his image.

—Johann Wolfgang von Goethe

I don't believe what you tell me. I believe what you do. Behavior is genuine. It is the purest form of the expression of your intent, your priorities, and your feelings. No matter what language you use to describe yourself, no matter what promises you make, no matter how sincerely you tell me you want my business, the truth about you will always emerge in how you act. You are how you behave—and you behave how you are.

If you are a sales clerk in a department store that prides itself on customer service but you really don't like serving customers, your lack of interest will show in the perfunctory way you answer my questions. If your company claims to put customers first, but your motivation as an account rep is to earn your commissions rather than help me solve my problems, then you will push me toward closure even when your solution or product is not right for me. If you consider yourself customer-focused but you are a senior executive who doesn't like spending time with key customers, then your lack of commitment will be evident on your calendar—and by your absence in my office. Conversely, if you are excited about and engaged by serving customers, your enthusiasm will show in how you behave toward me. It will be evident not only in your words but in the fact that you do more probing to understand my needs, bring me more ideas, take more time to help me, and go out of your way to take the extra steps that someone less committed to serving customers won't take.

Most people know what to do. The problem isn't lack of knowledge. In the past decade alone, thousands of books have been written about marketing, selling skills, managing customer relationships, and providing exceptional service. Billions of dollars have been spent training and educating everyone from senior executives to sales clerks on how to treat customers well. Does anyone today *not* know what to do? Yet there are countless examples of businesspeople behaving in ways that send—at best—the message that they are no different from other suppliers and—at worst—that they don't care about the customer or having the customer's business. Whether or not you care about your customers, it shows. You are how you behave.

We observed in Chapter 1 that you are on stage with your customers all the time. Like it or not, you are always either showing them that there is no difference between you and your rivals or you are behaving in ways that positively (or negatively) differentiate you from the other companies that want their business. You differentiate yourself from your competitors through acts of *commission* and *omission*—through the things you do and the things you don't do. Moreover, your customers are always comparing you to your competitors. When you enter into a relationship with a customer, you are constantly compared, behaviorally, with other suppliers the customer knows and is interacting with. There are no time-outs, grace periods, or honeymoons, and there is no opportunity to rest on your laurels. If you do, sooner or later your smarter competitors will outbehave you in ways that matter to the customer.

With customers, your behavior is always sending one message or another. Like words, signs, symbols, images, Morse code, and semaphores, behavior is a form of communication. In everything you do or don't do, you communicate whether you care, whether you are listening, whether you are responsive to the customer's needs and concerns, and whether you are placing your customer's interests ahead of (or behind) your own. Your behavior communicates what you think of customers, what you consider important, and whether you really want their business.

The environment in which you conduct your business also communicates. The way you package your products, decorate your office, design your brochures—these symbols say a lot about what your customer can expect. This is not news; but consider the impact on the customer when the message your business environment sends is incompatible with your behavior. Family doctors, for instance, try to create environments that appear clean, homey, and professional—physically, but not psychologically, sterile. The waiting room is usually pleasant and comfortable. On the walls are medical posters, diplomas or certificates, and Norman Rockwell prints or family photos. The message is that this is a place where you will be safe and comfortable, a place to ease your worry. The examination room is clean and well-lit. You generally don't see leftover gloves, used cotton swabs, or other alarming medical disposables lying on the counter. Instead, the tidiness and orderliness of the room says, "We know what we're doing. You're in good hands with the doctors and nurses who made this room so neat and professional."

So far, so good. Your initial impressions based on the environment are reassuring. Then the doctor walks in the room. If the doctor greets you respectfully, listens to you, cares about you and your health, is clean and well groomed, and offers effective treatment for your ailment, then the behavior will reinforce the message you received from the environment. But if the doctor is slovenly, has dirty fingernails, seems rushed, and gives you only a superficial examination before prescribing medicine you don't need, you will experience what psychologists call *cognitive dissonance,* which is a fancy way of saying you'll feel confused. Which message will have the greatest impact on you? The behavior, of course. It's what you'll remember most and will share with friends and family when they need to visit a doctor and are looking for a recommendation.

The good physician knows his patients through and through, and his knowledge is bought dearly. Time, sympathy and understanding must be lavishly dispensed, but the reward is to be found in that personal bond which forms the greatest satisfaction of the practice of medicine. One of the essential qualities of the clinician is interest in humanity, for the secret of the care of the patient is in caring for the patient.
—Francis W. Peabody, "The Care of the Patient,"
in *Journal of the American Medical Association*

We expect physicians to be knowledgeable, capable, and smart. We expect them to know what ails us and to provide competent help if they can. However, as Francis Peabody suggested in his landmark 1927 article for the *Journal of the American Medical Association,* we also expect them to be respectful, attentive, and caring.[1] We expect them to treat us with humanity. Indeed, these are the behavioral expectations we have of most of the people we interact with in business and professional settings: We want to be treated well.

What Customers Expect

It's obviously important for professionals and businesspeople to have a deep understanding of their customer's expectations. This idea is not new or profound, as Dawn Iacobucci, Kent Grayson, and Amy Ostrom noted in a 1994 article in *Sloan Management Review:* "'Customer satisfaction' may be a new buzzword, but the concept is not new. Striving for customer satisfaction is no different than good marketing. . . . Attempting to find out what customers want and then trying to deliver may be seen as striving for customer satisfaction or simply doing good marketing."[2] However, behavioral differentiation puts a new spin on this old concept. Understanding your customers' expectations of your products and services is one thing; understanding their expectations of your behavior is something else again. In part, customers may not know what they expect. They may never have been asked. Nonetheless, they can compare your behavior to your competitors' behavior because, in all likelihood, they will have experienced both. To help us understand behavioral expectations and customers' actual experiences, we surveyed a number of consumers of different kinds of professional services and will present our findings throughout this book. We will start here with what consumers expect from lawyers. Later in this chapter we'll describe how the lawyers' behaviors differentiate them positively or negatively from other lawyers. Table 3-1 shows a sample of the responses we received to the question, "What do you expect from a lawyer?" Note that only "competence" deals with technical expertise. All the other expectations are behavioral.

Do all lawyers exhibit the behaviors listed in Table 3-1? Oh, that this were true, but, alas, lawyers are human, and some are not the strong advocates their clients want. Some lawyers are not candid or compassionate, don't offer practical advice, are not clear and frequent communicators, and do not follow through on their promises. This means, of course, that the lawyers who do meet these behavioral expectations will differentiate themselves from those who don't. At the most basic level, then, you can differentiate yourself behaviorally from at least some of your competitors by understanding your cus-

Table 3-1. Customers' Expectations of Lawyers.

	Technical Expectations
Competence, Knowledge, and Experience	To have the core legal competencies To be competent and reliable To be an expert on the matter at hand To be smart in areas in which I am ignorant To continually update his/her knowledge To do appropriate research to support my case To understand and comply with basic court procedures so I don't get in trouble To provide expert legal advice To know the laws and explain them in terms I understand

	Behavioral Expectations
Client Advocacy	To be devoted to me as a client and to my cause To sincerely and genuinely care about me To look after and fight for my interests To care more about me and my situation than his/her fees To have my best interests in mind To be on my side—and zealously so—if he/she agrees to take the case To be an ardent advocate for my rights, when just To be focused on me as a client, not on billable time To be assertive with the bad guys
Honesty, Integrity, and Candor	To tell me everything I should know and to answer my questions To tell other people the truth and avoid taking advantage of them To give fair, honest, and truthful advice To be honest and trustworthy To use common sense To give me a realistic picture of my likelihood to get what I requested
Compassion	To be concerned about my situation To be patient and show understanding To be compassionate—to care about people To show empathy
Efficiency, Effectiveness, and Practicality	To be practical; to give actionable advice and guidance To be a diligent worker To give practical advice on how to respond to my issue To respond to my questions and needs efficiently and effectively; to avoid wasting my time or his/hers

(continues)

Table 3-1. (continued)

Communication and Responsiveness	To have strong communication skills
	To give me detailed explanations of all the ramifications of following or not following his/her advice
	To be available whenever I need him/her; to return my calls and make time available to meet with me
	To follow through on the things he/she commits to
	To answer all my questions in a timely manner so I can make the right decisions
	To comply with my reasonable requests for filings, motions, actions, and so on, or explain why he/she doesn't
	To respond to my communications with reasonable promptness
Professionalism and Confidentiality	To keep my matters confidential and protect my privacy
	To give me his/her undivided attention
	To demonstrate absolute professionalism

tomers' *behavioral* expectations and meeting them. It sounds easy, but it's not. If it were easy, then all but the most obtuse lawyers would meet the criteria in Table 3-1. The problem is that knowing what to do is not the same as doing it. The map is not the territory.

Another important point emerges from our discussion of consumers' expectations of lawyers: *Behaviors can differentiate you both positively and negatively.* In the various ways you behave toward your customers, you will show them either that you are better to work with than your competitors—or worse. Positive and negative BD can have a profound effect on a customer's willingness to work with you again. You can create a bias toward yourself that results in more business or a bias against yourself that can cost you not only the current customer but also many others whom the customer persuades to avoid working with you. Behavioral differentiation can be extraordinarily powerful.

Gaining Ground—Positive Behavioral Differentiation

Behavioral differentiators are positive when they enhance the customer's experience of you or your products and services and when they create, in the customer's mind, a favorable bias toward you. If all else is equal, in the future this customer will prefer doing business with you because you treated the customer distinctively different and better (however the customer defines it) than your competitors did. The following consumer's story illustrates how Marshall Field's created positive BD that will result in future bias toward their store:

I had an exceptional shopping experience at the old Marshall Field's store in Chicago. I hadn't been there before but was able to do some shopping while I was in Chicago on business. First, I was looking for a pair of shoes. I showed the salesman what I wanted to try on, and he brought those shoes out along with three similar styles he thought I might also like to consider. I stuck with my original choice, but those shoes didn't fit quite right. So he pulled out the lining, put in an inner sole, and put the original lining back in place. I haven't seen a shoe salesman do that since I was a kid—40 years ago!

I also shopped for some lingerie. I casually told the saleswoman that I lived far away and not close to a major department store. She gave me her business card and invited me to call her any time I needed something, and she would send it. Next, I browsed in the clothing department and found a top I liked. They had the right size but not the color I wanted. By the time I tried on that top in another color and confirmed the size, the saleswoman had already located the right color at another store. I didn't have to ask her to do this; she took the initiative and did it while I was still in the dressing room. Moreover, she arranged to send it to me at no charge. She explained that that was Marshall Field's policy when they didn't have what the customer wanted in the store.

Finally, I went to the furniture department because I knew Marshall Field's carried a particular line of fine wood furniture that is hard to find. After I found the coffee table I wanted, the saleswoman told me that they were holding a private sale in a few days that would give me 40 percent off. I left, thinking about the table, and then called her on the day of the sale after I returned home. I told her I'd decided to buy it. Since I didn't have a Marshall Field's account, she opened one for me on the phone, gave me an additional 10 percent off for establishing the account, and took care of everything. Weeks later, I even received a thank-you card from her.

The outcome of my experience is that I would always return to Marshall Field's any time I'm in Chicago. And I'd buy something—partly because it would be impossible not to find something wonderful there and partly because these experiences turned me into a loyal customer.

What's interesting about this consumer's story is the *consistency* of the behavioral impression created. In each of her four interactions with Marshall Field's salespeople, she experienced a similar degree of exemplary service—salespeople going out of their way to be helpful and to ensure that she got what she wanted. Each of the things these salespeople did individually would be considered excellent examples of customer service. Together, they form a pattern that creates, in her mind, the impression that Marshall Field's is a better place to shop—and it's an experience she wants to have again. Furthermore, it's not the kind of behavior she typically experiences in department stores, as she explains:

> Usually, you find what you need on the rack. If it's not on the rack, they don't have it. Then you search for a clerk and hand them your credit card. They process the payment, and you're gone. It's not that the clerks in many other stores are unfriendly, surly, or unhelpful; they just don't define their job any more broadly than completing the transaction.
>
> The people at Marshall Field's gave me the impression that meeting my needs was their highest priority. The shoe salesman went out of his way to make sure my shoes fit properly, and he did it so the shoes looked nice. The woman who called to find the right color top volunteered to do that—she didn't wait for me to ask. They all took the initiative to help me get what I wanted, and nobody seemed put upon. It's like, "This is how things are done at Marshall Field's."

As this example illustrates, one of the primary ways you create positive BD is to demonstrate that you want the customers' business and are earnest about solving their problems and helping them meet their goals. If you can convey this impression consistently, across a broad range of customer interactions involving a number of your people, you demonstrate the added value of working with you rather than your competitors. Here are some other ways positive BD is created:

When the customer knows that you have gone to extraordinary lengths to learn about them and understand their industry, company, and needs.

▲ If you're an online book retailer, you create a customer relationship management (CRM) system that remembers what your buyers have purchased in the past. Then you notify them about similar books they might be interested in. You also ask them to identify the current authors whose books they like. When those authors publish new books, you e-mail the buyers and offer prepublication discounts.

▲ If you're a manufacturer, your representatives live in your customers' stores or plants, conduct joint research on their markets, and co-design programs for improving how they reach their customers. You take an entire supply-chain view and partner with your customers to help them succeed.

▲ If you are a services company, you research your customer's industry thoroughly enough to know what challenges and opportunities they are facing, what they are trying to accomplish, and how their business model differs from competing models. On your own initiative, you publish a report for them that summarizes the insights you've gained during your research and then conduct a joint brainstorming session where you help them identify new opportunities.

▲ If you're an ad agency, before you make your first presentation to the client you survey their customers and learn how they view your client's products. Based on your survey, you already have preliminary thoughts on what the client can do to improve its advertising.

▲ Whoever you are, you do more homework than your competitors, have more insights, know more people (because you've talked to them), and show more interest in the customer's business.

When the customer perceives that you care about them and their business.

▲ You are a partner in a management consulting firm, and you track your client's financial performance metrics—showing concern when they decline and elation when they improve.

▲ You are a professional services firm. You purchase some of your customer's stock and hold it as an incentive for your team that is serving the customer. If the customer's stock rises within the specified period of the team's service to them, then the team receives the stock as a bonus.

▲ You lead a small engineering firm. You send representatives to your customer's industry conferences to learn more about their industry and competitors.

▲ You are a consumer goods manufacturer. You give your customers feedback on their Web site designs and offer consultation on how to improve their Web presence.

▲ No matter who are you, you are there when your customers need you, even if it's not convenient. You occasionally cancel a personal commitment in order to solve a customer problem or meet when it's most convenient for the customer.

▲ You are an attorney, an accountant, a doctor, a nurse, a consultant. You don't have a "charge-for-every-minute" mentality; you do some things gratis just because it's the right thing to do for your client.

When you are unusually thoughtful and considerate.

▲ You remember when the customer has had some personal trauma in his life and inquire about it in a way that is genuinely caring and not self-serving.
▲ You lend an ear when the customer wants to talk—about anything.
▲ You take the time to show her how to operate the equipment and give her tips on getting the most out of it.
▲ You remember the customer's birthday or other special occasion and send a personalized card or e-mail greeting.
▲ You remember the customer's name and the small facts about his life, and you inquire about them from time to time. To you, he feels like family, and that's how he sees it, too.

If you want to bring along some printed material, I will be a lot less impressed by your preprinted brochure than something that has clearly been put together for me. At least that shows a little thought, consideration.

—David Maister, "How Clients Choose,"
in *Managing the Professional Service Firm*

When you customize your product or service for them or otherwise show them that you are serving their needs specially.

▲ At no charge, you create a special piece of equipment the customer needs to solve a one-time problem.
▲ Without being asked to do so, you translate your operating manual into Spanish because you know there are some native Spanish speakers among your customer's operators.
▲ You modify your maintenance schedule to suit some customers' unusual hours.
▲ You create special package sizes to suit their consumers' needs.
▲ As a special favor, you mix and match pieces of your products that don't normally go together.
▲ You paint your products a special color, stamp the product with the customer's logo, or otherwise modify your product without additional charge to suit the customer.

When you have clearly gone out of your way to help them or to address their needs in ways that are above and beyond what your competitors would have done and beyond what the customer could reasonably expect.

▲ A customer leaves behind an important document. You send an employee to the airport to track him down and return the document before he boards his plane.

▲ You are a waiter. A customer orders a glass of wine with dinner; you refill the glass at no charge and then bring a complimentary glass of port at the end of the meal.

▲ To ensure that your customer has what he needs for his big meeting, you create the PowerPoint slides for him and hand-deliver them.

▲ You make a long-distance call to a customer to let her know that you've located a special item she was looking for—in one of your competitors' stores.

▲ With their permission, you take Polaroid pictures of your customers and add them to a bulletin board beside the door. They leave feeling like honored guests.

▲ Your customers are eating at your small café. They ask you where in your city they can buy some prints. You close your café and lead them half a mile on foot to the best print gallery in town. You know the shop is open because you phoned the owner and asked him if he would open his shop for your customers. When they are finished shopping, you return and lead them back to their hotel.

All these examples are real. The last one is especially poignant because it took place on a Sunday morning in four inches of snow. The proprietor of the café, an elderly Japanese woman, pulled on her boots and slogged through the snow to help her guests find what they wanted. Nearly thirty years later, her customers haven't forgotten her kindness.

> Delivering quality service means that you do well the things that are important to the customer. Doing things well that are not important has no impact. Actually, the only time customers are impressed by service is when it goes well beyond their expectations. Not meeting their expectations is their definition of poor service. Providing fabled service requires careful attention to the changing needs and desires of the customers, making them the drivers of your business.
>
> —Betsy Sanders, *Fabled Service: Ordinary Acts, Extraordinary Outcomes*

Positive behavioral differentiation has several important effects. First, it's memorable. When people go out of their way to do something helpful to us, we tend to remember them and what they did for us—largely because the experience was pleasurable. Second, positive BD causes liking. We tend to like the people who have been kinder, friendlier, more helpful, and more caring toward us. For the same reasons that we seek pleasure and avoid pain, we prefer to deal with people we like more than with those we don't. In his book *Influence: The Psychology of Persuasion,* psychologist Robert B. Cialdini observes that, "We most prefer to say yes to the requests of someone we know and like."[3] He maintains that liking is caused by a number of factors, including how physically attractive the seller is (why so many ads feature models), how similar we feel to the seller, how much contact we have with the seller (the reason face time is so important), and how cooperative the seller is. Whatever its causes, common sense tells us that people would prefer to buy from people they know and like (as opposed to people they don't know or don't like). Liking won't overcome a bad product or a bad deal, but if the competing products and prices are similar, then most buyers tend to buy from the salespeople and companies they like.

Earlier in this chapter, we gave the results of our research into people's behavioral expectations of lawyers (see Table 3-1). Table 3-2 identifies the positive experiences the same survey respondents had with lawyers. As you can see, many of their experiences involved liking—to the point that some respondents developed friendships with the lawyers working on their behalf. Clearly, competence and professionalism are also highly important to consumers of legal services.

In the minds of the people using legal services, lawyers' interpersonal behaviors (listening, caring, showing interest) are probably indistinguishable from their professional behaviors (being a strong advocate for the client's cause, having a "client-first" attitude, being responsive, following through, and meeting client expectations). These behaviors combine to form the whole of their experiences. Whether positive or negative, their experiences determine how people differentiate between the attorneys they will use again and the ones they won't. One of the respondents to our survey of BD among lawyers offered a convincing comparison:

> I'd like to offer my best and worst lawyer experiences. My best involved working with a nice, young lawyer who was eager to fulfill my needs. He was obviously new to the business and did not have a large client list. I simply needed some trademark assistance, and he bent over backwards to fulfill this request as well as satisfy the necessary government demands required to trademark a logo. He also assisted me with some business corporation issues—at no extra charge—because he

(Text continues on page 46)

Table 3-2. Positive Differentiating Behaviors of Lawyers

	Excellent Performance
Competence	They knew their job and the law. He was a powerful advocate and problem solver. She was very influential. He won the case and exceeded the award expectation. She was competent, confident, assertive, intelligent, intimidating, and humorous.

	Positive Behaviors
Responsiveness and Follow-Through	A local attorney completed a legal transaction for us recently; she was direct, pleasant, and responsive to our questions. He returned my phone calls promptly and did what he said he would do. He followed up with a call 90 days after the project to see how things were going.
Client Advocacy; manifesting a "Client-First" Attitude	After I divorced my husband, his credit card companies came back to me to pay his bills because they couldn't find him, even though it said in the divorce decree that I was not liable for them. The lawyer fought for me not to pay the bill and didn't charge me for the hours of work that he did. Instead, he charged the credit card company. He made me feel that even though I'd made a bad choice in husbands, there are still some people that will go to bat for me. They declined work when it would not be in the best interest of the company. Rather than accepting an assignment, they referred us to someone more knowledgeable to make better use of our money. I had an experience with an attorney once in which he actually told me how to accomplish my objective without using an attorney. It had to do with a real estate easement dispute. I was prepared to pay through the nose for the service. He told me that he could do it and frequently handled these types of issues, but he also told me I could request assistance from the county and not spend the money. I really liked that he helped me and did not behave as if he were doing it only because he didn't have time to handle my pesky little issue. He was interested in me as a person instead of a legal fee. He spent a lot of time on the phone on my

(continues)

Table 3-2. (continued)

	behalf, and sometimes didn't charge me for it because he genuinely cared.
Showing Caring and Taking a Personal Interest	He treated me with respect, made me feel important by focusing on my issues, and made me feel like he wanted to help. He showed some kindness and consideration. She treated me like a human being. He took the time to be a friend and understand how my personal life was being affected by the situation. She took an interest in me and in my problems. I had a woman lawyer who made it a point to come to my folks' home to handle their affairs and would call just to ask about their health. This fellow actually became a personal friend. We struggled through a maze of problems, but he kept his cool and he managed to have some fun along the way. She was very personable and listened to my concerns. The lawyer-CPA who handled my father's estate was very kind to me and shared with me some of his understanding of my dad and how he saw the family. This was healing.
Setting and Meeting Expectations	He quoted me a fee and stuck to it. He told me what he could and could not do, so I would know what to expect. Then he actually did what he said he was going to do and charged what he said he would charge.

knew we had limited financial capacity. He was willing to grow with us and essentially take some risks, for which I will be forever grateful.

Now for my worst experience. I met with an older lawyer before the previous story because I was entering into a business relationship with a group of wealthy people, and they were more astute than I was at the time. On someone's recommendation, I sought the advice of this particular lawyer and felt like the meter was running as soon as I sat down in his office. Whereas the trademark lawyer was warm and human and seemed sincere about solving my problems, this particular bottom feeder was arrogant and could not have cared less—at least that's how I felt.

Losing Ground—Negative Behavioral Differentiation

What makes BD so potent—and so dangerous to ignore—is that it can work against you, too. Figure 3-1 illustrates how behavioral differentiators can either attract or repel customers. Whether customers are buying medical services, appliances, management consulting, cardboard containers, or cold-rolled steel, they have a range of behavioral expectations regarding the people supplying those products or services. This range reflects how the providers they have preferred to work with or buy from in the past have treated them. Consequently, the norm defines their range of *acceptable* behaviors. The majority of providers in any field or industry fall within this normative range—the vast middle hump of the bell curve. Although there may be some variations in how they treat customers, these providers are behaviorally undifferentiated because everything they do is within the acceptable range.

When a seller's behaviors are noticeably *above* this normal range, the seller is positively differentiated from the pack, and the customer is *attracted* to the seller in much the same way that a magnet attracts iron. An invisible bond draws the buyer and seller together. As long as this bond remains strong, the buyer will be biased toward purchasing from the seller. When the seller's behaviors fall *below* the normal range, the effect is *repulsive*—negative differentiation keeps the two objects apart. We think this effect is more pronounced in BD than it is in other forms of differentiation. If you fail to differentiate your products on technical or service grounds, in the customer's eyes you fall into the emptiness of nondiscrimination, the twilight zone of blandness where you simply are no different from many other suppliers who sell the same thing you do. This is certainly one vision of commercial hell, but it's not as virulent or destructive as active repulsion, which can occur when badly treated customers are motivated to strike back.

In the years before the Internet, consumers' options for raising hell toward the companies they disliked were limited, but things have changed. The World Wide Web gives anyone with a computer *and the will to speak* out the ability to complain about the offending company to the entire Web world. Over the years, sites emerged as repositories for complaints against a broad number of companies. For example, www.baddealings.com, www.fuckedcompany.com, and www.thecomplaintstation.com are well-organized, long-standing complaint departments for the wired world. Baddealings.com even has a top ten list for the companies receiving the most complaints. Moreover, you can easily find hundreds of consumer complaint sites by using the keywords *consumer* plus *opinion* or *complaint* in any Internet search engine.

A number of other Web sites are dedicated to bashing particular companies: www.bestbuysux.org (bashes the discount retailer Best Buy), www.insurancejustice.com (Allstate Insurance), www.untied.com (United Airlines), www.walmartsurvivor.com (Wal-Mart), and www.Franklin Coveysucks.com (time management firm Franklin Covey). Of course, complaints against companies are not new, but now they have wings. At the time of this writing, FranklinCoveysucks.com had registered nearly 700,000 hits—that's a lot of people whose opinions are being influenced. In the year 2000, television's Dr. Laura Schlessinger angered the gay and lesbian community with prejudicial comments on her nationally syndicated talk show. The Web site created to protest her actions, www.stopdrlaura.com, registered over 60 million hits in just 10 months. That firestorm led Procter & Gamble and other sponsors to withdraw their support, and the show was banned in many places, including all of Canada. Such is the repulsive effect of negative BD. When your behavior toward customers is noticeably below the normal range as shown in Figure 3-1, you risk unleashing a virus that can infect many other potential customers.

Whether or not your company name becomes maligned on the Web, negative behavioral differentiators are clearly harmful—they cost you customers. They force you to find new customers because existing ones have gone elsewhere, which increases your cost of sales. Although this is patently obvious, the surprising news about negative behaviors is that they are so common—and

Figure 3-1. Behavioral Differentiation Bell Curve. The behaviors customers normally experience from sellers fall into the middle hump of the curve and do not differentiate. Behaviors at each extreme, however, are one or more standard deviations from the norm and will have a differentiated impact on customers, either positively or negatively.

commonplace. The complaints most often found on the Web are not about catastrophic service failures. Usually, they are about providers who have been unresponsive; who haven't listened; who haven't returned calls; or who have been rude, indifferent, or insensitive. Here are some typical examples of negative behavioral differentiators and the messages they send to customers:

▲ You are unable to repair an appliance and are indifferent toward the customer and so you say, "Hey, I've done all I can. Here's a number to call."
Message to the customer: "It's your problem."*

▲ You don't visit a customer for months and never ask how the expensive product they bought from you is working for them.
Message: "I don't care. I made my commission."

▲ You can't remember the customer's name.
Message: "You weren't important to me."

▲ You send your standard brochure with no handwritten note or other form of personalization.
Message: "This isn't a big enough deal for me to take the time."

▲ You insist on a receipt from your store and the manager's approval before you will allow a customer to return an item.
Message: "We don't trust you."

▲ You refuse to customize your product or otherwise agree to a customer's special request when the customer needs something slightly different than you offer.
Message: "Take it or leave it."

▲ You close promptly at 5 p.m. despite the fact that there are people waiting to be served.
Message: "We're more important than you are."

▲ You hope the customer doesn't notice that the package you're delivering has been dented on one side and whatever's inside sounds broken.
Message: "Hey, it's not my problem."

▲ You don't bother to tell customers that they could save money by buying the whole set as a package instead of purchasing individual pieces.
Message: "I hate this job and don't care about you."

---

*This true story is actually even worse than we've portrayed it. The consumer's electric dryer would operate for no more than five minutes before shutting off. The Sears repairman who serviced the appliance didn't test it after he worked on it to see if it would run longer than five minutes. When the consumer asked him to, he said, "I don't have time to stick around and test this. I have other calls to make." Although this is surely not representative of all Sears repair people, it left an indelible mark on this consumer, who told her story to many other people—and promptly purchased another dryer from a competing manufacturer.

▲ You don't return a customer's calls for weeks and then manufacture an excuse when the customer finally does get a hold of you.
Message: "You don't rate high enough for me to feel an urgent need to call you back right away. Take a number."

▲ You don't relay a customer's urgent message to others in your company who can help them, so the customer's needs are not met.
Message: "Who cares?"

These behaviors and the messages they send destroy customer relationships and can convert customers into vocal and active antagonists. Throughout this chapter, we've been tracking people's responses to lawyers' behavior. Table 3-3 shows the kinds of behaviors people cited when asked to describe their worst experiences with lawyers.

It will come as no surprise that the respondents to our survey said they would never use these lawyers' services again. People tend to remember negative experiences for a very long time. Being treated badly stings. We remember it the way we remember injuries to our body, and we tend to be unforgiving toward the people who have behaved in ways that fell below the range of acceptable behaviors, as shown in this consumer's account of a shopping experience in London:

> In Jermyn Street recently, I saw a tie in the window. We went into the shop to look for the tie. Not able to find it, we asked an assistant. He pointed to the rack and, in a very offhand manner, said: "They are all there." The shop had nobody in it, but the assistants were busy sorting out shirts. We asked another assistant and took him to the window. He looked at the tie and said: "I can tell you I haven't got one of those." He promptly went back into the shop and did not offer to get the one out of the window. The shop lost more than a tie sale. We would never go back and never recommend it to anybody.[4]

Most of us have had similar negative experiences, and our typical reaction is *passive*—we won't go to that establishment again, and we won't recommend it to anyone else. However, this consumer's reaction was active. He told the London *Evening Standard* about it. Negative BD often does more damage than positive BD does good because customers' reactions to bad experiences are emotional, not rational. When a product or services fail to meet our specifications it is noncompliant, and we have an intellectual justification for rejecting the product: "It wasn't what I wanted, so I didn't buy it." This is a fairly dispassionate and rational response, which providers can overcome

Table 3-3. Negative Differentiating Behaviors of Lawyers.

	Poor Performance
Incompetence	He was ignorant of the law and the case. She told me the wrong information and I had to pay bills my ex-husband should have paid. She didn't seem to know the relevant law or the judicial environment. He made erroneous filings and took erroneous actions that failed to comply with the court proceedings.

	Negative Behaviors
Arrogance, Condescending Attitude	He was a bellicose, arrogant blowhard who believed bluster is an adequate substitute for knowledge. She made me feel like I shouldn't have married my husband in the first place if I was going to divorce him. He was self-aggrandizing. She had inflated self-esteem; she was very narcissistic. He was sarcastic and condescending. He made me feel stupid for not understanding. She acted like she knew everything.
Mercenary and Self-Serving	He put off the court dates as long as he could and still charged me for extra hours to work on my case. This lawyer did research and charged me for it without telling me first. Just popped an expensive bill on me for a service I didn't want. He cared only about himself. He did nothing for me—and then overcharged me for it. She kept looking at her watch, and then billed me to the second. He considered me a billable hour rather than a client. He was interested in my case only if he would get a big fee.
Unresponsiveness	He did not follow through, did not respond to my phone calls, and did not complete the work he was hired to do. He had to be pushed every step of the way to comply with reasonable requests to move the case along. He procrastinated—took three times longer than it should have. She failed to return even simple phone calls. She was unwilling to hear me, take me seriously, or be open to my ideas.

(continues)

Table 3-3. (continued)

Poor Communication	He refused to answer my questions so I could understand what was going on. Basically, this lawyer didn't listen. He gave me the run-around and wouldn't be straight with me. He did a poor job of explaining the law in a way I could understand.
Uncompassionate; Lack of Respect	She was rude. He was unsympathetic to the possible negative outcomes of the trial for me. He had a total lack of compassion or a sense of what was right. She was in it only for herself. She had no concept of how others were feeling or what they needed. He seemed to have little time for my "petty" issues. He interrupted me a number of times to answer the phone. Plus, he never smiled or acted the least bit friendly.
Lackadaisical Attitude	He made me feel that my case was insignificant compared to his other cases. He was too passive, didn't cite established research, and lost interest in my case. She was dismissive and completely uninterested in helping me or even referring me to someone else. She was not committed to me and did not give me full attention. He was cavalier and showed no concern for me or my welfare. He didn't take my problems seriously. He wouldn't even make an appointment to meet with me.
Unprofessional	She gossiped about my case with a biased court clerk and told me to give up, though I eventually prevailed. He became angry at me and my case and withdrew from the case without warning me or arranging for another attorney. He was never on time for our appointments.

by showing that they've improved their product or service, that they've made changes that overcame the noncompliance issues. However, when we experience behavior so bad that it negatively differentiates the seller, we react emotionally, and the disappointment, frustration, and anger we feel are deeper and much longer-lasting. The emotional component of a negative experience cries out for relief—we are angry and need to tell people about it. As the lunatic newsman says in the film *Network:* "I'm mad as hell and I'm not going to take it anymore!"

Jack Browder, a former vice president for business development for Brown & Root, studied how long angry customers remained angry. The answer may depend on the nature of the business, but Browder's research showed him that angry customers stayed angry for 8 to 12 years. That's a long time to lose business, especially in tough markets when there aren't that many other prospects. The emotional impact of negative customer experiences can also be seen in some of the research on marriages. Professor John Gottman of the University of Washington has spent a career studying long-term marriages. In his 1994 book, *Why Marriages Succeed or Fail,* he reveals one of his more interesting findings: "As part of our research we carefully charted the amount of time couples spent fighting versus interacting positively—touching, smiling, paying compliments, laughing, etc. Across the board we found there was a very specific ratio that exists between the amount of positivity and negativity in a stable marriage. . . . That magic ratio is 5 to 1. In other words, as long as there is five times as much positive feeling and interaction between husband and wife as there is negative, we found the marriage was likely to be stable."[5] Such is the emotional power of negative emotional experiences—it takes five positive experiences to overcome a single negative one. Of course, in business it's worse. Marriage partners have generally made a strong emotional, social, and financial investment in making the marriage work, but customers don't have such bonds, and faced with a world of choice they will not tolerate negative behaviors for any longer than it takes them to find another supplier.

Why Positive Differentiating Behaviors Are Difficult to Imitate

If, as we have argued, positive behavioral differentiators create an invisible, attractive bond between buyers and sellers, and negative behavioral differentiators create an opposite, repulsive force, then it should be obvious to everyone that behaving well is good for business. Why doesn't everyone do it? Why isn't every company, professional firm, and corner drugstore a model of behavioral differentiation? The answer is that it takes more *skill, will,* and *leadership* than most organizations have. That's why the companies that are able to consistently create BD are truly exceptional. The enigma, as we said earlier, isn't that leaders don't know what to do; the enigma is that they know what to do but don't do it. In their book, The *Knowing-Doing Gap,* Stanford University professors Jeffrey Pfeffer and Robert I. Sutton studied this enigma at length. Here's how they described it:

> Did you ever wonder why so much education and training, management consultation, organizational research, and so many books and articles produce so few changes in actual management practice? Did you ever wonder why the little change that does occur often happens with such great difficulty? Why it is that, at the end of so many books and seminars, leaders report being enlightened and wiser, but not much happens in their organizations? . . . We wondered, too, and so we embarked on a quest to explore one of the great mysteries in organizational management: why knowledge of what needs to be done frequently fails to result in action or behavior consistent with that knowledge. We came to call this the knowing-doing problem—the challenge of turning knowledge about how to enhance organizational performance into actions consistent with that knowledge.[6]

Pfeffer and Sutton offer a number of cogent reasons why companies do or don't act on what they know they should do. Ultimately, it comes down to the fact that some people will always be more skilled at doing what they know should be done. Some people will have greater will. Call it drive, determination, persistence, vision. However you label it, will is usually the difference between a company that wallows in the twilight zone of undifferentiated blandness and one that emerges from the pack—and wins more than its fair share of business—by positively differentiating itself through its behavior.

A scene toward the end of the film *Jerry Maguire* illustrates why positive behavioral differentiators are so difficult to imitate. Sports agent Jerry Maguire (played by Tom Cruise) has just watched his only client, Arizona Cardinals wide receiver Rod Tidwell (Cuba Gooding, Jr.) play the game of his career against the Dallas Cowboys. After the game, Jerry is waiting for Rod to come out of the players' dressing room. Also waiting for Tidwell are dozens of reporters and photographers—and Maguire's nemesis, the oily and deceitful Bob Sugar, a rival agent. Sugar is standing in the hallway with one of his clients, a star athlete who had opted to hire Sugar instead of Maguire.

When Tidwell comes through the dressing room door, he is thronged by the press, but he doesn't want to be bothered by the media. He searches for

Jerry, and the two men celebrate their mutual success and their bond by hugging each other with obvious caring. Watching this, Bob Sugar's client says to him, "Why don't we have that kind of relationship?" Sugar pauses, looking like a deer caught in the headlights, and then awkwardly puts his arms out to hug his client. The athlete pushes him away in disgust. Bob Sugar isn't able to replicate Jerry Maguire's behavior toward his client because he doesn't care about his client in the way Jerry Maguire cares about Rod Tidwell and because nothing in his previous behavioral experience would prepare him to do what Jerry Maguire did. In other words, Sugar lacks both the will and skill to show that kind of authentic caring. Even when he's standing right there watching what Jerry's doing, he is unable to match Jerry's behavior because it's not authentic, and his client knows it.

The kinds of behaviors that truly differentiate you from your competitors are difficult to fake. It's hard to muster the will if it's not part of your nature. Herb Kelleher's antics, philosophy, and leadership at Southwest Airlines have been well documented over the past two decades, yet no other CEO in the U.S. airline industry has been able to replicate Kelleher's style or Southwest Airlines' success. Why? The answer isn't that they didn't know what to do. The answer is that they lacked the skill, will, and leadership to match Southwest Airlines' behavioral differentiators. Consequently, Southwest Airlines has been consistently on top of the U.S. airlines industry in numerous categories, has been a *Fortune* magazine Most Admired Company year after year, and has been profitable when the other U.S. airlines have not.

Your company's marketing image can be deceiving for a while. You can claim to be the best, fastest, most comprehensive, easiest to work with, most exciting, most luxurious, most personalized, most state-of-the-art, most advanced, and so on, but what customers will ultimately believe about you is what you deliver and how you behave toward them. You are how you behave—and you behave how you are.

Challenges for Readers

1. You are how you behave. How do your people behave toward customers—and how do customers perceive that behavior? Do you know for sure? Have you done customer focus groups? Blind surveys? Customer panels? Behavioral audits? Particularly important are how your behaviors toward customers differ from your competitors' behaviors. What is the difference?

2. What are you *not* doing now that could improve your behavioral differentiation? What opportunities do you have?

3. What does your business environment communicate to customers? Your facilities? Materials? Equipment? Landscaping? Art or decoration? Employee dress? What messages do customers receive from these visual symbols of your business? Is your behavior consistent with these symbols?

4. This chapter includes tables showing what typical consumers expect of lawyers, as well as some positive and negative experiences they've had with lawyers. If these tables reflected what customers in your industry expected and had experienced—both positively and negatively—what would the tables include? Rather than imagine how customers would answer these questions, go and ask them.

5. In what ways have the people in your company created positive behavioral differentiation? In what ways have they created negative behavioral differentiation? Do a candid appraisal of both and list as many positive and negative examples as you can find.

6. Sustaining behavioral differentiation requires skill, will, and leadership. If you don't have the degree of positive behavioral differentiation you would like in your company, which of these three requirements is problematic for you? Do some of your people lack the skill? The will? Or does your company lack the leadership to make it happen?

Endnotes

1. Francis W. Peabody, "The Care of the Patient," *Journal of the American Medical Association* 88 (March 19, 1927), pp. 877–882.

2. Dawn Iacobucci, Kent Grayson, and Amy Ostrom, "Customer Satisfaction Fables," *Sloan Management Review* 35, no. 4 (Summer 1994), p. 94.

3. Robert B. Cialdini, *Influence: The Psychology of Persuasion* (New York: William Morrow, 1984), p. 167.

4. "Customers are greeted with an alarming lack of courtesy," *Evening Standard*, London, April 12, 2001.

5. John Gottman, Ph.D., with Nan Silver, *Why Marriages Succeed or Fail* (New York: Simon & Schuster, 1994), p. 57.

6. Jeffrey Pfeffer and Robert I. Sutton, *The Knowing-Doing Gap: How Smart Companies Turn Knowledge into Action* (Boston: Harvard Business School Press, 2000), p. 4.

THE FOUR WAYS TO CREATE BEHAVIORAL DIFFERENTIATION

The correct way to play chess is to create an imbalance and try to build a situation in which it is favorable for you. An actual checkmate will follow once your opponent is helpless, or if the imbalances insist that an early kingside attack is the correct course. A deeper understanding of this statement shows that an imbalance is not necessarily an advantage. It is simply a difference. It is the player's responsibility to turn that difference into an advantage.

—Jeremy Silman, *The Reassess Your Chess Workbook*

Once I have decided which firms I will consider in the final set, my focus of enquiry shifts significantly. I am no longer asking 'can you do it?' but rather 'Do I want to work with you?' I am no longer interested in the institutional characteristics of your firm, but am now trying to form a judgment about you. By the fact that you are sitting here talking to me, you can assume that you have successfully marketed your firm: now the time has come to sell yourself.

—David H. Maister, *Managing the Professional Service Firm*

There is more than one way to skin a cat.

—Proverb

Jan Carlzon, the former CEO of Scandinavian Airlines, referred to customer interactions as "moments of truth." We call them "touch points"—those occasions when someone in a company interacts with or "touches" a customer. Carlzon estimated that his business, which serves the flying public, had millions of such touch points every year, but every form of business enterprise, no matter whom it serves, has hundreds or thousands of touch points each day. A salesperson calls on or talks to a customer. An accountant calls a customer's accounts payable department regarding a late check. A shipping manager calls to schedule a delivery. A customer service rep handles a complaint. An executive has lunch with one of the customer's executives. An engineer confers with the customer's plant manager. A company trainer teaches a group of customers how to use a software program. A proposal team submits a proposal. A business development team makes a formal presentation as their final and best effort to win a contract. Every one of these touch points is an opportunity for behavioral differentiation, but the way these individuals accomplish it may be quite different. There are, in fact, four types of behavioral differentiation—*operational, interpersonal, exceptional,* and *symbolic*—and we will explore these four types in this chapter.

The Four Types of Behavioral Differentiation

When retailers and business-to-consumer (B2C) service firms differentiate themselves behaviorally, they most often do it through superior customer service, though this is by no means the only way to create BD. The best of these firms—Wal-Mart, Disney, Nordstrom, Marshall Field's, Men's Wearhouse—institutionalize their behavioral differences through their operational practices, customer service policies and procedures, and employee education and training. We refer to this as *operational* behavioral differentiation because the differentiating behaviors become an integral part of how the company operates. This type of BD would include a company's policies for handling merchandise returns, responding to out-of-the-ordinary customer requests, communicating with customers (sending cards or thank-you notes, for instance), and other *standard operating procedures* for interacting with customers. Although these may be standard company policies—and therefore nothing special to the employees—customers often experience them as extraordinarily good treatment, so the behaviors resulting from these policies differentiate the company in customers' minds.

The second form of BD arises from employees' individual skills and attitudes. We call this *interpersonal* behavioral differentiation. As customers, we all have encountered people in a company we're buying from who listened well; showed genuine interest in us (as people, not just as buyers); were patient and responsive; and cared whether our needs were satisfied. These kinds of interpersonal behaviors cannot be operationalized *genuinely*. To be sure, sellers can ask their employees to behave this way. They can train them in good interpersonal skills and set the right expectations about how they should behave toward customers. But genuine interpersonal skill arises from the heart, not from policy. The employees who can differentiate themselves and their companies interpersonally are able to do it because it is genuinely part of who they are as people. You can't fake authentic caring. You can try, but most customers are savvy enough to see through the guise.

The third type of BD is *exceptional*. It occurs whenever employees go out of their way to help a customer. Exceptional treatment of customers is usually memorable to them because it exceeds their expectations in such positive ways that they recall, long afterward, the extraordinary way they were treated. One might argue that it's possible to operationalize exceptional treatment of customers, which begs the question, Is this really different from the operational form of BD we described earlier? We think it is because when employees do something exceptional for customers they often violate or ignore the company's policies and standard practices, which, by definition, makes their behavior exceptional. Or the company has no policy or practice to cover a situation that invites exceptional behavior, and employees act on their own initiative to do something exceptional. Of course, all differentiating behaviors are outside the norm of customers' experiences; otherwise, they wouldn't differentiate. But exceptional BD is beyond the high standard already established.

The final type of BD is *symbolic,* and it is in some ways the most subtle and interesting of the four—and sometimes the hardest to effect. These kinds of behaviors reflect your key product, service, or company messages and values—or your customer's messages and values. They symbolize what you are offering to provide to your customers or how your customers view themselves. When you create symbolic BD, you are aligning your messages with your behaviors—or your messages with your customers' values and messages. For instance, if you claim in your advertising to be the world's fastest shipping company *("Every shipment on time or before!"),* then your shipments must always arrive on schedule as promised—or sooner. Furthermore, if *speed* is one of your core messages as a company, a fundamental part of the identity you have created in the marketplace, then your behaviors should exemplify speed. You can't send an overnight package that arrives two days late. You can't promise to return a call on Tuesday and then not call until Wednesday. You can't schedule a sales meeting for 3:00 and then get stuck in traffic and fail to arrive on time. Your promise of speed becomes emblematic of how you operate. It is both an expressed and implied promise to your customers. Speed and promptness must therefore be reflected in *all* your touch points with customers, in *every* behavior they observe, not just with your shipments. If your competitors also promise prompt delivery, but they are not prompt in all their behaviors—and you are—you will be "walking the talk" and differentiating yourself symbolically.

The distinctions between these four types of behavioral differentiation are important because each represents an opportunity for companies to use behavior as a competitive asset. However, they must be deployed and managed differently. As we continue to explore these types of behavioral differentiators, we will offer examples of positive and negative behaviors for each type. Later, we will discuss how these four types are related and what the implications are for business leaders.

Why "great service?" What is wrong with "good service?" Good service isn't enough to insure differentiation from competitors, to build solid customer relationships, to compete on value without competing on price, to inspire employees to want to become even better at their work and at their lives, to deliver an unmistakable financial dividend.

—Leonard L. Berry, *On Great Service:*
A Framework for Action

Operational Behavioral Differentiation: Setting a New Standard

Operational BDs are those that have been codified and integrated into the standard operating procedures and policies affecting how employees *normally* interact with and serve customers. The word *normal* is important in this definition. If the company's *standard* procedures result in behaviors that clearly and positively distinguish the company from the behaviors customers experience with the company's competitors, then those standard procedures are differentiating and will help bias customers toward the company. Behavioral differentiators alone are insufficient, but if the company can offer competitive products or services at a price acceptable to its target customer segment, then positive BDs will create customer preference.

Operational BDs are the most tactical of the four types because they are deliberate choices you make about how to interact with customers and they can occur at most of your customer touch points. They reflect the moment-by-moment ways in which customers experience your company and its people. If they are *consistent* and *sustained*—if customers experience these behaviors with the majority of your employees the majority of the time—then they form the baseline of the customer's experience of you. As Figure 4-1 illustrates, they are the foundation of behavioral differentiation in any company. If your company is unable to integrate differentiating behaviors into your standard practices, it is unlikely that you will sustain BD in any other form.

It would be useful at this point to illustrate what positive operational behavioral differentiators look like. Clearly, they differ depending on the nature of the company and its customers, so what constitutes a behavioral differentiator for one company in its market may not seem like a differentiator to another company in another market. Remember, too, that behavioral differentiation is situational. Behavior doesn't differentiate unless the company's competitors don't normally behave that way.

Positive Operational Behaviors

▲ A "sales associate" greets customers at the front entrance and helps them find what they're looking for (if they need help).

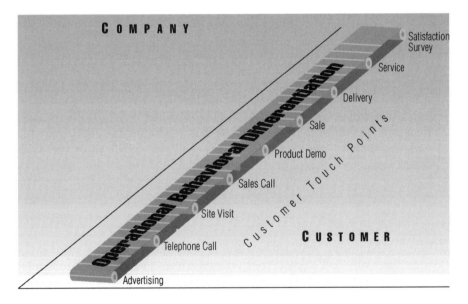

Figure 4-1. Operational Behavioral Differentiation. Operational BD is the foundation of all behavioral differentiation because it reflects standard behaviors that differentiate the company at most customer touch points. It should be a well-oiled machine, like a conveyor belt.

▲ As standard practice, your employees are trained to look for customers who seem to be lost or appear to need help and then to step up and offer assistance. If patrons are leaving the store empty-handed, employees ask if they could help them find what they were looking for.

▲ A store has a "no fault" return policy and salespeople are invariably friendly and eager to please customers—even to the point of accepting as "returns" some items the store doesn't carry.

▲ From your CEO on down, your executives are committed to having frequent face-to-face contact with key customer executives. Your account managers participate in these regular interactions and act as advocates for the customers' interests.

▲ Your salespeople send personal "thank-you" notes after every meeting with customers.

▲ Instead of bringing standard brochures and product or service descriptions to meetings with customers and prospects, it's your policy to develop high-quality, customized executive summaries that are focused on your customer's needs, key issues, and concerns.

▲ You know what your customers are interested in—hobbies and personal interests as well as business interests. You look for and send them things you know they'd enjoy seeing: newspaper clippings, journal or magazine articles, Web site addresses, books, videotapes, etc. What you send never has strings attached ("Let's have lunch and talk about our new. . . ."). Instead, you do it as a courtesy because you know they have these interests.

▲ If customers have problems installing or operating your equipment, you send a service rep to help them free of charge, and your rep stays with that customer until the problems are resolved and the equipment is working as it should.

▲ Your firm's practice is to open offices near your clients' largest regional locations so that your professionals are available locally to serve those clients.

▲ It is company policy for all executives—including the CEO—to visit some stores once a month. Whenever they are in a store, they serve customers along with the regular sales staff. Moreover, every executive is expected to model exemplary customer relationship skills—and they do.

▲ You regularly meet with your customer's consumers to learn more about what they want and expect from your customer's products. Periodically, you videotape some consumer focus groups and send the tapes, along with suggestions, to your customer. On a semiannual basis, you strategize with your customer about how they can better serve the consumers and how you can better serve them.

▲ You go out of your way to show the customer how to reduce costs, improve productivity, or otherwise improve their business operations or results. Your sales reps are called "senior consultants" and are trained to go beyond selling their products and provide active business consulting to the customer.

▲ You respond within one hour to every customer complaint and resolve problems quickly and at no additional cost to the customer.

▲ You collect consumer information and put it into a database so your systems "remember" consumer preferences. When consumers call, your representatives can quickly access each consumer's information, so you can "remember" what they've ordered, what they prefer, etc. Your representatives can call consumers by name, so you can personalize the call. [This used to be a powerful operational behavior; however, with the rapid growth of Customer Relationship Management (CRM) systems, this differentiator is rapidly becoming commoditized. In Theodore Levitt's words, this service feature is becoming the *expected* product. Soon, mail-order businesses that don't do this will fall below the service norm and be at a disadvantage.]

Operational BDs like these can and should be managed. They must be normalized so that every customer at every touch point receives and perceives special treatment. Unless you manage your people and processes so these behaviors are systematic and consistent, you won't create a sustainable behavioral advantage.

In Chapter 3, we introduced our research on behavioral differentiation in which we asked consumers three questions regarding various types of professionals they had interacted with:

▲ What do you expect of these professionals?
▲ In your best experiences with them, what happened?
▲ In your worst experiences with them, what happened?

In this chapter, we will report the findings of our research for waiters and waitresses. Table 4-1 shows what customers expect of these serving people.

Imagine for a moment that you are opening a new restaurant and are hiring and training your serving staff. Based on customers' expectations of waiters and waitresses, what would your restaurant's philosophy toward customers be? What standard practices would you establish for your serving staff? What qualities would you look for in the people you hire? At each touch point with your patrons, how would you ensure that your servers outbehave the servers in the rival restaurants around you? For each of the customer expectations in Table 4-1, there is a range of behavioral possibilities, as shown here for "knowledge of the product":

Normal or Expected Server Behaviors

▲ They know what's on the menu and can describe how each item is prepared.
▲ They know the daily specials.
▲ They can offer guidance about wine choices.
▲ Upon request, they can make menu recommendations.
▲ They know something about the restaurant and the area and can answer questions about them.

Negatively Differentiating Server Behaviors

▲ They don't know the menu well, and they aren't sure how items are prepared or incorrectly describe how items are prepared.
▲ They can't remember the daily specials and have to go ask; worse yet, they are annoyed when asked and tell you that the specials are written on the blackboard by the entrance.
▲ They drop the wine list on your table without comment and, when asked, have no clue about the wine choices and can't make recommendations.
▲ They don't know anything about the restaurant and don't seem to know the area.

Positively Differentiating Server Behaviors

▲ They know the menu inside out and can describe not only how each item is prepared but how their preparation differs from the normal way such a dish is prepared and why theirs is better. They are especially adept at describing the use of spices and garnishes and how the chef's selections enhance25 the meal.
▲ They know the daily specials by heart and can recommend a special based on a diner's likes and dislikes. Moreover, they know what specials are coming up and can recommend when the diner might want to return.
▲ Although they might not be wine connoisseurs, they know their restaurant's wine cellar well enough to recommend the best wine within the diner's price range. They can speak knowledgeably about the vineyards featured in their cellar.

Table 4-1. Customers' Expectations of Waiters and Waitresses.

	Technical Expectations
Knowledge of the Product	Being knowledgeable about the menu Being able to make good suggestions Knowing about the restaurant and what they have to offer guests Knowing the cuisine and wine choices Offering guidance about the menu and wine choices Knowing their product

	Behavioral Expectations
Prompt Service and Attention	Providing good service Being efficient; being there to serve diners Being attentive to me and my table Not allowing diners to be left waiting Being responsive to special requests Being attentive and having good memory Being there at our table when we need them Bringing the check in a timely fashion Being prompt Listening to what we would like and delivering it in a timely fashion Checking back with me quite a few times and, if I need something, bringing it right away Providing quick service with attention to detail Attending to me; I want to be acknowledged, not ignored Being accurate; getting orders right Noticing when patrons need service and presenting the check at the appropriate time Being attentive to the overall picture as well as the details Treating me and my party as though we were the only table they have at the moment
Friendliness	Being friendly; having a friendly manner Being engaging Having a good sense of humor Smiling Being personable and outgoing Being upbeat and approachable Being cordial Having a cheerful disposition Having a pleasant attitude and demeanor Being kind Being friendly without crossing the line

(continues)

Table 4-1. (continued)

Politeness and Courtesy	Being polite and cheerful Being courteous Being polite and maintaining good boundaries Refraining from interrupting conversations Being considerate, polite, and courteous Being patient Having common courtesy Asking what else I might want before bringing the check
Good Attitude	Appreciating my business Being happy (or appearing to be so) Being willing to make my dining experience positive Acting like they like their job—that they chose it Being there to serve Being willing to do whatever it takes to make my experience positive; the best ones look at your dining out as an event and try to dazzle you with their service Making the experience enjoyable for me; a friendly waiter or waitress can add so much to the enjoyment of a social evening dining out; when they take everything in stride and crack jokes, they add to the fun of being out Taking pride in their work and their restaurant
Honesty	Being honest about the taste of the food Telling me if the fish is three days old and that's why it's on special Being honest enough to warn me what not to select on the menu
Miscellaneous	Being resourceful and problem solving so my dining experience is the way I want it Being in tune enough to realize when I want constant attention or want to be left alone Asking if I want coffee before they pour it in my cup Being neat and clean

▲ They know the history of the restaurant and any interesting features about it, as well as the history and attractions of the area. When asked, they can provide fascinating bits of information.

Given the option, no sensible restaurateur would want anything other than these positive differentiating behaviors, which are more satisfying to patrons and will cause them to return. Are these kinds of behaviors difficult to achieve? We don't think so, but you have to decide that you want exemplary service—that this is important to you in how you will serve your customers—and you must set appropriately high standards as part of your operating philosophy. In short, you have to make your *behavior* toward customers an important element in your value proposition. Then you have to hire the right people and educate them—in your menu choices, in how the food is prepared, in the contents of your wine cellar, in the history and interesting features of your restaurant, and so on. That's how you operationalize exceptional behaviors from your serving staff.

Companies whose operational behaviors are no different from their competitors' represent the vast middle ground of standard operating procedures and practices. From a behavioral standpoint, they are undifferentiated, so they need to compete based on other factors, such as product differences (if they can sustain them), service guarantees, location and access, or price. Companies that fall below the norm in their operational behaviors are in an even more precarious position because customers eventually will recognize that buying from these companies entails a price beyond the cost of the goods or services—they have to contend with behavior that makes the buying experience unpleasant or worse. Here are some examples of operational behaviors that negatively differentiate the seller.

Negative Operational Behaviors

▲ Customers wander around your store looking for help but can't find anyone to help them.

▲ Your wait staff is required to clear tables as quickly as possible, particularly during the busy lunch and dinner periods. As soon as patrons look like they have stopped eating, your waiters and waitresses clear their plates, even if food remains on them.

▲ Your employees have little authority to handle customer complaints or problems and must seek a manager's approval to resolve many customer issues.

▲ Your company has a strong engineering focus. The sales reps are treated like second-class citizens and have trouble gaining the respect or cooperation of others in your company, including senior management. Customers sense this and know that your sales reps don't have the power or authority to solve their problems, although they mostly see the sales reps.

▲ You have a long, automated menu on your customer telephone lines, and customers are forced to go through multiple options to find what they need.

▲ To discourage returns, your "unofficial" policy is to frustrate customers who are returning an item or who call to file a complaint. You have deliberate procedures for making the process difficult. For instance, customers returning items are required to have receipts and must fill out a lengthy form indicating the reasons for the return. All returns require a supervisor's approval.

▲ You understaff your customer service department and install an automated system to handle customer calls. However, the "help" line is nothing more than an automated answering system that provides answers to frequently asked questions. Customers don't have another number to call, and this one does not enable them to reach a human being.

▲ Your company has a strict thirty-day policy on receiving payments. If a customer's check is not entered into your system by the end of that period, the computer automatically generates a threatening "late payment" notice. If payment is not received within fifteen days of that notice, customers are sent a "collections" notice and the account is turned over to a collection agency.

▲ Customers have difficulty locating the "right" person in your company who can help them. They are referred endlessly to others or are given other numbers to call—which are frequently busy.

▲ Your field sales and service representatives have limited decision-making authority. They must go through four levels of management to seek exceptions to policy or get approval for major cost expenditures to solve problems with customers' equipment.

These examples, which are not unusual, result from standard policies or practices that companies have put in place—often with the best of intentions—to run their operations more efficiently or to solve problems. Whether through misapplication, benign neglect, or a management team more concerned with running a tight ship than delighting customers, these kinds of policies lose their purpose over time and devolve into thoughtless, often bureaucratic behaviors that annoy and frustrate customers. The result is a buying experience that is below the norm most customers experience, so the unintended consequence of what may once have been sensible policies is negative behavioral differentiation. On the other hand, we're giving some businesses more of the benefit of the doubt than they deserve. As consumers, we all have experienced some airlines, restaurants, movie theatres, and retail stores that are not focused on customers and that implement operational policies and practices that are almost deliberately antagonistic toward the people who patronize them. They may survive in the market for other reasons (cost, location, convenience), but they will not engender customer loyalty and are unlikely to survive when their customers find alternatives.

Operational BDs are closely tied to a company's business model and reflect the company's values and attitudes toward serving customers. Hence, they reveal the philosophy and vision of the company's leaders. Wal-Mart would never have gained its prominence among retailers had it not been for Sam Walton's attitude toward customers. He said, "There is only one boss. The customer. And he can fire everybody in the company from the chairman on down, simply by spending his money somewhere else." Walton understood something so fundamental about people that it seems embarrassingly commonplace to cite it: He understood that when you *connect* with people, when you engage them on a human level, it makes them feel good—about themselves and about you—and they will be more inclined to shop at your store because they like you. Of course, Walton also knew that he had to offer the right products at attractive prices in convenient locations. His business model was sound, but so were the business models of many of his rivals when he founded Wal-Mart. So he added a differentiator that has made *the* difference at Wal-Mart: the 10-foot attitude.

When Sam ran for class president in college, he found a simple way to connect with people: "I learned that one of the secrets to leadership was the simplest thing of all: Speak to people coming down the sidewalk before they speak to you."[1] He won that class election and later operationalized this simple human relations principle as he taught the "10-foot attitude" in his stores. Whenever he visited his associates, he asked for a pledge: "I want you to promise that whenever you come within 10 feet of a customer, you will look him in the eye, greet him and ask if you can help him."[2] Wal-Mart's 10-foot attitude begins with the associate who greets every customer at the door and extends to all associates whom customers encounter as they shop. This BD seems simple, and it is. Many of them are. What makes them powerful is that they help make a customer's shopping experience more satisfying and less stressful—and different enough from their experiences at other retailers for them to return to Wal-Mart. Harry Cunningham, the CEO of S.S. Kresge, who opened the first Kmart discount department store in 1962, said admiringly of Walton, "Sam's establishment of the Walton culture throughout the company was the key to the whole thing. It's just incomparable. He is the greatest businessman of this century."[3]

Operational BDs have to be consistent and sustainable. By *consistent,* we mean that customers must experience them no matter which employee they encounter. If some Wal-Mart associates manifest the 10-foot attitude but others don't, then the customers' experiences will not be consistent enough for them to form the impression that "Wal-Mart is different." Instead, they'll assume that some associates are friendlier and more helpful than others. For operational behaviors to differentiate, customers must experience them all of the time (or close to it). Furthermore, they have to experience those differentiating behaviors over time, so operational BDs must be *sustainable,* which requires leadership, education, and processes for perpetuating the desired behaviors and attitudes.

Their consistency and sustainability make operational BDs visible—not only to customers but also to competitors—so they can have a short half-life. Operational behaviors that truly differentiate can be studied and emulated to some degree. In benchmarking studies, these kinds of behaviors are often cited as best practices, so operational BDs run the risk of losing their differentiation and becoming commoditized as more of a company's competitors learn to adopt the behaviors customers are responding to. However, this doesn't detract from the power of operational BDs or from a company's need to discover how it can differentiate itself behaviorally and operationalize those differentiating behaviors. Failing to find and implement operational BDs is akin to throwing in the towel. You must do it even if your competitors do copy your best practices. However, as we noted earlier, even when they know what you're doing, they often fail to emulate those practices successfully enough to blunt your competitive advantage.

Interpersonal Behavioral Differentiation: Showing That You Care

A completely different kind of behavioral differentiation arises not from policies, procedures, and standard operating practices but from something deep within individual employees. At first glance, what we describe as interpersonal BDs may seem commonplace and undistinguishing: listening carefully, being respectful, showing care, being sensitive to what customers want, attending to them patiently, and being good-humored and pleasant. What's so remarkable about that?

Well, the remarkable thing is that many, many people in business don't behave this way with customers, including those whose jobs place them on the front lines of customer sales and service. As customers, we all have encountered people in the companies we're buying from who are warm and engaging, take a personal interest in us, and make us feel good about interacting with them. But we've also experienced the opposite—those salespeople, executives, customer service reps, and engineers who are cold, distracted, uncaring, impatient, and oblivious to our needs except on a superficial level. Sometimes, their behaviors are not offensive; they are just so focused on the task that they make no human connection at all. We might as well be interacting with a machine. As we said in Chapter 3, our experience of other people's behavior resembles a bell curve. The vast, undifferentiated hump in the middle represents how we experience most people: they are civil, moderately friendly if engaged, moderately helpful if asked, and they observe the normal social customs of the region where they live. Our interactions with them, whether we meet them socially or in business, are normally unremarkable.

On the lower end of the bell curve are those people whose interpersonal skills are obviously below the norm—who are cold, don't listen, don't care, and can't be bothered. Their behavior is so far outside our normal behavior that we notice it and are typically put off by it. When we encounter these people in a buyer's organization, they differentiate themselves—and their company—negatively. The reverse is also true. Those people on the upper end of the bell curve, who exhibit exceptional interpersonal skills, create positive behavioral differentiation. We generally like them more, feel good dealing with them, and would welcome meeting them again. Assuming that the bell curve for interpersonal behavior among the general population is normal—and this is a safe assumption—then about one person in six has the skill and the will to consistently relate to other people in ways that differentiate them interpersonally. Of course, we all have our good and bad days, and it's likely that interpersonal behavior fluctuates, even among those who excel at it. On some days they may be exceptional and on other days just noticeably above or below average.

Emotions are contagious.
—Daniel Goleman, *Emotional Intelligence*

There is a growing body of evidence that interpersonal skill is a form of intelligence and that those who possess more of it have an advantage. In his book *Emotional Intelligence,* Daniel Goleman argues convincingly that emotional intelligence is a distinguishing factor in success: "Much evidence testifies that people who are emotionally adept—who know and manage their own feelings well, and who read and deal effectively with other people's feelings—are at an advantage in any domain of life, whether romance and intimate relationships or picking up the unspoken rules that govern success in organizational politics."[4] Goleman's work derives in part from research by Howard Gardner and others at the Harvard Graduate School of Education who developed the theory of multiple intelligences, including interpersonal intelligence. According to Gardner, "Interpersonal intelligence builds on a core capacity to notice distinctions among others; in particular, contrasts in their moods, temperaments, motivations, and intentions. In more advanced forms, this intelligence permits a skilled adult to read the intentions and desires of others, even when these have been hidden."[5]

As we were researching this book, we interviewed the owner of a large, independent bookstore that is renowned among book buyers and readers for its comfortable atmosphere; huge inventory of books; and friendliness toward customers, even those who spend the day in the store, reading on a comfortable sofa without buying anything. The owner said that when she goes into a store she hates it when a salesperson rushes up and says, "Can I help you?" Like many shoppers, she often wants to browse in peace and prefers to ask for help if she needs it. So her philosophy in her bookstore is to offer to help customers only if they appear to want help. We asked how she knows that. "You have to read the customer," she said. "You have to listen with your eyes and ears and watch their body language. If they look lost, then go see if they need help. If they're deep in thought, don't disturb them."

People who are highly skilled interpersonally are able to read others. Furthermore, because they are sensitive to others, they are also sensitive to the impact they have on others, and they know how to manage that impact. They use the tools we all learned in childhood—smiling, maintaining eye contact, leaning forward, gesturing in friendly ways, and so on—to moderate their interactions and respond to the signals others are sending. As Daniel Goleman says, "People who make an excellent social impression . . . are adept at monitoring their own expression of emotion, are keenly attuned to the ways others are reacting, and so are able to continually fine-tune their social performance, adjusting it to make sure they are having the desired effect."[6] Of course, there are people in business, especially salespeople, who believe they can be consistently successful by "turning on the charm" when they have to. We've all encountered these people. They really don't care about people, but they flip on the "charm" switch as they approach customers and keep it on just long enough to fulfill their personal agenda. The stereotype of this manipulative charmer is the car salesperson, but whether they are selling cars, IPOs, beef, or cold-rolled steel, their insincerity masks a deep cynicism that only the most naïve of buyers fails to sense. When we speak of positive interpersonal behavioral differentiation we are excluding these con artists because even moderately sophisticated buyers read their insincerity and know them for what they are, which, ironically, creates negative interpersonal differentiation.

Positive interpersonal behaviors are obviously crucial during the sales process. However, being sensitive to others, reading their intentions and desires, and making a good social impression are important at all customer touch points, not just during sales calls and executive lunches. Yet in numerous instances employees are at best indifferent toward customers and at worst antagonistic. We saw the contrast in our research on behavioral differentiation when we asked respondents to cite their best and worst experiences with waiters and waitresses (Tables 4-2 and 4-3).

(text continues on page 78)

Table 4-2. Positive Differentiating Behaviors of Waiters and Waitresses.

	Excellent Performance
Competence, Knowledge, and Experience	She is always friendly and competent. She checked back several times during our meal—not too many times but also not too few. She got it just right. He gave his personal opinions of the food selections and spoke highly of less expensive items. One waiter offered suggestions for wine with specific entrees and gave us a thorough rundown of the menu and the specials. He made sure our drinks were refreshed at all times, was sociable with the group, and let us hang around as long as we liked.
	Positive Behaviors
Prompt Service and Attention	For one great waitress I remember, nothing was too much to ask. She checked back frequently and was truly sorry if we ordered an item they were out of. She went out of her way to make sure I was happy and taken care of. She did this with genuine sincerity—not because she had to. She paid attention to our conversation and was sure not to interrupt or ask a question while we were eating. She was extremely efficient and speedy, yet she appeared to slow down when approaching the table and interacting with me. She was very personable and outgoing; kept us up to date on the preparation of the meal, checked on our reactions to it when the food arrived, and gave us an after-dinner drink free.
Friendliness, Pleasant Attitude	Several of us go to a Mexican restaurant at least once a week, so we are familiar with the wait staff. One waiter in particular always brightens our day by teasing us about what we order (it's usually the same each time) and if we want margaritas to get us through the rest of our day. It is a positive experience for us since his mood is infectious and gets us in happier mood. Some wait staff seem to intuitively understand that they are an important part of the experience of eating out. Friendliness and a great sense of humor are the qualities that have added the most to my experiences of eating out.

(continues)

Table 4-2. (continued)

	When they are cheerful, it makes me glad I'm there.
	A friendly greeting, smile and attitude can make a meal that is just average seem extraordinary. Asking if everything is all right and giving the impression that you are their most important customer makes you feel good.
	The waitress always remembered my name, habits, and likes. She also was perpetually friendly, even when I knew she was having a hard time. In a way she became a role model for me on how to meet adversity with grace.
	In addition to great service, which is a must, a great waiter/waitress should have a cheerful disposition, establish eye contact and smile, use my name, look and act in a professional manner. One waiter in Albuquerque made up a little poem for my daughter and sang it at the table while we were waiting. That was a nice touch.
Attentive, Sensitive, and Caring	She always picks up on those "unspoken cues"—for example, if I seem frustrated with my food or unhappy with my seat, she asks how they can make it better. If I am unable to read the menu because I forgot my glasses, she is willing to help read the offerings. And she offers a free dessert if my meal is unpleasant.
	On a business trip, dining alone at a fine restaurant in the Regent Hotel in Hong Kong, the waiter, who had already graciously engaged me in conversation to make me feel less alone, offered to take me on a tour of the Regent's wine cellar between the courses of my meal. He spent 20 minutes showing me everything in that incredible cellar. When I came in, I was feeling a little down from missing my wife at that meal. But he turned my lonely evening into a very memorable one.
	The best experience I ever had was with a waitress who truly showed every customer that she absolutely enjoyed her job. She took the time to greet us, sincerely ask how our morning had been, and then made sure that we felt like we were dining in her

own home. The key element to her success is that she treated all of her customers well and catered to their needs like no one else was around or mattered.

The waitress noticed that we had left a good portion of our meal and asked if our meal was good. We said it was fair. She immediately said that the meal was on the house and gave us a voucher for a free dinner for two. Later, the manager called and apologized and invited us to give them another try. That was 11 years ago. Now we eat there at least three times a month and have not had a bad meal since.

A few things can make a big difference. When dining with young children, we had some waiters/waitresses that would automatically bring crackers for the kids when we arrived at the table, and they would make sure the kids' food got there right away—before the adult meals. That way we could get the kids started, and then eat our food when it arrived a few minutes later—while it was still hot!

I have restaurants that I like to go to mostly because of the waiters or waitresses. There's a waitress that works at the Doubletree who always spends a little time shooting the breeze before taking orders. She miraculously remembers what I've ordered in the past and comments when I don't order it. "Oh, you like the pasta, don't you? It's especially good tonight if you want to change your mind." And if I order dessert, she brings out this huge piece of pie or dish of ice cream. She gets great tips from us.

There is nothing more irritating to me than to receive rude, uncaring, or just generally inadequate service. Once, I sat through the worst meal in my life and really didn't complain or walk away angry. I was willing to give the restaurant a second chance because I felt appreciated. They wanted my business and went out of their way to let me know that. I guess it's like being invited to someone's home and feeling real hospitality.

Table 4-3. Negative Differentiating Behaviors of Waiters and Waitresses.

	Poor Performance
Incompetence	She didn't realize that the food was improperly prepared. He didn't know the menu. She was totally unhelpful. He was very unprofessional. He didn't know what the specials of the day were, and he couldn't tell us how some dishes were prepared.

	Negative Behaviors
Rudeness	Our waiter was rude and hostile. He was obsequious and condescending. I will never go back there. He was very rude. We were in a small town having lunch. My husband was drinking iced tea, and when he got to the bottom of his glass, he found a dead spider in it. When we brought this to the waitress' attention, she said, "It wasn't there when I filled it." My husband said he didn't put it in there and asked her for a new glass. She said that she would rinse out his glass but not give him a new one. Unbelievable. He was sloppy in appearance and behavior. He almost slammed our plates down on the table when he brought them. I was dining alone on a business trip at a very expensive restaurant in New York City. During the entire meal, the waiter seemed resentful that I was there (like I was taking up valuable space) and acted like I was unfit to dine in their restaurant. He was rude, unhelpful, and condescending.
Apathy	She had a no-care attitude ("I don't want to be here today."). She just didn't care. She was unbelievably awful. We asked her about an item on the menu, and she said, "I don't know" and then didn't bother to go find out. She was defensive about the food and didn't care that we didn't like it. His service was poor, and he had excuses for everything. He was unappreciative. He seemed concerned only about the size of the bill so he would earn a bigger tip.

She didn't treat me as a guest.

She was slow with no apparent reason, and she didn't communicate about the service.

She sent the signal that she would rather have been elsewhere. She neglected simple tasks like filling water glasses and replacing linen. Later, she asked how our food was but then failed to respond when I said, "Just okay." She seemed to think that apathy is good service, and then she expected a 15% tip.

The service was just terrible. None of the help staff seemed to care.

She refused a special request (salad dressing on the side).

Bad Attitude	He had a bad attitude and gave sarcastic answers to our questions.
	She acted perturbed when asked to correct wrong orders.
	The waitress had a very nasty attitude.
	She had a surly attitude.
	He seemed to feel that being a waiter was far below his true lot in life. Our request for service seemed to insult his capabilities because his affect conveyed a deep-seated resentment that we would expect him to do things like take our order and carry food. Watching him, one had to wonder how he ever survived even one evening as a waiter. Needless to say, we haven't been back to that restaurant. They should have paid us by the hour for having to deal with him.
	She seemed offended when I asked for a piece of missing silverware.
Inattention, Unresponsiveness, Forgetfulness	He was a space cadet—just totally out of it.
	We were ignored for about half an hour.
	The service was very slow; she just ignored us.
	He was inattentive to the point of being absent—until it was time to give us the bill.
	We waited 30 minutes at the table just to get our drink orders taken.
	Their service was very poor; they had no concern for my happiness.
	She kept forgetting things.
	We waited forever for the check.
	She spent more time talking with her coworkers than waiting on patrons.

(continues)

Table 4-3. (continued)

	He took our order but then didn't show up again until I called him over to the table.
	The waitress didn't turn in our food order. At least 45 minutes later we asked her about it and she didn't apologize or appear to care.
	I felt totally neglected.
	We had to call him over to our table in order to get service.
Miscellaneous	The waitress had long, greasy hair, which she managed to dangle in my food, leaving souvenirs.
	He had dirty hands and touched the food.
	The waitress wasn't sociable at all, which put me off.
	The waiter kept interrupting what was obviously a very private conversation.

Note in Table 4-2 the observed behaviors that reflect a high degree of interpersonal intelligence: picking up on the "unspoken cues," noticing when a large portion of the meal remains, giving the impression that the diner is important, handling adversity with grace. Also notable is how much importance respondents placed on the serving person's disposition. They give high marks for servers who are personable, outgoing, and friendly. As Daniel Goleman observed, emotions are contagious. When employees are friendly and outgoing, they tend to elicit similar feelings and behaviors among customers—and vice versa, as Table 4-3 shows.

Remarkably, more than ninety percent of the negative experiences diners cited in our study resulted from servers' poor *behaviors*—or *attitudes,* which are the precursors of behavior. This suggests that mastering the technical content of a job is relatively easy compared to the behavioral content. Further, when customers become annoyed with a company or an establishment, it's generally because of how they're treated. Behavioral differentiation, whether positive or negative, can have an enormous impact on your business, but you have to be aware of the impact, either way, and manage it.

Interpersonal behavior is part of virtually every customer communication and interaction, even in written communications. At every customer touch point, you have the opportunity to differentiate yourself interpersonally. In this respect, interpersonal BDs are like operational BDs, as Figure 4-2 shows. However, the two forms of BD are different. Operational BDs are systemic and reflect a company's policies, procedures, and standard practices. Inter-

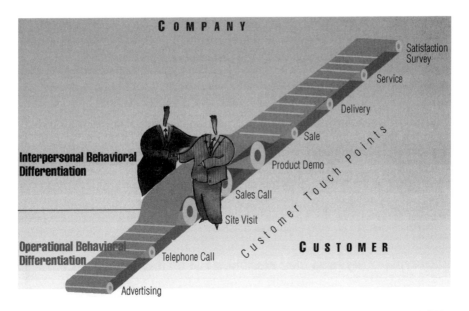

Figure 4-2. Interpersonal Behavioral Differentiation. Interpersonal BDs operate in parallel with operational BDs. They may or may not occur at customer touch points because they rely on the individual attitudes and skills of each employee. They have an amplifying effect on operational behaviors.

personal BDs emerge from employees' personalities and temperaments and are reflected in their interactions with customers. To illustrate the difference, consider the Tale of Two Bellhops.

Tom and John are two bellhops working for the same hotel. The hotel manager understands operational BD and establishes some behavioral standards for her employees, including escorting guests to their cars in the underground lot, bringing a complimentary coffee and tea service to guests' rooms in the morning, and running errands for business guests who are busy during the day. Guests don't experience this kind of behavior in other hotels they've stayed in, so these behaviors positively differentiate the hotel. Both Tom and John learn these behaviors during their orientation training and exhibit them as they interact with guests. However, Tom is naturally friendly and outgoing. He has exceptional interpersonal skills. John is more distant and lacks Tom's warmth. Guests who encounter the two are pleased with the service each provides but feel even better when interacting with Tom. His warm and engaging personality gives them an extra lift.

What if Tom and John worked in a hotel that did not differentiate itself operationally? If there were no operational BDs, Tom would still—due to his extraordinary interpersonal skill—be differentiating himself interpersonally. *Interpersonal and operational BDs are independent of each other but can be mutually reinforcing.* Employees with high interpersonal skills will enhance the behavioral differentiation caused by a company's operational policies. Similarly, when a company's operational policies allow for the exceptional treatment of customers, employees are likely to feel better during their interactions with customers, which will support and encourage employees with outstanding interpersonal skills.

Both staff and customers tend to stay with organizations that enable them to experience positive, meaningful, and personally important feelings, even if the organizations cannot always provide everything they want or solve all their problems.

—Janelle Barlow and Dianna Maul, *Emotional Value*

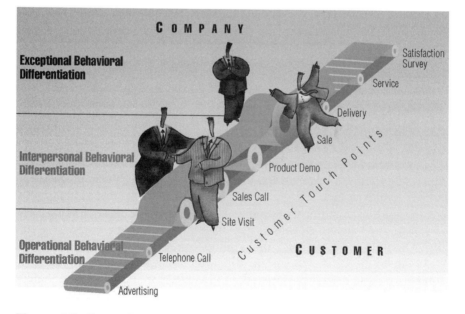

Figure 4-3. Exceptional Behavioral Differentiation. Exceptional BDs are an outgrowth of operational BDs. They can occur when companies and company leaders enable employees to "break the rules" and provide exceptional service to customers. Their amplifying effect is typically even greater than interpersonal BDs.

Only one person in six has the degree of *innate* interpersonal skill that is truly differentiating; however, as Daniel Goleman argues in *Emotional Intelligence,* "temperament is not destiny."[7] About two-thirds of people have average interpersonal skills, but those skills can be improved through expectation setting, education and training, and on-the-job reinforcement. Beyond hiring, training, and setting high standards, companies have to create an environment where interpersonal BDs can be sustained, and it's hard to sustain this level of interpersonal performance if the company is understaffed and employees are too busy to take the time to care. We will have more to say later about sustaining interpersonal behavioral differentiation as we discuss Michael Abrashoff and other leaders who routinely excel in this area, but one final point before we move on: Interpersonal BDs are as portable as employees' feet. If the atmosphere and working conditions in a company are unsatisfying to people with high interpersonal intelligence, they will vote with their feet and find better places to work. Although interpersonal behavioral differentiation resides in the individual skill and will of employees, it can be managed by creating an environment that retains employees who delight customers with their warmth, caring, and engaging personalities. They are, in spirit and deed, caring professionals, and that makes a huge difference with customers.

Exceptional Behavioral Differentiation: Breaking the Rules

Exceptional BDs are just that—the rare exceptions—even by behaviorally differentiated standards. They generally involve a real or apparent deviation from standard procedures, so they can be an outgrowth of operational BDs, as shown in Figure 4-3. Because they go beyond normal operational procedures, they may incur costs that can't be sustained for a lengthy period. So these behaviors are usually exceptions to normal policy—breaking the rules in ways that do something extraordinary for customers. Or they may be even more exceptional, behaving positively in extraordinary ways the rules don't even cover.

Positive Exceptional Behaviors

▲ Four of your hotel guests are talking in the lobby about where to go for dinner. They don't know the restaurants in the area but are sure they don't want to go to the chain restaurant near the hotel. One of your employees, who is about to go off shift, overhears them and offers to drive them to a better restaurant and pick them up when they are through.

▲ You are a nurse whose shift has ended, but one patient who is undergoing a difficult procedure the next morning is frightened. You spend most of your evening with the patient—talking, reading to her, reassuring her about the procedure, and leaving only when she's asleep.

▲ You are a teacher. Although you are not highly paid and need the money for your own family, you buy supplies and textbooks for eight students whose families can't afford them.

▲ You pull some strings for a customer—getting tickets that are hard to come by, helping his child get an interview or get accepted at a university, or going out of the way to introduce him to someone important.

▲ You don't have what the customer wants, so you obtain it from one of your competitors in order to satisfy the customer's needs.

▲ You are a dentist. At the end of every day, you telephone the patients you saw that day at their homes and ask how they are doing.

▲ The customer left something important in your office. You drive to her home that evening and return it.

▲ You work in a large department store. A client of one of your customers has flown into town for an important job interview, and the airline has lost his luggage. It's Sunday, the store is closed, and the interview is at 8:00 Monday morning. You open the store by yourself on Sunday evening, escort the client to all appropriate departments and get him what he needs, hem his trousers at no extra charge, and ensure that he will be well dressed and ready for his interview the next morning.

▲ The customer buys a self-installation item but has trouble installing it. You go to the customer's business location or home and help install it at no charge.

Exceptional BD occurs when customers experience treatment that is truly more than would normally be required or expected. Whether treatment is exceptional or not is in the eye of the beholder, of course. The preceding examples reflect behaviors that different customers felt were exceptional at the time. It requires an extra effort on the part of employees. They must go out of their way to provide greater service, or take more time to do something (typically at no benefit to themselves beyond the intrinsic satisfaction of helping others), or give more than is required, often at personal expense or sacrifice. Customers generally recognize that the employee's behavior is exceptional, which can create a bond reminiscent of the bond between close friends. This occurs because there is no surer sign of caring than an employee's willingness to behave in an exceptional way toward a customer. It's not unusual, in fact, for such exceptional behavior to lead to enduring friendships. Exceptional BD has the kind of impact that can cause intense and vocal customer loyalty and turn customers into advocates.

The flip side of exceptional BD is apathy, as reflected in these negative examples of exceptional BD:

Negative Exceptional Behaviors

▲ Employees notice a customer in need but choose to do nothing about it, and the customer senses this.

▲ Employees know that something should be done but decide, "It's not my job."

▲ Employees could do more for customers, but it would interfere with their breaks.

▲ Employees feel that customers should be more self-sufficient. They manifest the attitude that if customers can't figure it out, that's their problem.

▲ Employees are angry with the company and take it out on customers, which they regard as the company's problem, not theirs.

▲ Customers have an extraordinary need and employees don't do anything about it, although they could if they really wanted to. Their excuse is that "it's against our policy."

When you fail to do something exceptional for customers, they sense that you have passed on the opportunity and are unwilling to step outside the real or virtual boundaries you have established for serving their needs. Of course, there are customers who will press every advantage and practically demand special treatment. You may have to impose sensible boundaries with them or they'll consume you, your employees, and your business. Goodwill in the interchange between buyers and sellers depends on an unspoken *quid pro quo:* "If you treat me right, I'll treat you right." This sense of reciprocity extends not only to the exchange of value in product for price (as a customer I want to receive fair value for my money) but also to the social interaction (I want to be treated with courtesy and respect). When either party violates this unspoken *quid pro quo,* goodwill suffers and each party becomes more defensive. Sellers become less willing to do anything exceptional for customers, and buyers take their business elsewhere (or create "revenge" Web sites).

Although there are legitimate reasons for setting boundaries and protecting the business from unscrupulous customers, companies should nonetheless find ways to create an environment where exceptional behavioral differentiation is possible when appropriate. Exceptional behaviors generally depend on the initiative of individual employees, but companies can encourage and support those initiatives by trusting them to make sensible decisions and giving them the latitude and responsibility to exercise their judgment. Ritz-Carlton is one of the finest examples of a company that encourages exceptional treatment of customers. In its employee training programs, Ritz-

Carlton sets high standards for customer service and is clear about employees' responsibilities in achieving those standards: **"Instant guest pacification** will be ensured by all. React quickly to correct the problem immediately. Follow-up with a telephone call within twenty minutes to verify the problem has been resolved to the customer's satisfaction. Do everything you possibly can to never lose a guest."[8] Ritz-Carlton does more than preach the gospel; it authorizes each associate to spend up to $2,000 to satisfy a guest. This is literally "putting your money where your mouth is." At the same time, the hotel encourages employees to behave responsibly in solving problems and to protect the hotel while ensuring guest satisfaction: "Protecting the assets of a Ritz-Carlton Hotel is the responsibility of every employee."[9]

Like many companies that excel at BD, Ritz-Carlton has operationalized many of its differentiating behaviors. These operational BDs reflect the hotel's vision and philosophy, are taught and reinforced during training sessions and employee meetings, and are embodied in the daily behaviors of the hotel's 22,000 employees. Wisely, Ritz-Carlton has also made it possible for employees to go beyond normal operational excellence and provide exceptional levels of service when required.

Ask any Harley® rider—they'll gladly share their experiences. These experiences of motorcycling create the thoughts, images and emotions of which dreams are made. So when we say, "We fulfill dreams through the experiences of motorcycling," we're talking about "E" business—Harley style . . . the Experience Business.

—Jeffrey L. Bleustein, Chairman and CEO,
Harley-Davidson, Inc.

Symbolic Behavioral Differentiation: Walking the Talk

We learned a powerful lesson about symbolic behavioral differentiation years ago when we were faculty members for an educational firm that offered writing programs to corporations. Our fellow faculty members were skilled at writing, but many of the other employees of this firm were not, including the direct sales force. Annually, they mailed thousands of letters and proposals to clients and prospects, and at least a half dozen times a year a prospect who received one of their documents returned it with the grammatical, punctuation, and spelling errors circled in red. Occasionally, these returned letters included a caustic appraisal of both the author and the firm: "And *you* want to teach *me* how to write!" This is negative symbolic BD.

Symbolic BD is fundamentally about alignment—the *internal* alignment of a company's messages with its behavior or the *external* alignment of a company's behavior with its customers' values, products, or image. In the simplest terms, alignment means walking the talk—behaving in ways that reflect and reinforce your messages or are aligned with your customer's messages. If you claim that you can offer the customer an experienced and knowledgeable project team, then your team's behavior should reflect their depth of experience, they should demonstrate their knowledge in their customer presentations and responses to questions, and they should act like a team. If you claim that your firm is highly creative, then your concepts had better be fresh and original, and so should your people—in appearance, energy, temperament, and actions. Your messages are promises of what's to come, and your behavior is often the first concrete evidence customers have that you will fulfill those promises.

In *Frames of Mind,* Howard Gardner notes how humans use symbols to convey meaning: "Symbols and symbol systems gain their greatest utility as they enter into the fashioning of full-fledged symbolic products: stories and sonnets, plays and poetry, mathematical proofs and problem solutions, rituals, and reviews—all manner of symbolic entities that individuals create in order to convey a set of meanings, and that other individuals imbued in the culture are able to understand, interpret, appreciate, criticize, or transform."[9] Gardner's context is literature, science, and academia, but he would be no less correct if his examples included company names, logos, print or television ads, marketing slogans, product brochures, proposals, business letters, office furnishings, business cards, and dress codes. These are all examples of means by which companies create emblems to represent themselves to potential customers. The BMW logo, the Goodyear blimp, "Intel Inside," Colonel Sanders' image, Prudential's rock, and the Energizer Bunny—these symbols communicate who a company is, what the company does, and what customers can expect from them.

Business symbols, like the symbols of government, religion, and pop culture, are so ubiquitous in our lives that they become largely subliminal. We are aware of them—and influenced by them—mostly on a subconscious level. Yet the messages they convey can have a powerful effect on buyers' decisions to choose one product over another. Because one of the primary aims of business is to find and retain customers, most business symbols convey a promise of benefit. Sometimes these promises are implied, but they are often explicit—especially in ads, slogans, and proposals. Even the most fundamental emblem of a company, its name, can express a promise to customers: Best Buy (see Figure 4-4), Quik Lube, Comfort Inn, Federal Express, Budget Rent-A-Car, Humana (which suggests *humane*), Super Value Stores, and The Sharper Image. Other organizations' *names* don't express the benefit customers should expect to receive, but their *brand image* does: Coca-Cola, Disney, Goodyear, Sony, Versace, Marks & Spencer, McKinsey & Company, Harvard University, Pricewaterhouse- Coopers, the New York Stock Exchange. We know what to expect from these organizations because their brand is an emblem of their promise. Finally, consider company slogans. These slogans appear in the company's ads, or on their Web sites, or in their brochures. Like names, logos, and brands, these slogans convey the company's central theme, its distinguishing message to the market, what it thinks of itself and what it wants customers to remember:

Bank of America	Embracing ingenuity
Porsche	Driving the future
Harley-Davidson	Experience Business
Eli Lilly	Answers that matter
Ford Motor Company	Striving to make the world a better place
General Electric	We Bring Good Things to Life
Credit Suisse	Sharp ideas. Tailor-made solutions. Flawless execution.
Fluor Corporation	A passion to build

Figure 4-4. Best Buy's Corporate ID. Best Buy is an example of a company that makes its promise of value to customers evident in its company name, logo, and image. Consequently, customers know what to expect when they enter a Best Buy store—the "best buy" or greatest value for their money. Used with permission.

These slogans suggest what we should expect from these companies and their people and products—although, in some cases, that message may not be immediately clear. From Bank of America, for instance, we would expect ingenious solutions—and smart, ingenious people. From Porsche, we would expect futuristic automobiles—cutting edge, beyond state of the art, the cars of the future today—and forward-thinking people, not stodgy, conservative traditionalists. From Harley-Davidson, we would expect a lifestyle experience—and people in every position at the company who reflect that experience. Fluor's slogan is particularly interesting. Here is how they elaborate upon it:

> **A Passion to Build** captures the essence of our company. It is inspired by our legacy of leadership, experience, respect and pride. It describes our promise for the future expressed through our noble purpose as a business, our corporate vision, our objectives, our core values, and the principles that guide our actions.[10]

Lofty stuff! Should we take it literally? Yes, because the people at Fluor view themselves as master builders. It's their message to prospective customers. It's the promise they make about how they execute projects. If we hire Fluor Corporation to build our chemical plant, we can reasonably expect the Fluor people we meet to show their passion for building, to demonstrate leadership and pride, and to deal with us and our project as though they were fulfilling a noble purpose. In other words, there should be alignment between the messages they convey and the way they act. They should walk the talk.

Symbolic BD is in some ways the most intellectual and challenging of the four types because it requires a great deal of thoughtfulness about what messages the company is sending and how to ensure that the company's behaviors match its messages. Symbolic BD often takes time to establish because the messages must be reflected in the practices and behaviors of many people; this requires considerable leadership and self-conscious attention to detail, as well as monitoring of current employees' behaviors and an effective program for educating new employees and aligning them behaviorally with those messages as quickly as possible. Here are some examples of positive symbolic BD, where the behaviors are well aligned with the messages:

Positive Symbolic Behaviors

▲ You manufacture and sell a line of men's mid-range business wear, including a brand of suits, trousers, and sport coats called Everprest. True to their name, they don't wrinkle, even after extended wear. Your male employees who come in contact with customers, including sales reps and executives, wear your line of clothing, and their suits, jackets, and pants are never wrinkled.

▲ You claim to excel at project management—and your presentations begin and end on time. You demonstrate good project management in everything you do with the customer. You never miss deadlines.

▲ Your establishment promotes cleanliness and courteous service—and your facilities are always clean and your people always courteous.

▲ You run a health club—and your managers, trainers and other employees are themselves trim and physically fit.

▲ You sell network services and equipment—and your company has a state-of-the-art network.

▲ You sell productivity software. You use the software yourselves and are models of high productivity in everything you do.

▲ You advertise authentic Mexican food in your restaurant—and your servers speak Spanish and the food is Mexican, not Tex-Mex.

▲ You emphasize the safety of your operations. Everything on your project sites is safe, and your people emphasize safety in everything they do.

▲ Part of your ad slogan is "fast and efficient service"—and customers never have to wait more than a few minutes to be served.

▲ You say your coffee is always fresh—and it always is.

▲ Your slogan implies that the flight attendants on your airplanes are friendly—and they invariably are.

Of course, the danger in making promises is not keeping them, which can convert customers into cynics. Customers expect you to walk the talk. When you don't, they become jaded. They question whether they are receiving a fair exchange of value for their money and whether any of your promises can be trusted. Consider these situations in which a company's implied or expressed promises are not reflected in their behavior:

Negative Symbolic Behaviors

▲ You claim to be an international firm and have excellent knowledge of local conditions around the world, but your representative doesn't speak the local language and is unaware of an impending ministry change that could affect the customer's business.

▲ You run a major car rental company that takes pride in the quality of its service. Everything in the image you create is first rate. However, customers frequently experience long lines and haggard representatives at your counters and have difficulty finding an attendant to check them in when they return cars. What's even more exasperating is that your employees take their breaks in plain view of returning customers, so it appears that your people don't care if customers are kept waiting.

▲ You create a trendy restaurant, co-owned and promoted by famous Holly-wood stars, that capitalizes on the Hollywood mystique. However, the food is unremarkable, the décor is undistinguished from other trendy restaurants, and after the initial hoopla fades, patrons rarely see anyone from Hollywood in the restaurants.

▲ In your proposals, you claim to be state of the art, but you don't have the latest technology and don't seem to be aware of advances one of your competitors just made.

▲ You are a search firm and claim to excel at cross-border searches, but your offices operate autonomously. Actual cross-border searches often do not produce the best candidates in a reasonable period of time because your compensation and election policies reward completion of local searches and building of the local office. There are few actual incentives to cooperate with offices in other countries except the goodwill of your professionals, which is inadequate more often than you want to admit.

▲ You claim to offer fast, courteous service, but your receptionist is abrupt with people on the phone, and your executives don't return calls promptly (in fact, sometimes not at all).

▲ You claim to be experts in investment management. However, my plain vanilla stock index fund has performed much better than the funds you have managed for me, and I get better information on stock trends and potential investments from The Motley Fool (www.fool.com) than I do from you.

Walking the talk can be difficult because a company's messages are usually conceived by its leaders, aided by marketing managers and creative teams from ad agencies, and there may be little actual correspondence between those messages and the living values, attitudes, processes, and actions of the hundreds or thousands of people who do the company's daily, front-line interacting with customers. Any executive who's tried to drive a major change program throughout a company knows how time-consuming and difficult a task it can be—and the legions of books on change management testify to how frequently it fails.

To this point, we have focused on internal symbolic BD—the alignment (or misalignment) of a company's messages with its behaviors as customers perceive them. Another powerful way companies can create symbolic BD is to align their behavior with a customer's values, products, or image. We will illustrate this with the Tale of the Yellow Pages. Years ago, a large computer systems company was bidding on a multibillion-dollar contract from one of the baby Bells. There were more than 25 bidders, so the baby Bell asked for executive summaries instead of full proposals as a way to narrow the field.

When the shortlist was published, the computer systems company was surprised to learn that they had not made the cut. Because they were such a major player in the industry, they asked the customer to reconsider, and they were given ten days to resubmit their executive summary.

In retrospect, it was clear why they failed so miserably the first time. Their executive summary was a typical engineering-focused description of their capabilities. It showed little insight into the customer's needs or key issues and concerns. Moreover, it looked dull—a plain vanilla presentation with few visuals and little distinctive formatting. It was mediocre in every way, and it looked it. Beyond the obvious—focusing on the customer's issues and clearly addressing their needs—the proposal team realized they had to do something more dramatic in their resubmittal, or they risked being lost in the crowd again. They chose what seemed like a risky course of action—they designed their new executive summary so it looked and felt like their customer's Yellow Pages. The text was presented in multi-column blocks. The visuals—and there were plenty of them—looked like display ads. The front and back cover mimicked the style and format of the customer's Yellow Pages. Beneath the new façade was a nearly complete overhaul of the story they told in the first summary. Now focused almost exclusively on the customer, the new summary told the story from the customer's perspective and put all of the company's product and service features in the context of how they could meet the customer's needs and solve their problems. Shortly after submitting their new executive summary, they received calls from the customer asking for many additional copies of the summary because a number of the customer's employees wanted their own copy.

Whether or not their solution seems gimmicky, it worked. They were ultimately successful in their pursuit because they grasped the need to symbolize their connection to the customer. The Yellow Pages format they adopted became a symbol of the deeper alignment they achieved in the link between their customer's core needs and problems and their company's capabilities and solutions. Sometimes, the symbols companies choose are simple, and these symbols achieve the goal if the deeper alignment they imply is real and meaningful to the customer. Empty symbols are pointless and can even damage the relationship, but when chosen and executed well, symbols can create a resonance with the customer that is profoundly differentiating for the company.

Because they operate on such a broad scale, symbolic BDs are the most strategic of the four types of BD. They can build trust and credibility with customers very rapidly if the customers judge them to be authentic. Most importantly, symbolic BDs are ubiquitous and will always either reinforce or contradict the company's core messages to the marketplace. This occurs because the behaviors customers perceive will always either be congruent or incongruent with the promises expressed or implied in the company's messages to its markets.

The Relationships Among the Types of Behavioral Differentiators

Figure 4-5 illustrates the relationships among the four types of BDs. The most direct and sustained experience customers have occurs with the day-to-day operational behaviors that are evident at most customer touch points, so operational BDs are the foundation of behavioral differentiation. If you can differentiate yourself in your *standard operating policies and practices,* you will create the impression that, as a rule, your company is more satisfying and attractive to do business with. Without creating a baseline of operational BDs, it's unlikely that the other forms of BD will have enough sustained impact to convince customers that your company itself consistently behaves in

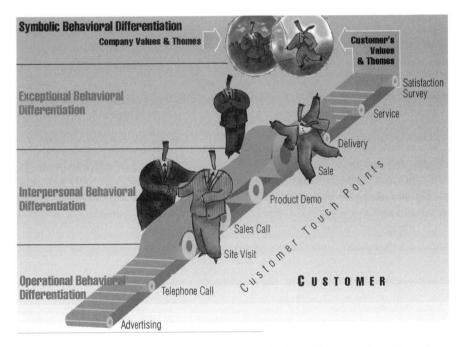

Figure 4-5. Symbolic Behavioral Differentiation. The complete BD picture includes symbolic behavioral differentiation, which reflects the alignment of your and the customer's values and themes. All four types of BD could be present at any touch point.

ways superior to your competitors. Consequently, the first task of a company's leaders is to try to operationalize behaviors that distinguish the company from its rivals. Business leaders like Sam Walton and Herb Kelleher were able to do this through an almost fanatical vision of how to serve customers and the strength of will to drive that vision down through every part of the company and model the differentiating behaviors themselves.

Exceptional BDs generally grow out of the operational BDs—they are extraordinary extensions of policy or authorized exceptions that individual employees undertake, often on their own initiative, to solve a customer's problem or meet a customer's need in an exceptional way. Although we speak of them as "breaking the rules" because they are the exception rather than the rule, in fact the companies that do this well enable and empower employees to behave exceptionally when, in their judgment, it's the right thing to do for customers.

In Figure 4-5, we show symbolic BDs as a field encompassing operational and exceptional BDs. Symbolic behaviors form the *background* within which these other forms of BD may occur. The outlying type of BD is interpersonal. It is independent, relying as it does on the social skills and temperaments of individual employees, but it can reinforce or enhance the effect of other types of BD, and vice versa. The other types of BD can have a halo effect on interpersonal behaviors. Companies that establish the other types create an environment that enhances employees' self-respect and builds trust between the company, its employees, and its customers. When they can serve customers exceptionally well, employees get more positive reinforcement from customers, which increases job satisfaction. Consequently, they tend to be more positive. They become friendlier and smile more, which enhances the customers' experiences, and so on. This virtuous cycle is, in Daniel Goleman's words, a subtle dance: "When we see a happy face (or an angry one), it evokes the corresponding emotion in us, albeit subtly."[11] In the end, these types of BD tend to be mutually reinforcing.

In this chapter we have explored the four types of behavioral differentiation but have not discussed how companies create and sustain these types. In the next four chapters we will do that, primarily by examining how companies that excel in each type of BD have been able to do so.

The Four Types of Behavioral Differentiation

Operational	Set a new standard.
Interpersonal	Show that you care.
Exceptional	Break the rules.
Symbolic	Walk the talk.

Challenges for Readers

1. In this chapter, we introduced the concept of touch points—those moments and events when anyone in your company interacts or communicates with a customer. What are the touch points for your company? Try to identify every single one of them. We'll warn you ahead of time that this is challenging. There will be more touch points than you imagine.

2. Does your company have any operational BDs? Remember that these must be standard policies, procedures, or practices that positively differentiate you from your competitors, and they must be sustained and consistent. Examine your customer touch points. Where do you have opportunities to create more or better operational BDs?

3. What does your company do to encourage and support the kinds of interpersonal behaviors from your employees that would differentiate you from your competitors? What is your level of interpersonal intelligence or skill? In your interactions with customers, do you differentiate yourself interpersonally? If not, what can you do about that? How can you improve the interpersonal behaviors of all your employees?

4. Do you differentiate yourself through exceptional behaviors toward customers? How? What does your management do to enable and encourage employees to "break the rules" now and then to do something exceptional for customers?

5. What core messages does your company send to the marketplace through your symbols: name, logo, brand, slogans, advertising, brochures, etc.? Are your behaviors congruent with those messages? Do you walk the talk?

Endnotes

1. Sam Walton, quoted in "Sam's Way," Wal-Mart Web site, November 15, 2001.
2. Ibid.
3. Harry Cunningham, quoted in Wal-Mart Web site, November 15, 2001.
4. Daniel Goleman, *Emotional Intelligence* (New York: Bantam Books, 1995), p. 37.
5. Howard Gardner, *Multiple Intelligences: A Theory in Practice* (New York: Basic Books, 1993), p. 23.
6. Goleman, p. 119.

7. Ibid., p. 215.
8. Pat Mene and Natasha Milijasevic, "The 20 Ritz-Carlton Basics," in "Best Practices of a Leader in the Hospitality Industry," in Stanley A. Brown, ed., *Breakthrough Customer Service: Best Practices of Leaders in Customer Support* (Toronto: John Wiley & Sons Canada, Ltd., 1997), p. 381.
9. Howard Gardner, *Frames of Mind: The Theory of Multiple Intelligences* (New York: Basic Books, 1983), p. 301
10. Fluor Corporation Website, November 20, 2001.
11. Goleman, p. 137.

5

THE GOLD STANDARDS
IN BEHAVIORAL
DIFFERENTIATION

We sell service. We sell an experience. If we sell service, we can go into any type of business because there are many opportunities where people experience terrible service.
—Robert George, Corporate Director of Training and Development,
Ritz-Carlton Hotel Company

We emotionally engage our employees, and we engage our customers by establishing a personal contact with the idea of creating a product that is exactly what they want—an exceptional hotel and exceptional service. The key is not what we do but how we execute what we do. That is what differentiates us. We have a very well-defined process for creating extraordinary service and a bond with our customers.
—Leonardo Inghilleri, Senior Vice President and Brand Executive,
Bulgari Company Hotels and Resorts

A four-year-old girl had attended the Teddy Bear Tea with her mother at Ritz-Carlton's Buckhead property in Atlanta and had left her teddy bear behind. Her mother later phoned the hotel and asked the concierge, Carter Donovan, if they could find the bear. Donovan located it and told the girl's mother that she would hold it behind the front desk. But several days later, when the four-year-old returned, this time with her grandfather, Donovan discovered that the bear had vanished. "She was four and had huge, big brown eyes," Donovan recalls. "When she and her grandpa asked for the bear, I said, 'Oh, yes,' and then could not find it. How could I tell them that we'd made a mistake? I just knew that that bear was her world. For me not to have the bear would be too hard for her. These things are very real for them. You can't just say, 'Gee, I'm sorry that happened.' It's like a child losing a favorite blanket. You can't just buy a new one. It's not the same thing."

Excusing herself, Donovan rushed into the Room Executive's office and told him what had happened. He said, "Carter, do what you have to do." So she ran to the gift shop, found another bear—a larger one because there were none exactly like the one the little girl left behind—ran outside, avoiding the front desk and lobby, and threw the bear into the backseat of the hotel's limousine. When she returned to the lobby, she could see that the grandfather knew something was up.

"I knew I had to talk to her and not her grandfather," Donovan says. "So I grabbed her hand and said, 'The bear's arrived! It's here—let's go! It's been out driving around waiting for you to come back.' She came out with me and I said to myself, 'Please, God, let it work.' When I opened the limousine door, she peered inside and said, 'Look how big you've gotten while staying at the Ritz-Carlton!' It was one of those moments. That's the thing about life, and this is what I tell everyone at orientation: You want to be able to look back on life and ask, 'Did I make a difference?' 'Did I make a contribution?' I tell everyone, we have the gift and the opportunity to go out and touch somebody's life and create a memory and say, 'I did make a contribution.' We all ask the big question, 'Why am I here?' but not everyone gets the opportunity to make a contribution. That's why I feel so blessed. I get a chance every day to contribute to somebody's life."[1]

Carter Donovan fits the classic mold of a Ritz-Carlton general manager. She was hired in the 1980s as a concierge. Since then she has made beds, washed dishes, done laundry, tended bar, waited tables, and carried luggage (and sometimes still does). Today, as the General Manager of the Ritz-Carlton Sarasota, she has a strong view about what is important: "The biggest thing about being a general manager is being able to read people's body language and anticipate what their needs are going to be. You've got to love people and be able to get inside of them. I'm there to provide a service for them, and I want to be certain that I provide them with an experience."[2] Carter Donovan represents one of the fundamental principles that differentiates Ritz-Carlton Hotels from most other hospitality companies—the ethic of *anticipating* guests' needs and acting before those needs are expressed. Day by day, guest by guest, employee by employee, touch point by touch point, no one does a better job of operational behavioral differentiation than Ritz-Carlton Hotels. They *are* the gold standard.

We chose Ritz-Carlton Hotel Company as an exemplar of behavioral differentiation not only because their people behave in ways that positively differentiate their hotels from rival hotel chains but also because Ritz-Carlton is a high-performing organization in every respect, and operational behavioral differentiation is the principal reason for their success. Consider these facts:

▲ Since its founding in 1983, The Ritz-Carlton Hotel Company has become a multibillion-dollar property management company, with 22,000 employees and 40 hotels worldwide.
▲ Their properties have won top honors from *Travel + Leisure* every year since 1997.
▲ They have fourteen properties in the Top 100 World's Best Hotels.
▲ In 1999, their hotel in Cancun won the first ever AAA five-diamond rating.
▲ In 2002, twelve Ritz-Carlton hotels in North America and the Caribbean earned AAA five-diamond ratings.
▲ In a Hewitt Associates study of employers in Asia (excluding Japan), the Ritz-Carlton Portman in Shanghai was #1 on the list and their Millenia property in Singapore was #3.
▲ Brand Keys created a customer loyalty index and asked 16,000 travelers to rate the five major carriers and hotel chains. Among hotels, Ritz-Carlton was far ahead of all others, both on exceeding guests' expectations and exceeding staff expectations.

By every external measure of excellence in the hospitality industry, Ritz-Carlton hotels are rated as the finest or among the finest year after year.

Most impressive, however, is that Ritz-Carlton is the only company in the hospitality industry to win the prestigious Malcolm Baldrige National Quality Award—and they have won it twice, in 1992 and 1999. No other company in the service category has ever won the award twice. Ritz-Carlton's journey toward the Baldrige Award began in 1988 when Horst Schulze became president and COO of the hotel company. Schulze was convinced that the responsibility for quality could not be delegated. Faced with the rapid development of new hotels, he created and then led the team that developed Ritz-Carlton's Gold Standards, which include the simplest and most elegant motto we have seen in any service business: "We are ladies and gentlemen serving ladies and gentlemen."

In 1990, Schulze hired Brian Kaznova, a consultant who had helped IBM's Rochester office win the MBNQA, and teamed him with Pat Mene, Ritz-Carlton's vice president of quality and purchasing. Using the Baldrige Award criteria as their roadmap, this core team embarked on a quality improvement odyssey that failed to win the award in 1991 (although the results yielded an insightful blueprint for quality improvement), but did win it in 1992. Their feedback report in 1992 identified seventy-five further "opportunities for improvement," and this became the basis for their quest to improve quality beyond 1992. Baldrige Award winners cannot apply for the award again for five years, so as they waited to reapply, Ritz-Carlton focused on improving their processes, measuring the results, and educating their employees. In 1999, they won the award again. This time, their report listed only twenty-two further "opportunities for improvement," and those have been instrumental in shaping Ritz-Carlton's current seven-year strategy.

What distinguishes the Ritz-Carlton Hotel Company from most other hospitality companies is not their commitment to continuous improvement. It would be difficult to find seriously competitive companies today that don't embrace continuous improvement. What distinguishes the people of Ritz-Carlton is their passion for behaving in extraordinary ways, both toward their guests and toward each other, and the remarkable attention they pay to every customer touch point. Their director of quality statistics and projects, Randy Dickson, has calculated that for normal Ritz-Carlton guests they have 1,100 opportunities each day to do well or to "mess up." Not all of those touch points are human interactions. Many of those points occur in the kitchen, or the offices, or the garage. These are points at which decisions are made or work is done that will eventually affect a guest—positively or negatively. For meeting planners, Dickson estimates that they have 1,300 such opportunities per day. So, on any given day, throughout their forty properties and among their 22,000 employees, the total number of possible defects is over one million. This means that, on average, each Ritz-Carlton employee has 64 opportunities every workday to delight customers—or disappoint them. We are discussing Ritz-Carlton in this chapter because 92 percent of the time, customers' reactions to those opportunities is delight, and the only way a company can accomplish this extraordinary level of satisfaction is through operational behavioral differentiation.*

---

*Gallup surveys rank Ritz-Carlton number one in customer satisfaction. Their most recent satisfaction rate is 92 percent (their closest competitor is 57 percent). Their goal is 97 percent, which they believe will be achievable at an estimated cost of $300 million. Achieving customer satisfaction rates higher than 97 percent is probably not feasible, in their opinion, because some guests will never be satisfied and the investment required to rate higher than 97 percent is not justifiable.

In Chapter 4 we said that operational behavioral differentiators are those that have been codified and integrated into the standard operating procedures and policies affecting how employees *normally* interact with and serve customers. Customers' impressions of your company form moment by moment, touch point by touch point, as your employees greet them, interact with them, answer their questions, respond to their requests, meet their needs, handle their complaints, and bid them farewell. To differentiate yourself behaviorally, you must ensure that your customers' experiences with you and your company are consistently better than their experiences with your competitors. Everyone has occasional lapses, but those lapses must be rare exceptions, not the norm. At Ritz-Carlton, the lapses are rare because they are passionate about managing every customer touch point. It is instructive to see how they do it, and it begins with their Gold Standards.

Ritz-Carlton's Gold Standards

At the root of human and organizational behavior is a self-concept. How we behave depends to a large extent on how we think of ourselves and how we define our purpose and our relationships with others, including our customers and employees. Ritz-Carlton's self-concept is clearly articulated in its credo, shown here in Figure 5-1 as part of their Gold Standards. Theirs is a place "where the genuine care and comfort of our guests is our highest mission."[3] The operative word here is *genuine,* which implies more than the routine levels of customer service one finds in most hotels; it implies an authentic service motive in employees, a personal fulfillment that comes from helping others have an extraordinary experience. It means having a select group of employees, those for whom service *is* the end, not a means to the end. Clearly, not every prospective employee is up to this (so they need not apply at Ritz-Carlton). Furthermore, the Ritz-Carlton experience "enlivens the senses, instills well-being, and fulfills even the unexpressed wishes and needs of our guests." Those who stay there "will always enjoy a warm, relaxed yet refined ambience."[4]

The Gold Standards (or Credo Card) shown in Figure 5-1 have effects that are both mundane and sublime. First, let's look at the mundane. The Credo Card captures the essence of Ritz-Carlton's identity, mission, and service principles—all in eight business-card–sized panels, which can be folded easily and fit into a wallet or pocket. Employees can easily carry it with them, teaching them, reminding them, guiding them, and reinforcing the basic principles of behavior toward Ritz-Carlton guests. Item 14 of "The Ritz-Carlton Basics" is surprisingly specific: "Use the proper vocabulary with our guests and each other. (Use words such as-'Good morning,' 'Certainly,' 'I'll be happy to' and

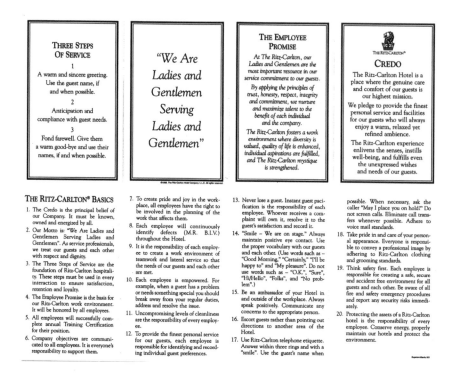

The following are the four panels shown at the top of the figure:

THREE STEPS OF SERVICE

1
A warm and sincere greeting. Use the guest name, if and when possible.

2
Anticipation and compliance with guest needs.

3
Fond farewell. Give them a warm good-bye and use their names, if and when possible.

"We Are Ladies and Gentlemen Serving Ladies and Gentlemen"

THE EMPLOYEE PROMISE

At The Ritz-Carlton, our Ladies and Gentlemen are the most important resource in our service commitment to our guests.

By applying the principles of trust, honesty, respect, integrity and commitment, we nurture and maximize talent to the benefit of each individual and the company.

The Ritz-Carlton fosters a work environment where diversity is valued, quality of life is enhanced, individual aspirations are fulfilled, and The Ritz-Carlton mystique is strengthened.

CREDO

The Ritz-Carlton Hotel is a place where the genuine care and comfort of our guests is our highest mission.

We pledge to provide the finest personal service and facilities for our guests who will always enjoy a warm, relaxed yet refined ambience.

The Ritz-Carlton experience enlivens the senses, instills well-being, and fulfills even the unexpressed wishes and needs of our guests.

THE RITZ-CARLTON® BASICS

1. The Credo is the principal belief of our Company. It must be known, owned and energized by all.
2. Our Motto is: "We Are Ladies and Gentlemen Serving Ladies and Gentlemen". As service professionals, we treat our guests and each other with respect and dignity.
3. The Three Steps of Service are the foundation of Ritz-Carlton hospitality. These steps must be used in every interaction to ensure satisfaction, retention and loyalty.
4. The Employee Promise is the basis for our Ritz-Carlton work environment. It will be honored by all employees.
5. All employees will successfully complete annual Training Certification for their position.
6. Company objectives are communicated to all employees. It is everyone's responsibility to support them.
7. To create pride and joy in the workplace, all employees have the right to be involved in the planning of the work that affects them.
8. Each employee will continuously identify defects (M.R. B.I.V.) throughout the Hotel.
9. It is the responsibility of each employee to create a work environment of teamwork and lateral service so that the needs of our guests and each other are met.
10. Each employee is empowered. For example, when a guest has a problem or needs something special you should break away from your regular duties, address and resolve the issue.
11. Uncompromising levels of cleanliness are the responsibility of every employee.
12. To provide the finest personal service for our guests, each employee is responsible for identifying and recording individual guest preferences.
13. Never lose a guest. Instant guest pacification is the responsibility of each employee. Whoever receives a complaint will own it, resolve it to the guest's satisfaction and record it.
14. "Smile – We are on stage." Always maintain positive eye contact. Use the proper vocabulary with our guests and each other. (Use words such as – "Good Morning," "Certainly," "I'll be happy to" and "My pleasure". Do not use words such as – "O.K.", "Sure", "Hi/Hello", "Folks", and "No problem".)
15. Be an ambassador of your Hotel in and outside of the workplace. Always speak positively. Communicate any concerns to the appropriate person.
16. Escort guests rather than pointing out directions to another area of the Hotel.
17. Use Ritz-Carlton telephone etiquette. Answer within three rings and with a "smile". Use the guest's name when possible. When necessary, ask the caller "May I place you on hold?" Do not screen calls. Eliminate call transfers whenever possible. Adhere to voice mail standards.
18. Take pride in and care of your personal appearance. Everyone is responsible to convey a professional image by adhering to Ritz-Carlton clothing and grooming standards.
19. Think safety first. Each employee is responsible for creating a safe, secure and accident free environment for all guests and each other. Be aware of all fire and safety emergency procedures and report any security risks immediately.
20. Protecting the assets of a Ritz-Carlton hotel is the responsibility of every employee. Conserve energy, properly maintain our hotels and protect the environment.

Figure 5-1. Ritz-Carlton Gold Standards. This card, which every Ritz-Carlton employee carries, defines the hotel's purpose and mission, its promise to guests and employees, and the basics of providing extraordinary service to guests. The continuous reinforcement of these messages is the foundation of Ritz-Carlton's operational behavioral differentiation. Copyright 1999 The Ritz-Carlton Company. All rights reserved. Reprinted with the permission of The Ritz-Carlton Hotel Company, L.L.C.

'My pleasure.' Do not use words such as-'O.K.,' 'Sure,' 'Hi/Hello,' 'Folks,' and 'No problem.')"[5] Specifying the language to use, both with guests and with each other, creates an air of formality and the "refined ambience" the hotel seeks. In so doing, the hotel is teaching employees how to behave at the touch point level. *These are not abstract customer service ideals; these are guidelines for managing every customer touch point, and that is how you operationalize behavioral differentiation.* The Gold Standards reflect the *standard* way of behaving. Moment by moment, day by day, this is how to behave toward guests and each other if you work for Ritz-Carlton.

Now for the sublime. Throughout the Gold Standards, the hotel addresses not only how to behave toward guests but also how employees should behave toward each other—and how the institution will behave toward them (see "The Employee Promise" in Figure 5-1). This is not a one-sided admonishment about how to serve customers. This is a social contract between the institution, the people who work for the institution, and the people the institution and its employees serve. Very few organizations make their social contract this explicit, and none that we know of except Ritz-Carlton puts it in a form employees are expected to carry with them day in and day out. Further, the Gold Standards paint an empowering picture. They define the expected experience for all guests, an experience that differentiates Ritz-Carlton Hotels from most other places guests will have stayed in their lives. The Ritz-Carlton experience is the ideal outcome for guests. Knowing this is liberating for employees because when they encounter situations where guests' needs or expectations are not being met—where the ideal outcome is not being achieved—they don't have to go find a supervisor to know what to do (or get approval to do it). They are orchestrators of the experience, on a par with the general manager of each property and all other Ritz-Carlton employees. Most of Ritz-Carlton's competitors define jobs by function, responsibilities, and limits on authority; Ritz-Carlton defines jobs in terms of the ideal outcome for guests. Disney does this, too. *A growing number of companies are recognizing the need to move from exceptional customer service to exceptional customer experiences.*[6]

When you consider the Ritz-Carlton ethic toward its customers and employees, the contrast with a corporation like Enron is startling. As we write this, the Enron collapse is still being investigated. Analysts conclude that the senior executives of what once was the seventh largest corporation in the U.S. were arrogant and greedy. Writing for *Fortune,* Bethany McLean quoted an Enron insider who worked for former CEO Jeff Skilling, "More than anywhere else, they talked about how much money we would make."[7] Enron's purpose seems to have been to enrich its leaders, not to serve its customers or shareholders. It also seems clear that those leaders had little genuine regard for employees. As McLean notes, "Skilling is usually credited with creating a system of forced rankings for employees, in which those rated in the bottom 20% would leave the company. Thus, employees attempted to crush not just outsiders but each other."[8] When you create a cutthroat environment, employees are not motivated to behave in ways that differentiate you positively. They are too busy scheming and watching their backs. Ritz-Carlton, with an admirable purpose and a sound social contract, is an exemplar of positive behavioral differentiation; Enron, with an ignoble purpose and a Darwinian social contract, exemplified the opposite. Behavioral differentiation begins with core values and beliefs that engage and motivate people, and Ritz-Carlton's are spelled out in their Gold Standards.

Recruiting and Selection

Although the Gold Standards are the foundation for behavioral differentiation at Ritz-Carlton, people make it happen, so recruiting and selection of new employees is critically important to the hotel. According to Pat Mene and Natasha Milijasevic, "New employees are recruited into each of the 120 hotel-specific standard job positions available using a highly predictive instrument known as 'character trait recruiting.' This tool is used to determine the capability of a candidate to meet the requirements of the job he or she is applying for. It is based on the attributes of employees who have been successful in that role in the past."[9] Hiring is not an isolated event performed by human resources. The hotel incorporates current employees into the interviewing process, so everyone feels responsible for the person hired and the team as a whole. Furthermore, they look for employees who exhibit "relationship extension," which is defined as their willingness and ability to anticipate customers' needs. Ritz-Carlton's success in hiring and employee retention is evident in an aggregate 2001 turnover rate for all Ritz-Carlton properties of 26 percent (down from 77 percent in 1989). The industry average was 84 percent in 1995 and more recently has been around 55 percent.

Fundamentals win it. Football is two things; it's blocking and tackling. I don't care about formations or new defenses or tricks on defense. If you block and tackle better than the team you're playing, you'll win.

—Vince Lombardi

Employee Orientation and Continuing Education

Find the right people. Then educate them. According to Robert George, a corporate director of training and development, before new employees can begin their jobs—no matter how shorthanded a hotel might be—they must attend a two-day orientation and pass their appropriate certifications for the job. The certification process is task-specific as well as philosophical: they must demonstrate that they can do the job *and* that they understand and are committed to the Gold Standards. Cultural buy-in is considered to be equally important, if not more so, than any technical expertise they gather during the orientation session. Furthermore, many of the hotels invite new employees to stay at the hotel as a guest so they can experience great service and thus know what it looks and feels like from guests' perspectives.

All senior property leaders attend the orientation sessions. In fact, if senior leaders are unavailable, then they will delay the orientation session until they are available. Ritz-Carlton considers senior leader participation critically important in aligning new employees with the company's goals, vision, and service expectations. In many cases, new employees are expected to make significant behavioral changes—to behave and speak more formally than they have before; to treat each other and their guests as ladies and gentlemen; to demonstrate more grace, if you will, than may have been asked of them in the past; and to adopt a genuine service mindset, one that results in authentic caring about guest welfare and contributes to guests' Ritz-Carlton experiences. Senior leaders, along with other Ritz-Carlton members present during the orientation, act as models of the behaviors they expect to see.

After twenty-one days of employment, all new employees return for a follow-up orientation session conducted by the general manager and other senior property leaders. Besides repeating the Gold Standards and soliciting feedback and questions, the general managers may ask questions like, "Is it true that you are treated with respect?" or "What have you uncovered that we should revisit?" Ritz-Carlton refers to this follow-up meeting as "Day 21," and they view it as an important milestone for new employees. Citing the psychological literature that suggests that habits must be created or broken within twenty-one days, they expect to know by "Day 21" whether new employees are exhibiting the desired behaviors and have extinguished the undesired ones. Mario Dones, also a corporate director of training and development, says that they believe they can't wait longer than three weeks for this check-in because, by then, employees will either buy into the culture, feel apathetic, leave, or even begin to work against the organization. Only one of those outcomes is tolerated at the three-week mark.

After one year or "Day 365," new employees meet again to discuss the Gold Standards, revisit their goals, exchange stories of exceptional service, and be tested on technical proficiency and adherence to the Ritz-Carlton philosophy. Along with these orientation sessions, employees participate in a remarkable amount of continuing corporate education. Robert George indicates that new employees undergo 310 hours of training with their first year and a minimum of 125 hours in subsequent years. Managers have as much as 300 hours of training and education annually. Every year, Ritz-Carlton spends between 3.5 and 4.5 percent of its payroll on training and education. Among top hotels, the industry average for spending on employee education ranges from 2 to 3.5 percent of payroll.[10] Clearly, one of the primary ways Ritz-Carlton operationalizes extraordinary behaviors, then, is through an extraordinary commitment to new employee orientation and ongoing employee education and training, especially around the core values, behaviors, and expectations set forth in the Gold Standards.

The Daily Lineup

When you drop a stone into a pond, waves ripple away from the center, gradually diminishing in amplitude as the energy dissipates. The farther away you are from the center, the less impact the waves will have on you. Those closest to the center feel the greatest effect; those farthest away may be aware of the ripples but are not greatly moved by them unless something happens that amplifies the effect. So it is with orientation sessions, corporate communications from the top, and education and training. If the values, beliefs, attitudes, and messages are not reinforced, the effect on employees far from the corporate center—where such things usually originate—will gradually fade away. At Ritz-Carlton, the daily lineup ensures that no one is ever far from the center.

Daily lineups are required of *everyone, everyday.* Departments schedule their own time for these meetings, based on guest needs or other considerations, but within each hotel in each department for each shift there is a "town hall" meeting. A different member of the department acts as the daily facilitator, which ensures that everyone carries the torch at one point or another. They follow a weekly agenda, which corporate officers prepare, that includes a subject of the week, a Gold Standard of the week, and a basic of the day. Every Ritz-Carlton property follows the same agenda, which ensures that all employees get the same message. In addition, the daily lineups feature typical corporate announcements of new policies, employees' anniversary dates or birthdays, rewards or recognition, and so on. What is most interesting about them, however, are the stories of exceptional behavior toward guests. In every daily lineup, employees are encouraged to share stories of exceptional customer care. Beyond the sharing of best practices, these stories are carriers of the culture, the emblems of the Ritz-Carlton experience. The emotional power and poignancy of the best stories linger. Like the campfire stories told throughout the ages by bands of hunters, these stories reinforce the group's purpose and mission, fill each person's imagination with possibilities, and inspire them to behave in ways the group would approve of. Ultimately, the stories are elements of the group's mythology. The great stories are remembered and repeated, passed on through generations of employees and across the worldwide archipelago of Ritz-Carlton properties, communicating not only what's possible but also what's expected. It is an extraordinary form of peer pressure and cultural reinforcement, and it occurs *daily,* not annually in company retreats or monthly in newsletters, as in most organizations. These lineups not only foster BD through the sharing of experiences and building of the tradition of service at Ritz-Carlton, they are a behavioral differentiator in and of themselves. They create and reinforce internal alignment while substantiating and causing BD with customers. Ritz-Carlton does it every single day, which is how they build operational behavioral differentiation and why they are an exemplar of it. Few of their competitors have the discipline or the resolve to match these operational practices.

Purpose Over Function—and the Authority to Resolve Problems

Ritz-Carlton's second of the "Three Steps of Service" (see Figure 5-1) is to anticipate and comply with guest needs. The operative word here is *anticipate*. Former COO Horst Schulze said, "The main thing is to have a vision of purpose, not a vision of function."[11] A chef's function may be to prepare food, but that's not his purpose; a desk clerk's function may be to check guests into and out of the hotel, but that's not her purpose. In an interview, Leonardo Inghilleri, formerly the vice president of human resources for Ritz-Carlton and currently a senior vice president at Bulgari Hotels and Resorts, explains further:

> There are three types of service. Bad service is what you get when your wishes are not complied with, when you want something and don't get it. Ordinary service happens when you ask for something and get it— i.e., you ask for a glass of water and the waiter brings it to you. This type of service can be either mediocre or very good, but still it is just based on compliance with the customer's needs. The third type of service is the extraordinary one. This happens when service instills the "wow" factor through the *anticipation of customer needs*. The hotel or service provider fulfills your wishes before you have a chance to express them. Extraordinary service is accomplished in part through technique, but technique is never enough. You need employees who have the "desire" to do so!
>
> Anticipating customer needs deals with mind reading. I don't know how to hire mind readers; therefore, I must have a workforce that understands the difference between their daily function and the purpose of their job. The waiter's function is to run food in and out of the kitchen. The waiter's purpose, on the other hand, is to create a memorable dining experience for his customers. If workers clearly understand that their purpose is not to take meal orders or clean rooms but to create a memorable experience, to instill a sense of well being in the customers, then the enterprise can and will deliver extraordinary service and establish unparalleled customer loyalty.[12]

We spoke earlier about the stories of exceptional customer care that are told during daily lineups. Robert George tells the story that occurred at one of Ritz-Carlton's Florida properties. A beach attendant was busy stacking chairs and putting them away for the evening. A guest asked him to leave one out because he was going to propose to his girlfriend that night. The beach attendant was happy to oblige but went much further than simple compliance with the guest's wishes. He rented a tuxedo and purchased flowers, candles, and champagne so he could create a special environment for the couple. When his guests arrived, he escorted them to the chairs, presented the special things he had arranged, and made himself available as their personal butler for the evening. What enabled this beach attendant to create an extraordinary experience for his guests was the latitude every Ritz-Carlton employee has to make decisions independent of policies or management without the fear of retribution or criticism, so long as it contributes to a guest's experience, and this applies especially to guests with problems or complaints.

One of the daily basics requires every employee, regardless of job function, to take ownership of complaints that customers bring to their attention, and they are allowed to spend up to $2,000 per guest to resolve complaints or problems. They might need to spend some or all of that $2,000, but the spending threshold is not what Ritz-Carlton considers important (in practice, managers are more likely to throw money at problems than staff members are), and sometimes all a customer wants is acknowledgement that a problem has occurred and an apology. What's important is delighting the customer by resolving the difficulty without having to go through a chain of command to do so. Customers with complaints are not passed along to "the person who can help you," as usually happens in companies that serve the public. Instead, the person who received the complaint, regardless of his or her normal function, promptly resolves the problem.

What's most impressive about this Ritz-Carlton policy is not the employee empowerment it creates but the fact that the hotel does not include these costs on their P&L statements because they don't want them subject to financial scrutiny by cost-conscious managers. Ritz-Carlton is not willing to reduce these costs, so it does not put them on the chopping block. The message they want to send to employees is, "We trust you to do the right things."[13] This spending policy and feeling of ownership it creates leads to a sense of pride and responsibility among employees, which is a critical link to customer loyalty and, ultimately, to Ritz-Carlton's growth and profitability. For Pat Mene, the most rewarding moments occur when people understand that profitability is a result of developing customer loyalty and employee satisfaction. In Mene's words, "The best investment you can make is customer and employee loyalty. I love it when people say there's a relationship, and they see it. There are lots of ways to make money, but when people see it so fundamentally, I'm proud."[14]

The Management of Measurement

As one would expect from a company that has won the Malcolm Baldrige National Quality Award twice, Ritz-Carlton has sophisticated systems for measuring virtually every aspect of their performance. The Baldrige Award criteria and process were both a catalyst and a blueprint for the systems of measures and controls they created. Although this may be true for other companies as well, Ritz-Carlton has an almost fanatical determination to measure performance and to drive quality improvements through every aspect of their operations. Here are some of their more notable measures:

▲ A database that encourages employees to identify and report defects before guests find them. Housekeepers, for instance, who discover that a lamp is broken or a window pane is cracked would enter that defect into the computer so that the problem can be fixed. Ritz-Carlton has a culture of rewards and recognition for employees who are proactive about quality assurance, so the more defects employees report, the more rewarded they are. Although the system is voluntary, it encourages employees to be quick in reporting defects in processes as well as materials.

▲ A second, guest-initiated database for reporting and fixing material defects. If guests complain to any Ritz-Carlton employee about a material problem—a broken television, a loose doorknob, a mini-bar that won't open—that employee is required to report it and then take responsibility for fixing the problem or ensuring that it is fixed.

▲ An automated database that monitors the quality of guests' experiences. When an event occurs that indicates a problem with service quality, that event automatically counts in the hotel's daily point value. The database tracks "the 10 most serious defects that can occur during the regular operation of a Ritz-Carlton hotel."[15] For example, housekeeping deficiencies receive one point each, meeting event problems receive five points each, and unresolved guest difficulties receive fifty points each. Each occurrence of a problem is multiplied by the number of points for that type of problem, totaled, and then divided by the number of days over which the data was collected. The result is a daily average score, which is sent to all employees of the hotel. The goal is to achieve the lowest possible score. The daily reports ensure that everyone, not just management, is aware of the hotel's quality performance, which gives the entire staff a sense that they own the problem and share in the pride when they achieve and sustain a 0 score.

▲ A customer relationship management (CRM) system that captures and communicates customer preferences, such as whether they prefer Diet Coke or Diet Pepsi, cream or milk in their coffee, the *Wall Street Journal* or *USA Today,* or rooms near an elevator. Entries are also employee-generated based on their interactions with guests, and there is also a culture of rewards and recognition for employees who contribute the most to this system. In addition, this database automatically tracks how many times guests have stayed at a Ritz-Carlton hotel, how much they spend in the restaurants, how much they purchase from the mini-bar, and so on. Many companies have CRM systems; what Ritz-Carlton does exceptionally well is to engage employees in recording information so the entire system of Ritz-Carlton properties becomes smarter about its returning guests, especially those who stay frequently.

In addition to these measures, Ritz-Carlton surveys its employees twice a year and has hired Gallup to measure guest satisfaction every month. They learned that guest comment cards are not reliable measures of guest satisfaction because those cards are submitted primarily by guests who are not totally satisfied. So Gallup conducts telephone surveys of guests every month. The hotel's goal with these measures is to increase employee and customer loyalty, and they have done so every year since Horst Schulze became president and COO.* They pay extraordinary attention to these details in part because they do not own the hotel properties. Ritz-Carlton is a management company. Their value proposition lies in the leadership, values, culture, and processes that make these properties successful, and they perceive a link between customer loyalty and employee loyalty. If employees feel pride and joy in their work, then they will behave in ways that cause customer loyalty, and employees will feel that pride and joy if they see their leaders behaving in exceptional ways, if employees participate in planning the work that affects them, and if everyone acts like a CEO. This last point is not trivial. By it, they mean that housekeepers should behave like the CEOs of the rooms they take care of, waiters should act like the CEOs of the tables they serve, and front desk clerks should be CEOs of the front desk. With quality and responsibility come pride and joy; with pride and joy come genuine caring and commitment to guests; with gen-

---

*Most people credit Horst Schulze with building the Ritz-Carlton mystique and shaping the hotel's vision and identity. The motto, "We are ladies and gentlemen serving ladies and gentlemen," was his creation. Legend has it that as a youngster in grade school in Austria he was required to write an essay about what ladies and gentlemen are, and that lesson remained with him for a lifetime. When he retired in 2001, hundreds of Ritz-Carlton employees and their families are said to have lined the path between his office and his car, nearly half a mile away, and many wept as he departed.

uine caring and commitment come behaviors that translate into exceptional experiences for guests. And with continuous and sustained exceptional guest experiences comes positive behavioral differentiation.

Ritz-Carlton has over one million customer touch points every day, and they are meticulous about managing each one of them. They view themselves as an elite institution (they target the top 1 to 3 percent of luxury travelers) whose mission is to create an exceptional experience for their customers and joy and pride among their employees. They are careful in selecting new employees, and then they devote an extraordinary amount of time to orientation and ongoing education and training. They manage their mission and their culture in daily lineups for every employee at every property (and in corporate headquarters), and they have a commitment to quality that some other organizations may equal but none can surpass. They manage details like few other organizations do, and they reward employees for taking initiative and solving problems. They are strongly process-driven, and they measure everything. These are the leadership behaviors that create operational behavioral differentiation. Recently, they opened their Leadership Center to outsiders, allowing non-Ritz-Carlton participants to study their principles of legendary service. But they are not concerned about losing their behavioral differentiation. "People will copy what we do," said Robert George. "But they'll never be able to copy the relationship between our leader and people, between our people and our guests. Our customers leave with a feeling, a memory. The importance of the experience is huge."

Tom's and Shane's Trip from Hell

In contrast to the Ritz-Carlton experience, consider the tale told by Tom Farmer and Shane Atchison. Shane is the CEO and Tom the director of strategy for ZAAZ, Inc., a Seattle-based web design and technology consultancy that serves clients nationwide. In November 2001, they had the kind of trip from hell that most frequent business travelers have at one time or another, but they decided to do something about it. We warned in Chapter 3 that the Internet gives anyone with a computer *and the will to speak out* the ability to complain about the offending company to the entire Web world. What we are about to share with you is the object lesson to end all object lessons. After a trip to Houston, in which a hotel treated them very badly, Tom and Shane created a PowerPoint presentation to register their complaint. They sent their presentation to the hotel chain's headquarters and a few friends. The rest of the story is now an Internet legend. What follows is the slide show they created (see Figure 5-2). At their request, we have changed the name of the of-

(text continues on page 118)

Figure 5-2. Tom's and Shane's Protest. This PowerPoint presentation became an Internet underground sensation. It illustrates the danger of poor customer service in an age of true mass communication.

Yours is a Very Bad Hotel

A graphic complaint prepared for:

John Doe
General Manager

Jane Smith
Front Desk Manager

Anon Business Hotel
One Major Freeway
Houston, Texas

*In the Early Morning Hours of
November 15, 2001, at the Anon Business Hotel
Houston, We Were Treated Very Badly Indeed.*

- We are Tom Farmer and Shane Atchison of Seattle, Washington.
- We held guaranteed, confirmed reservations at the Anon Business Hotel for the night of November 14-15.
- These rooms were held for late arrival with a major credit card.
- Tom is a card-carrying Anon World Traveler VIP Member
- Yet when we arrived at 2:00am… *we were refused rooms!*

Refused Rooms... Even When We're "Confirmed" and "Guaranteed"?

- ◆ Chuck, your Night Clerk, said the only rooms left were off-limits because their plumbing and air-conditioning had broken!
- ◆ He'd given away the last good rooms three hours ago!
- ◆ He'd done nothing about finding us accommodation elsewhere!
- ◆ And he was deeply unapologetic!

Quotations from Night Clerk Chuck

"Most of our guests don't arrive
at two o'clock in the morning."

-- 2:08 am, November 15, 2001

Explaining why it was
OUR fault that the Anon Business Hotel
could not honor our guaranteed reservation

(continues)

Figure 5-2. (continued)

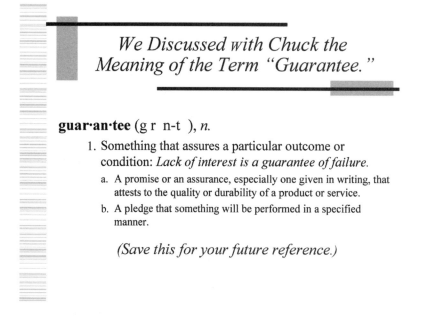

We Discussed with Chuck the Meaning of the Term "Guarantee."

guar·an·tee (g r n-t), *n.*

1. Something that assures a particular outcome or condition: *Lack of interest is a guarantee of failure.*

   a. A promise or an assurance, especially one given in writing, that attests to the quality or durability of a product or service.

   b. A pledge that something will be performed in a specified manner.

   (Save this for your future reference.)

Chuck Didn't Much Care.

♦ He seemed to have been betting that we wouldn't show up.

♦ When we suggested that the least he should have done was line up other rooms for us in advance... Chuck bristled!

Quotations from Night Clerk Chuck

"I have nothing to apologize to you for."

-- 2:10 am, November 15, 2001

*Explaining why we were wrong
to be upset that our "guaranteed"
rooms weren't saved for us*

The Career Path of Night Clerk Chuck
(He peaked last week.)

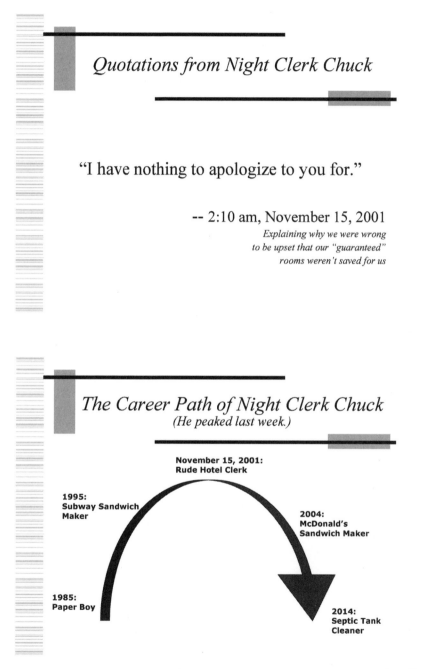

November 15, 2001:
Rude Hotel Clerk

1995:
Subway Sandwich
Maker

2004:
McDonald's
Sandwich Maker

1985:
Paper Boy

2014:
Septic Tank
Cleaner

(continues)

Figure 5-2. (continued)

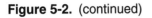

Chuck Wasn't Too Optimistic About Finding Us a Place to Sleep.

• 2:15 in the morning is a heck of a time to start looking for two spare hotel rooms!

• Chuck slowly started dialing around town.

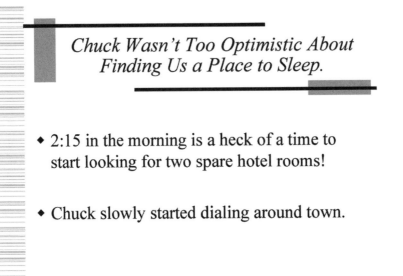

Quotations from Night Clerk Chuck

"I don't know if there ARE any
hotel rooms around here... all these
hotels are full."

-- 2:12 am, November 15, 2001

*Just starting to look for alternate
accommodation for us, even though he'd filled
his own house up by 11:00pm*

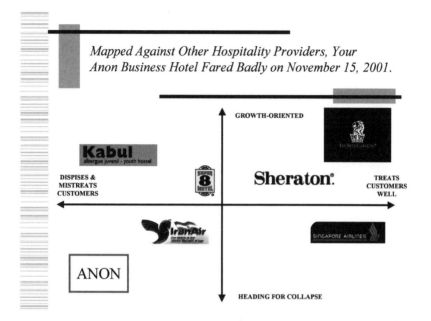

Mapped Against Other Hospitality Providers, Your
Anon Business Hotel Fared Badly on November 15, 2001.

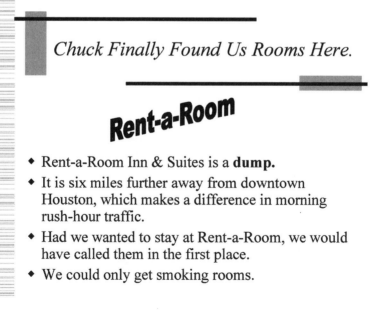

Chuck Finally Found Us Rooms Here.

- Rent-a-Room Inn & Suites is a **dump.**
- It is six miles further away from downtown Houston, which makes a difference in morning rush-hour traffic.
- Had we wanted to stay at Rent-a-Room, we would have called them in the first place.
- We could only get smoking rooms.

(continues)

Figure 5-2. (continued)

> ## The Experience Chuck Provided Deviated from Usual Treatment of a World Traveler VIP Member.

Expected World Traveler VIP Member Benefits	Actual Benefits Provided by Anon Business Hotel
Confirmed reservation	Ignored reservation
Upgraded room when available	No room available
Free continental breakfast	Free confusing directions to shabby alternate hotel
VIP points *plus* frequent-flyer miles	Insolence *plus* insults

> ## Even After We Left the Anon Business Hotel, Our Troubles Weren't Over, as This Timeline Shows.

Jon, a colleague, was arriving in Houston on an overnight flight and coming to join us at the Anon Business Hotel first thing in the morning. As we had to go stay elsewhere, we wrote Jon a note and left it in care of Chuck the Night Clerk.

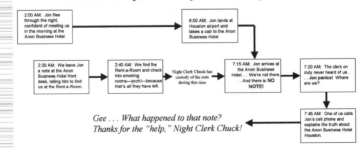

Gee . . . What happened to that note?
Thanks for the "help," Night Clerk Chuck!

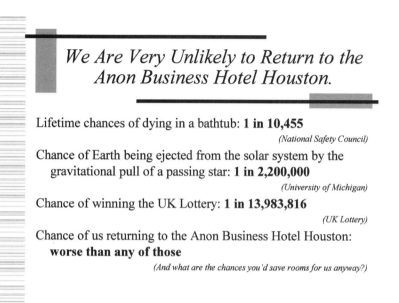

We Are Very Unlikely to Return to the Anon Business Hotel Houston.

Lifetime chances of dying in a bathtub: **1 in 10,455**

(National Safety Council)

Chance of Earth being ejected from the solar system by the gravitational pull of a passing star: **1 in 2,200,000**

(University of Michigan)

Chance of winning the UK Lottery: **1 in 13,983,816**

(UK Lottery)

Chance of us returning to the Anon Business Hotel Houston: **worse than any of those**

(And what are the chances you'd save rooms for us anyway?)

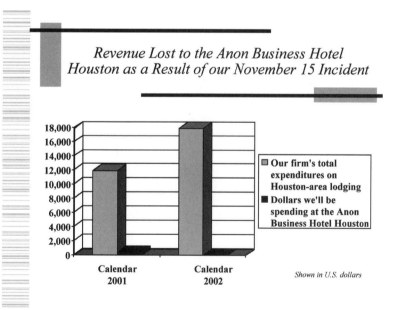

Revenue Lost to the Anon Business Hotel Houston as a Result of our November 15 Incident

- ☐ Our firm's total expenditures on Houston-area lodging
- ■ Dollars we'll be spending at the Anon Business Hotel Houston

Shown in U.S. dollars

(continues)

Figure 5-2. (continued)

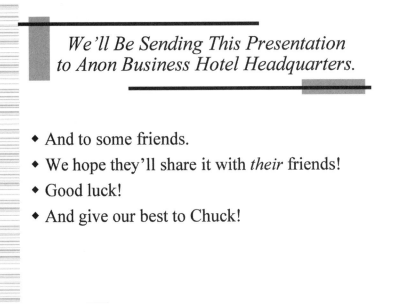

We'll Be Sending This Presentation to Anon Business Hotel Headquarters.

* And to some friends.
* We hope they'll share it with *their* friends!
* Good luck!
* And give our best to Chuck!

fending hotel chain and the names of the guilty parties (the sanitized name we chose, "Anon" stands for *anonymous*). However, readers would recognize the hotel chain; its parent corporation is one of the major names in the hospitality industry. Here's the story Tom and Shane had to tell (printed with their permission).

As we said earlier, the authors e-mailed this presentation to the hotel and a few of their friends. They envisioned that twenty people might see it, but those twenty sent it to their friends, who sent it to more friends, and like a rabid chain letter it spread far and wide. In their original slide show, Tom Farmer included his E-mail address, and he was soon deluged with responses. He later wrote, "I am stunned at how far this little PowerPoint file has circulated. Since it left my desktop November 21, I've been contacted by well over 3,000 amused, sympathetic hospitality professionals, marketing/PR people, business school professors . . . you name it. Without my help, it found its way to the highest levels of the [Anon Business Hotel] empire; a credible third-party source told me that by the week before Christmas, the PR director of [Anon's corporate parent] had received the file by e-mail more than 80 separate times."[16] At last count, the authors had received e-mail reactions to their slide show from people on six continents. Bear in mind that the 3,000 responses they have had is the tip of the iceberg. Most people who received a copy of this slide show from friends will not send the authors a message. Typically, less than 1 percent of the people who see such things are moved to respond. It would be fair to estimate that over half a million people saw this PowerPoint presentation. *USA Today* picked up the story (January 4, 2002) and *Travel Weekly* ran an article on the incident as well. If ever there were a cautionary tale about negative behavioral differentiation, this is it. In this Internet age, even a single, unrepentant lapse in behavior toward customers can bring notoriety far beyond the scale of the offense, and it will cost you money as well as customer loyalty.

> **The blunders are all there on the board, waiting to be made.**
> —Savielly Tartakover, International Grand Master

The World's Most Customer-Centric Company

In the parlance of the Internet age, Ritz-Carlton is a B2C company (a business serving consumers), and it would be tempting to conclude that operational BD is easier in the B2C interface where touch points are clearly identifiable and the customer service norms and procedures can be carefully controlled. However, operational BDs are just as evident in B2B interfaces, and our exemplar of this is EMC Corporation, a Massachusetts-based information storage firm that *Fast Company* labeled "the world's most customer-centric company."[17] Until the third quarter of 2001, EMC's market cap growth streak had been the envy of Wall Street. The New York Stock Exchange recognized EMC for achieving the highest single-decade performance (the 1990s) of any listed stock in the history of the exchange. EMC topped *The Wall Street Journal's* top performer list, with an 82 percent average compound annual total return during the decade. Had you invested $1,000 in EMC at the end of 1990, your stock would have been worth nearly $400,000 by the end of 2000. The last half of 2001 was not kind to any information technology company, and EMC suffered along with everyone else. By early 2002, however, things began turning around for them. Despite the market ups and downs, EMC has an exceptional performance record, and it is based in large part on operational behavioral differentiation and a remarkable turnaround engineered by executive chairman and past president Michael Ruettgers.

Founded in 1979 by Richard Egan and Roger Marino (the E and M in EMC), the company focused on add-on memory for microcomputers. Revenues grew rapidly through 1984; by 1988, however, marketplace changes and defective components led to a net loss of $7.5 million. Michael Ruettgers joined the company in 1989, quickly instituted a continuous improvement program, and helped to accelerate the transition to a provider of storage solutions. In that same year, the newly refocused EMC took on IBM, which controlled the mainframe market for storage through proprietary disk drive technology. EMC introduced RAID (Redundant Arrays of Independent Disks), which linked groups of inexpensive 5.25-inch drives together to replace mainframe storage that relied on 14-inch proprietary disks. By 1990, EMC added intelligence (software programs that added data management, protection, and business continuity features) to its storage systems and took over market leadership in mainframe storage.

In 1995, EMC created the first platform-independent storage system. This system allowed companies that had data on different computing platforms such as mainframes, UNIX servers, and smaller Windows NT to use the same storage device. This move into enterprise storage continued into the more recent open storage concept: storage units that can sit separately on networks and supply data to a variety of servers, even if they are made by different manufacturers.[18] EMC's open infrastructure is very helpful to customers because any hardware products they are using will interface with EMC storage, and they don't have to figure out what does or doesn't work together. Although software is not a new effort, recently EMC has placed a serious focus on developing a software-based approach to storage in the networked storage arena. This emphasis has been especially prominent since Joe Tucci came aboard as CEO in 2001. Tucci believes that customers are looking to software solutions to more efficiently use the storage capacity that they already have.[19] Three-quarters of the EMC billion-dollar annual research and development budget goes into software development.

How EMC Differentiates Itself

EMC's differentiation begins with a singular focus on information storage technology.* Competitors like IBM and Compaq have a much broader array of products and services, so EMC's strategic focus on information storage enables it to devote its resources and energy to this area of information management. As an innovator and thought leader in the handling of mission-critical business information, EMC develops technology advances in direct

---

*Much of this information comes from interviews conducted in March 2002 with the following EMC executives: Joseph Walton, senior vice president of Global Services; Leo Colborne, vice president of Global Technical Support; Walter Rietz, vice president of Global Services Customer Satisfaction, Inside Sales, Product Management; Al Lanzetta, vice president of Global Customer Service, Field Operations & Support; Al Coarusso, director, Worldwide Customer Support Centers; Cynthia Curtis, director, Global Services Marketing; and Don Potter, HR operations manager. Printed with their permission.

response to the needs of its customers. The recent focus on software development is a response to customers' needs for automated information management and an open systems strategy (software designed to run storage hardware from many companies). As Joe Tucci states, "We are delivering what customers need most today: networked storage and consolidation, open management software, business continuity solutions, and lower total cost of ownership."[20]

EMC has a unique approach to delivering customer service through involvement in product and service development. Former CEO Mike Ruettgers believed that "customer loyalty is built on investing in the exact product and service attributes that customers value most," so EMC brings customers into the heart of their product/service development cycle. The goal is to "turn customer outreach into collaborative innovation." EMC accomplishes this collaboration through customer advisory councils. These are unique gatherings, not traditional sales or user groups. Eighty to one hundred carefully selected customers in different geographies who are key decision makers, strategists, or visionaries are invited to come together for intensive discussions, having made a minimum 18-month commitment and signed nondisclosure agreements. These sessions are designed to create a forum for collaborative innovation, but also to better understand product requirements, validate product concepts, and develop long-term business directions.[21] In *X-Engineering the Corporation,* James Champy calls these councils an "impressive exercise in customer pull" that allows EMC to define its process push with pinpoint accuracy.[22]

EMC may not have invented "staying close to customers and innovating in direct response to their needs," but they execute this strategy as well as any company in the world. From early on, EMC has involved key customers in the product development cycle and monitored customer satisfaction through structured processes such as internal and external surveys. Recently, according to EMC sources, they have added the metric of customer loyalty. Loyalty is significant for long-term, profitable relationships, and customer satisfaction by itself is no guarantee of loyalty. As a number of studies have shown, companies can have satisfied customers but do not automatically retain them, so customer loyalty deserves separate attention. EMC measures where customers score on the loyalty dimension and then develops strategies to address loyalty issues on every account management plan.

EMC's Unique Services Model

Most differentiating for EMC is how the company has institutionalized customer service through its unique services model—and these practices make EMC an exemplar of operational behavioral differentiation. Customers whose business depends on the availability, manageability, and security of data for competitive advantage want a seamless process for information storage. Their worst nightmare is downtime, yet technology does change, it needs updating, and it sometimes fails. Quick response time is the name of the game, because customers can lose thousands of dollars for every minute mission-critical data is unavailable. Therefore, EMC promises to be "the world's best caretaker" of that information. The company delivers on this promise in a number of ways that form the operational foundation of their BD.

Customer Service as an Investment

At EMC, customer service is viewed as an investment in customer satisfaction, not as a profit center. Consequently, Field Services and Technical Support can concentrate on finding the right and best solution for customer problems, regardless of the cost impact to EMC. In most IT service organizations, technical support has two conflicting goals: to provide the best service and support while trying to minimize costs and maximize the company's profits. EMC's approach represents a substantial investment and a fundamental difference in mindset.

Rapid Escalation of Problems

EMC has instituted procedures and an unusually high degree of accountability for prioritizing and resolving customer problems quickly. This requires a team effort on the part of field engineers and the willingness to involve others by escalating a customer's concern up the service chain. If a problem is not resolved in eight hours, it is escalated to Joseph Walton, senior vice president of the Global Services Division, who then becomes actively involved in resolving the matter and working with the customer. If the problem is not resolved within two more hours, it is escalated to Joe Tucci, the CEO. This degree of senior executive involvement in problems that are not resolved quickly is unusual, to say the least.

Global Service Deployment

EMC provides a global network of technical, field, and support personnel available 24/7/365 to solve problems and provide support. EMC has both centralized support centers and local customer engineers to respond to customer issues through team efforts. There are remote service centers for equipment and SACs (Software Assistance Centers) for software in Hopkinton, Massachusetts; Cork, Ireland; Tokyo; and Sydney (see Figure 5-3). This network of global support centers allows EMC to have a "follow the sun" sup-

Figure 5-3. EMC's PSE Lab in Hopkinton. Sophisticated remote diagnostics and repair capabilities at EMC's Product Support Engineering Lab resolve most issues before a problem occurs.

port model, which means they can focus their resources around the globe and around the clock, and they can respond rapidly to calls during time periods in each part of the world when call volumes are highest.

EMC has also invested in an Intelligent Contact Management System developed by Cisco Systems. This system is a call distribution and management system that allows calls to be routed by support availability globally and also by skill set. Through this system, they have greatly reduced call hold and resolution times. The system also facilitates the real-time response to software customers who have Severity Level 1 issues (severe business impact issues). These customers do not wait for a call back; their needs are addressed immediately.

Phone-Home Capability

EMC takes a preemptive approach to technology problem solving that helps them identify and resolve many pending technical problems before customers become aware of them. A sophisticated "phone-home" capability allows remote support for system monitoring and troubleshooting 24/7/365. Each EMC storage box has a laptop interfaced with it whose function is to monitor the well-being of the storage device, including physical conditions such as the temperature of the unit and the proper functioning of drives and cache boards. The laptop is connected to a modem that allows it to relay a warning to the remote support center if a critical diagnostic incident occurs. With this notification system, EMC technicians can take action quickly and resolve most problems before they affect a customer's business. In many cases, EMC field technicians can hot-swap parts without down time. It's important to note that, although the features we are describing are technical differentiators, to customers they feel behavioral. EMC's "phone-home" technology is an enabler of what customers will experience as a behavioral difference. Charles Brombaugh, manager of Design Automation for Thomson Consumer Electronics and a customer of EMC, makes this point: "The best part of EMC's service organization is that they monitor the systems for me. I've received calls from support technicians to let me know when there's a problem, what they're going to do about it, and how long it will take to fix it. EMC responds proactively—service technicians have actually shown up telling us there was a warning that we had a bad disk, and we never knew it. They replaced it without any downtime. I was flabbergasted. This was based on a warning, not an error. EMC's service organization is second to none."[23]

Guilty Until Proven Innocent

EMC is willing to own problems even before it is established whether their products caused the problems. They call this policy "guilty until proven innocent." Rather than wasting time debating the cause of the problem, EMC deploys its field support technicians to resolve the issue and get the customer back online as quickly as possible. Furthermore, if a problem can be attributed to another supplier's product, EMC will work directly with that supplier to resolve the problem, so the customer doesn't have to. EMC claims it has more rapid escalation up some other suppliers' service chains than the suppliers themselves do.

Few vendors have supported us the way EMC has. Typically, vendors drop off their equipment and leave the rest up to us. EMC understands our application, and what we're trying to do. EMC treats our business as if it were its own. Not many companies step up to the plate like that.

—Jon Prall, Vice President of Operations, Excite@Home

Change Control Without a Hitch

Handling change control efficiently and effectively is important to customers in today's dynamic IT environments, where upgrades and configuration changes are frequent. At EMC, change control is managed by a Code, Configuration, and Change Control Team (C4 Team) and is moving toward increased automation with a Change Control Automation (CCA) system. According to the Gartner Group, EMC's automated system and dedicated support team handles up to 1,800 changes per week globally, with more than 99 percent first-time accuracy.[24] To ensure that changes are made without a hitch, EMC has invested an unprecedented $2 billion in an interoperability lab that, according to Joseph Walton, SVP of Global Services, contains "everybody's everything" (see Figure 5-4). This lab allows EMC to test and perfect change processes using any configuration of IT equipment and software, which is essential in today's multivendor IT environments.

In Chapter 4, we noted that best-in-class companies operationalize their behavioral differentiators and consistently behave in ways that differentiate them from their competitors. The service processes we've just described do that for EMC. Their mindset toward service—concomitant with their day-to-day standard procedures for resolving customer's problems, anticipating hardware failures, and making seamless equipment changes and upgrades—makes them best in class. In *The Discipline of Market Leaders,* Michael Treacy and Fred Wiersema argue that operationally excellent companies are

Figure 5-4. Joseph Walton, senior vice president of Global Services. Walton launched EMC Global Services in November 2000. He is now responsible for all EMC services and customer satisfaction worldwide.

not interested in one-time acts of heroism. They prefer to change their operating procedures so they realize systematic improvements.[25] The key to operational BD is having a vision of behavior toward customers that surpasses what your competitors are able or willing to do and then having the will and the skill to create and implement systems and procedures that yield consistently better treatment of customers than they receive from your rivals. As executive chairman Mike Ruettgers said, "Customer loyalty is built on doing hundreds of small things right—over and over again."[26]

Measuring Customer Satisfaction

EMC believes that customer feedback is critical to their ability to respond to customer needs and issues and to ensure satisfaction with EMC products and services. So they have developed customer surveys and check-in visits that are reminiscent of Ritz-Carlton's guest surveys. The thoroughness and consistency with which they gather and process this information is a clear behavioral differentiator for EMC, as it is for Ritz-Carlton Hotels. Customer feedback programs are labor intensive and cost EMC between three and four million dollars a year. However, as Walter Reitz, VP of Global Services Customer Satisfaction, argues, "Customers have high expectations and view customer service as a core competency for EMC. For us to slip in this area diminishes our overall value proposition." Among the list of customer feedback mechanisms from EMC Global Services is a satisfaction survey conducted by an external research firm.

This global survey is conducted annually to provide feedback about overall satisfaction with EMC and its products and services. The person selected to complete the survey must be closely involved with the decision-making process and understand EMC's performance as a supplier, as well as be familiar with EMC sales representatives, systems engineers, and customer engineers. Reitz says that more than 70 percent of their customers participate in this survey. Previously, the survey had been done by telephone, but in response to customer feedback they are now developing an online version to make the survey faster and easier to complete.

Staff performance and compensation are directly tied to customer satisfaction ratings, which motivates the staff to do whatever it takes to exceed customer expectations. The company provides extensive training and mentoring programs to help employees acquire the skills they need, including training on developing presence with customers and building relationships with them. Like Ritz-Carlton's new employee orientation program, EMC has a "Fast Start" program meant to accelerate the process of cultural assimilation and buy-in and to help new hires be fully functional by the end of their first quarter.

Helping Save Customers' Businesses After 9/11

The measure of a company's attitude and behavior toward customers is most evident in a crisis, the most tragic of which in recent memory was the terrorist attack on September 11. As a significant player in the IT infrastructures of major companies, EMC recognized, only minutes after the attacks on the World Trade Center, that many of its customers in the New York area might be affected. Phone calls began pouring in through the phone-home capabilities at customer sites. Within thirty minutes of the second tower's falling, EMC had an operational command center up and running in Hopkinton to direct and manage EMC's response to this crisis. Both local and global resources were mobilized to help resuscitate affected businesses. In most cases EMC was the first or only vendor on-site. Because of their tight operational procedures, they were able to locate and ship needed equipment from all over the country.

> I think the term "hero," which has been used very frequently in the media over the past month, is rightfully bestowed on those who are working to save lives. And not for a minute should we lose sight of what true loss really is. In this case, it is not data. However, while we couldn't do anything specific about the tragic loss of human life with our customers, we could and did help resuscitate our customers' businesses.
> —Joseph Walton, SVP Global Services, EMC, October 2001

In the immediate area of the attacks, under grueling physical and emotional conditions, EMC team members went to work helping people wherever they could, and assessing the information storage infrastructure status at numerous customer locations. They moved and configured replacement systems and set up secondary disaster recovery sites. The discipline and processes that are part of the normal way of life for EMC staff stood them in good stead under these extraordinary crisis conditions.[27] For example:

▲ Failing power supplies in lower Manhattan threatened the operation of the whole IT infrastructure of two subsidiaries of a global investment services corporation. They were relying on backup diesel generators to supply power to their critical IT systems. Within days, one subsidiary had to move its production center out of New York. This move required bin file changes, reconfigurations, and new installations. Despite the difficulty of getting into lower Manhattan, EMC engineers Pat Fagan, Tony Picciuti, and Herman Byng managed to get to the first site to replace its power supply. Making their way through five more devastated city blocks to the other data center, they installed bin files and launched SRDF. They remained at the site until the data transfer was totally operational and only then walked another half-mile out of the affected area. By then, it was midnight.

▲ The New York City data center of a major European bank was buried in debris and had major structural damage, including a ten-story hole in the front of the building. The data center contained twenty-three Symmetrix systems, and EMC was the first supplier on-site. The majority of the production systems were protected with SDRF, but some were not. The EMC team had to recreate the open systems environments and mainframe development environments to get this customer operating at its only remaining data center in New Jersey. On September 12, EMC account manager Tom Malone ordered two Symmetrix 8830 systems that arrived early the next morning. Global Services readied the systems and put them into operation later that day, thirty-six hours after the attack.

▲ On the morning of September 11, Ron Breuche of EMC Professional Services arrived at the offices of his customer, a wireless Internet service provider located near the World Trade Center, just like any other morning. As the terrorist attacks and rescue efforts unfolded outside, the building's air conditioning failed, threatening his customer's mission-critical systems. Ron kept these systems running, spending the night in the basement data center, which had also become a temporary shelter for hundreds of people. Even when the customer was able to get one of its own people on-site to relieve Ron, he didn't leave until the cooling situation was under control.

EMC's efforts to keep its customers' systems working may pale beside the stories of heroism and sacrifice on 9/11, especially by the hundreds of firefighters, police, and rescue workers who fought to save lives. Nonetheless, EMC kept its focus on its customers throughout that tragedy and worked hard to minimize the damage to its customers' mission-critical systems and data. What enabled EMC to respond so quickly and effectively were its operational structure, systems, and procedures and the people who, day in and day out, behave in ways that operationally differentiate EMC from its competitors.

In contrast, consider this sign we saw in a local restaurant: "To-go orders do NOT include complimentary chips and salsa. If you have any questions, see our management, NOT our employees." The manager of this restaurant may think he is acting chivalrously in shielding his wait staff from frustrated customers, but in the process he has absolved his employees of the responsibility and authority to resolve customer complaints. The policy he instituted virtually ensures that his employees will not behave in ways that differentiate his restaurant from others in the area. We saw another sign at a dry cleaning establishment. It was printed on a card taped to a small brass urn sitting on a shelf behind the counter, and it read, "Ashes of problem customers." The message to customers is clear: "In this place, if you don't treat us the way we want to be treated, we will cremate you, at least symbolically." When management behaves this way, it sends an unmistakable signal both to employees and customers that the company is more important than the customer. Contrast this behavior with the extraordinary behavior Ritz-Carlton and EMC manifest toward their customers, consistently, every day, in every location. That is what makes them exemplars of operational BD.

Challenges for Readers

1. Ritz-Carlton is the gold standard for customer service in its industry. Who is best-in-class in your industry? Day in and day out, which company does the best job of managing customer touch points so that their behavior toward customers is consistently outstanding? What do they do to achieve operational BD?
2. Ritz-Carlton uses the Malcolm Baldrige Award criteria to drive their quality improvement process. What process do you use? Can it help you identify opportunities to implement or improve your operational BD?
3. Ritz-Carlton uses a number of tools to institutionalize its operational behavioral differentiators, including the Credo card, daily lineups, and rigorous training programs. What tools do you use? What tools *could* you use?
4. Ritz-Carlton's operational excellence is based on the ethic of *anticipating* guest needs and a policy that expects employees to assume responsibility for resolving guest problems and gives them the authority to do so. How does it work in your company? Are all employees responsible for solving customer problems? How much latitude do they have to do that?
5. EMC's customer advisory councils form an extraordinary customer outreach program. How does your company develop a level of customer intimacy that enables you to understand how their business is changing, anticipate their needs, and demonstrate your commitment to serving them? A number of companies have programs for getting close to customers. What can make that behavior differentiating is the consistency of your customer outreach and the investment you make in staying close to them. How do you fare on those criteria?
6. EMC treats customer service as an investment rather than a profit center, and employees are measured primarily on customer satisfaction. Their op-

erational BD is an outcome of these elements of their corporate strategy. What are the behavioral outcomes of your corporate strategy?

7. If customer problems are not resolved within ten hours, EMC's CEO is notified and remains involved until the problem is fixed. This is an extraordinary level of attention from senior management. How long does it take for your CEO to become involved when your customers have problems with your products or services? How much attention from senior management do your customers receive?

Endnotes

1. Carter Donovan interview with Laurie Voss (March 19, 2002).
2. Ruth Lando, "Carter Donovan: As excitement builds around Sarasota's new Ritz-Carlton, the hotel's top executive talks about service—and smiles," *Sarasota Herald Tribune* (October 7, 2001), p. 60.
3. "The Gold Standards," The Ritz-Carlton Hotel Company (1999).
4. Ibid.
5. Ibid.
6. For an excellent discussion of this phenomenon, see B. Joseph Pine II and James H. Gilmore, *The Experience Economy: Work Is Theatre & Every Business a Stage* (Boston: Harvard Business School Press, 1999).
7. Bethany McLean, "Why Enron Went Bust," *Fortune,* 144, no. 13 (December 24, 2001), p. 61.
8. Ibid.
9. Pat Mene and Natasha Milijasevic, "Best Practices of a Leader in the Hospitality Industry: The Ritz-Carlton Hotel Company," in Stanley A. Brown, *Breakthrough Customer Service: Best Practices of Leaders in Customer Support* (Toronto: John Wiley & Sons Canada, Ltd., 1997), p. 383.
10. Cris Prystay, "Best employers in Asia: People equal profit—Ritz Carlton banks on investing in staff," *Asian Wall Street Journal,* September 6, 2001, p. N1.
11. Horst Schulze, www.lodgingnews.com/lodgingmag/ 2000_08/2000_08 _92.asp. (February 21, 2002).
12. Leonardo Inghilleri interview with Laurie Voss (February 13, 2002).
13. Much of our information here comes from educational programs given at the Ritz-Carlton Leadership Center by Robert George and Mario Dones.
14. Pat Mene interview with Laurie Voss (March 2002).
15. The Ritz-Carlton Hotel Company, L.L.C., *1999 Application Summary for the Malcolm Baldrige National Quality Award,* p. 12.

16. Tom Farmer e-mail message to Terry Bacon (January 16, 2001).
17. Paul C. Judge, "EMC Corporation," *Fast Company* (June 2001), p. 138.
18. David Kirkpatrick, "In the New Age of Data, EMC Rules," *Fortune* (August 1999), www.fortune.com/indexw.jhtml? doc_id=201101&channel=artcol.jhtml&_DARGS= (December 7, 2001).
19. "EMC's Joe Tucci: Betting on Storage Software," *VarBusiness* (December 2001), www.varbusiness.com/sections/research/research.asp? ArticleID=31908 (January 24, 2002).
20. EMC press release, January 24, 2002.
21. Michael C. Ruettgers, "I Pledge Allegiance to This Company: From Customer Satisfaction to Allegiance," *Chief Executive Magazine* (December 7, 2001). www.chiefexecutive.net/mag/147/article3.htm
22. James A. Champy, *X-Engineering the Corporation: Reinventing Your Business in the Digital Age* (New York: Warner Books, 2002), p. 60.
23. Charles Brombaugh, www.emc.com/global_services/cs_quotes.jsp? openfolder=cs (April 1, 2002).
24. The Gartner Group, "EMC Launches Integrated Global Services," *Vendor Analysis* (March 29, 2001).
25. Michael Treacy and Fred Wiersema, *The Discipline of Market Leaders* (Reading, Mass.: Addison-Wesley Publishing Company, 1995).
26. Ruettgers, ibid.
27. "In crisis, EMC comes through," *EMC.NOW* 3, 12 (December 2001), pp. 4–5. All of the stories told here are from this document. Reprinted and edited with permission.

6

RANDOM ACTS OF KINDNESS

Being treated with respect and dignity by one company raises the standard everywhere, not just in the same environment or in comparable businesses. Customers tend to use their most satisfying experiences as their benchmark.

—Betsy Sanders, *Fabled Service*

Relationships, whether business or marriage, seem to be subject to the Second Law of Thermodynamics: unless maintained, they gradually deteriorate and wear down.

—Art Weinstein and William C. Johnson,
Designing and Delivering Superior Customer Value

In just about every case, my sailors were not born with anything remotely resembling a silver spoon in their mouths. But each and every one of them was trying to make something meaningful of their lives.

—D. Michael Abrashoff, former captain of the *USS Benfold*

Bill Hardin remembers an evening with a potential customer that did not go as planned. His company had four prime seats behind home plate at the Astrodome, and he and his associate had arranged to meet the customer's proposed project manager, John, and an engineering manager for dinner at Willie G's before heading to the ball game. It was to be one of those evenings with the boys: dinner, beer, cigars, jokes, and nine innings of baseball. In the engineering and construction business, this was how you got to know your customers and how you bonded with them before they had to decide which company they wanted to work with. So Bill was surprised when John arrived at the restaurant not with the engineering manager, who had another commitment, but with a 7-year-old girl, who turned out to be John's daughter. His wife had had to leave town unexpectedly, and rather than canceling their meeting John decided to bring her to dinner and then send Bill and his associate off to the game by themselves.

"As he apologized for the inconvenience," Bill said, "we could see that the little girl was interested in the Astros. She said Jose Cruz was her favorite player." So Bill insisted that all four of them go to the game. John consented but was worried that they might have to leave before the end of the game if she got tired. He suggested they take separate cars so he and his daughter could leave without inconveniencing Bill and his associate.

"No big deal," Bill said. "Let's go in one car. We're glad to have you as our guests, and we will treat you as our guests." The young lady ended up having the time of her life that evening. She faded during the seventh-inning stretch, and the men carried her out of the Astrodome in their arms. When the bid went in months later, it was a dead heat technically and commercially, so the customer made the decision based on other factors. You can probably guess who won.[1]

Interpersonal BD is often little more than a random act of kindness: a smile where it wasn't expected, a helpful accommodation that didn't need to be made, an uncommon degree of sensitivity toward someone else, a show of caring that transcends commercial considerations. Most people have average interpersonal skills. They may display emotional brilliance now and then, but their skills are for the most part unremarkable and indistinguishable from most other people. They are in the vast hump in the middle of the bell curve (see Figure 6-1). About one-sixth of the population excels interpersonally (those with statistically significant skills on the right wing of the bell curve), and about one-sixth has inferior interpersonal skills (the left wing of the curve).

We develop our interpersonal skills very early in life: in learning how to cope with and relate to our parents and siblings; in what we are taught in school, church, youth groups, sports, and other organized activities; and in learning how to form friendships and even more intimate relationships with our peers. However, to some degree our interpersonal skills are a product of our innate disposition toward others: how outgoing we are, how comfortable we are with strangers, how open we are to sharing our feelings, how interested we are in other people, and so on. People who are not outgoing, who don't like strangers, who don't share their feelings, and who aren't interested in other people are unlikely to manifest good interpersonal skill. They will

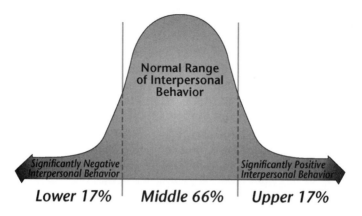

Figure 6-1. The Interpersonal Bell Curve. Interpersonal behavior is likely to follow a normal distribution. Noticeably negative and positive behaviors fall on either wing of the bell curve, and this is where interpersonal BD occurs.

probably fall on the left wing of the bell curve (see Figure 6-1), and if they work for you, putting them in positions with significant customer interaction may be unwise. However, our conclusion begs the question: Do significantly greater or lesser interpersonal skills in your people really have an impact on how customers view your business? We think the answer is a resounding "Yes," and in this chapter we are going to explore the impact of interpersonal BD, not only in business but in any organization. Our examples include "Chainsaw" Al Dunlap, Leona Helmsley (the Queen of Mean), former Atlanta Braves pitcher John Rocker, and naval officers whose careers reflect opposite ends of the interpersonal spectrum.

What People Want

To understand how to differentiate your interpersonal behavior with customers, you must first understand what people want in their interactions with others. Clearly, we cannot fathom individual motives or desires, but we can describe what *normal* people in *normal* situations in *most* cultures expect from other people. That may seem like a lot of caveats, but we have to exclude what abnormal people want, and what people who are angry or upset or otherwise in an extreme emotional state may want from others. Further, there are cultural, gender-related, or age-related expectations that complicate what people want from others. So we will confine ourselves to exploring what people expect of others in *normal* circumstances. Here, in a nutshell, is what people want:

▲ People want to feel welcome. When they come to a new place, they want to feel accepted by the people who are already there and welcomed to that place. They don't want to remain strangers. Even in transactional situations, like stopping at a gas station on a road they have never traveled before and may never travel again, customers have a more positive experience if the people working there welcome them and make them feel at home.

▲ People want to be accepted as themselves. They don't want to be labeled, stereotyped, or pigeonholed by someone else's preconceptions. They don't want to be branded and treated differently because of assumptions others make based on first impressions or superficial observations. They don't want to wear a façade in order for others to accept them. They want to be treated equally and fairly.

▲ People want to feel involved. They want to participate, to be meaningfully engaged, to be asked for their opinion, and to have their opinion count. Few things feel worse to most people than exclusion.

▲ People want to feel excited. Ralph Waldo Emerson said, "Every great and commanding moment in the annals of the world is the triumph of some enthusiasm." When people are excited, they are more engaged. The experience is more fun. That's why well-designed theme parks are always such a draw. It's why Chuck-E-Cheese has been so successful in attracting children. It's why McDonald's starting building children's play stations in their restaurants. Smart companies make what they do exciting for customers and employees.

▲ People want to feel respected. Respect is about honoring basic human dignity. It requires empathy—the ability to put yourself in others' shoes and recognize that they aren't so different from you. No matter what one's station or predicament in life, we are all human, and to recognize the essential humanity in others is to accord them the respect they deserve as human beings.

▲ People want to feel encouraged and appreciated. They want to believe that their efforts are succeeding, that they are on the right track, that there is reason to feel good about themselves and their work. On the other hand, they don't want to be patronized or pandered to. They want *genuine* encouragement when it is warranted. When they contribute something or do something well, they want to be noticed and acknowledged, and, for customers, *contributing* may mean nothing more than doing business with you. When they do you a favor, failing to appreciate it is likely to reduce their willingness to do more favors for you. Appreciation is the basic currency of reciprocation.

Computers, which can personalize products, cannot humanize them. For that you need humans. With every transaction, people become more important in the process. That's because the ability to customize a product to the individual makes the relationship with the customer the key transaction. Gathering information, and above all developing trust, have become the key source of sustainable competitive advantage.
—Gary Heil, Warren Bennis, and Deborah C. Stephens,
Douglas MacGregor, Revisited: Managing the Human Side of Enterprise

▲ People want to feel cared for. To care means "to guard or protect." When someone cares about us, we feel guarded and protected. We know this person will help us if we need help. To *receive* care you have to *give* care because caring is reciprocal. It stands to reason, then, that if you don't care about your customers, they won't care about you. However, David Maister's research in professional service firms reveals a shocking outcome about caring. He has asked thousands of professionals how they feel about their clients. He gives them three ways to classify how they feel:

1. "I really like these people. I enjoy serving them."
2. "I can tolerate them. I'm responsible and I give good service, but there is no real difference between today's client and tomorrow's client."
3. "These people are idiots who work in a boring industry."[2]

According to Maister, only about 20 percent of professionals say they really like their clients, 60 to 70 percent of professionals give the second response, and 10 to 20 percent say they can't stand their clients.[3] These statistics are discouraging, to say the least. However, they essentially conform to the shape of the bell curve we showed in Figure 6-1. Only about one-sixth of professionals truly care about their clients, and they are the ones likely to behave in the statistically significant right wing of the bell curve. The ones who don't like their clients are likely to fall into the left wing of the bell curve because their behavior will reflect their lack of caring. It always does.

▲ People want to feel informed. They like to know what's going on. No one wants to feel that everyone around them is well informed while they are left in the dark. You can't make smart decisions with incomplete information.

▲ People want to feel trusted. No one likes being on trial or suspected of wrongdoing when they have done nothing wrong. We don't like being watched or having people on their guard around us, especially if we have done nothing to warrant their distrust. Being trusted feels good and secure. It gives you confidence in yourself, and it helps you be more trusting of others. So when businesses behave as though they can't trust their customers, then customers become more distrustful themselves. However, it would be naïve to assume that you can trust everyone. Some people do lie, cheat, and steal. Anti-theft devices in retail stores are an unfortunate necessity, but stores should be careful not to alienate all customers by assuming that everyone is dishonorable.

▲ People want to feel understood. They want to be listened to and feel that people understand and appreciate their perspective. At heart, when people seek to be understood they are seeking both acknowledgement and empathy. They want to know that they are not alone and that their opinions are valued.

In the course of normal social interactions, this is what everyone wants. People with strong interpersonal skills instinctively understand this and behave in ways that make others feel welcomed, trusted, listened to, respected, cared for, and so on. In other words, they create an emotionally satisfying environment for the people they interact with. According to Daniel Goleman, such people are highly emotionally intelligent. He argues that emotional intelligence is a greater factor in success in life than IQ, and there is growing evidence from a number of researchers to support his contention. Emotionally intelligent people know how to manage the *emotional exchange* that occurs when they interact with others, and this creates a more satisfying interaction for both parties.

We think it's possible for organizations to be emotionally intelligent as well. We have already cited two prime examples: Ritz-Carlton and EMC. In later chapters, we will describe how other companies have been able to create environments for their employees and customers that differentiate the companies behaviorally. In many of those examples, emotional intelligence is a key factor. Essentially, it means understanding what people want in human interactions, including business meetings and calls, and finding the people and building the systems that will give customers a satisfying emotional experience. When you understand what people want, it is not difficult to design systems and protocols for serving customers that meet their basic emotional needs. Beyond systems, however, you need employees at every significant touch point with customers who understand how people want to be treated and who behave accordingly. Operational BD is a function of systems, rules, procedures, traditions, and standard practices, but interpersonal BD is a function of each employee's own values, attitudes, and behavior.

The Bell Curve of Interpersonal Behavior

Figure 6-1 illustrates the normal distribution of interpersonal behaviors, which we presume to reflect the range of behaviors present in any interaction. The middle hump of the curve shows the range of average or normal behaviors, and these constitute about two-thirds of all interpersonal behaviors. In other words, what we experience two-thirds of the time from people is behavior we would consider normal, although there might be great variations in those behaviors. Some people listen better than others, but unless we encounter people who are remarkably worse or better listeners than normal, we would say that their listening behavior falls in that vast middle hump. The wings on either side of the bell curve reflect the negative and positive behaviors that would be one standard deviation beyond the norm. In a normal distribution, each of these wings would include one-sixth of the behaviors we observe. So, statistically, one-sixth of listening behaviors are significantly worse than normal and one-sixth are significantly better. To make our point more concretely, we will examine each of the three areas of this bell curve in more depth and will look at the types of behaviors one might find there. First, we will look at the vast middle hump (Figure 6-2). This is the normal range of interpersonal behavior.

Customs obviously differ, but it would be fair to say that in any part of the world people would normally be civil with one another: returning a greeting when one is given, answering when asked a question, being polite according to the customs of politeness in a particular culture, being reasonably friendly and responsive, and so on. This is especially true in business contexts, where the behavioral standards are higher than they would be, for instance, at a football match. In the normal course of business, customers would expect people to listen to them, be honest and forthright, maintain appropriate eye contact, and be respectful. In the average business encounter, these behaviors would occur but would be unremarkable, which is to say they would not behaviorally differentiate. It's what happens most of the time, and although it may satisfy customers it probably won't delight them. Merely doing what is expected may satisfy customers, but most suppliers can do that, so satisfaction alone is not differentiating. It's the price of admission.

Occasionally, however, customers experience the kinds of behaviors shown in Figure 6-3. This is the left wing of the bell curve, the negative one-

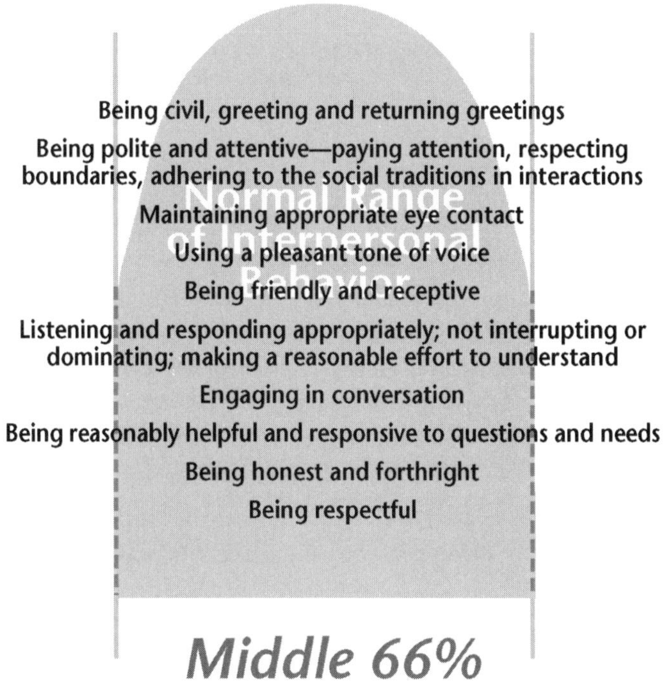

Figure 6-2. Average Interpersonal Behaviors. The middle of the bell curve represents the norm of interpersonal behavior. About two-thirds of the people we encounter normally behave this way. Whenever we interact with others, these are the kinds of behaviors we expect.

sixth of behaviors that are one or more standard deviations below the norm. These kinds of behaviors are remarkable. When we experience them as customers, we notice them because they are so far outside our normal expectations, and they negatively differentiate the people behaving this way. These behaviors range from apathy (at the top of Figure 6-3) to hostility and deceit. Given the importance of retaining customers, it is amazing that people in business can behave this way, but they sometimes do. Throughout this book we report the results of our research on BD, and as our research shows, lawyers, physicians, nurses, waiters, new car sellers, and others who ought to know better sometimes treat customers so badly that the customers vow never to use those providers again. Many of the negative behaviors we cite in our research are interpersonal in nature and are reflected in Figure 6-3.

At the other end of the interpersonal bell curve (Figure 6-4) are positive behaviors that are significantly beyond our normal expectations. Because these

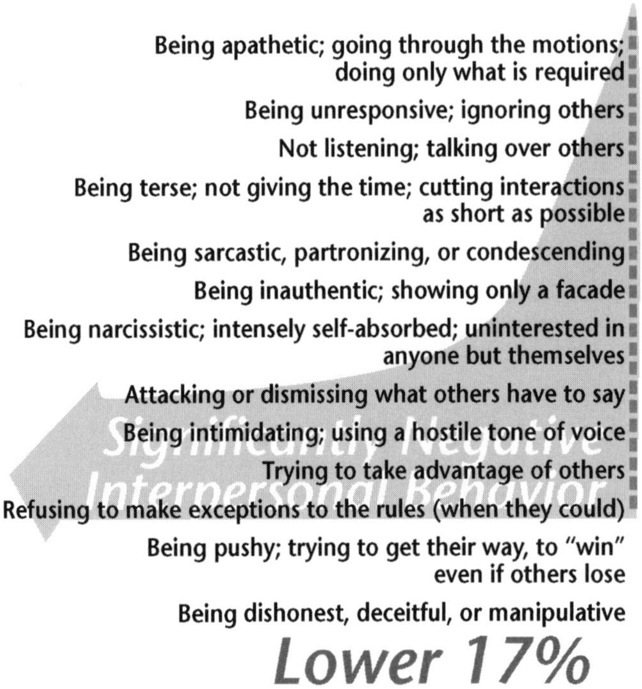
Being apathetic; going through the motions; doing only what is required
Being unresponsive; ignoring others
Not listening; talking over others
Being terse; not giving the time; cutting interactions as short as possible
Being sarcastic, partronizing, or condescending
Being inauthentic; showing only a facade
Being narcissistic; intensely self-absorbed; uninterested in anyone but themselves
Attacking or dismissing what others have to say
Being intimidating; using a hostile tone of voice
Trying to take advantage of others
Refusing to make exceptions to the rules (when they could)
Being pushy; trying to get their way, to "win" even if others lose
Being dishonest, deceitful, or manipulative
Significantly Negative Interpersonal Behavior
Lower 17%

Figure 6-3. Negative Interpersonal Behaviors. The left wing of the bell curve represents behaviors that are one standard deviation below the norm. These kinds of employee behaviors negatively differentiate the company and have a repulsive effect on customers.

behaviors exceed our expectations and create a more satisfying emotional environment, they tend to be memorable, too. When we experience these behaviors as customers, we feel better about the interaction, we like the people who treated us so well, and we are inclined to return to them and their company when we need more of what we bought from them. Positive interpersonal behaviors, like all BD, have an *attractive* effect on customers (negative behaviors have a *repulsive* effect). In our research on BD, we asked consumers of healthcare to identify their worst and best experiences with nurses and physicians. Here are some typical responses, listed as elements of the left and right wings of the interpersonal bell curve:

Negative Interpersonal BD (left wing of the bell curve)	Positive Interpersonal BD (right wing of the bell curve)
Lecturing and being condescending; treating patients as though they were unruly children	Being a thoughtful listener, explaining thoroughly, then ensuring patients understand
Being patronizing and judgmental	Remembering patients' preferences and needs from one visit to the next
Being impatient and rude; not responding when spoken to; having a short temper	Standing up for the patient and ensuring that excellent care is received
Being unfriendly; lacking warmth; having cold hands and a cold manner	Being willing to communicate bad news and do it in a compassionate way
Not caring; being unconcerned about patients or their lives	Showing genuine caring; asking about the patient's life and family
Having a superior attitude; being arrogant	Arranging a cake for a patient having a birthday in the hospital
Treating patients like things on an assembly line; running patients through the mill	Devoting the time required; doing research on the problem; then following up on the treatment
Making patients wait, then rushing through a diagnosis	Focusing on patients' general well being, not just the illness
Utterly lacking in compassion; being apathetic about patients' problems	Giving patients a home telephone number to call if they have questions or problems
Being a poor communicator; not answering patients' questions and not telling them what they need to know about their illness and care	Remaining singularly focused on the patients being helped; not being distracted
Having poor personal hygiene; being sloppy and unkempt; wearing dirty clothing; smelling bad	Following through; remaining engaged through all aspects of recovery
Not returning phone calls for long periods	Telephoning former patients periodically to see how they are doing

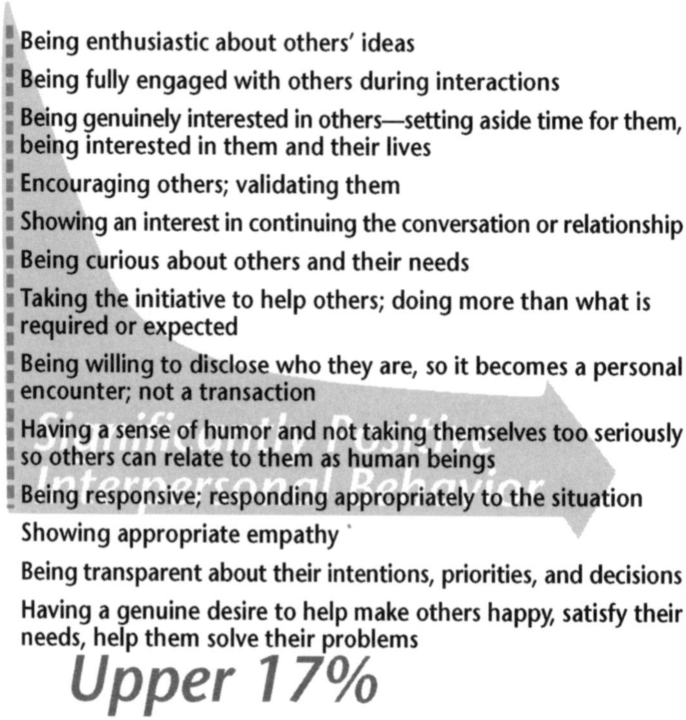
Being enthusiastic about others' ideas
Being fully engaged with others during interactions
Being genuinely interested in others—setting aside time for them, being interested in them and their lives
Encouraging others; validating them
Showing an interest in continuing the conversation or relationship
Being curious about others and their needs
Taking the initiative to help others; doing more than what is required or expected
Being willing to disclose who they are, so it becomes a personal encounter; not a transaction
Having a sense of humor and not taking themselves too seriously so others can relate to them as human beings
Being responsive; responding appropriately to the situation
Showing appropriate empathy
Being transparent about their intentions, priorities, and decisions
Having a genuine desire to help make others happy, satisfy their needs, help them solve their problems
Significantly Positive Interpersonal Behavior
Upper 17%

Figure 6-4. Positive Interpersonal Behaviors. The right wing of the bell curve consists of behaviors that are one standard deviation above the norm. Employees who exhibit these behaviors positively differentiate the company, which has an attractive effect on customers.

> If you hire the wrong people, your vision will be dashed at every turn. You simply cannot make "not nice" people want to treat the customers—and each other—well. As difficult as it is to define, you have to hire people with the right attitude because it cannot be trained, mandated, or motivated into being.
>
> —Betsy Sanders, *Fabled Service*

Chainsaw Al and the Queen of Mean

It is not difficult to find examples of business leaders whose interpersonal misbehavior makes them the object of fear and loathing. The media loves stories of people behaving badly, particularly when they fall from their lofty positions. What happens to them can serve as an object lesson for the rest of us. A decade ago, the person everyone loved to hate was Leona Helmsley, the billionaire wife of real estate magnate Harry Helmsley. Dubbed the "Queen of Mean" by the media and "the wicked witch" by New York mayor Ed Koch, Helmsley was notorious for her arrogance and nastiness toward everyone she considered beneath her. Her own attorney described her as "a tough bitch with an explosive temper." Although she and her husband were extraordinarily wealthy, they ran afoul of the law when it was discovered that millions of dollars in renovation bills for their Greenwich, Connecticut, home had been falsely charged as business expenses to their Manhattan office buildings.

Harry was deemed too ill to stand trial, so Leona faced tax evasion charges alone. During the trial, much of her negative interpersonal behavior surfaced. In fact, it became her lawyer's explanation for the crime: "The novel defence was that staff so feared her wrath that they independently resorted to faking invoices to minimise the time they had to spend in her company. The court heard that when it was brought to her attention that a contractor she had refused to pay had six children to feed, she retorted: 'Why didn't he keep his trousers on? He wouldn't have so many problems.' Her past sins were paraded daily."[4] During the trial, Helmsley's maid testified that Leona had said, "We don't pay taxes. Only the little people pay taxes." She was convicted of tax evasion, fined, and sentenced to four years in prison. She served eighteen months and was freed with the stipulation that she perform hundreds of hours of community service, which, it was later reported, she had had her servants do for her.

At the time of her trial, *Newsweek* ran a story about Helmsley. Her face was featured on the cover with the headline, "Rhymes with Rich." Subsequently, her rise and fall were featured in a trash TV movie starring Suzanne Pleshette entitled "Queen of Mean." On our bell curve of interpersonal behavior (Figure 6-1), Leona Helmsley's behavior is so far to the left it may not belong on the same scale as "normal" bad behavior. She is a prime example of someone whose interpersonal behavior negatively differentiated her, and the consequences of that behavior include being pilloried in the press, turned into the butt of many jokes on late-night TV, testified against by people who worked closely with her, and being shown little remorse by the legal system. Indeed, when she complained to the trial judge that she was too ill to go to prison, he made the offhand remark that the prison he was sending her to had a hospital wing.

Another business figure people loved to hate in the last decade was Al Dunlap, self-styled corporate tough guy and ruthless king of downsizing. Dunlap made a name for himself as an aide to British billionaire financier Sir James Goldsmith but is most noted for his stints at Scott Paper and Sunbeam.

At both corporations, his strategy was to slash and burn—to ruthlessly cut products and employees in an effort to maximize shareholder value. In an era of radical cost cutting, Wall Street applauded his moves. Scott Paper's stock rose 225 percent, which added $6.3 billion in value to the company. However, critics felt that in the process of cost cutting he trimmed as much muscle as fat. Shortly after Kimberly-Clark purchased the company (a merger in which Dunlap pocketed $100 million), Scott Paper began to look like an empty shell. According to one observer, "His 'miracle' at Scott was accomplished in less than two years. However, it took only one quarter for Kimberly-Clark to find out it had purchased a prettied-up 'pig-in-a-poke.' Scott's buyer discovered that Dunlap and his henchmen increased earnings by cutting and closing critical plants, deferring all maintenance on plants and equipment, and building inventories for the sole purpose of booking sales. None of what he accomplished at Scott was designed to build for the future, only sell off the present, all in the name of adding shareholder value."[5]

In 1996, he was appointed CEO of Sunbeam. According to *Business Week's* John Byrne, at his first executive meeting Dunlap verbally attacked Spencer Volk, head of international business, for being one minute late to the meeting. "The old Sunbeam is over today! It's over! It's over! It's over!" Dunlap kept repeating. He then forced the senior officers to beg to keep their jobs, part of what P. Newton White, who joined the team from Scott Paper, described as Dunlap's "piss all over them and then we'll build them back up" policy.[6] Byrne said that some of the senior officers were more than ready to get out of there. "At least then they could take their severance pay and walk away from what was surely going to be a living hell, working for an impulsive and abusive loud mouth."[7] True to his slash-and-burn nature, Dunlap cut 12,000 jobs at Sunbeam, shut down two-thirds of its eighteen manufacturing plants, and engaged in a business practice known as "stuffing the channel," which means persuading retailers to buy more products than they need by offering huge discounts. This adds a lot of revenue to the books very quickly, and, indeed, Sunbeam's stock jumped after Dunlap took over and made his first moves. This house of cards came tumbling down in 1998 when retailers, overloaded with Sunbeam products, stopped purchasing, and revenues plummeted.

Later, under Chapter 11 proceedings, Sunbeam was forced to restate its financial results for six quarters ending March 31, 1998, which covered most of Dunlap's tenure at Sunbeam. Early in 2002, after years of legal wrangling and investigation, "Chainsaw Al" agreed to pay $15 million to settle a class action lawsuit by Sunbeam shareholders, which had accused him and three other former Sunbeam executives of securities fraud. (Interestingly, as part of the same lawsuit, accounting firm Arthur Andersen, famous now for the debacle at Enron, agreed to pay $110 million to settle claims with Sunbeam shareholders.)

Of course, this is more than a tale of corporate mismanagement and downsizing run amuck. It's really a tale of misguided leadership and the consequences of interpersonal behavior so deplorable that it ruins companies as it ruins lives. Al Dunlap fancied himself a tough guy, a Rambo in pinstripes, who was there to set people straight. In an interview with PBS, he said, "I'm a no-nonsense person. I'm not coming there to listen to all the excuses which they've been giving. That's what got them into trouble to begin with. I'm not there to hear what can't be done. I'm there to get results. I'm there to challenge people beyond what they've ever been challenged before. And so, if that's tough, then yes, I am tough."[8] But there's a difference between tough and tyrannical. Jack Welch was also tough, but he knew how to build a company and inspire a leadership team. Welch also downsized and focused a large organization by selling underperforming units. However, in the process he built a strong culture, a leadership engine that remains the envy of many companies, and a high-performing enterprise. Welch trained a generation of business leaders who went on to lead other companies, and he left a powerful legacy. Dunlap left burning hulks.

Other Examples of Negative Behavioral Differentiation

Chainsaw Al and the Queen of Mean are two of the more blatant examples of business leaders who paid a price for their abusive behavior toward others, although cynics would point out that both are multimillionaires, and their negative interpersonal BD didn't ruin them. Still, it would be wrong to assume from their example that clawing your way to the top and abusing people around you is a recipe for success. Helmsley and Dunlap were public figures whose caustic behavior brought them notoriety, and they did pay a penalty for it. What is less obvious are the ruined lives and fortunes of thousands of lesser-known business leaders whose negative behavior derails their careers and brings indeterminate harm to the people and companies they have been responsible for. We *can* measure some of the damage.

Sexual harassment, for instance, is clearly one form of negative interpersonal BD. In our schema of negative interpersonal behaviors shown in Figure 6-3, sexual harassment would fall under "being intimidating," "trying to take advantage of others," "being pushy," and perhaps "being manipulative or deceitful." Most business people are not guilty of sexual harassment, so the few who *are* negatively differentiate themselves based on their behavior. The consequences? According to the Equal Employment Opportunity Commission, more than 15,000 sexual harassment complaints have been filed with the agency every year since 1995. In 2001, the monetary benefit to those filing the complaints was $53 million. In that same year, more than four hundred sexual harassment lawsuits were filed, and the monetary benefits of those suits exceeded another $50 million.[9] As we write this, the cost of settling a single sexual harassment complaint has reached a new high. The average cost to defend against a complaint is $300,000, and the average settlement is around $280,000.[10] That is a lot of money to pay for hostility, immaturity, and poor judgment.

Less blatant than sexual harassment, but even more costly to business, are executives' negative interpersonal behaviors that alienate customers, demotivate employees, disrupt teams, and cause the executives themselves to derail. In the context we are using the term, *derail* means to be fired or demoted or to plateau in one's career below the level one should have attained. As its railroad metaphor implies, when executives derail, they fall off the career track. Why does this occur? A study of 300 middle- to upper-level managers by Michael Lombardo and Cynthia McCauley uncovered six common reasons for derailment: problems with interpersonal relationships, difficulty molding a staff, difficulty making strategic transitions, lack of follow-through, overdependence, and strategic differences with management.[11] Three of these six factors involve interpersonal competence or what Daniel Goleman has labeled emotional intelligence.

According to Lombardo and McCauley, the category *problems with interpersonal relationships* includes "adopts a bullying style under stress," "isolates him/herself from others," and "has left a trail of bruised people."[12] Managers who derail because of poor interpersonal skill, then, are people who don't handle stress well and become bullying or authoritarian when the going gets tough. They exclude others, don't allow enough participation, make decisions without consultation, and are aloof or distant from the people they manage. Finally, they may be abusive, threatening, intimidating, or too hard on people. As coaches, we are frequently asked to counsel executives who have become known as "people killers." At their worst, these bullies negatively differentiate themselves by being insensitive to others, demanding inhuman sacrifices of time, harshly criticizing in public even the most minor offense, and blaming others for their own failures.

Lombardo and McCauley's second factor, *difficulty in molding a staff,* includes "is not good at building a team," and their last factor, *strategic difficulties with management,* includes "could not handle a conflict with a bad boss or one he/she disagreed with."[13] Clearly, these three major causes of derailment involve a host of interpersonal problems. Every manager may be guilty of bad behavior from time to time, but when it becomes a *pattern* of abuse or neglect, when it is repeated often enough to have a long-term negative impact on the manager and the people he or she manages, then it constitutes negative interpersonal BD.

How many managers are at risk of derailing? Another study of more than two thousand executives determined that a significant percentage were derailing or already had. In "Recovering Executives at Risk of Derailing," Barbara Spencer Singer reports in a Lore International Institute study that tracked the careers of 2,171 executives and discovered that "30 percent were being promoted faster than their peers, 35 percent were at risk of derailment in the near future, and 12 percent had already derailed."[14] This study also said that 22 percent of executives were on track. Oftentimes, derailed executives leave the company they were working for, but some don't. In either case, the costs are staggering:

> Not all derailment leads to exiting a company—a person might be offered a consultancy or be reassigned to a new job—but when the person is forced to leave, it typically costs a company 16 to 18 months' of that person's pay to replace him or her. . . . The person might also just stagnate. Sometimes, derailed executives are put into 'placeholder' positions where they won't do much damage. This practice leads to inefficiencies and reduced productivity—and costs the company much more in the long run. Finally, additional costs are incurred through lost sales and lost customers. Executives that have left the organization or have become disgruntled often impact customer loyalty. Clearly, executive derailment is an enormous financial burden, costing corporations billions of dollars a year.[15]

The internal impact of managers who are abusive, abrasive, and interpersonally inept is substantial. The external impact on customers must also be enormous, but it is impossible to calculate. Managers and employees of companies who behave badly toward customers directly affect sales. However, inept interpersonal relationships internally also indirectly affect sales by demotivating employees and creating apathetic and even hostile interactions with customers.

The Jackass Defense

Bullies with bad tempers are not confined to the business arena. Sports has had its share of prima donnas, Neanderthals, and bad boys in uniforms. Dennis Rodman comes to mind, but he dressed up (once in a bridal gown), talked tough, and behaved outrageously as a way to get attention. Rodman is an exhibitionist and a showman. For serious negative BD, we have to turn to John Rocker, the former Atlanta Brave, former Cleveland Indian, and then Texas Ranger whose racist remarks disrupted his team, incensed fans, and prompted the baseball commissioner to impose a stiff suspension and fine. Rocker created so much animosity that a Web site was created called www.rocker sucks.com in which one fan wrote: "You are a disgrace to the game of baseball. Maybe you should think before you shoot off your big fat mouth. You are an immature punk who is lucky to be in the majors. Get some class!"[16]

Rocker's career started auspiciously enough. He was heavily scouted as a high school player and he opted to go into the draft instead of attending college. He graduated from high school in 1993 and was drafted by the Atlanta Braves, who saw him as an excellent pitching prospect. He developed in the Braves' system and behaved himself until September 1999, when he came in as a relief pitcher against the New York Mets and saved three games. Mets fans were understandably resentful at Rocker's performance and let him know it. Rocker went on record as saying Mets fans were stupid and "a tired act." His talented pitching in September meant the Mets and Braves would meet again for three games in October, and the winner of the series would win the National League East title and compete for the championship. In October, Mets fans booed Rocker; threw beer bottles, batteries, and water at him; and made vulgar remarks about his mother and his girlfriend. Rather than ignore the crowd, he returned fire—with insults of his own (see Figure 6-5).[17] However, his sentiments were not yet fully captured in print. The Braves won the

Figure 6-5. John Rocker Incites the Fans. The pitcher's volatile temper and abusive comments ignited a firestorm of controversy. Photo courtesy of Al Tielemans/ Sports Illustrated.

first two games in their October battle for National League East title. The hostility erupted again when Rocker saved game three, a win that put them one game away from the National League Championship Series.

In game four, Rocker was put in to clinch the Braves' 2–1 lead and save the game, but he failed. One Mets batter hit a Rocker pitch that scored two runs. After that, Rocker lost what composure he had left. One reporter later called him a one-man psycho circus. He spit at Mets fans and gave them the finger. After the game he blamed the loss on his teammates and the Mets hitter who had cost him two runs. He said the Braves shortstop was too old to "make that kind of play," and he discredited the hit by claiming that it was "one of the more cheaper hits I've given up my entire life."[18] He took no responsibility for the loss, blamed his teammates, and bad-mouthed the Mets hitter who won the game. Rocker's outbursts strained his relationship with his teammates and added fuel to the Mets fans' fire. The Braves won the series in six games, but were later swept by the New York Yankees in the World Series. As the baseball season ended, the feud between Rocker and Mets fans had gained enough momentum to make an interesting story, and Jeff Pearlman of *Sports Illustrated* invited Rocker for an interview. It was an opportunity Rocker should have passed up.

In Pearlman's article based on that interview, Rocker came across as a foul, loudmouthed, intolerant buffoon. Worse, his comments about New York and its people were blatantly racist. Here are two of Rocker's most infamous remarks:

> *On ever playing for a New York team:* "I would retire first. It's the most hectic, nerve-racking city. Imagine having to take the [Number] 7 train to the ballpark, looking like you're [riding through] Beirut next to some kid with purple hair next to some queer with AIDS right next to some dude who just got out of jail for the fourth time right next to some 20-year-old mom with four kids. It's depressing."
>
> *On New York City itself:* "The biggest thing I don't like about New York are the foreigners. I'm not a very big fan of foreigners. You can walk an entire block in Times Square and not hear anybody speaking English. Asians and Koreans and Vietnamese and Indians and Russians and Spanish people and everything up there. How the hell did they get in this country?"[19]

During the interview, Rocker also referred to an unnamed Atlanta Braves teammate as a "fat monkey." The fallout from the *Sports Illustrated* story was immediate. Although Rocker later apologized, it was not enough to assuage the anger and disgust many people felt. Among the reactions were these:

▲ Baseball commissioner Bud Selig demanded that Rocker undergo a psychological evaluation and would consider the results before deciding on disciplinary measures.

▲ A number of major league baseball players were outraged at Rocker's remarks. New York Yankees shortstop Derek Jeter said, "I wouldn't sit in the same room with him. I wouldn't sit with someone who's a racist. He says he's not a racist, but he makes racist comments."[20]

▲ Protestors marched in front of CNN's Atlanta headquarters, angry that the Atlanta Braves had taken no action against Rocker. (CNN's parent, Time-Warner, owns the Braves.)

▲ Braves first baseman Randall Simon, who is from the Dominican Republic, said he knew Rocker was talking about him when he described a teammate as a "fat monkey." In an interview with Morris News Service, Simon said, "I swear to you if he said that to my face I'd tear him up, and one of us would be suspended right now."[21]

▲ Teammate Chipper Jones worried that the distraction Rocker was causing was hard on the team and could bring even more trouble: "It seems like we always have our distractions and adversity every year, but this year has been the worst. . . . We have twenty-four guys in there that have lived with this distraction every day, and we didn't ask for any of it. You get asked about him so much, and then there's the safety issue. I think about it all the time. You don't know what's going to happen. How easy would it be for someone to sneak something in any stadium and take a pot shot at somebody?"[22]

▲ Heavy metal rock band Twisted Sister objected to the Braves' use of their song, "I Wanna Rock," to introduce Rocker when he came onto the field. Guitarist Jay French said, "We've got Hispanics in this band, Italians in this band, people who are Polish and Russian. We're all immigrants, all foreigners—quote unquote—and this is our way of saying his comments were not acceptable."[23]

Before the dust had settled, sports analysts were speculating about whether Rocker could remain with the Braves and, indeed, if he had any baseball career prospects at all. The only hope for Rocker, it seemed, was to play dumb, as commentator Frank Deford suggested: "Presumably, Rocker will, in some fashion, try to construe the hateful remarks he made to Jeff Pearlman of *Sports Illustrated.* The words he spoke are themselves, of course, in no way defensible, nor can he repair the hurtful damage he has done. But it is possible that Rocker can at least seek to mitigate the sins of his tongue—and his heart—by pleading that he is not so racist, not so vile, not so hurtful, but instead that he is simply a showoff and a dimwit. This might be called the jackass defense."[24] In the end, the Braves traded Rocker to the Cleveland Indians, where he remained for a difficult season. Later, Rocker was a reliever with the Texas Rangers. It's anybody's guess whether the hullabaloo he caused has made him wiser, but in May 2002 he traveled with the Rangers to Cleveland and pitched against the Indians. He was relieved in the eighth inning, and on his way to the dugout Cleveland fans began booing. Instead of spitting, cursing, or making obscene gestures, Rocker just smiled and tipped his hat to them.

> **People all say that I've had a bad break, but today—today I consider myself the luckiest man on the face of the Earth."**
> —Gary Cooper (as Lou Gehrig) saying farewell to a stadium full of fans in *The Pride of the Yankees*. Gehrig was one of the Yankees' most beloved players. He left the game after being diagnosed with amyotrophic lateral sclerosis.

The John Rocker story raises an interesting point about negative interpersonal BD. When you behave badly toward people, they develop a bias against you that can take on a life of its own. You become the galvanizing object of their wrath. Even when you are no longer behaving badly, their negative bias toward you lingers. They expect the worst and will not give you the benefit of the doubt. This is why a single bad experience can drive customers away from your business and keep them away for years. Anger and disappointment die hard.

A Tale of Two Captains

In Herman Wouk's Pulitzer Prize-winning novel, *The Caine Mutiny*, the abrasive captain of a minesweeper is relieved of command by his executive officer during a typhoon. Like Captain Bligh in *Mutiny on the Bounty*, Captain Queeg (played in the film version of the story by Humphrey Bogart) is a petty tyrant who ignores his crew's advice, ridicules officers and sailors publicly, and explodes in anger over trivial matters. Captain Queeg takes over a sloppy ship and is determined to turn it into one of the Navy's finest. To do that, he will need help from his officers, but in his first meeting with them (see Figure 6-6), he lets them know that he goes strictly by the rules and won't tolerate debate. "I am book man," Queeg says. "Deviate from the book and you'd better have half a dozen good reasons, and you'll still get an argument from me, and I don't lose arguments on board my ship. That's one of the nice things about being captain." Merrick, the executive officer, tries to tell the captain that the crew of the *Caine* is not used to doing things by the book. Im-

Figure 6-6. The Caine Mutiny. Humphrey Bogart as Captain Queeg letting his officers know that he doesn't lose arguments on his ship. Photo courtesy of Bettmann/CORBIS.

plicit in his warning is that change will have to be managed carefully, but Queeg won't hear it: "You can tell the crew there are four ways to do things on my ship—the right way, the wrong way, the navy way, and my way. If they do things my way, we'll get along."

Queeg knows the book, but he doesn't know how to lead men. He is mercurial, becomes angry when challenged, and is easily distracted by trivial matters. During an exercise in which his ship is pulling a target, he orders the ship to turn and then sees a sailor with his shirttail hanging out. He had seen this infraction of the rules earlier and admonished the officers and crew never to let it happen again. When it does, he becomes obsessed with disciplining those responsible and loses sight of the ship's movements. The helmsman tries to warn him that they are sailing in a circle and risk cutting their own towline, but the captain angrily tells him to shut up. When they do cut the towline, the captain blames it on faulty equipment and refuses to accept the responsibility for the incident. Queeg is a perfectionist who won't tolerate any questioning of his authority. He won't tolerate criticism and won't admit mistakes, and his crew quickly learns that to avoid his wrath they have to keep silent. It's an intolerable situation, and when Queeg freezes during a typhoon and the ship is in danger of foundering, the executive officer forcibly relieves the captain of his command.

The Caine Mutiny is fiction, but the events on board the *USS Florida* were not. The *Florida* is a Trident submarine, one of the most lethal weapons ever built. Nearly two football fields long, with a crew of 154, the *Florida* carried twenty-four long-range missiles with 192 nuclear warheads. It was one of America's most potent nuclear deterrents. In September 1996, the *Florida* got a new captain, Michael Alfonso. It was his first command, and like Captain Queeg he quickly established who was in charge. He told the crew he was going to push them hard, and he did, but they were not prepared for his loud, abrasive style. Captain Alfonso was a screamer, and *that* is highly unusual in the confines of a nuclear submarine whose mission is to run submerged and silent for months at a time. Like Queeg, Alfonso berated officers and enlisted men publicly, often for minor infractions. The ship's morale plummeted, and the crew began comparing themselves to the unfortunate crew of the *Caine*. In midsummer of 1997, the Navy investigated the reports of problems aboard the *Florida*, and Rear Admiral Paul Sullivan, perhaps worried about low morale on board a nuclear missile submarine, took the unprecedented step of relieving the captain of his command. The admiral had lost confidence in Alfonso's ability to lead the officers and men on board the *Florida*.[25] Table 6-1 shows more of the parallels between these two captains and their ships.

By this example, we don't mean to imply that leaders who are abrasive, petty, and mercurial will always suffer the consequences of their negative interpersonal BD. Competent jerks sometimes succeed because the benefits they bring to an organization outweigh the damage done by their behavior or because the organization is afraid to remove them for some other reason. Richard Tedlow reminds us, too, that the giants of American industry were not always the nicest of people: "I'm not going to make the case in this article that the legendary titans of American business offer a template of leadership lessons for all of us to follow. Many were individuals we wouldn't want to emulate, at least in every particular. They could be scheming and, more than occasionally, ruthless. Indeed, in many instances they were as titanic in the problems they created—especially the interpersonal problems—as in the empires they built."[26] What do we conclude from this? It is possible to behave badly and still succeed, but if you decide to go that route, you'd better have Andrew Carnegie's resources, or Bill Gates' timing, or John D. Rockefeller's connections, because the odds are against you. More and more, employees as well as customers won't tolerate it.

Table 6-1. A Comparison of Captains Queeg and Alfonso.

Captain Queeg of the USS Caine	Captain Alfonso of the USS Florida
Upon taking command, told the officers he would go strictly by the book.	Upon taking command, told the crew he would push them hard.
Harshly reprimanded anyone whose performance he felt was lacking, regardless of rank.	Harshly reprimanded anyone whose performance he felt was lacking, regardless of rank.
Frequently yelled at the crew.	Was known as a "screamer," which grates on crews in the confines of a nuclear submarine.
Had an abrasive manner and did not listen; people were afraid to tell him when something was wrong.	Had an abrasive manner and did not listen; people were afraid to tell him when something was wrong.
Would not tolerate non-regulation dress; reprimanded a sailor for having his shirt tail out.	Would not tolerate non-regulation dress; reprimanded an officer for wearing a non-standard hat.
Officers used humor to cope; one made up a song about the captain called "Old Yellow Stain Blues."	Officers used humor to cope; one joked about the USS Florida diet plan—getting your ass chewed every day.
Ordered punitive measures when his wishes were not complied with quickly (no liberty for 3 months because some men were not properly dressed during battle drills.)	Ordered punitive measures when his wishes were not complied with quickly (ordered the crew to repeatedly clean an area even after it was spotless).
Became enraged when a quart of strawberries went missing; ordered a middle-of-the-night investigation and then a strip search of all crewmen to locate a fictional missing key.	Became enraged when the soda dispenser that should have con-tained Coca-Cola had Mr. Pibb instead. Ordered three senior officers to appear and then shouted obscenities at them.
Arrived late for a movie being shown on deck; was enraged that he hadn't been notified of the film, a western. A sailor reminded him that he said he was sick of westerns,	Arrived for lunch one day and was angry that the potato soup was not being served on time; ordered a drill, which took all sailors away from their meals. If the captain

but the captain suspended all movies for 30 days.	couldn't eat on time, no one could.
Was relieved of command at sea during a typhoon by his executive officer, Merrick.	Was relieved of command by an admiral after an investigation found sufficient cause due to ship problems and poor morale.
Had his defenders. Some people felt that Merrick erred in relieving him of command.	Had his defenders. Some people felt that he was a just an old-style officer in a new navy.

If you don't like certain people, it's easier than ever to escape them. If you are a lousy person, it's harder than ever to keep people around you.

—Tim Sanders, "Love is the Killer App"

The Best Damn Ship in the Navy

Gourmet chefs? A welcoming plan for new recruits with their bunks assigned and linens waiting for them? An America Online account so sailors can keep in touch with their families through the Internet? Music videos projected onto the side of the ship when it's in port? Karaoke contests and an Elvis impersonator? This is definitely not your father's navy.

Welcome to the *USS Benfold.* From June 1997 to 1999, it was commanded by one of the most innovative ship captains in the U.S. Navy, D. Michael Abrashoff (see Figure 6-7). The story of the *Benfold* under his command is a story of the power of positive interpersonal BD. It's also a story of phenomenal leadership and how it can transform an organization. In the 21 months Abrashoff commanded the *Benfold,* he and his crew turned it into the best damn ship in the navy.

The *Benfold* (DDG 65) is a guided missile destroyer, one of the technological marvels in the U.S. Navy's Arleigh Burke class. It is a multimission surface combatant with responsibility for antisubmarine, anti-air, and anti-surface warfare. Like the larger Ticonderoga class cruisers, guided missile destroyers like the *Benfold* have a combat systems center built around the sophisticated Aegis combat system and the SPY-ID multifunction phased array radar. These destroyers can be fitted with forward and aft vertical launching systems, advanced antisubmarine warfare systems, advanced anti-aircraft

Figure 6-7. Michael Abrashoff. His behavior as captain of the *USS Benfold* differentiated him from the previous captain and helped him create the best damn ship in the navy. Photo courtesy of Michael Abrashoff.

missiles, two radar-controlled Phalanx close-in weapon systems, Harpoon antiship missiles, and Tomahawk cruise missiles (which featured so prominently in the Gulf War and the war in Afghanistan). According to the navy, the *Benfold* is one of the most powerful surface combatants ever put to sea.

The ship joined the Pacific Fleet for duty in March 1996. It was the fifteenth of the navy's thirty-five Arleigh Burke class guided missile destroyers. When Mike Abrashoff assumed command in June 1997, he was one of the youngest naval officers ever appointed to command this type of ship, and the magnitude of the challenge facing him became apparent as he watched the departing captain leave the ship. It is customary when a ship changes captains for the event to occur amid much fanfare and celebration. Families and friends are on hand. The band is playing, and guest speakers extol the virtues of the ship, its crew, and its departing captain. However, when the public address system announced this captain's departure, there were catcalls and jeers from some of the crew who were clearly glad to see him go. Abrashoff was shocked at the disrespect they showed the former captain and vowed that that would not happen to him when he left the ship.

An Arleigh Burke class destroyer has a crew of 300 men and women. These sailors, some of whom have not graduated from high school and many of whom are not college graduates, must operate and maintain highly sophisticated propulsion, communication, sensing, and weapons systems—and do it during stressful conditions. Commanding such a crew is like managing a company of 300 underpaid volunteers who are separated from their families for prolonged periods, who must be ready to perform flawlessly at a moment's notice, and who may lose their lives if they are not successful (and sometimes even if they are). By comparison, running a company is a Sunday picnic.

For Mike Abrashoff, however, commanding a ship was the culmination of a lifelong dream. An Annapolis grad, he had been working his entire career for the opportunity to run his own ship. Beyond his naval training and experience, the one thing he brought to the *Benfold* was a deep commitment to leading people the right way, even if it meant bucking 225 years of U.S. Navy tradition and never being promoted again. As far as he was concerned, he had already climbed as high as he'd planned. He credits his success with the fact that his attention wasn't on his own career and personal advancement and that was what allowed him to concentrate his full attention on the success of his crew. "All I ever wanted," he says, "was for the ship to be the best, for everybody to get something out of it themselves, and for it to be a life-forming experience for them. They repaid me with outstanding performance."[27]

Behavioral differentiation has its origins in leaders and their values and in the culture and values of the organization and the people in it. What distinguishes Mike Abrashoff as a leader—and what makes him an example of interpersonal BD—is the human touch he brought to commanding a naval warship. He had an inclusive attitude about the experience of serving on the *Benfold*, and he knew he could not successfully manage a complex, modern warship on his own:

> Our ships cost a billion dollars to build these days, and they are so technologically complex, it's incredible—all these computers, tremendous weapons systems, and the ship's engines, which are the same engines that propel 747s—and all of this is being maintained by people who do not have college degrees. Only the officers for the most part have college degrees. We've got to manage all this information coming at us, making intelligent decisions and directing people to do the right things. It's absolutely impossible for one person to stay on top of it all. It just can't be done, whereas twenty years ago one person could stay on top of it. So that meant I needed to get smarter myself and train my people so they could run their mission areas knowing my vision and philosophy, knowing what my orders are, and knowing when to bring me in on what they were doing. I couldn't be involved in every aspect of the ship's operation, so they needed to know what was important to me so they could call me when they hit a milestone.[28]

This meant building a crew that would be self-directed, that would understand the mission and do what it took in their areas to perform as expected. It meant having people who knew enough to trust their own judgment and who would act appropriately because they knew the captain trusted them. Abrashoff understood that for a 300-person team to act this way, each person had to feel involved in the broader mission. "You have to get them to believe in the purpose of the organization," he told us. "And they have to believe that what they are doing is important, that it is critical that they perform properly to successfully achieve your purpose. One of the things I succeeded at was getting them to understand that our success was not about me; it was about all of us, and I needed every one of them contributing 100 percent all the time in order to achieve it."[29] So a key behavioral difference is the leader sublimating his ego and defining success in terms of how it rewards everyone in the team. This is not a new idea. Robert Greenleaf called it "servant leadership." However, it is still uncommon in command-and-control and traditional hierarchical management environments.

Like George Zimmer of Men's Wearhouse and Herb Kelleher of Southwest Airlines, Abrashoff came to believe that the command-and-control approach is not the best way to tap people's intelligence and skills. He learned that lesson when he decided to get to know every sailor on the ship: "When I first took charge of the *Benfold,* I was having trouble learning the names of everyone in the crew, so I decided to interview five people a day. Along with Master Chief Bob Scheeler, the senior enlisted guy on the ship, I met with each person individually and asked three simple questions: What do you like most about the *Benfold?* What do you like least? What would you change if you could?"[30] Asking those questions helped Abrashoff identify a number of areas of the ship's operation that could be improved, but it had a more profound effect on him as a leader:

> What happened from that is that I came to respect my people as I never had before. I used to view them as just people to be ordered about to get a mission accomplished, to reach our bottom line. When I interviewed them and got to know them, I realized they had as much on the ball, if not more, than me. And that they wanted to do great things. They had loved ones they wanted to take care of. They had goals they wanted to achieve. I started thinking, who am I not to create the climate that helps these people achieve their goals? Before, I never knew them, never cared about them, just assumed they were out to screw me over, and I thought I had to micromanage them. But after I got to know them, I came to respect them and then wanted to help them achieve their goals.[31]

Taking a personal interest in those you are leading is a differentiating behavior for leaders because many don't. Treating your direct reports with humanity and respect, listening to them and valuing their ideas, and creating the conditions in which they can achieve great things—these behaviors sound like leadership clichés. Anyone who has read anything on leadership knows these best practice behaviors, but the fact is that few leaders do them consistently well. *That's* what makes the behavioral difference. Like thousands of other naval commanders, Abrashoff knew the basics. What made the difference is that he saw his sailors as human beings. He had the interest and took the time to get to know them. He cared about their lives and their aspirations as individuals. That's why he is an exemplar of interpersonal BD. To his sailors, the difference was interpersonal: he *listened* to them, he *cared* about them, he *respected* them, and he went out of his way to help make their personal and professional lives more fulfilling.

Mike Abrashoff says he learned some important lessons from exit interviews of people leaving the Navy. He had always assumed that low pay was the primary reason why the Navy did not have a higher retention rate, but that proved not to be true. "The top reason was not being treated with respect and dignity; second was being prevented from making an impact on the organization; third, not being listened to; and fourth, not being rewarded with more responsibility."[32] Low pay was ranked fifth. As a ship captain, Abrashoff had a mostly indirect effect on sailors' pay, but he could affect whether they were treated with respect, whether they were allowed to make an impact, whether they were listened to, and whether they were rewarded with more responsibility. Those are areas of leadership where he could make an impact. He also felt that quality of life was an important issue, and he could affect that as well. Here are a few of the innovative things Abrashoff did to help make the *Benfold* "the best damn ship in the navy" and, coincidentally, to differentiate himself as a ship's captain:

▲ He listened to sailors' complaints about the food on board the ship. Instead of saying, "This is the Navy, and you'll eat what the Navy gives you," he explored the alternatives and found that he could save money by purchasing name brand, higher-quality food instead of using more expensive naval provisions. The money he saved allowed him to send five of the ship's cooks to culinary school, which improved both the meals and the morale on board ship.

▲ He discovered that a number of sailors wanted to go to college, but many of them had not taken the college entrance exam. He polled the ship and discovered that forty-five sailors would be interested in taking the exam if he would arrange it. So he found an SAT administrator and flew him out to the ship to give the test.

▲ He created a welcoming plan for new recruits. He realized how lonely and intimidating it can be for 18- or 19-year-olds to join the navy, complete boot camp, and arrive at a new ship scared and friendless. On the *Benfold*, when new recruits arrived, they were welcomed aboard, taken to their assigned bunks (with blankets and linen already there), shown their lockers (which already had their names on them), encouraged to call home to let their folks know they had arrived, and then matched with a "running mate" whose job was to take them on a tour of the ship, show them how things worked, and make them feel at home. For their first five days aboard ship, new recruits stuck with their running mates.

▲ On a port call at Dubai, he learned that the sailors on shore leave were frustrated because the bus drivers didn't speak English and wouldn't deviate from their routes. So Abrashoff rented fifteen minivans, assigned a petty officer to each van, and sent the crew off on a shore leave they would find satisfying instead of frustrating.

▲ To help crewmembers stay in touch with their families while at sea for months on end, he established an AOL account for the ship that connected through a communications satellite.

▲ He made a list of his crew's spouses' birthdays and sent them a specially made birthday card that read, "The Officers and Crew of the *USS Benfold* wish you a happy birthday." He signed each card, "Love, Mike. P.S. Your [husband or wife] is doing a great job." Crewmembers often dropped by his cabin to thank him for sending those cards. They helped make the crew's families feel like they were part of the *Benfold*.

▲ Whenever sailors did a particularly great job, Abrashoff sent a letter to their parents. He tells this story of one such letter: "One young man who wasn't star material was working on a project with four outstanding sailors. I debated whether he deserved one of my letters; because he was part of a stellar group, I went ahead. His parents were divorced, so I sent a letter to each parent. About two weeks later, the sailor knocked on my door with tears streaming down his face. 'What's wrong?' I asked. 'I just got a call from my father, who all my life told me I'm a failure. This time, he said he'd just read your letter, and he wanted to congratulate me and say how proud he was of me. It's the first time in my entire life he's actually encouraged me. Captain, I can't thank you enough.'"[33]

▲ He instituted a monthly karaoke happy hour. When the crew discovered that K.C. Marshall, the ship's navigator, was a pretty good Elvis impersonator and had a great voice, they made him part of the ongoing entertainment. One Christmas Eve, Marshall dressed in a glittery white pantsuit and imitated Elvis singing "Blue Christmas."

▲ One sailor suggested they get a stereo system for the ship, and soon it became commonplace to gather on the flight deck at sunset and listen to jazz. Of course, alcohol onboard ship is forbidden, but another sailor suggested smoking cigars while they listened to jazz. Before long, Thursday nights became jazz and cigar nights on the *Benfold.*

▲ On Saturday nights in the Persian Gulf, they showed a double feature, always a comedy and then an action thriller. Sailors brought beach chairs, pillows, and blankets, and the ship provided soft drinks and popcorn.[34]

Lest all of this sound like so much fun and games, Abrashoff's philosophy was that "having fun with your friends creates infinitely more social glue for any organization than stock options and bonuses will ever provide."[35] He was determined to improve the quality of life for the small community he was responsible for and make that a reason people might want to remain in the navy. Did he succeed? Consider this. It costs American taxpayers $35,000 to recruit and send each sailor through a nine-week boot camp, which some don't finish. Full training to acquire the skills to operate the complex communications, propulsion, and weapons systems aboard a ship costs a minimum of $100,000 per sailor. Of those who survive their first tour, fewer than 30 percent reenlist. That's a lot of taxpayers' money wasted. On the *Benfold* under Abrashoff, 100 percent of the career sailors signed on for another tour, saving the Navy (and taxpayers) $1.6 million in personnel-related costs in 1998.[36]

Beyond quality of life and retention, Captain Abrashoff also succeeded in making the *Benfold* one of the finest, most combat-ready ships in the navy. He did it by trusting his crew, giving them greater responsibilities, and helping them own the process. Their certification for deployment to the Persian Gulf was an affirmation of Abrashoff's approach. The fleet began preparing for certification six months in advance. In this readiness assessment, the different areas of the ship and crew are tested and come out earning a level 1, 2, 3, or 4. Most ships come out at level 1. When the *Benfold* first started preparations, Abrashoff wanted to push the envelope a little bit and shoot for level 2. He soon realized that his crew would have no problem reaching level 2, so he pushed them to go to level 3. At this point, the crew rolled their eyes, thinking he was asking the impossible. However, they rose to the challenge, and level 4 came within reach:

> "I put on the push to get level 4 and it turned out we didn't have enough senior people to present all the areas that needed to be presented. So I said to my combat systems officer, 'Let's go for the second- and third-class petty officers and have them do it.' And he said, 'But only officers and chiefs have ever done this.' I said, 'What's the worse that can happen to us? We come out at level 1? So let's go for it.' So we empowered junior people to step up to the plate, and darned if their areas of super-

vision didn't get higher marks than a lot of the areas that were supervised by officers and petty officers. Because they were motivated to do it, because nobody at that level had ever been given that level of responsibility, and they responded by busting their butts and doing great work, which far exceeded my expectations. I was expecting, in my wildest dreams, they would come out in level 2 in those areas, but in every area that was supervised by a junior petty officer, we came out at level 4 because they owned the process, and they were going to work hard to make sure that it succeeded."[37]

The ship received the highest scores ever on that inspection and achieved a level 4 in combat readiness. While Abrashoff was at the helm of the *Benfold,* the ship gained the reputation of being the best ship in the Pacific. That reputation was formalized in 1998 when the ship won the prestigious Spokane Trophy for having the best combat readiness in the fleet. It was the first time an Arleigh Burke class guided missile destroyer had won that honor. When Abrashoff left the *Benfold,* there was a long waiting list of sailors who wished to transfer to the ship. For most, it would be a long wait because few sailors who served on the *Benfold* wanted to leave. With pride and affection, they all referred to it as "the best damn ship in the navy."

We have devoted the last part of this chapter to examining a leader whose behaviors endeared him to the people he led and inspired them to perform to the full extent of their abilities. Mike Abrashoff is a powerful contrast to other military and business leaders whose behavior falls on the opposite end of the interpersonal bell curve. Interpersonal BD is a function of each individual's values, attitudes, and behavior. You cannot mandate strong interpersonal skills throughout a large organization and expect those skills to extend to every customer interaction every day. It simply doesn't work that way. However, like Mike Abrashoff, you can choose to treat people well. You can model the behaviors yourself. You can establish processes for handling interactions between people. You can create customer-friendly policies. You can devise ways and means of dealing with customers that will behaviorally differentiate you, and you can teach employees those ways and means. But superior interaction skill is not a process. It's an attitude, an operating style, and a learned set of behaviors and beliefs set in childhood and reinforced through one's formative years.

In the end, if some people are not inclined to be friendly and helpful toward customers and are not motivated to do so, then no amount of modeling, education, coaching, or arm twisting is likely to convert them. Some people just can't be bothered. Some are constitutionally sour, unengaged, and unhelpful. Some are arrogant, aloof, and self-serving. If you have some people like that in your company, especially in your managerial ranks, then you have a decision to make. You can consign them to places where they have little or no customer interaction, you can get rid of them, or you can get them some intensive coaching. If you are one of these people, then you should do some soul searching because, as Tim Sanders pointed out in *Fast Company,* "What's really different about the [current] economy is that lousy guys finish last":

> There are two tough-minded reasons for this soft-hearted reality. The first is the abundance of choice in business—choice of products, schools, media, and career paths. Choice spells doom for villains. At a time when more of us have more options than ever, there's no need to put up with a product or service that doesn't deliver, a company we don't like, or a boss whom we don't respect. The second reason is what I call the "new telegraph." It's almost impossible for a shoddy product, a noxious company, or a crummy person to keep its, his, or her sad reality a secret anymore. There are too many highly opinionated and well-informed people with access to e-mail, instant messaging, and the Web.[38]

Challenges for Readers

1. By and large, customers interpret your employees' behaviors as your company's behaviors. How would your customers view your company's interpersonal behaviors? In which part of the interpersonal bell curve (Figure 6-1) do your company's behaviors normally fall?
2. How emotionally intelligent is your organization? How emotionally intelligent are your leaders? Your employees? Do your policies and procedures and your culture support and encourage interpersonal behavior toward employees and customers that would differentiate you from your competitors?
3. In this chapter, we discussed the high price of sexual harassment and other forms of negative interpersonal BD. How much of such behavior occurs in your organization, and what price are you paying for it? How much money are you losing from poor behavior that alienates customers, demotivates employees, disrupts teams, and causes executives to derail and have to be replaced?
4. Misbehaving prima donnas are a problem in many organizations. Although they are talented and do great work, they often run roughshod over "lesser mortals" in the organization and are sometimes arrogant and dismissive with customers. Do you have any people like that in your com-

pany? Ultimately, these people do more damage than good, but they generally have some supporters (especially some customers), and it takes courage to get rid of them. How do you handle your destructive prima donnas?

5. Think about the leaders in your organization. Are they more like Captain Queeg or Captain Abrashoff? Leaders set the tone in an organization. If, like Mike Abrashoff, they demonstrate superior interpersonal and leadership skill, they will model for others how to behave. What do your leaders model?

Endnotes

1. Bill Hardin interview with David G. Pugh, 2001. Story used with permission.
2. Alan M. Webber, "Are All Consultants Corrupt?" *Fast Company* (May 2002), p. 134.
3. Ibid.
4. Hugh Davies, "Queen Meanie faces prison for $1.2m dodge," *The Sunday Telegraph,* London (March 15, 1992), p. 15.
5. "'Chainsaw' to the rescue? Think again!" www.saperston.com/financial/chain (May 15, 2002).
6. John A. Byrne, *Chainsaw: The Notorious Career of Al Dunlap in the Era of Profit-at-Any-Price* (New York: Harper-Collins, 1999), p. 3.
7. Ibid.
8. Al Dunlap, "Running with the Bulls, Managing Corporate Change: Cutting to the Core," *Surviving the bottom line with Hedrick Smith,* http://www.pbs.org/bottomline/html/dunlap.html (April 22, 2002).
9. U.S. Equal Employment Opportunity Commission, www.eeoc.gov/stats (May 20, 2002).
10. Gilbert F. Casellas and Irene L. Hill, "Sexual Harassment: Prevention and Avoiding Liability," *Fall 1998 SHRM Legal Report,* Society for Human Resource Management, www.shrm.org/whitepapers/documents (May 17, 2002).
11. Michael M. Lombardo and Cynthia D. McCauley, "The Dynamics of Management Derailment," Technical Report Number 34 (July 1988), Center for Creative Leadership, p. 3.
12. Ibid.
13. Ibid.

14. Barbara Spencer Singer, "Recovering Executives at Risk of Derailing," *The White Paper Series by Lore International Institute,* Durango, Colo. (2001), p. 1.
15. Ibid., p. 2.
16. Jeff Pearlman, "At Full Blast," *CNN Sports Illustrated Online,* sports illustrated.cnn.com/features/cover/news/1999/12/22/rocker (December 23, 1999).
17. Ibid; Murray Chass, "Baseball remarks could hurt Rocker most of all," *The New York Times,* www.nytimes.com (December 24, 1999).
18. Pearlman, op cit.
19. Ibid.
20. Derek Jeter, "Jeter latest to rip Rocker for comments," *CNN Sports Illustrated Online,* sportsillustrated.cnn.com/baseball/mlb/news/2000/01/26/jeter_rocker_ap (January 26, 2000).
21. Randall Simon, "He's Lying: Braves' Simon finding it hard to accept Rocker's apology," *CNN Sports Illustrated Online,* sportsillustrated.cnn.com/baseball/mlb/news/2000/01/15/rocker_simon_ap (January 16, 2000).
22. Seth Livingstone, "Brave cat, great kid," *Baseball Weekly* (May 31–June 6, 2000).
23. "We're not gonna take it: Heavy metal band objects to Rocker's remarks," *CNN Sports Illustrated Online,* sportsillustrated.cnn.com/baseball/mlb/news/2000 /01/17/twisted_rocker_ap (January 17, 2000).
24. Frank Deford, "Rocker's fate rests with teammates," *CNN Sports Illustrated Online,* sportsillustrated.cnn.com/inside_game/deford/news/2000/01/12/deford (January 19, 2000).
25. Thomas E. Ricks, "Deep Trouble: A Skipper's Chance to Run a Trident Sub Hit Stormy Waters," *The Wall Street Journal* (November 20, 1997), p. A1.
26. Richard S. Tedlow, "What Titans Can Teach Us," *Harvard Business Review* (December 2001), p. 70.
27. D. Michael Abrashoff interview with Donna Williams (May 4, 2002).
28. Ibid.
29. Ibid.
30. Polly LaBarre, "The Agenda—Grassroots Leadership," Fast Company www.fastcompany.com/online/23/grassroots. html.
31. Abrashoff, op cit.

32. D. Michael Abrashoff, *It's Your Ship* (New York: Warner Books, 2002), p. 6.
33. Ibid, p. 143.
34. LaBarre, op. cit. These stories are also told in D. Michael Abrashoff, *It's Your Ship* (New York: Warner Books, 2002).
35. Abrashoff, *It's Your Ship*, op cit., p. 189.
36. LaBarre, op cit.
37. Abrashoff interview with Donna Williams, op cit.
38. Tim Sanders, "Love is the Killer App," *Fast Company* (February 2002), p. 66.

7

EXCEPTIONAL VALUES

A piano played by a live person is Nordstrom's signature service for engaging a customer's senses. If shoppers need any kind of special assistance, a concierge is at the ready with helpful information about the store or to call a cab for you or to recommend a restaurant. Need to send a fax? They'll do that for you. Need to check your coat, umbrella, and packages with the concierge? No problem.

—Robert Spector, *Lessons from The Nordstrom Way*

Don't play with fear in your heart. If you play with courage, the worst thing that can happen to you is a loss. Since we will all lose many games in our lifetime, we might as well go down with honor and make every game as instructive as possible. Playing passively and getting routed is no fun at all and teaches you nothing.

—Jeremy Silman, *The Amateur's Mind*

By definition, any behavior that is positively differentiating is exceptional to some degree because it goes beyond what customers normally expect. It would be fair to assume that exceptional behavior occurs in nearly all companies, at least occasionally. However, in some companies—such as Ritz-Carlton, EMC, Volvo Cars, Men's Wearhouse, Southwest Airlines, Hall Kinion, and Heidrick & Struggles—exceptional BD occurs more than occasionally. Why is that? Are these companies led by exceptional leaders? Do they have a culture that encourages exceptional behavior? Do they have policies, procedures, and processes that result in exceptional treatment of customers? Do they have more exceptional people working for them than other companies do? The answer is—all of the above. Companies that differentiate themselves behaviorally usually have inspired leadership; a culture that encourages employees to treat customers exceptionally well; policies, procedures, and processes that support these efforts; and service-minded employees who were attracted to these companies and were hired because they enjoy serving others and are inclined to be friendly and helpful without having to be told to do so.

The word *exceptional* means "deviating from the norm," "forming an exception," and "being better than average." In this book, we are using *exceptional behavioral differentiation* to describe the kinds of behaviors that customers find extraordinary, even from companies where the behavioral standard is already beyond what customers normally expect from suppliers of a particular product or service. Here are some examples:

The Missing Suitcase

Craig Silverman relates this story of an event that occurred when he was with Hall Kinion (a placement firm) on the west coast. Hall Kinion had flown a job candidate to San Francisco from New Jersey to interview for a very high-level position, and the airline lost his luggage. "He was scheduled to have the interview of his life the next morning," Craig told us. "He was to meet with the venture capitalists and the board of directors. It was extremely important to him. So our recruiters got on the phone and called Nordstrom. The store manager was more than willing to help. At 7:00 the next morning, we had a car service pick up the candidate at the hotel and take him to Nordstrom, where the store manager was waiting, although the store did not open for several more hours. They got him totally outfitted: suit, tie, shirt, belt, shoes—the works. They even hemmed and pressed his trousers. Then they put him back in the limo and got him to the 9 a.m. appointment on time. At the end of the day, he got the offer."[1]

An Important Proposal

At one of Ritz-Carlton's Florida properties, a beach attendant was busy stacking chairs, putting them away for the evening. He was approached by a guest, who asked him to leave two chairs out because he was going to propose to his girlfriend on the beach that night. The beach attendant was happy to oblige but went far beyond what the guest expected. The attendant rented a tuxedo for himself, purchased flowers and champagne, and brought candles to the beach in order to create a special environment for the guest and his girl-friend. When the couple arrived later, the formally attired attendant met them at the beach and escorted them to the chairs. He presented the flowers, lit the candles, and served the champagne to an astonished pair of guests. Then he told them that he would be their personal butler for the evening, and if they needed anything to let him know. As the couple left the beach later, the attendant learned that she had accepted the young man's marriage proposal.[2]

Preparing for the Olympic Games

Kathie Lyons, who headed up a team of 20 people responsible for moving EMC spare parts around the world, knew that her unit would be challenged during the 1996 Summer Olympic games in Atlanta. The city center, including Atlanta's business district, where several EMC customers housed their computer operations, would be snarled by security checkpoints and traffic for weeks. If a customer's system went down during the Olympics, EMC would be unable to meet its service guarantee if they could not get spare parts to the customer's location on time. So Lyons stationed bicycle messengers at two dozen locations and stocked each one with EMC parts. As a backup, she hired two helicopters and kept them on standby during the games. "She never had to use them," says Frank Hauck, who ran EMC's customer service at the time. "But nobody ever said to her, 'Waste of money.'"[3]

Getting Mutzy into Australia

Gerry Roche, senior chairman and 40-year veteran of executive search firm Heidrick & Struggles, was engaged to find a new CEO for one of the largest companies in Australia. Roche had it narrowed down to a stellar candidate, a man who was currently president of a large company in the U.S., and who we will call John Smith. "We had him all set to go," said Roche. "Everything. We had someone who took him around to meet board people all over the world. The arrangements were very sophisticated. Not many people appreciate what it takes to get *every* board member in the world of a company of that size to interview candidates. It was a huge logistical challenge. But we got everything all lined up, and he was accepted." Smith's hiring was announced in the newspapers. He got everything ready for the move; packed up his home; and made arrangements to send the furniture, family, and Mutzy, the family's beloved dog, to Australia. "But then," Roche continued, "we learned that the dog could not get into Australia because of a mandatory quarantine, and *Mrs.* Smith said, 'If the dog doesn't go, I don't go!'"

Roche reflects, "I can still remember afterwards writing a letter to John Smith telling him what we went through to line up a Four Seasons–type offshore hotel for dogs where Mutzy could wait in quarantine for six months. So, until Mutzy could get into the country, John would have to do this and that, and follow this procedure and that rule, and so on. Here was this long letter from the senior chairman of Heidrick & Struggles talking about getting a dog into Australia. At the end of the letter, after I had gone through all the intricate details of the process, my last sentence was, 'I hope this does the job, John. Best regards, Gerry.' And then 'P.S. Has my job come down to this?' He sent it back with 'YES. Thanks,' in big, bold, black lettering."[4]

Each of these examples illustrates someone going the extra mile for a customer, doing things that are not in the policy manual or part of normal operating procedure. The recruiters at Hall Kinion were not expected to resolve a candidate's lost luggage problem, or call Nordstrom to arrange for emergency clothing for the candidate, or hire the car service to ferry him from one location to the next. The store manager at Nordstrom did not have to open several hours early and then personally outfit the candidate, including hemming his trousers. He was not paid extra for that. The beach attendant at Ritz-Carlton did not have to rent the tuxedo, buy the champagne and flowers, and spend the evening looking after a young couple. In fact, he was off work that night. He created a special experience for those guests on his own time. Katie Lyons of EMC took extraordinary measures in advance of the Olympic games in Atlanta to ensure that if problems did arise with customers' systems, EMC could live up to its service promise. In fact, nothing happened, but she was prepared if something had. Finally, Gerry Roche did not have to assume personal responsibility for taking care of a candidate's dog through the quarantine period. He did it to make his candidate's—and his candidate's family's—move and transition to Australia easier while the candidate was undertaking a new and substantially bigger job. These are all service behaviors that fit our definition of exceptional BD.

> **If you build a differentiated product, the world will not automatically beat a path to your door. Better products don't win. Better perceptions tend to be the winners.**
>
> —Jack Trout, *Differentiate or Die*

Perhaps, as a customer, something like this has happened to you. You receive the kind of service and care from people in a company that is clearly beyond what they normally do and beyond what you could reasonably expect. They have gone out of their way to make your experience more pleasurable, more satisfying, and more memorable. *That* is exceptional BD. By and large, exceptional BD occurs because individual employees decide to go the extra mile for customers. However, this will not happen with any frequency unless companies create the conditions in which exceptional behaviors can occur. Those conditions include an environment that allows employees to behave exceptionally from time to time and a culture that supports and encourages exceptional treatment of customers. This is an important point because employees of some companies are prohibited from making exceptions to policy. They are discouraged from going the extra mile, perhaps because management fears that if they do make exceptions for *some* customers then *all* customers will start demanding extraordinary treatment and, heaven forbid, then they might have to treat *everyone* really well. In this chapter, we are focusing on two companies that do it right: Volvo Cars and Men's Wearhouse. Although these companies could not be more different in many ways, each has attitudes and cultures that encourage their employees to treat customers exceptionally well and to make customers' experiences memorable.

The Value of *Medarbetarskap*

Welcome to Volvo Cars, the pride of Sweden, one of the most socially responsible and progressive companies in the world, and the home of *medarbetarskap*. No direct English translation for this Swedish word exists. The word has broader meaning than any single word in English conveys. *Medarbetarskap* is a value central to Volvo's behavioral differentiation, and it involves being proactive and constructive. It encourages all employees to take the initiative and embodies the freedom to do so. It involves knowing how your work fits into the larger scheme of things and emphasizes measuring the critical processes. It requires living and working responsibly, in a manner that advances the well-being of individuals, the corporation, and the country.[5]

Here are the facts. Volvo was founded in 1927 by Assar Gabrielsson and Gustaf Larson. The company is headquartered in Göteborg, Sweden, and has manufacturing plants in Sweden, Belgium, The Netherlands, South Africa, Malaysia, and Thailand. It employs over 27,000 people, competes in more than 160 markets through 1,800 dealers, and since 1999 has been part of Ford Motor Company. Its market niche is luxury automobiles, so it competes with Lexus, BMW, and Mercedes Benz. One of the hallmarks of Volvo Cars is quality. The median life expectancy of all Volvos in service is 18.6 years. Volvo Cars is the only car company with a high mileage club, which recognizes owners with over 100,000 miles on the odometer. The company honors owners who reach progressive benchmarks: 200,000 miles, 300,000 miles, and so on. The record is astounding, even to Volvo: "We never expected anyone to reach 1,000,000 miles, but it happened. In 1987 we recorded the first

Volvo in North America to reach the million-mile plateau. This feat, in itself, is amazing. But even more astonishing is that the million miles were accumulated in only 23 years. That's more than 300 cross country trips and an average of better than 40,000 miles every year! Now that's durability. That same Volvo is still on the road with now over 1.8 million miles!"[6]

What's missing in this factual description is the heart and soul of the company, which is its emphasis on quality, safety, and environmental care. Volvo Cars takes very seriously the idea of being a good corporate citizen. In its annual reports on corporate citizenship, the company reports on the health of all entities it affects, including employees, the Swedish government, customers, and suppliers. Volvo Cars' reporting on profit is no more important to the company than its reporting on efforts made to sustain and protect the environment and to look after the safety of drivers, passengers, and pedestrians. As cofounder Gustaf Larson once said, "Cars are driven by people. The guiding principle behind everything we make at Volvo Cars, therefore, is and must remain—safety."[7] That philosophy of social responsibility has driven Volvo, if you will pardon the pun, from the outset and remains a staunch value and commitment seventy-five years later. In part, Volvo's social consciousness reflects the country of its origin, but there are also practical business reasons for being a good corporate citizen internally and externally. Hans-Olov Olsson, Volvo Cars' president and CEO, explains:

> Good relations are essential to running a business and, thereby, generating development which is important to the company, society, and its individual members alike. According to a recent survey (the Millennium Poll), 40 percent of the world's population has considered refusing, or has actually refused, to buy products from companies which do not meet their standards of corporate citizenship. In North America, the figure is 70 percent. In this light, corporate citizenship must not be regarded as a 'luxury' to be indulged in when times are good, but as an essential condition for achieving our business goals. [And yet] corporate citizenship is not a project to be completed within a given timeframe; it is an attitude and a frame of mind which must imbue everything that we do.[8]

Behavioral differentiation at Volvo Cars begins with that attitude and frame of mind. It begins with a philosophy that the people at Volvo Cars firmly believe separates them from most other car companies. Charlotta Källbäck, strategy manager in the president's office, reflects the pride and passion we experienced from all the Volvo Cars people we spoke to: "I think that the closer you come to our company, the more passionate people you will meet: engineers who love what they do, factory workers who are proud and strive for improving things, designers who have traveled the world and end up at Volvo Cars, and marketers who love the brand."[9] Like the people at Harley-Davidson, the people at Volvo Cars love the products they create and love the fact that they can do it in a socially responsible way.

Behaviorally, Volvo Cars is distinct from its competitors because the company's founders—and current executives—made explicit their public commitment to care for people. They see themselves as more than just a car manufacturer. They are stewards of the environment. They are champions of safety for all car passengers (and even pedestrians who are in danger of being injured by cars). Like their competitors, they strive to make their cars exciting, comfortable, and sophisticated, but their first priority is their commitment to people. Volvo Car Corporation designs cars based on their desire to care for human beings locally, nationally, and globally, and their company philosophy underscores the importance of the behaviors they want to represent: "The difference between Volvo Cars and other car manufacturers is a commitment and a philosophy which has characterized the company for many decades. Volvo's founders, Assar Gabrielsson and Gustaf Larson, established at a very early stage that the company's operations should be based on care for human beings. Safety, quality, reliability and responsibility are the core of our operations, our products, and our behaviour."[10]

Daring ideas are like chessmen moved forward. They may be beaten, but they may start a winning game.

—Goethe

From this corporate emphasis comes some exceptional behavior. First, many Volvos are assembled based on individual job orders from car buyers, which helps the company establish a direct connection with the people buying their cars. Buyers generally work through a dealer, but the car specifications go to a Volvo Cars factory, so the factory workers who assemble the car quite literally know who will drive home their finished product. They may observe the new owner's first glimpse of their new car, see their reactions to the product, and witness the first test drive. They will know firsthand the new owner's excitement and pride at owning a Volvo. They know that their craftsmanship will be appreciated, and they go to great lengths to ensure that each detail has been carefully looked after. Nerissa Morris Hampton, vice president of human resources and a veteran of the auto industry, explains:

> Our manufacturing process places a different focus on customers than is typical in the automotive world. Volvo Cars has a high mix of direct customer orders. This way of manufacturing allows employees to feel

more of a connection to customers while they're producing the vehicles. They work in teams, and that team really takes responsibility for the quality of the vehicle. It's quite different to know that the vehicle coming down the line has a particular customer, and they might even be coming to the plant to pick it up. That makes a big difference in the work that they do. They say to themselves, "I know that there's somebody waiting for this car." You can order online or go through a dealer, but since dealers have very limited stock, the majority of our orders are specific customer orders.[11]

One of the effects of this closer connection with car buyers is a more collaborative approach to serving customers. In Sweden, and in Volvo Cars, there is less distinction and more cooperation between what would traditionally be called blue-collar workers and white-collar professionals. Nerissa Morris Hampton elaborates:

There is less of a distinction at Volvo Cars regarding policies and operating guidelines between blue collar and white collar than you'd find in American industries. Here there are lines, but not as bold. They allow development opportunities to be extended further into the organization. There's some overlap in the teaching and teamwork, and this overlap extends from blue collar to white collar and vice versa. Therefore, everyone is working much closer to the manufacturing process. I visited a plant in Belgium, for example. When you go into the plant, you begin with an orientation of the priorities of the plant and how teams have been organized to address customer needs—and specifically customer concerns. The whole orientation is around improving the process for the customer. They can say, "We know what the needs are and we organize around these needs and concerns and we're responsible—not the supervisors or area managers—in the team." Blue-collar employees take responsibility for tracking the quality process and developing metrics for quality. They can resolve issues that contribute to problems. If you go into a typical US assembly plant, you'll find many lines of demarcation. Here you have three lines, and as a result they can fix problems much faster because they don't have to wait for someone from a different area. Volvo Cars has taken away barriers to people delivering.[12]

In recent years, the expression "customer intimacy" has become fashionable as companies strive to get closer to customers. Too often, customer intimacy is not a philosophy grounded in the values and beliefs of the company but a bit of hyperbole, a defensive reaction to loss of market share, and the sudden realization that if they do not learn how to get closer to their customers they are going to be beaten soundly by smarter competitors who are already "intimate" with those customers. But Volvo's philosophies are deeply rooted and reflect their behavior toward each other as much as their behavior toward customers. Moreover, people at Volvo Cars are self-conscious about their behavior, as Sven Eckerstein, Senior Vice President for Human Resources, explains:

> We think about how to act and how to create a product. Before you buy a car, you want to know not just about a car as such, but how it expands to the behavior of the company. You want to know how we act towards each other. I know that everyone I hand over something to is a customer of ours. When we meet with customers we tell them more than just about the car. We tell them about the way we behave, the way we do things, the way we produce the cars, and the way we treat each other. Customers say this is more interesting than just hearing about the car. They say, "It helps me be connected to you. I would be proud to be a driver of a Volvo, a member of the Volvo family, and I would drive your car even if it were a lousy car." You should enjoy going to our dealership. It's an experience we hope that you have.[13]

The Volvo experience is indeed unique. If you ask one hundred people on the street about their last experience buying a car, you are likely to hear more negative than positive stories. By and large, the automobile industry is an unlikely place to experience exceptional BD. The traditional, glad-handing salespeople who tell you they have to go speak to their manager to get any offer approved have become the most common car-buying experience, at least in the U.S. Although the people in the dealership are all smiles, the process feels detached and transactional, and many buyers feel beaten up afterward. However, Volvo Cars has found a way to go well beyond the common experience and delight car buyers. The company invites customers to visit Sweden to pick up and test-drive their customized, newly minted vehicles. Furthermore, Volvo Cars pays for the trip. It's an experience that *feels* exceptional every step of the way, as this American Volvo Cars customer attests:

> Volvo treated us like kings and queens. We had waited a long time to buy the car. For years, we've been looking for a Volvo. When we got to the point where we had saved the money, we contacted the Volvo dealership closest to us. The dealer gave us Volvo's Web site address so we

could customize our order. We had to give the local dealer a down payment and, 30 days before we left, we had to pay for the whole car. However, Volvo paid for my airline ticket (I paid for my son's) and our first night's lodging in a first-class hotel. We saved about 7 percent on the price of the car—*plus* a free trip.

Volvo picked us up at the hotel in a limousine, took us to their factory, and treated us to a sit-down meal that was very fancy. They've got hospitality and manners down pat. They never acted like *they* were doing us a favor. Just the opposite. They brought our specific car out, and we tested it on their racetrack. They watched as we drove it around, like they were excited for us. The price of the car included two weeks of insurance, and had I been braver, I could have driven the car anywhere in Europe and then returned it to factory for shipping. They were just so nice. At the same time, my neighbor was buying a Dodge at the local Dodge dealer. My son and I would call my husband from Sweden and talk about our great time while our neighbor would drop in to tell my husband that she had been "beaten down" that day at the local car dealer. The contrast between our experience and hers made our deal seem even better.[14]

In the end, this customer got not only a new car but also a memorable experience and a relationship with the manufacturer. No other car manufacturer offers a car-buying experience as positive and distinctive as Volvo Cars' experience. This story exemplifies both exceptional BD (the customer felt like royalty) and interpersonal BD ("they've got hospitality and politeness down pat" and "they never acted like they were doing the favor"). The experience of buying and owning a Volvo is meant to be exceptional, and Volvo Cars works hard to make that happen for *every* customer. When asked to comment on this customer's comparison between her experience at Volvo and her neighbor's experience at a local dealer, Sven Eckerstein said, "Ah, yes. That's how we would like it to be. We train our people to provide a good experience. Scandinavians are rather socially conscious and hopefully that will come out in the way we act toward our customers. We expect and hope that they will experience our values."[15] For Hans-Olov Olsson, CEO and president of Volvo Cars, the exceptional behavior that customers see can occur only when the company's internal interpersonal behaviors (what customers do not see) are outstanding:

The first priority on our agenda is customer satisfaction. You won't be number one unless you are exceptional. The definition of exceptional is that you deliver more than the individual expected from you, and that is also the heritage at Volvo Cars. The company was founded seventy-five years ago. The founders had an idea about caring for people—employees and customers. That's why they said that since we are designing cars, it is always important to care for people. With our heritage, we have a lot of stories to tell—and when it comes to safety we have a lot of exceptional stories to tell. A couple of years ago we began collecting "survivor stories." People write or call and tell me how they survived a car accident in a Volvo. These are product-related stories, but they reflect what we stand for, and these stories need to be repeated in the organization. To the outside world, these are the kinds of things that develop identity. Inside the organization, you cannot compromise on how people are treated. Inside, it's very much an interpersonal relationship. A car company is a complex system from product development to production to logistics, and it repeats itself in great volume. You have to have precision in everything you're doing, and you create precision through excellent interpersonal interactions. So I would say that exceptional behavior is what we aim for with the outside world, and we get that with exceptional interpersonal relationships on the inside.[16]

We try to do things just about the opposite of every other company.

—George Zimmer, founder and CEO of Men's Wearhouse

Suits and Servant Leadership

When a history of business in the twentieth century is written, it will no doubt end by describing the creation of high-tech giants like Microsoft and Oracle, the growth of the Internet and e-commerce, the meteoric rise and fall of dot.com companies, and the longest bull market Wall Street has ever seen. Sadly, it will also document the crisis in confidence brought on by the duplicity and greed that came out of the Enron, Arthur Andersen, and Global Crossing scandals. These are the "sexy" stories that attract media attention. In the glow of e-commerce it is easy to overlook more run-of-the-mill business stories like the remarkable rise of Men's Wearhouse (MW). This is a story of the triumph of servant leadership, and it occurred in men's retail clothing, an unlikely place in the dot.com era to find business innovation. However, since George Zimmer founded MW in 1973, the company has become a billion-dollar enterprise while the rest of the retail clothing industry has sagged. Zimmer accomplished this feat by defying conventional business wisdom and, like Volvo Cars, by behaving in exceptional ways toward his employees and his customers (Figure 7-1).

Figure 7-1. George Zimmer.
Founder and CEO of Men's
Wearhouse, Zimmer turned the
tables on traditional retailing
and created a company with
heart and soul.

When he founded his new company in Houston, George Zimmer had only $7,000 to capitalize his venture and a cigar box to use as a cash register. He also had the cockeyed notion that he could build a successful men's retail clothing chain by hiring full-time employees; paying them a decent wage; giving them training and education; and creating a culture based on trust, self-fulfillment, and servant leadership. To understand how revolutionary this was, consider the facts. In the late 1990s, about 16 percent of America's workers (20 million people) were employed in retail. Salaries for average retail salespeople vary between $22,000 and $31,000. It is a low-wage, low-skill, high-turnover industry.

However, the *entry-level* salary for a full-time MW wardrobe consultant (the equivalent of a salesperson in any other clothing store) is $32,000, and the average MW employee receives 40 hours of training annually, including courses at SUITS University. In 2002, MW was named as one of America's Best 100 Companies to Work For by *Fortune* (for the third year in a row). That year it was also named by *Forbes* as one of the Best Big Companies in America (again, for the third year in a row). In 2001, MW received a Workforce Optimas Award for success in a changing industry. These awards recognize human resource initiatives that have positive results for the organization receiving the award. MW's award citation says, "The Men's Wearhouse has ignored and broken the rules of retailing that make it a place of low pay, little training, and lots of part-time work. It makes a heavy investment in employee training and development and has created a workforce that can sell just about anything and can adapt and flourish in virtually any changing business environment."[17]

Behavioral Differences at Men's Wearhouse

George Zimmer attributes much of the company's success to integrating his servant leadership values into the corporate culture. He developed the company's mission statement based on those values and has encouraged all employees to live and work by it. The company's financial success and corporate values of collective honesty, sincerity, integrity, responsiveness, authenticity, mutual goodwill, and caring for each other have become a primary focus for Zimmer as CEO. He decided early on that the company was really in the people business rather than the suit business, and this idea is manifested in extensive training programs for employees and a focus on self-development and self-fulfillment. Zimmer felt that he had to create trust-based relationships with his employees, and he was confident that that trust would then be passed on to customers. Employee loyalty and long-term relationships with the company were necessary precursors to customer loyalty and their long-term relationships with MW. Zimmer's genius was to recognize that men do not like to shop, especially for their own clothing, because they don't know what to buy. So if every time they go into a men's clothing store they encounter a different part-time sales clerk who doesn't know enough to be able to provide expert assistance, why should they return to that store? To make the MW shopping experience more compelling for men, Zimmer did a number of things differently, and it's important to recognize that shoppers experience these things as behavioral differences:

▲ Instead of sales clerks, he hires *wardrobe consultants,* and the difference is more than semantic. Wardrobe consultants at MW are trained in men's clothing. They know what many male shoppers don't: what looks good with different body types, what clothing to wear for what occasion, how to select a tie, what goes with what and what doesn't, and so on. At MW, a wardrobe consultant *is* a consultant, not just a sales clerk. They are taught to be consultative and to provide more value-added assistance than the typical men's clothing store sales clerk is *expected* to provide (and is *capable* of providing). Their goal is to gather information about a customer's current clothing needs and fill them painlessly and quickly. They help customers maximize their wardrobes by showing them how to coordinate a few key garments as well as working within budget constraints. Wardrobe consultants are empowered to provide exceptional service by doing things like personal delivery of clothing items, keeping stores open later or opening earlier than scheduled hours, and locating unavailable items in other stores. This emphasis on consultative sales and development of long-term relationships with customers is a strong behavioral differentiator for Men's Wearhouse in comparison to other retail stores.

▲ The wardrobe consultant position at MW is a full-time, higher-paying position than comparable positions at other men's clothing stores. Zimmer did this to reduce turnover and retain his trained employees. Consequently, shoppers returning to an MW are likely to encounter the same people who served them before, which results in the kind of employee-customer relationships that build customer loyalty and increase employee satisfaction.

▲ MW offers professional tailoring at every location. Because MW operates in the tailored clothing niche, providing quality, professional tailoring is a key element of the service package and creates another opportunity for behavioral differentiation during the customer's shopping experience. Many department stores have exited the men's tailored clothing market because of the costly customer service demands of it. MW, however, guarantees the availability of professional tailoring in every location. The company also does the following:

- Provides emergency tailoring on request, 24 hours a day.
- Hems pants while the customer waits.
- Makes minor repairs to clothing if needed.
- Re-alters at no charge any garments that have been altered once.
- Offers free lifetime pressing of any clothing purchased at any MW location nationwide.
- Guarantees that customers will be satisfied with how their clothing fits.

Furthermore, unlike most retail clothing stores, MW's tailors are not relegated to a back room; they are considered part of the upfront customer service team. From a customer's perspective, this array of clothing services feels like a strong commitment from MW. "We want you to look good," the company's behavior says. "Not just now but into the future."

▲ Many aspects of the MW store setup are geared to make the shopping environment more responsive to the preferences of male shoppers. Stores are of average size (current average size is 6,000 square feet), so they are not overwhelming. They are located in strip malls or other locations with convenient access from a parking lot. An inviting, relaxed, fun atmosphere is provided through sporting events on television, putting greens, nerf basketball, ping pong, and free coffee. This is not your normal shopping experience.

▲ MW has a Business Club Rewards program, which is an MW credit card that rewards customers with a $50 merchandise certificate for every $500 spent at MW. In many competing customer loyalty programs, the rewards are too small to be motivating to buyers or are inconvenient (discounts only on overstocked merchandise). MW's program, however, is generous and is considered a "best bet" among rewards programs.[18]

⋏ MW has a group sales service that allows groups to set up appointments after hours. It also offers free seminars to groups to help men become more knowledgeable about clothing decisions and men's fashions, and it produces free videos on wardrobe topics.

The cumulative effect of these behaviors is a demonstrated commitment to making customers' shopping experiences informative, painless, and predictable, which is what most men want. MW's after-sales service is particularly differentiating.

A Web Site with Soul

MW's Web presence is among the most unique in the industry. They call it *e-service* rather than *e-commerce*. Developed in 2000, the MW Web site differentiates the company through both site content and its impact on an online customer's experience. It is not just a vehicle for online sales but rather a way to strengthen the bond with customers and an opportunity to enhance customers' lives. It also provides a forum for other stakeholders, such as community and business leaders. In this way, MW hopes to shape the quality of relationships not only in the business community but also in the extended global community. George Zimmer believes we all have a responsibility to contribute to society and says, "You might say it's our common cause."[19]

MW's Web site (www.menswearhouse.com) includes provisions for shopping online, but these are not remarkably different from competitors' online shopping areas. However, the site has two features that help customers in unique ways. The first is Guy'dLines, a section offering advice to men on clothing and other lifestyle issues. There are articles on dressing for success, wearing casual clothing, going formal, organizing your closet, taking care of your clothing, choosing the right tie, and so on. Users can also read lifestyle tips like "6 Reasons She Won't Have Dinner With You Again," and can ask questions of the "Guy'dLine's Guru." Previous questions and answers are available in a searchable archive. For the average guy trying to enhance his look, this free service from MW is a huge differentiator. By comparison, the Brooks Brothers (www.brooksbrothers.com) and Federated Department Stores (www.federated-fds.com) Web sites are little more than online shopping areas. As of this writing, they offer no helpful hints to men and provide no value added except for shopping online. It's important to recognize that what MW does on its Web site is a *behavioral difference to customers.* The message is this: "Men's Wearhouse wants to help you look better. We will go the extra mile and do more for you because we are committed to helping you make the right clothing choices and look the best you can look."

The second value-added feature on MW's Web site is "Common Threads," an area devoted to information on and discussion of values and philosophy in work and life. As MW describes it, "The Men's Wearhouse is committed to providing value to all of its stakeholders. We know that, in fulfilling this commitment, our employees are the primary determinant of success or failure. That's why, over the last quarter century, we've been participating in an experiment—searching for ways to motivate, support, and inspire the best from each member of our corporate community. Common Threads will focus on ideas about building community within companies and organizations . . . creating workplaces of trust, achievement, compassion, inspiration, celebration, and financial security."[20] This section of the Web site presents MW's philosophy, the elements of which include gaining fulfillment at work, balancing work and family life, recognizing the value of emotional intelligence, having fun at work, honoring commitments, creating fearless and energized workplaces, hiring the person rather than the resume, treating employees as customers, being willing to make mistakes, being optimistic, looking for win-win opportunities, taking advantage of people's strengths, being a servant leader, and so on. Also in Common Threads are opinion polls ("What makes a job most rewarding to you?"); articles by guest contributors (such as "Leadership for a New Millennium" by David Ryback); links to featured organizations, such as The Families and Work Institute; and reviews of books on leadership, work-life balance, emotional intelligence, having fun at work, and related topics.[21]

> I don't think any other retail companies have ever existed where the executive vice president in charge of Store Operations, which includes the guts of our business, is a clinical psychologist with a PhD.
>
> —George Zimmer

It should be clear from this discussion that MW is not your average company. This is a values-driven organization that seeks nothing less than the betterment of society, and it's not just talk. The philosophy at MW is evident in many behaviors and reflects the principles of servant leadership, an idea first proposed by Robert Greenleaf in 1970. He said, "The servant-leader is servant first. It begins with the natural feeling that one wants to serve. Then conscious choice brings one to aspire to lead. The best test is: Do those served grow as persons; do they, while being served, become healthier, wiser, freer, more autonomous, more likely themselves to become servants?"[22] This concept is so fundamental to the way MW operates that it is difficult not to see it everywhere one looks. It is all over the MW Web site, it is discussed and presented in training programs and meetings throughout the company, and it is evident in the company's commitment to employees. It is evident in MW's policy that all managers participate in cleaning and inventory. If an executive is in a store and a customer needs assistance, the executive steps in to assist. *Everyone* is trained to respond to situations with the question, "What can I do to help?"[23]

Emotional Intelligence in Action

A key element of MW's philosophy is building exceptional relationships with all stakeholders, and they believe that that requires high degrees of emotional intelligence, or EQ, which is the foundation of MW's relationship training. EQ is an ability that, combined with self-awareness, allows a person to nurture positive relationships with others. MW recognizes that relationships are built one interaction at a time, so there are many opportunities to make or break them. This point is brought home in training programs at SUITS University and in daily interactions among managers, employees, and customers. MW teaches and reinforces these EQ principles in its training:

▲ Promote active listening between all levels of employees.
▲ Encourage true feelings to be voiced as part of any process.
▲ Encourage empathy with teammates and customers.
▲ Interact with others without using sarcasm or derogatory remarks.
▲ Emphasize conflict resolution practices that promote compromise and build consensus.
▲ Promote optimism over negativity.
▲ Encourage moments of silent reflection (before responding) as part of any interaction.
▲ Promote the consideration of all possible alternatives (and their consequences) before making decisions.
▲ Immediately acknowledge employees who use Emotional Intelligence.[24]

Like so many of the companies that exemplify behavioral differentiation, MW is self-conscious about behavior: its behavior toward employees, first and foremost, and its behavior toward customers. Although the underlying philosophy emanates from George Zimmer, the architect of much of MW's behavioral focus is his childhood friend, Charlie Bresler, now Executive Vice President of Store Operations, Human Development, and Marketing (see Figure 7-2). A clinical psychologist and former director of Behavioral Medicine at the

Figure 7-2. Charlie Bresler. Zimmer's childhood friend, Bresler introduced behavioral consulting at Men's Wearhouse and increased the average ticket sale by 13 percent.

California School of Professional Psychology in Fresno, Bresler instituted behavioral training programs for corporate and store employees and developed the Employee Relations department and facilitated its integration with Store Operations. Bresler believes that his goal, and the goal of the company, is not only to help employees realize their potential in selling men's clothing but also to develop their potential in all aspects of their lives, helping them become self-actualized individuals:

> We believe that people have more potential than they have evidenced, and we have a responsibility to create an environment in which they can evidence some of that potential. The interaction of their potential and our environment can create something better in that human being than existed before. I think this mindset, which is empathic, gives people more opportunity to prove themselves, leads to more intense training because you believe it will pay off, and creates more tolerance and a willingness to give people second chances because you understand that it takes multiple times before people become comfortable.[25]

Giving people second chances is a cornerstone of MW's employee philosophy and is one reason MW's turnover is lower than the industry average. Mistakes are part of the learning process, and Bresler believes the company has to exercise judgment and tolerance when people err. It's part of what he calls "contextual management," which means looking at all the variables in a situation and weighing them differently depending on the context. When decisions are made in context, Bresler believes, there are very few rules that cannot be broken. He recounts one incident in which a regional manager named Tom had just fired a wardrobe consultant:

> I called Tom and said, "Why did you fire Joe?" And he said, "Because he stole a suit." I said, "So?" He said, "Well, what do you mean?" I said, "Well, you didn't have to fire him because he stole a suit. You could have demoted him. You could have disciplined him in some other way. I'm not suggesting in any way you were wrong to fire him. Most often that's the appropriate thing to do. I'm just saying you didn't *have* to fire him." He said, "Huh, I never thought about that. I really didn't want to fire him." I said, "Well, maybe you need to call him up and tell him you really don't want him to steal anymore, but he doesn't need to be fired." So he did and the guy is working reasonably successfully with us, and I don't think he's stolen a suit since.[26]

Of course, there are some rotten apples in the barrel who will never deserve the trust the company gives them and will never be high performers. Invariably, they leave the company or are let go. MW's goal is not to make the entire workforce high performing, which they view as impossible, but to turn average performers into *above*-average performers. They segment the workforce into the top 20 percent, the bottom 20 percent, and the middle 60 percent. The top 20 percent are already high performers and will thrive in an empowered environment; the bottom 20 percent are not likely to fit and will leave or be fired. "What George Zimmer has been able to do," says Bresler, "is to help the retail worker who is in the 60 percent get better. It is one thing I think George does exceptionally well. He doesn't look to do what's right in some abstract way; he looks to do what would make the situation better. That is the essence of why he has been so successful."[27]

Another critical element of Zimmer's philosophy is that "if the customer thinks he's right, he is right!" This is certainly not a novel idea, but the extent to which this principle is operationalized in the shopping experience at MW is remarkable, and they adhere to this principle even if unscrupulous customers occasionally take advantage of them. George Zimmer explains how he arrived at this position:

I can remember when I first started in business and worked in our stores. When people came in for refunds and exchanges, I would be very tough about it. I always did what I thought was very fair but sometimes not from the customer's point of view. "Tough," I would say. "You've worn this garment for a year. Don't you think it's a little ridiculous to return it!" And the customer would say, "Absolutely not! I never liked it!" And I would say, "You know what, sir, go to hell!" Over the years we've come to a different position, which is, in effect, if the customer thinks he's right, then he is right. That opens up a small opportunity for a very small minority of customers to take advantage of us. They come in and they buy a tuxedo on Friday and they bring it back on Monday for a refund. We might want to say, "Why didn't you just rent one from us?" Well, our position is that we can't run the risk of alienating any customer, so we instruct our people that if the customer thinks he's right, then he is right.[28]

Another stakeholder group that MW manages exceptionally well is vendors. In the retail world, vendors face a constant struggle with the customers they sell to. Many retailers take advantage of them, which obviously breeds distrust. George Zimmer listened to their complaints early in the company's history and resolved to treat them honestly and fairly and to build long-term, loyal relationships with his suppliers. Zimmer explains:

When goods don't sell, retailers force the vendors to take back the goods, and if the vendor doesn't do it, then they threaten the vendor that they won't be a vendor anymore. They ask the vendors to help pay for the advertising of the product or when a good doesn't sell, they call up the vendor and ask for markdown allowances. We took the position, after hearing vendors complain about this all the time, that we would do things a little differently. So we don't ask our vendors for markdown allowances or co-op advertising. Nor do we ask our vendors to buy us dinner or get us tickets to Broadway shows. In fact, our buyers are instructed to pick up the checks, and we provide tickets to our vendors, rather than vice versa. Actually, over the years we have taken to a great degree what are normally vendor-customer relationships and turned them into reciprocal friendships, which are authentic.[29]

Men's Wearhouse believes that it has commitments to five stakeholder groups: employees, customers, vendors, communities, and shareholders. Of those, employees are considered the most important. According to George Zimmer, long-term shareholder value is a natural consequence of doing the right things for the other shareholder groups: "If you take care of your employees, customers, vendors, and communities, then your shareholders are going to have long-term value unless you have something structurally wrong with your company. The mistake a lot of people on Wall Street make is to put shareholders first. Yeah, you can always squeeze out more shareholder return at the expense of other stakeholders and that will work for a couple of quarters, but it's not going to work for a couple of decades, not even for a couple of years."[30]

Representing the Customer

The premise at MW is that employees come first. If you create a fulfilling environment for them, they will in turn create fulfilling experiences for customers. MW does this by paying higher wages, elevating the status of its front-line customer service group to "wardrobe consultants" instead of "sales clerks," making tailors part of the customer service team, providing an extraordinary amount of education and training, striving to live the principles of servant leadership, and creating a culture of self-actualization. The goal is for MW employees to represent the customer, and this means subordinating self-interest to the needs of the customers. In most retail clothing stores, this would be difficult because salespeople make most of their living from commissions, which forces them to compete with one another. At MW, as George Zimmer explains, the emphasis is on team selling:

> We train our people that when you're not waiting on a customer and somebody else is, we want you to assist even though you're not going to get any commission. You're going to do that because tomorrow, when you're waiting on a customer, and the other guy isn't, he's going to assist you. What does assist mean? Well, if I'm standing with you in a fitting mirror or at one of our lay-down tables where wardrobes are assembled, it's not easy for me to go to another part of the store to get another piece of merchandise that would fit your needs. But if I have someone helping me, I can say, "Would you go get me the trench coat in the fly front, charcoal gray, in a 42 long?" Then he can go get that while I continue my presentation. When it comes to coordinating shirts and ties, we have found that rather than having one salesperson spending the entire time one-on-one with a customer, we bring a *sales associate* into the sale. That's a euphemism for *cashier* in our store, except that they're not just cashiers. They're also trained in coordinating the shirts and ties that go with the suits and sport coats we sell. So we get this kind of yin-yang balance between men and women, older people

and younger people, working in groups with our customers. The customer's experience is both conscious and unconscious. Maybe he's just unconsciously picking up the scent that this is not a pure commission situation, the way he's used to, because there are three people involved in his transaction. We think this behavior is one reason our stores do a lot more volume than most of our competitors.[31]

The idea of putting the customer's interests first is well established in professions like management consulting, but it is a foreign concept in most retail businesses where commission structures are the primary governors of employee behavior and customers are too often viewed as a means to an end. Of course, this attitude is not universal in retail. Nordstrom and Marshall Field's, to name two exemplary companies, have quite a different view of customers. Nonetheless, what distinguishes MW from most of its competitors is its consultative approach to serving customers' needs. "I used to say, when you go to greet a customer, for the first three seconds before you open your mouth, imagine that this is an acquaintance of yours," says George Zimmer. "Not a friend, but an acquaintance who has never been to the store but has been threatening to come see you for months and now is showing up. And what you want to do is show him the good stuff! Show him the best deal that you as an insider know of. You want to be that person's representative. I think customers pick that up."[32]

Exceptional BD at Men's Wearhouse

At the beginning of this chapter, we said that companies that differentiate themselves behaviorally usually have inspired leadership; a culture that encourages employees to treat customers exceptionally well; supporting policies, procedures, and processes; and employees who were hired because they enjoy serving others and are inclined to be friendly and helpful without having to be told to do so. We also said that *exceptional behavioral differentiation* describes the kinds of behaviors that customers find extraordinary, even from companies where the behavioral standard is already beyond what customers normally expect from suppliers of a particular product or service. MW is a fine example of a company that has managed to provide exceptional service consistently because it has the right leadership, culture, processes, and people. Ultimately, exceptional BD is the result of individual moments where employees "go the extra mile" for a customer and do something the customer finds extraordinary. It will not happen, however, unless the stage has been set and the leaders model the exceptional behaviors they want to see in employees. Charlie Bresler recalls such a moment:

I remember a customer calling up and needing a pair of shoes. I drove the shoes myself to the customer's office, which was forty minutes out of my way. You know, people in the store saw that. The senior managers everywhere in our company do these kinds of things. So one of the ways we get employees to do extraordinary things for customers is by just doing it ourselves, and that's a very important way. It's a critical part of the training process. It's what we talk about: selling with soul, going the extra mile for our customers.[33]

Men's Wearhouse has numerous stories like this—shirts ruined by the local cleaners that MW replaces at no charge just before a man has a critical job interview, dress clothes that are fitted after hours when a man is promoted and needs to be well dressed the following morning, tailored suits purchased and ready in less than half an hour, crisply pressed tuxedo shirts delivered to a hotel just in time for a black tie event, and so on. George Zimmer receives between one to two hundred messages a week from customers commenting on the remarkable service they received at an MW store. He sends nearly ten thousand letters every year to employees who are mentioned in these messages.

Why Doesn't Everybody Do It?

If there is a mystery in this story, it is not why or how MW consistently differentiates itself from its competitors through exceptional behavior. The mystery is why its competitors don't copy what MW does. The company shares openly and in great detail its "secrets of success." It invites other organizations to participate in dialogues about issues involving the philosophy and values for unleashing human potential. Its best practices are readily available on the MW Web site. The company is generous about sharing what it does to create a more empowered and engaged workforce and to behaviorally differentiate itself with customers. Why others don't emulate MW is baffling to George Zimmer, too. "I've joked about that for over a decade," he told us. "Why is it that a company like ours that started with seven grand and nothing else, and is now the dominant force in its field, why is it that no one copies what we do? Okay, so maybe it took awhile for them to figure out, but we've been doing this for thirty years. The reason I'm so generous with our ideas is because I've learned that nobody is ever going to copy the idea. Nobody seems to think it will apply in their business, or I don't know what it is . . . it's the most amazing thing."[34]

Charlie Bresler believes there are two reasons why MW's competitors do not copy its behavioral differentiators. The first reason is practical. "For one thing," he said, "you have to create an infrastructure, not only a cultural in-frastructure but also a financial infrastructure operating margin that can support what we do. They can recruit people away from us, but if they are not prepared to develop the infrastructure, then they aren't going to be success-ful." The second reason is more philosophical, and consequently more diffi-cult to embody in practice without a significant culture change: "What dif-ferentiates us is that we have a consulting culture and we expect our people to be consultants. That's what our customers feel. If it's done well, they feel they've had a wonderful experience."[35]

Challenges for Readers

1. Exceptional BD occurs more often when companies have a culture that en-courages employees to treat customers exceptionally well, which often means "breaking the rules." Does your culture allow employees to "break the rules" in order to give customers an extraordinary experience?
2. Both Volvo Cars and Men's Wearhouse are companies with high ideals and a strong sense of purpose. They pride themselves on being good cor-porate citizens that promote important social values. There appears to be a direct correlation between the strength of a company's social values and its capacity for exceptional behavior. How values-driven is your company?
3. Companies that behave exceptionally are likely to be self-conscious about their behavior. At Men's Wearhouse, for instance, the executive responsi-ble for store operations is a clinical psychologist. MW teaches its people to be more emotionally intelligent and is deliberate in crafting an experi-ence for customers that they will find more satisfying. How self-conscious are you about how your employees behave toward customers? And toward each other? How could you be more self-conscious about your behavior and its impact on customers?
4. Al Dunlap and George Zimmer are a study in contrasts. Chainsaw Al slashed and burned at Scott Paper and Sunbeam, radically cutting people and products in the name of shareholder value. George Zimmer believes that if you take care of your employees, customers, vendors, and commu-nities, then your shareholders will receive value. Which of these two op-posites best reflects your company's perspective? What impact does your perspective have on your ability to create exceptional BD?

Endnotes

1. Craig Silverman interview with Terry Bacon (July 25, 2001).
2. Robert George lecture during *Legendary Service at the Ritz-Carlton (I),* Ritz-Carlton Leadership Center, Atlanta, Georgia (January 14–15, 2001).
3. Paul C. Judge, "Best Performers: The World's Most Customer-Centric Company," *Fast Company,* 47 (June 2001), p. 144.
4. Gerry Roche interview with Meredith Ashby and Stephen Miles (Spring 2002).
5. Charlotta Källbäck interview with Laurie Voss (February 22, 2002).
6. Volvo Car Company Web site, http://new.volvocars. com/whyvolvo/why_high_mile_club.asp (May 30, 2002).
7. *Company Philosophy,* Volvo Car Corporation, Göteborg, Sweden.
8. Hans-Olov Olsson (April 4, 2002) http://www.citizenship.volvocars. com/frontweb/2_0.asp?secId=2.
9. Källbäck, ibid.
10. *Company Philosophy,* op cit.
11. Nerissa Morris Hampton interview with Laurie Voss (January 29, 2002).
12. Ibid.
13. Sven Eckerstein interview with Laurie Voss (April 2, 2002).
14. Louise Powers-Ackley interview with Laurie Voss (December 17, 2001).
15. Eckerstein, op cit.
16. Hans-Olov Olsson interview with Laurie Voss (May 2002).
17. "Men's Wearhouse Named One of Best Companies to Work for by Fortune Magazine for Second Consecutive Year; Company Also Receives Award from Human Resources Magazine," *Business Wire* (January 2001), p. 1.
18. "A Few Customer Loyalty Programs Are Worth the Effort," *The Salt Lake Tribune* (August 22, 2000), p. C5.
19. www.menswearhouse.com/home_page/common_threads (April 17, 2002).
20. "Common Threads," www.menswearhouse.com/home_page/common_threads (April 9, 2002).
21. Ibid.
22. Larry C. Spears, "Ten Traits to Develop in Becoming a Servant-Leader" (April 9, 2002). www.menswearhouse.com/home_page/common_threads/ct521_article.asp.

23. George Zimmer, "Building Community Through Shared Values, Goals and Experiences," www.menswearhouse. com/home_page/common_ threads (April 17, 2002).

24. "The Value of Emotional Intelligence," www.menswearhouse.com/ home_page/common_threads (April 17, 2002).

25. Charlie Bresler interview with Pamela Wise (April 16, 2002).

26. Ibid.

27. Ibid.

28. George Zimmer interview with Pamela Wise (April 15, 2002).

29. Ibid.

30. Ibid.

31. Ibid.

32. Ibid.

33. Bresler, op cit.

34. Zimmer interview with Pamela Wise, op cit.

35. Bresler, op cit.

8

LIVING THE PROMISE

All men dream, but unequally. Those that dream at night in the dusty recesses of their minds awake the next day to find that their dreams were just vanity. But those who dream during the day with their eyes wide open are dangerous men; they act out their dreams to make them reality.

—T.E. Lawrence

Whatever you do, you need courage. Whatever course you decide upon, there is always someone to tell you you are wrong. There are always difficulties arising which tempt you to believe that your critics are right. To map out a course of action and follow it to an end requires some of the same courage which a soldier needs. Peace has its victories, but it takes brave men to win them.

—Ralph Waldo Emerson

Sales manager Jim Hanna had good reason to be worried. Although his company, General American Telecom (GAT), was among the major telecommunications companies in the U.S., business in his district had been slow, and they had lost several key bids in the past year.[1] If they were unable to put some food on the table soon, the district would be forced to lay off a substantial number of people. So Jim was relieved when he learned that the Northern State College and University System (NSCUS) planned to replace its aging telephone system and that a Request for Proposal (RFP) would be released in the next few months. NSCUS was responsible for managing eleven four-year colleges and universities and fifteen two-year colleges. Building an integrated telecommunications system for that number of institutions would be a project of significant size—enough to pull his district out of the doldrums if they won the award.

In their first meeting to discuss this opportunity, Gina Labattaglia, the district manager, and Calvin Story, the network operations manager, agreed that the NSCUS project was critically important to the district. They did not have to review the other opportunities in their pipeline to know that this was the largest opportunity they would face in the coming year. To Labattaglia, their priorities were clear: "We need to bet the farm on this one," she told Hanna. "Put everything you have behind winning this work." The account manager responsible for NSCUS was Kimberly Hansen. She was one of the new breed of account managers GAT had been hiring lately—young, ambitious MBAs with enough pluck to make up for their lack of experience. Hansen had been with GAT for just two years, but she impressed customers and had a good head on her shoulders. Moreover, when you gave her a project, she grabbed it with both hands and ran with it. Hanna figured that was just what the district needed, so he pulled a pursuit team together—led by Hansen—and told them, "Come hell or high water, *we are going to win this contract.* Be bold. Be creative. Do whatever you need to do. Just win this."

We said in Chapter 4 that symbolic BD is about alignment—the *internal* alignment of a company's messages with its behavior or the *external* alignment of a company's behavior with its customers' values, products, or image. In the story that follows, we are going to illustrate how a company behaved in ways that symbolized its understanding of and connection with a customer. Symbolic BD is not always self-evident; the symbols may be subtle and their messages may resonate just below the surface of awareness. But if this sounds obscure, let us assure you that the process of creating symbolic BD is anything but. Creating symbolic BD is a thoughtful and deliberate linking of a company's products and solutions with a customer's issues, needs, and priorities. Moreover, it is *living the promise*—behaving in ways that symbolize your understanding of and empathy toward the customer's values and needs.

GAT's Competitive Challenges

Kim Hansen's team included Don Stovall, the service manager for the district, and Dennis Steinberg, the systems manager. Along with Calvin Story, these technical managers would design the integrated telecommunications system and write the technical proposal. Soon after learning about the opportunity, Hansen and Steinberg visited NSCUS, introduced themselves to some of the key people, and gathered preliminary information on NSCUS' needs and expectations for their new system. What they learned was both encouraging and discouraging. The project would occur in two phases. During phase I, the supplier would build an integrated telecommunications system only for the eleven four-year colleges and universities (phase II would encompass the fifteen two-year schools). The new system would include voice, data, messaging, and networking. In addition to replacing the old telephones, switches, and other equipment, the contractor would also install a fiber-optic network and create a system that linked all the schools in one fast, high-bandwidth network. For a technology company like GAT, this was a relatively simple task; GAT could easily meet the technical requirements and offer a state-of-the-art solution at a reasonable price. That was the encouraging news. The problem was that their competitors could do the same. GAT's desire for a "plain vanilla," low-risk solution meant that every major contender would be able to meet the technical requirements, so neither GAT nor any other company would be able to win this competition through technical merit alone.

During one of her customer meetings, Hansen confirmed what she suspected from the moment she learned of the opportunity: that the local "Baby Bell" telephone service provider would be competing for the contract. The Baby Bell owned the installed system at the NSCUS campuses. Although that system was aging, it nonetheless gave the Baby Bell a lot of presence on campus; a thorough knowledge of the people, systems, and equipment in place; and a jump start in the customers' confidence. The Baby Bell was the incumbent, and incumbents always have an advantage, even if they have some performance problems. For one thing, the incumbent has an installed base of equipment, including a proprietary architecture that can be expanded rather than totally replaced: this would create a potential cost savings, but *only if done by the incumbent.*

In this case, the situation was worse because the Baby Bell was well regarded by the schools. Moreover, when the professors and administrators went home at night, they used the Baby Bell's systems and services. GAT was a brand name, but it lacked the kind of local presence the Baby Bell had. The two other major competitors were also strong. One was a large telecom company in Canada; the other was a nationwide contender in the U.S. market. Both would field good teams and excellent solutions. Still, the most formidable competitor was the Baby Bell, and as the insiders in this horse race, they could be counted on to have a head start, great legs, and a strong finish.

The Consultant from Houston

The final key challenge arose when Hansen learned that NSCUS had hired a consultant to run the contractor selection process. Named Robert Loesch, he ran a one-man telecom system consultancy in Houston, and no one in GAT had ever worked with him. As far as they knew, he had not worked with any of the other competitors either, but this was bad news no matter how they looked at it. Loesch was an unknown quantity to them (and vice versa) and the team had a number of questions about him: Did he have any favorites among the competing suppliers? What did he know about GAT's products and systems? What did he consider important? How would he view the technical choices GAT had made? Most importantly, how much influence would he have on the selection?

As they learned more about Loesch, they became convinced that he had been a good choice for NSCUS. Born near London, he was an electrical engineer who had spent much of his career with British Telecom. He was technically competent and experienced in advising academic institutions on telecommunications systems. NSCUS was unlikely to have anyone in their system as knowledgeable about telecom systems as Robert Loesch, so it made sense that they would hire someone like him to lead their selection process, and it was no surprise when Hansen learned that Loesch would write the RFP himself.

The Selection Process

As the RFP was about to be released, however, Hansen did get a surprise. She learned from contacts in NSCUS that a selection committee had been formed. It would consist of Loesch and one representative from each of the eleven four-year colleges and universities in the NSCUS system. This group of twelve would decide which bidder won the award. The surprising part was not the *fact* of the committee but its *composition.* The representatives from the academic institutions included vice presidents of administration (usually the campus person responsible for the physical plant), directors of computer services, registrars, and librarians. The people in these positions might have technical backgrounds, perhaps in computer science, but few of them would know the technical intricacies of modern telecommunications systems. So it seemed increasingly clear to Hansen's GAT team that Loesch himself would be the primary technical evaluator.

Could he be the *only* technical evaluator? They weren't sure, but the hot debate topic at their morning meetings became how to influence those eleven institutional representatives. They were likely to have different questions, issues, and priorities than Loesch. Moreover, they would have their own institutions in mind as they read the proposals, so it was important to understand what each of them considered important and what each would be looking for in the supplier they chose. You can't influence people without knowing what is important to them, so Hansen and her team each selected several represen-

tatives and sought to learn as much about them as they could in the time remaining. They had just completed their visits to the campuses and interviews
with key people when the RFP hit the streets. They estimated that the scope
of work described in the RFP would yield a project of about $110 million (for
phase I), and they had three weeks to write their proposal. In those three
weeks, Hanna remembers saying to the team, they would either save the district or close it down.

Success is the child of audacity.

—Benjamin Disraeli

The Think Tank

Their initial assessment of their chances looked grim. Although they had
an excellent technical solution, it would not differentiate them from their rivals. Neither would their price. Even at the maximum discounted price allowed by corporate, they were unlikely to undercut their competitors' prices
enough to gain a price advantage. Besides, their competitors would probably
offer discounted prices, too. Since learning of the opportunity, they had introduced themselves to the consultant and the institutional representatives on
the selection committee, but the Baby Bell with the installed base knew the
customers much better and had a great reputation. Although the team had a
"never say die" attitude, they also understood the magnitude of the challenge
facing them. They tackled that challenge by forming a think tank to develop
their win strategy. In addition to their core team, they brought in technical and
marketing specialists from around the company. Housed in a small room in
the basement of their building, the think tank had walls and walls of white-
boards and corkboards. In the weeks to come, these boards would be filled
with brainstormed lists, diagrams, crudely drawn charts, Dilbert cartoons,
sandwich orders, and an occasional plea for help.

First, they discussed the proposal itself. If they could not win on technical
merit, then what was their proposal supposed to accomplish? Some of the
diehard technicians from the systems and networking groups insisted that
GAT did have a better technical solution and should try to win based on the
sophistication of their system and the advanced features they could offer the
customer. Hansen said, "Great. Make the case to us, and if we buy it, that's
what we'll pitch to the customer." She established a faux customer panel consisting of Don Stovall, Dennis Steinberg, Calvin Story, and a senior systems
engineer who used to work for the Baby Bell, and she had the technicians
make their case. "It frustrated the hell out of them," she recalls, "because the
panel shot down every claim they made. They knew enough about our com-

petitors' systems, products, and architecture to show that, although our solutions are great, in the end there were few real differences between what we can do and what our competitors can do. And you're kidding yourself if you think otherwise. It was a tense afternoon. When it was over, everyone was convinced that we could not win this by trying to convince NSCUS that we are technically better than the other guys are."

The brainstorm came from Don Stovall, who had met with the consultant, Robert Loesch, the preceding week. "Loesch comes across as a real buttoned-up kind of guy," Stovall told the group. "A stickler for details. Everything nice and tidy. He kept talking about what he wants to see and how he wants to see it. I think the way to win with this guy is to give him exactly what he asks for—no more, no less." That became the team's strategy for the proposal: to be absolutely compliant with Loesch's specifications and proposal instructions. They knew that Loesch had created a checklist for scoring the proposals, a checklist based on the specifications and scope of work. So their goal was to get the highest technical score, and the way to do that was to give the man every piece of information he asked for, in the order in which he asked for it. Stovall, who describes himself as a maniacal Boston Red Sox fan, put it this way: "We want a clean inning. No hits, no runs, no errors, and no one left on base." Somebody wrote that on the white board and circled it in red. That became the team's mantra. Keep it simple, they told themselves. Answer the mail. Don't deviate from the script. "The RFP says there are a thousand technical points," Hansen remarked, "and we want nine hundred and ninety of them."

Another brainstorm came from Hansen herself. She had met with four of the institutional representatives and was struck by the fact that their perspectives about the new system were so different. At first, she considered this a problem. "I thought, 'These schools can't figure out what they want! How are we ever going to give them a system that satisfies everyone?' Then I realized that this was actually a great opportunity for us." In essence, the team decided to *think globally and act locally,* as the saying goes. They would propose the global integrated solution the consultant had specified, but they would find a way to address each school's issues, needs, and priorities. This concept raised an intriguing question for the group: How do you address each evaluator's individual concerns when you are writing a proposal that must adhere absolutely to the specifications and allows no room for additional thoughts? If not through the proposal, then how? Once the RFP was released, state procurement integrity laws prohibited bidders from contacting the eleven institutional representatives. So they had no apparent way to communicate with the academic evaluators until after the proposals were submitted—and perhaps not until the decision had been made.

"Let's create something besides the proposal for the school reps," someone suggested.

"Like what?"

"Like an executive summary."

"Can we do that?"

"No one said we couldn't."

The idea did not gain immediate acceptance on the team. There were too many unknowns. What form would this summary take? Would the consultant allow it? Would the academic evaluators even read it? After some debate, they decided that it was the best solution, largely because they couldn't think of anything else. Someone suggested that they call the consultant and ask if it was all right to include a summary with their proposal, but Jim Hanna vetoed that. He was concerned that they might tip their hand too early. They didn't know Loesch that well, Hanna reasoned, and they couldn't trust that he wouldn't tell the other bidders what GAT planned to do, especially if he favored one of their rivals. So the team decided to develop an executive summary on a wing and a prayer and then call the consultant just days before the proposals were due to seek permission to include it. It was the kind of bold move Hanna had been looking for, but there were misgivings among some team members. It would cost them nearly $40,000 to create this executive summary. If Loesch did not allow it, they could be stuck with very expensive mementos of a pursuit gone bad.

The Summary Design

Their first design decision was to create a four-color brochure. Four-color printing raised the price, and there was some concern that the academic institutions might consider it a wasteful expenditure, a sign of GAT's extravagance. In the end, however, they concluded that a tasteful brochure with color was more professional and classy than creating something too "plain vanilla." NSCUS' motto was "centers of merit," and their own public relations materials were printed professionally in muted pastels. So the team felt that submitting a tasteful but professional brochure in light pastel colors would reflect NSCUS' image and create a subtle correspondence. Their decision to submit an executive summary was itself a behavioral differentiator (their rivals were not likely to do it), but their decision to use pastel colors to reflect NSCUS "centers of merit" concept was an explicit act of symbolic BD. It tied together the customer's self-concept with the image GAT wanted to project. The symbolism here might be subtle, but it was not the only thing they did to symbolize their alignment with the customer.

To show that they understood the special needs and concerns of the eleven academic evaluators, they also decided to devote one full page in the summary to each school. *Think globally. Act locally.* The brochure would have sixteen pages, five of which would tell the overall story. The other eleven pages would tell eleven different stories, each tailored to a particular four-year college or university in NSCUS. The message GAT wanted to send to each of the academic evaluators was this: "We understand and care about your special needs. Your institution is as important to us as the other ten. We have taken the time to learn what you want from your new telecommunications system, and you can be assured that you will get it." The messages that companies send in their marketing communications, meetings, presentations, and proposals are promises of what is to come. GAT could have simply said, "We will pay attention to each of the eleven institutions and address your individual needs." However, this stated promise pales beside the impact of their behavior when they investigate each school's individual needs and devote one full page in their summary to each of the eleven schools. In GAT's case, their behavior manifested their promise. It was far more convincing than simply stating the promise *because they were already behaving as they promised they would*—such is the impact of symbolic BD.

The next decision concerned what they would put on the pages dedicated to the individual colleges and universities. Before the RFP was released, they had spoken to key people at each of the schools and knew what they wanted and needed from this new telecommunications system. They understood how each of the schools envisioned using the technology to accomplish their mission and improve their educational, research, and community programs. So it made sense to address each institution's specific needs on the page devoted to that institution. Beyond that, they were not sure what to do with those pages until Jim Hanna suggested that they include photographs of each institution.

"What would be the point of that?" someone asked. "They already know what their buildings look like."

"The point," Jim said, "would be that we know what they look like. We've been there. And we don't just buy stock photos, which anyone can do. We send a photographer to each campus, who takes shots of the buildings and surroundings that are not your standard public relations shots." It was an infectious idea. Soon everyone was brainstorming.

"They should be from unusual angles."

"Right. Not your usual well-composed picture. It should be like snapping someone's picture and cutting off the top of their head."

"When readers look at a photo, they have to wonder where the photographer was standing in order to get that shot."

Figures 8-1 and 8-2 illustrate what these photos looked like. They are not breathtaking pictures; in fact, they are rather mundane. However, the unusual composition sends an important message: "We cared enough about you and your school to make a special trip to take this photograph. The investment we have already made in getting to know you reflects the kind of investments we make in our customers to ensure that we understand them and will meet their needs." These photographs created a kind of intimacy that is not possible with stock photos. It was one of GAT's most effective uses of symbols.

The team also sought to show how and where they had supported NSCUS programs and events in the past. The goal was to establish that, although GAT was not the current service provider, the company had long supported the colleges and was not just showing interest now because of the contract. GAT had funded a number of research projects through the years and was an annual supporter of one of the most recognized sports events in the state—the annual Northern State Marathon, which is sponsored by the Northern State Medical College and the regional cancer society. Figure 8-3 shows how this connection was highlighted in the executive summary. Many of the pages dedicated to one of the eleven institutions had artwork illustrating a connection between GAT and the institution.

Figure 8-1. One Illustrative Campus Photograph. It's not a classic, well-composed photograph, but it communicates that "We were here."

Figure 8-2. Another Illustrative Campus Photograph. The GAT team wanted readers to wonder where the photographer had been standing in order to get this kind of shot.

As the institutional pages in the executive summary came together, the team decided to devote one of the remaining pages to their team and its qualifications. The system they were proposing might be high tech, but systems are built, delivered, installed, operated, and maintained by people. So it was important that the evaluators feel comfortable with the people who would be serving them if GAT won the contract, and here the team found another opportunity for a symbolic connection with the customer. Instead of using the standard mug shot of each team member, they decided to take group photos, and in those photos they wanted to look accessible and friendly, the kind of people NSCUS would want to work with: professional, yes, but also casual. Later, when Hansen was putting together their resumes, she was amazed to discover that all but one of their proposed team had graduated from NSCUS schools. She thought, "If they hire us, they're hiring their own graduates." That became one of their themes in the executive summary: "We are not strangers; we are your alumni; we are you." Figure 8-4 illustrates how they conveyed this connection in their group photos.

The GAT team was writing the proposal and the executive summary simultaneously. The plan was to finish the executive summary two weeks be-

GAT has supported
the Northern State
Marathon for more than
20 years. Calvin Story,
our network manager,
finished 59th in the
2001 race, with a personal
best time of 2:20:19.

Figure 8-3. Northern State Marathon Art. Art like this was used to show the connections between GAT and the NSCUS institutions.

Clockwise, top right:
Don Stovall,
Service Manager,
U of N;
Dennis Steinberg,
Systems Manager,
Cal State Fullerton;
Calvin Story,
Network Operations
Manager, NSU;
Kim Hansen,
Account Manager,
NSC-Bingham

Figure 8-4. Part of the GAT Team. This is not the typical posed photograph. It's meant to convey that these are real people, the kind of people you would want to work with.

fore the proposals were due so they could concentrate on technical and price proposals in the final weeks. As they were completing the executive summary, they had one final idea for showing the symbolic connection between GAT and NSCUS. Both organizations' logos are circular. Beneath NSCUS' logo is the motto "Centers of Merit." Their system operates as a meritocracy, and each institution is a center of merit in its own way. As the team considered how to display the logos on the back cover, Don Stovall said, "Why don't we center both logos above the motto?" Their schools are centers of merit, and so are we." That idea had a slow start but gained momentum as team members reflected on the message it sent. It was the final visual connection, the last thing the evaluators would see as they turned over the last page on the executive summary. Figure 8-5 shows how this appeared. Was this a risky thing to do? "I worried about it," said Hansen. "We were messing with their logo, in a sense, and that's always risky. In the end, we thought the power of the symbolism outweighed the risks. Besides, if you say you're going to be bold, then you have to make bold moves. You have to live the promise."

Drum Roll, Please

It was now four days before the proposals were due. The printed executive summaries—three hundred of them—had been back from the printer for a week. It was now time to call the consultant and request permission to include the executive summaries with their proposal. Kim Hansen and Jim Hanna had been rehearsing the call for several days. People throughout the district headquarters building were anxious as the call was placed. Hansen told Loesch

Figure 8-5. The Aligning of the Symbols. The final image in GAT's executive summary showed that they are also a center of merit.

that they were concerned that some of the institutional reps on the selection committee might not understand everything in the technical proposal, so GAT wanted to submit a separate executive summary for their benefit. Loesch thought about it for only a moment before saying, "Fine." Calvin Story later commented that everyone had been holding their breath, and when news of the call was broadcast on their phone system, the collective exhaling of breath practically blew the windows out.

That was their last big hurdle. If Loesch now told anyone about their executive summary, they didn't think their competitors would have time to create a good one. Besides, Loesch knew only that they would submit an executive summary. He didn't know what it contained or what it looked like. They felt that they were as close to having an edge with this summary than they were likely to get. Two days later, Hansen called Loesch again. "It occurred to us," she said, "that some of the institutional members of the selection team may want some extra copies of the executive summary to take back to their campuses. We are submitting twelve copies of the proposal. Would it be all right if we sent more than twelve copies of the executive summary?" Loesch did not object to that, so on the day of submittal, they hand-carried twelve copies of the proposal and two hundred copies of the executive summary.

Now they had to wait. For three weeks, they heard nothing from Loesch or NSCUS. Then a call came, not from Loesch but from the head of NSCUS. He asked if they could send sixty more copies of their executive summary because they wanted the Northern state legislature to know what they were doing. Although the winner had not been announced, Hansen and her team were confident that they had won—and that their executive summary had played a major role in the victory. Her assumptions were confirmed several weeks later when they were officially notified that they had been awarded the phase I contract. Subsequently, they also won phase II.

The Power of Symbolic Behaviors

Why did GAT win? They scored highly on the technical proposal evaluation but not enough to clearly differentiate them from the pack. Their rivals were equally competent. Likewise, their price was not a distinguishing factor. They were lower than the highest bidder and higher than the two lowest bidders. They beat the incumbent—but not because the incumbent faltered. They won, according to NSCUS sources who later spoke to them about the competition, because they had a sound solution, because authorities at each of the campuses felt that GAT understood their priorities, and because their executive summary told a compelling story:

▲ It clearly identified and addressed their key issues.
▲ It communicated the proposed system in a nontechnical way that allowed other people on the campuses to understand what was being proposed, how it would work, and how it would benefit them.
▲ It convinced them that the GAT team would be good to work with.
▲ It addressed each of the school's needs in an egalitarian way.
▲ It gave them a level of comfort they didn't have with the other offers.

In our telling of this story, we have focused on how the GAT team used symbols to tell a compelling story. We have not stressed their technical capabilities, but it should be evident that they would not have been selected had they not been a world-class supplier with the staff, skills, and resources to successfully complete a project of this kind. As we said earlier, behavioral differentiation is not a substitute for substance. You won't win unless you offer products or services that meet customers' needs at a price they are willing to pay. GAT had a good technical story to tell, but its rivals also had good stories. GAT won because Kim Hansen and her team used the symbols of NSCUS and its constituent schools to reflect their understanding of the project and the customer's vision and goals. They won because their behavior showed that they were aligned with the customer in some very fundamental ways. Behavior is the great architect of impressions, and on this opportunity GAT's behavior enabled them to show perfect alignment.

Harley-Davidson and the Experience Business

The story of how GAT won the NSCUS contract is an example of *external* symbolic behavioral differentiation—where a company's behaviors reflect the values and beliefs of the customer. When we introduced symbolic behavioral differentiation in Chapter 4, we also discussed the *internal* form of symbolic BD, and we said this occurs when a company's behaviors reflect its own values and beliefs. Our exemplar for internal symbolic BD is Harley-Davidson, the company *Forbes* magazine named Company of the Year for 2001. In just the last four years, Harley-Davidson's net sales have increased by 65 percent (from $2 billion in 1998 to $3.3 billion in 2001). During that same period, earnings grew by 104 percent. Harley-Davidson has had sixteen consecutive years of record revenue and earnings but still will not add capacity fast enough to satisfy the worldwide demand for their products. During the tech boom, investors couldn't throw enough money at dot.coms. They should have thrown it at Harley. According to *Forbes,* "Since Harley went public, its shares have risen 15,000%. Intel? A mere 7,200% since 1986. GE? A paltry 1,056%."[2]

Woman in a bar: "Hey, Johnny, what are you rebelling against?"
Johnny: "What've you got?"

—Marlon Brando, as Harley biker leader Johnny
in *The Wild One*

Harley-Davidson has its own definition of e-business. They say that they are in the **Experience Business**. The motorcycle is the vehicle, but the product is a lifestyle. It's an attitude, a way of being, a brotherhood and sisterhood of common interests, a perspective on life that has its antecedents not when Bill Harley and Arthur Davidson built the first motorized bicycle in 1901 (to take them to the local fishing hole) but even earlier, when explorers, cowboys, adventurers, and vagabonds set off across the mountains and plains of the American West on their horses. The lore about Harley-Davidson is as rich and textured as the history of America. Although the motorcycle is an Industrial Age icon, it has its roots in the leather saddle of the old West (the seat on a motorcycle is known as the *saddle* and some motorcyclists today have *saddlebags* on their bikes). Harley-Davidson historian Dr. Martin Jack Rosenblum explains the Harley mystique:

> To be a bikerider is to be a Harley person, almost by default. No other brand or marque embodies so completely and consistently the bikerider aesthetic, and it always has. . . .
>
> The Harley-Davidson spirit is the strength and courage that comes from devotion to personal freedoms. It is individuality. Riding a Harley is the stuff of adventure and legend, and it inspires these feelings in people. The resultant sense of identity, the merging of heritage and experience, is lived from the saddle and taken into everyday affairs. The lore of Harley-Davidson is the ride.[3]

In its article on the company, *Forbes* said, "Harley-Davidson is a cult brand and that demands a certain adherence to traditions."[4] Is it a cult brand because it adheres to traditions or has its adherence to tradition made it a cult brand? Which came first? The Harley mystique has been carefully managed for nearly a century. It emerged from the founders' personalities and the turn-of-the-century roughneck optimism in which the company was born. It was nearly destroyed by AMF, who bought the company and tried to manage it like the other recreational product lines AMF owned. AMF grew production too quickly, and quality suffered. Harley was on the verge of extinction when thirteen Harley executives, including Jeffrey Bleustein (the current CEO) bought Harley-Davidson in a leveraged buyout and began the process of reconstruction. Through the bad and good times, the company has never lost touch with the mythos of its founding and has always seen itself as more than a manufacturer of motorcycles. From its official founding date of 1903 through today, Harley-Davidson has behaved in ways that symbolize its vision and values. Here are a few of the ways it does that:

▲ The company's products are proudly and self-consciously traditional. They have a retro look that harks back to an earlier era and reflects the individualism and freedom of the American frontier. Regardless of other design trends and fads through the 50s, 60s, 70s, and other later decades of American life, Harley-Davidson has steadfastly maintained that retro ethic in the look, feel, and sound of its products. Like the swoop fenders, teardrop gas tanks, and miles of chrome, the famous "potato-potato-potato" sound of Harley pipes is no accident. They carefully design their engines, frames, and exhaust pipes so that a Harley-Davidson motorcycle sounds like no other.

▲ It has exploited its brand to create a customer community unlike any other in the world. Since 1913, Harley has been putting its brand on other products. The company markets its own line of branded clothing, and it licenses a broad array of products featuring the Harley-Davidson name or logo, including shirts, sweaters, jackets, jeans and pants, eyewear, boots, and headgear. You can buy Harley-Davidson tattoo designs, flags, belt buckles, coffee mugs, jewelry, votive candles, cologne, neckties, sweaters, jackets, pants, scarves, and skirts. You can drive a Harley-Davidson–branded pickup and eat at a Harley-Davidson café. The Harley-Davidson name and logo are among the most recognizable brands in the world because the company has aggressively promoted its image. A combination of clever marketing and fierce customer loyalty has enabled Harley-Davidson to map its values and themes onto its customers, making them willing accomplices in an acculturation process that distinguishes the community of Harley owners from everyone else in the world and that communicates that identity to the marketplace. Wearing leathers at motorcycle rallies is a symbol of membership in the Harley-Davidson cult. Among owners, the black-and-gold emblem—whether it's worn on your T-shirt, baseball cap, belt buckle, or skin—is both a statement and a symbol of pride. Harley-Davidson understands the power of these symbols and consciously uses them to communicate the company's vision and the values (the Harley experience) and to build customer loyalty. The millions of people around the world who display the Harley-Davidson name and logo are proud co-conspirators in the company's symbolic behavioral differentiation.

▲ The company supports and encourages one of the world's largest organizations of product owners—the Harley Owners Group or H.O.G. The 660,000 members of H.O.G. form an extended family that stretches around the globe, drawn together by the many Harley-sponsored rallies, road tours, festivals, and celebrations. In 2002, Harley announced a 14-month-long Open Road Tour, which they describe as "a 25-acre traveling festival of pure Harley-Davidson adrenaline."[5] Featuring exhibits, movies, biker fashion shows, entertainment, activities for kids, and miles of leather and chrome, the Open Road Tour punctuates a year-long, worldwide celebration of Harley-Davidson's hundredth anniversary. In organizing and supporting the Harley Owners Group and its many activities and events, the company is behaving in ways that symbolize the rider's experience and reflect back to its customers the loyalty the customers have shown toward the brand.

▲ The company provides an extraordinary level of support to dealers and suppliers. Harley-Davidson's dealer support may not be qualitatively different from the support Honda, Kawasaki, and Suzuki provide to their dealers. All offer training, merchandising, advertising and display support, and so on, but Harley-Davidson brings with it a broad network of like-minded businesses that reinforce the spirit of the brand in ways none of its rivals can copy. Moreover, more than 50 percent of Harley-Davidson employees own the product (purchased the same way other owners purchase their motorcycles). Because so many employees drive Harley-Davidson motorcycles, the company has a built-in "focus group" numbering in the thousands. The company and its employees, dealers, suppliers, and owners form an extended community of shared interests, identities, and experiences that few other product brands can boast.

> Early on, Harley created bikes and gear that gave you the impression that you are part of Old West mythology. Their products became symbols of freedom, adventure, and escape. It's John Wayne at the end of the movie. Two wheels and an engine and a great deal of mythology—that's all Harley-Davidson is.
>
> —Ultan Guilfoyle

Motorcycles and those who ride them have until recently been on the fringes of mainstream America. In popular culture they have traditionally been the symbols of rebellion and disaffection. We see them on our movie screens and in our dreams—a cast of cultural icons that includes the loners (baseball-playing Steve McQueen in *The Great Escape*), the hippies (Peter Fonda and Dennis Hopper in *Easy Rider*), and the outlaws (Marlon Brando in *The Wild One*). But today's riders are more likely to be pro-establishment than anti-establishment. Rich Urban Bikers or RUBs used to be a disdainful term for yuppies who had the money and leisure time to get into motorcycling. Today, they make up a large segment of Harley owners. Years ago on a business trip, Terry stayed at a hotel in Phoenix where a number of bikers were also staying. They were attending a rally, and the hotel parking lot was filled with rows of glittering Harley-Davidson motorcycles. Bikers clustered in small social groups around the property, similarly attired in the uniform of revolt—black leather jackets and pants, leather gloves and squared-toed boots, bandannas, and mirrored sunglasses. A sign posted by the hotel in the lobby read, "Don't be alarmed by the appearance of our guests who are attending the Harley-Davidson rally. Many of them are doctors and lawyers."

As Harley-Davidson has become more mainstream, one quintessential fact has not changed—the name symbolizes a unique experience, not only of riding on the open road but of belonging to something deeply rooted in the American experience. Harley-Davidson is well aware of this and self-consciously behaves in ways that are congruent with the expressed and implied messages it communicates to the marketplace. Furthermore, the company knows that what distinguishes it and its products from those of its rivals are not the machines themselves, whose features can be copied, nor its marketing strategies, which are well known, nor its distribution or product support infrastructure, whose particulars can be duplicated. What differentiates Harley-Davidson from its rivals is its symbolism, which it carefully cultivates through the management of the rider's experience. As the company said in one of its recent annual reports, "That experience is no accident; it is nurtured by dealers, employees and suppliers alike, brought to life by the passion of our loyal customers. Harley-Davidson is in the business of creating the unique experiences of which dreams are made. We create moments in time that live on long after they are gone. And that's something no one can copy."[6]

Walking the Talk with God

In our final discussion of symbolic behavioral differentiation, we are going to venture away from business and focus on an area of life whose purpose is inherently symbolic and where positive behavioral differentiation is the normal expectation. Religious leaders do not have *customers* as we normally think of the word, but they must cultivate followers whose buy in is as important to the church as it is for businesses trying to woo customers. Every successful religious leader has built a following and inspired the kind of customer loyalty that most businesses would envy. So as we researched behavioral differentiation we chose to include religious leaders in our survey. We asked *consumers* of religious leadership what they expected of religious leaders, what happened in their best experiences of religious leaders, and what happened in their worst experiences of religious leaders. The results are shown in Tables 8-1, 8-2, and 8-3.

As we noted earlier in our discussions of this research, people's expectations are largely behavioral, not functional. When they reflect on their best and worst experiences with lawyers, physicians, car salespeople, or religious leaders, 90 percent of their observations focus on the *behavior* of the person interacting with them. Whether we are getting a new car, legal advice, an annual physical, or salvation, we judge our interactions with the *providers* of these products and services principally by how they treat us. Religion is a special case because we expect our religious leaders' behavior to be congruent with the messages they preach. Because they purport to represent the teachings of God, we expect their behavior to reflect a supremely high standard. What happens, then, when their behavior is not aligned with their teachings? In recent years, the Catholic Church in the U.S. was rocked by a growing scandal of priests who were accused or convicted of sexual crimes—many of them against children—and bishops or cardinals who covered it up.

Leaders in other religions have also been accused or guilty of similar crimes from time to time, so this problem is not confined to Catholics. It's also important to keep the magnitude of the problem in perspective. The U.S. has approximately 47,000 Catholic priests. The vast majority of these men are living symbols of the religion they practice, but in any group of this size there are bound to be some whose behavior betrays their mission. The most infamous case at the moment centers on former priest John J. Geoghan, who was sentenced to nine to ten years in prison for indecent assault on a 10-year-old boy but is suspected of molesting as many as 130 children. In the past five decades, hundreds of priests have been suspected of sexual crimes. Some have been expelled from the church and a handful have gone to prison, but evidence is mounting that the church has routinely swept priestly misconduct under the rug, quietly paying hundreds of millions of dollars to settle claims and pay off the victims. By the time the dust settles, some estimates place the total liability for these claims at over one billion dollars. At the center of the storm in Geoghan's case was Cardinal Bernard Law of the Archdiocese of Boston, who, it was reported, had a longstanding policy of handling allegations of sexual crimes within the church instead of notifying civil authorities.[7]

Cardinal Law also figures into the case of Reverend Paul Shanley, the ex-priest who was charged with three counts of the rape of a child. According to the charges, the rapes began when the child was six years old, continued until he was thirteen, and sometimes occurred in the church confessional. Reports published in the *Boston Globe* indicate that Cardinal Law and his deputies in

(text continues on page 216)

Table 8-1. Customer Expectations of Religious Leaders.

	Functional Expectations
Knowledge, Wisdom	To be well educated To have broad experience with the world To be wise as well as knowledgeable To have a firm knowledge of his/her religion To have an understanding of real-life issues To be intelligent To be worldly as well as spiritual To be a life-long learner To have a deep understanding of the human animal
Community Service	To take public stands for what is right To get involved with community programs To care about and do something about the disenfranchised To be of service to the community, whether or not they are all members of his/her congregation To demonstrate a love of God and his/her fellow man
	Behavioral Expectations
Honesty and Integrity	To have integrity above all! To foster truth To abide by the laws they preach privately as well as in public To live in such a way there need be nothing to hide To have a devotion to their faith and live their lives as a testament to that faith
Efficiency, Effectiveness, and Practicality	To show professionalism To be charismatic To have good personal hygiene and dress professionally To demonstrate good leadership skills To be enthusiastic with their mission To be inspiring
Congregant Advocacy, Confidentiality, Candor	To be a true confidant and advisor To have a strong ability to keep communications confidential To show personal interest in my spiritual well being To be warm and always interested in all aspects of my life To show me genuine concern

Compassion	To show concern for the people in his/her religious community To be caring To be sensitive to the world but also to individuals who come to him/her To radiate warmth To be kind, especially to those who seem undeserving To be nurturing
Communication and Responsiveness	To be a good communicator To ask questions To be a good listener To be open To not assume they possess the only answers To be able to counsel wisely
Congruous with Teachings	To ensure that his behavior is consistent with his espoused beliefs To live what they teach To be spiritual and live the beliefs they express To exhibit faith-promoting actions To practice what he/she preaches
Humble	To share the stage with others To possess humility To recognize that they are not perfect or above the rest of us To not be condescending To show they know they are still human, too
Tolerance, Understanding	To be flexible and open-minded To be tolerant of other beliefs To be accepting of who I am To have respect for all living beings To have an openness to opposing views without judgment To avoid judging and finding fault

Table 8-2. Positive Differentiating Behaviors of Religious Leaders.

	Excellent Performance
Dedication	He was ready to lower the boom when asked advice about something that just was not done appropriately, as that act or deed impacted someone else. She was kind and loving and never preached to us, but demonstrated the kind of "compassion in action" that has always been her trademark. She far surpassed my expectations. When issues arose within our community that needed someone to speak out for justice, his was the voice.
	Positive Behaviors
Communication	He is a compelling visionary who can share that vision and communicate it effectively to his followers. She made some remark about how the greatest gift you can ever give is compassion. Although I'm not a Catholic, I think it may have changed my life. He has always been ready to discuss religious matters with me and put them in language that I can understand. She is an excellent listener, able to ask the right questions and therefore find the right answers.
Demonstrated Humility	He was not afraid to let us know that he was human, too. He has never made me feel like he thinks he's above his congregation. He openly gave out the kind of message in his life that his creed provided in its dogma.
Showing Caring and Taking a Personal Interest	She showed personal interest in my spiritual well-being. He was warm and always interested in all aspects of my life During a counseling session one day I was being elusive. She was able to read between the lines to discover the true nature of my difficulty and as a result she was able to help me through it. She was an important person and I didn't think she would be able to make time for a few students, but she invited us to walk to Mass with her and she spent the time asking us questions about who we were and what we wanted to do with our lives.

He generously gave his best personal and spiritual energy to me and my family during our time of need.

He has taken consistent, personal interest in our family.

Honesty, Integrity, and Consistency	He expects model behavior and that is what he portrays to us.
	He sets an example by living righteously.
	She lives a moral life, is honest, ethical, and holds herself to the highest standards.
	His personal behavior is consistent with his teachings to us.
	She has deep conviction and integrity, yet also doesn't judge and find fault.
	He has shown openness to opposing views without becoming judgmental.

Table 8-3. Negative Differentiating Behaviors of Religious Leaders.

	Poor Performance
Incompetence	He was indecisive and lived a careless life.
	He was sloppy in appearance and in thought.
	She didn't seem to have a firm grasp on her religion. She didn't know the facts.
	He was unable to understand the challenges of real life.
	She was completely uninspiring.

	Negative Behaviors
Hypocritical	He was drunk on Saturday night and the picture of piety on Sunday morning.
	He talked about doing one thing but he did another.
	He didn't live the beliefs he expressed.
	He did not truly believe what he preached and you could tell he just wanted out of his job.
	She talked the talk, but she didn't walk the walk.
Dishonest, Unethical, Self-Serving	He used the power of his position for unethical purposes.
	She used religious explanation for her own personal gain.
	She had her own political agenda and used people to get ahead in the parish.
	He was a charismatic charlatan who put his own spin on religious teachings to justify his acquisition of 7 million dollars of his constituency's money.

(continues)

Table 8-3. (continued)

	He was dishonest and was only in it for power and money.
	He sexually abused members of his congregation.
	She was interested only in meeting her own needs.
Poor Communication	He was pompous, a grandstander.
	I was told that I needed to "repent," that I needed to abolish all my impure thoughts. I was young, but even to think of it now—as if!
	She saw herself as the top rather than a tap, a resource.
	He was a preacher, but not a listener.
	She told me I was going to hell if I wasn't "saved."
Intolerant, Rude	He showed bigotry and prejudice.
	She was closed-minded, acting as if she had all the answers and had a corner on the truth.
	He was disrespectful of any thoughts that veered away from his teachings.
	He was inflexible in acceptance of differing beliefs.
	She was not open to new ideas.
	She made me feel guilty for not feeling the way she did.
	He was rude.
	She discriminated against some members of the congregation based on their appearance.
Uncompassionate, Disrespectful	She lacked feeling, character, and personality.
	He was egotistical.
	He was uncaring and uncompassionate.
	She didn't relate well with people and didn't seem really interested in helping them.

the Boston archdiocese were aware of Shanley's misconduct and the allegations of sexual abuse but did not report his criminal behavior to authorities. Indeed, Cardinal Law appears to have protected Shanley, even after the archdiocese paid settlements to some of his victims, and recommended him for assignments in other areas. Although he was certainly aware of Shanley's sexual abuse of children, in a letter to Shanley dated February 29, 1996, Law wrote, "Without doubt over all of these years of generous and zealous care, the lives and hearts of many people have been touched by your sharing of the Lord's Spirit. You are truly appreciated for all that you have done."[8] Another of Shanley's victims, anguished as much by Law's cover-up as the abuse he suffered, lashed out at the church at a news conference in April 2002: "If the

Catholic Church in America does not fit the definition of organized crime, then Americans seriously need to examine their concept of justice. Bernard Law and [archdiocese attorney] Wilson Rogers have behaved throughout this catastrophe with a deviousness, cunning, and lack of good intent that crossed long ago into the realm of criminality, however much the ever-elastic niceties of the law protect them."[9] Indeed, in a deposition Law was forced to give regarding the Shanley case, he claimed that his subordinates had handled the matter, and he was not personally aware of it. Adolf Eichmann, Richard Nixon, and, more recently, Slobodan Milosevic made the same claim.

> It really is a rape of your soul. It is not just physical abuse, it's a betrayal of your faith. It's the most damaging thing imaginable. I can't have faith now, and if I wanted to, I have no place to turn.
>
> —Victim of John J. Geoghan, quoted in *Newsweek*

Whether you take a generous or skeptical view of the church's actions may depend on your emotional and spiritual investment in organized religion in general and the Catholic Church in particular. But it seems clear, in either case, that hiding these crimes and trying to settle the claims quietly runs contrary to the spirit of Christianity and is especially ironic, in this case, because the Catholic Church advocates confession as one of its core religious practices. What's good for the parishioners ought to be good for the institution, but apparently that has not always been the case. No doubt, Cardinal Law thought he was acting in the church's best interests by handling these problems discreetly, but the unintended consequence of his actions, and the actions of other church leaders like him, has been to perpetuate the careers (and hence the crimes) of men like John Geoghan and Paul Shanley and to deepen the wound already inflicted by pedophile priests. In the nonbusiness arena, there is probably no better example of negative behavioral differentiation, and the price the church is paying for it includes disaffected parishioners; declining church membership; and the public shame of a noble institution whose behavior has, in this instance, betrayed its purpose.

Symbolic behavioral differentiation is the alignment of your behavior with your purpose and values or the purpose and values of your customers. When you achieve that alignment, you are walking the talk. Most people place a high premium on consistency between words and actions, so you are satisfying their subconscious need for congruence. If you fail to achieve that alignment, however, you may come across as hypocritical and are likely to be viewed with suspicion or disdain. Customers will sometimes overlook the fact that you don't walk the talk, but if they have reasonable choices and can buy your products or services elsewhere, failing to be congruent with your messages will eventually undermine your business, your profession, or your calling.

Challenges for Readers

1. What are your company's purpose and core values? What messages do you consciously send to the marketplace about yourself, your products and services, and your relationships with your customers?
2. What internal and external behaviors would reflect your core values and messages? In other words, how should you behave based on your espoused principles?
3. Do you live the promise? Are your company's behaviors aligned with your purpose and values? Ask your employees and customers these questions.
4. How could you change your company's and employees' behaviors in ways that would positively differentiate you from your competitors and symbolize your messages to the marketplace?
5. GAT did an outstanding job of behaving in ways that symbolized their understanding of and alignment with the goals and vision of NSCUS and its constituent four-year schools. Think about how you present yourself to your customers. Do you have similar opportunities for symbolic behavioral differentiation? For a moment, set aside your preconceptions about how you sell your products or services and imagine what would be possible if you were to behave during the selling process in ways that reflected your customer's purpose and values. What would that look like?

Endnotes

1. This case study is based on a real telecommunications company and a real contract competition in which we acted as consultants. However, we have changed the names and the key facts of the case to preserve confidentiality. The organizational and individual names used are entirely fictional and are not meant to suggest any real persons or companies. Likewise, the state system of higher education is fictional, as is the Northern State itself. Be that as it may, events like these did occur, and the symbolic behavioral differentiators we describe represent the types of strategies companies have actually used to win bids. The dialogue cited here is recalled from actual conversations with the key participants in the case.

2. Jonathan Fahey, "Love into Money," *Forbes* 169, no. 1 (January 7, 2002), p. 60.
3. Martin Jack Rosenblum, "Foreword," in Herbert Wagner, *Harley-Davidson Lore: 1903-1965 Origins Through Panhead* (San Francisco: Chronicle Books, 1999).
4. Jonathan Fahey, op cit., p. 65.
5. www.harley-davidson.com/EX/ANV/en/openroad tour.asp (March 8, 2002).
6. *2001 Harley-Davidson Annual Report.*
7. Lisa Miller and David France, "Sins of the Fathers," *Newsweek* (March 4, 2002), pp. 43–53.
8. Walter V. Robinson and Thomas Farragher, "Shanley's long record ignored," *The Boston Globe,* http://www.boston.com/globe/spotlight/abuse/stories/040902_shanley_record.htm (April 9, 2002).
9. Thomas Farragher, "Alleged victims detail torment," *The Boston Globe,* http://www.boston.com/globe/spotlight/abuse/stories/040902_victims.htm (April 9, 2002).

9

THE ENGINES THAT DRIVE BEHAVIORAL DIFFERENTIATION

Executives use phrases such as customer driven, customer focused, market oriented, and so forth to motivate their people to do a better job serving the customer. While the idea is sound, too often it is just "lip service" or talk rather than a major investment for improving all facets of the organization and its business culture.

—Art Weinstein and William C. Johnson, *Designing and Delivering Superior Customer Value*

What is important is not so much what we do—the specific people management techniques and practices—but why we do it—the underlying philosophy and view of people and the business that provides a foundation for the practices.

—Jeffrey Pfeffer and Robert I. Sutton, *The Knowing-Doing Gap*

Would Wal-Mart have become Wal-Mart without Sam Walton? Would Southwest Airlines have outperformed all the major airline companies without Herb Kelleher? Would Ritz-Carlton have won the Malcolm Baldrige National Quality Award twice without the culture Horst Schulze shaped when he said, "We are ladies and gentlemen serving ladies and gentlemen"? Would Harley-Davidson's share price have increased 15,000 percent since it went public if Harley had not found effective ways to sell the *experience* rather than

the product? Business behavior that truly differentiates a company from its rivals is, by definition, exceptional. Customers may experience exceptional behavior with *any* company from time to time, but companies are unlikely to sustain behavioral differentiation and create a significant competitive advantage for themselves unless some guiding forces drive their behavioral differences. Those guiding forces are leadership, culture, and process.

The most important of these driving forces is leadership. Without the will of the company's leaders, extraordinary behavior throughout an organization could not be sustained, even if it occasionally happened, because in the long run most people in the organization would tend to behave in ways that reflect the norm of human behavior. It's what they *normally* experience, so it's how they would *normally* behave. That vast hump in the middle of the bell curve (see Figure 3-1) exists because it is how most people in most businesses behave most of the time. Consistently behaving in extraordinary ways requires the vision, guidance, teaching, and modeling of leaders like Sam Walton, Herb Kelleher, George Zimmer, and Horst Schulze. What these leaders possess is not simply a commitment to treat customers extraordinarily but the determination to make it happen consistently and the will to see it through, even in the face of opposition and early failures. Southwest Airlines is a case in point. In its formative years, Herb Kelleher and his partners faced daunting opposition and nearly failed to get the new airline off the ground. It took courage and a fierce commitment to the vision for Kelleher to prevail. John Viney argues this point about successful leaders in *Drive: Leadership in Business and Beyond:* "There seems no question that leaders must have an unshakeable belief in the cause, or body, they represent. If they do not have faith, why should those who follow them have faith? Conviction alone does not a leader make, however, for a follower may be every bit as convinced of the justice of the cause as their leader. The distinguishing feature by which we may know a leader is courage."[1]

Leaders like Herb Kelleher and Sam Walton were extraordinary themselves, and they built extraordinary companies because they had the courage to ignore the standard, successful business models in their industries; the self-confidence to invest in their vision; and the determination to persist in the face of doubters, skeptics, and those who actively opposed them. Moreover, like Horst Schulze, they understood that behavior can be a key differentiator for their companies—and this truly sets them apart as business leaders. The standard MBA approach to business leadership is analytical and focuses on such things as product innovation, distribution channels, marketing, organizational structure, asset management, strategic and financial planning, risk analysis, and other analytical and managerial areas of expertise. Clearly, these are important, but we believe they miss the real point about getting and keeping customers. For the most part, these technical facets of business management constitute the "hardware" of a business. The products you produce, the distribution channels you use, the facilities you have, the resources you need—these are dictated to a large extent by the type of business you are in and by customers' expectations of anyone who sells your types of products or services.*

Of course, there is tremendous variability in how different companies deploy and manage their "hardware," but all companies are as constricted in their "hardware" as Dell, Compaq, Gateway, and IBM are constricted in the desktop hardware they manufacture or assemble. Ritz-Carlton is in the hospitality industry, for example. It rents hotel rooms to guests and provides them with other amenities, the nature of which is dictated in large part by guests' expectations. Ritz-Carlton may provide a more upscale hospitality experience than most other hotel providers, but they are nonetheless constricted in their choices of what they provide and how they provide it. As long as Ritz-Carlton remains in the hotel business, their guests will expect certain things when they stay at a Ritz-Carlton (a room, a bed, a telephone, a place to dine, somewhere to park the car, etc.), and Ritz-Carlton cannot deviate from those basic expectations without penalty. At one time, Harley-Davidson tried to expand its business through a line of recreational vehicles (RVs) called Holiday Rambler. Though the RVs they sold were a sound product line, they did not fit the Harley-Davidson culture. No one in the marketplace (and probably few in the company) accepted the concept. Holiday Rambler was a perennial under-performer in Harley-Davidson's lineup and did not fit in the product mix, so Harley divested the unit and sold it to Monaco Coach Company in 1996. The business adage that you should "stick to your knitting" derives from the realization that the "hardware" of business offers little flexibility. Market expectations limit your options.

Companies have considerably greater leverage with the "software" of their business—their people, policies, and processes, which manifest the company's values and culture. Horst Schulze instinctively understood that he

---

*For the most part, business schools focus on the hardware—the analytical, tangible, and cerebral parts of running a business. They don't do as well focusing on the soft side—the human, intangible, psychological, moral, and spiritual aspects of business, although most business schools now have a few courses in these areas. For this reason, MBAs and the management consultants or venture capitalists they often become are sometimes seen as being heartless and insensitive. The human side of an enterprise is considerably more complicated and difficult to manage than the hardware, which is probably why so many otherwise-good companies are unaware of the impact of their behavior on their business or seem incapable of leading employees to raise their behavioral bar, so to speak.

could gain the greatest leverage at Ritz-Carlton on the soft side of the enterprise: whom you hire and where you put them, what expectations you set, what responsibilities you give them and what degrees of freedom you allow, how you educate them and reinforce their education, what you reward and how you motivate people, and how you design both their work and their interactions with customers. Leaders who excel at building and sustaining behavioral differentiation invariably focus more of their time and attention on the soft side. Ram Charan and Geoffrey Colvin argue that many companies mistakenly cut the soft side during hard times: "We hope it's no longer necessary to argue that [people are] increasingly your company's only source of competitive advantage. Yet when times get tough, many companies ease up on recruiting, figuring a slow economy will drive more applicants their way, and they spend less on training as a way to raise profits quickly without doing immediate damage to the business. That's just dumb. People do become obsolete; they also grow."[2]

> Observed techniques are not the process of servicing the customer; they are the outcome of a process that has its origin in the commitment of the leader.
>
> —Betsy Sanders, *Fabled Service*

In Chapter 2, we discussed how the second law of thermodynamics applies to markets. The second law, which defines entropy, also applies to companies. In a closed system, there is a natural tendency toward increasing disorder unless energy is applied to impose order. Unless you expend energy to maintain your house, it will eventually become decrepit, and unless leaders in a company expend energy to sustain behavioral differentiation, their company's behaviors will eventually devolve toward the middle of the bell curve. A vast sameness pervades all industries. Most companies will tend to be uniform and essentially indistinguishable from each other except for those that are inspired by leaders whose vision and determination provide the energy that keeps the company operating at the positive, upper end of the bell curve (see Figure 3-1).

It would be a mistake, however, to assume that leadership alone will suffice. Leaders come and go. Moreover, leaders are not always visible, day-to-day, to the people in the field who interact with customers at various touch points. Their presence is often more symbolic than real, so leaders need the complementary forces of *culture* and *process* to sustain BD and ensure that it occurs in the majority of customer interactions. Culture is particularly important because it forms the basis for how most people in an organization behave most of the time. Culture is the map that shows people what the territory looks like, where things are, and how to get there. It establishes behavioral expectations and sets the boundaries one should not cross. Culture is the carrier of values, although there may be a difference between the espoused values of the culture and the values in action. In strong cultures, like that of Southwest Airlines, what the founding leader created is perpetuated through the collective behavior, values, and will of the employees who remain after the leader has gone. Whether Southwest Airlines will be able to sustain its BD without Herb Kelleher at the helm is a question we will address in Chapter 10.

The other driving force that helps leaders sustain BD is *process*, which includes the internally focused systems and processes for recruiting, educating, managing, and rewarding people, and the externally focused systems and processes for getting and keeping customers, communicating with them, serving their needs, and managing customer relationships. Processes are the workhorses of BD because they establish the behaviors that should occur during normal interactions with employees and customers. EMC's process for escalating customer problems up the chain of command if they are not resolved quickly is an example of a behaviorally differentiating process that was driven by leadership. When Ruettgers took over as CEO he centralized the management and dispatching functions of all service activities and decided to implement the rapid-escalation system. He and his team devised this process so they could differentiate themselves from their competitors and show their customers the kind of commitment they were making to protect customers' mission-critical information.

Together, leadership, culture, and process are the forces that drive behavioral differentiation. As Figure 9-1 illustrates, leaders provide the direction and energy that shapes the culture and the values of the organization. They also create or inspire the systems and processes that guide behavior day to day. The companies we have studied that exemplify BD have leaders (who may also be founders) who understand that how they treat their employees and how their company treats customers can give them a significant competitive advantage. These leaders create cultures that shape attitudes, values, beliefs, policies, and behaviors that result in extraordinary experiences for customers, and they build processes that institutionalize the exceptional. Throughout the rest of this chapter, we will explore these drivers of BD more fully. We will also examine the drivers of negatively differentiated behaviors in companies.

The Leadership Engine

While speaking at a conference on quality, Jan Carlzon, former CEO of Scandinavian Air System (SAS), told the story of a trip to London. He had a

Figure 9-1. The Engines that Drive BD. Leadership provides most of the power for behavioral differentiation in an organization.

reservation at a hotel where, by his estimate, he had stayed at least fifteen times. Yet when he checked in, the clerk acted as though it were his first visit. He asked Carlzon for his name, looked up the reservation in the hotel's computer, then asked Carlzon to write his name, address, telephone number, and other particulars on a lengthy form, just as he had fifteen previous times. "Imagine," Carlzon said, "if the manager gathered his employees in the morning and said, 'Today, Jan Carlzon is coming. He's been here fifteen times. I also remember he likes antique fairs.' So, when I arrive, the clerk asks for my name. I tell him and he says, 'Welcome, Mr. Carlzon. We are proud to have you here for the sixteenth time. Please sign this form that we already completed for you from past records. By the way, we put some brochures about antique fairs in your room because we know you are interested in them.'"

What Carlzon is suggesting is now commonplace at Ritz-Carlton, Four Seasons, and other, mostly upscale hotel chains that have implemented "customer intimacy" programs, but most hotels still do not "remember" guests from one visit to the next. We chose to open this section with a story about Jan Carlzon because he exemplifies the type of business leader who is likely to inspire BD. Before customer intimacy became a buzzword, he was transforming a failing business by instituting the kinds of attitudes and behaviors that would differentiate SAS behaviorally. Like many airlines that lost money in the late 70s and early 80s, SAS had a succession of poor years prior to 1981, when Carlzon became CEO. He took a number of radical measures to restore the airline to profitability: breaking down the silos between departments, removing large numbers of middle managers, and empowering the people on the front line to make decisions that improved flyers' experiences with SAS. But he also turned the concept of management on its head—literally, by reversing the normal top-down organization charts of the day, putting himself at the bottom of an inverted pyramid and the frontline customer service people at the top. In his view, management's principal function is to facilitate the efforts of those in contact with customers. They are the difference between the sublime and the mundane. If customers walk away saying, "That was an incredibly positive experience," they will do so because the people who served them at every touch point did an exceptional job.

"Thirty thousand passengers, a lot of them on business, fly SAS every day and come face to face with our people about five times a trip," said our President Jan Carlzon, "and that's a hundred fifty thousand encounters a day, moments of truth that can make or break us and I don't control a single one of them." So what did Carlzon do? He turned control over to the ticket agents, cabin attendants and others who really need it. "If a passenger has a problem," he said, "don't worry about protocol or a few pennies. Just fix it. And I will back you 100%." How many chief executives do you know who trust their frontline people enough to give them that kind of power? Can you imagine what that did for morale, and service? Within two years, Scandinavian Airlines was named Airline of the Year.

—Anders Bjork, Director, Southwest Area, SAS

Carlzon was one of the business leaders who emerged during the 1970s who instinctively understood that behavior is a powerful source of competitive advantage. He recognized that in highly competitive industries, where so much of what a business has to work with is commoditized, the company's behavior at every touch point can be a strong enough differentiator to cause customers to prefer doing business with SAS. He also understood that the airplane is not the ride. When customers think of your company, they don't think of the "hardware"; they think of the experience. What is memorable to them is not what they purchased; it's how they were treated. What customers experience at every touch point (or *moment of truth*, as Carlzon called them) is the basis of their impression of your company. It governs what they will tell others about you, it influences what they are willing to pay for your products or services, and it determines whether they will be back. Sam Walton understood this. So did Herb Kelleher. And George Zimmer, Horst Schulze, and Mike Ruettgers.

Our conclusion from studying the companies that exemplify BD is that they are led by business leaders who are themselves above the norm. Average business executives—the ones in the middle of the bell curve—are unlikely to inspire their employees to behave in ways that will behaviorally differentiate the company in the eyes of its customers. It seems to require that the leaders themselves behave exceptionally. Exceptional behavior begets exceptional behavior. Beyond what behaviorally differentiated leaders do, they appear to have the following perspectives on customers and on the companies they lead:

▲ They understand both the competitive power of behavior as well as its inescapability. They know that customers and employees will observe and evaluate your behavior no matter what you do. Further, they know that your behavior reflects your beliefs. No matter what you say, your behavior reveals the truth about how you feel, what you value, and how you prioritize. In short, BD leaders truly grasp that *you are how you behave and you behave how you are,* as we discussed in Chapter 3. Your behavior toward your employees *is* your character; your company's behavior toward customers *is* the mirror to your company's soul. Knowing this, the kinds of leaders who inspire BD attend to the moments of truth Carlzon spoke of and put the power to behave exceptionally in the hands of those who are most in contact with customers. We often say of people who are exceptionally good with customers that they have "good customer hands."

▲ They view behavior as an element of strategy. They understand that behavior is more than customer service and that it can be a rich source of competitive advantage. Typically, they are highly sensitive to their customers' expectations and normal experiences, and they are driven to differentiate themselves by providing a richer experience for their customers. They view the customer's experience, rather than product design or channel strategies, as the ultimate source of competitive advantage. They also understand that one of the best ways to compete in highly competitive markets (such as air travel) is not to compete directly with competitors but to raise customers' expectations of what the experience should be. By raising those expectations, they are raising the bar on the competition, and it may be one the competitors will find difficult to clear.

▲ They understand that companies do not have attitudes and beliefs about customers, individual employees do. So they place an extraordinary amount of emphasis on screening and hiring of new employees. Typically, they care less about a person's technical qualifications and experience than they do about the person's attitudes and demeanor. Skills can be learned; character and disposition can't.

▲ They know the difference between espoused values and values in practice, and they know that their behavior must be aligned with their values. So they work hard to ensure that the rules of behavior throughout the company are congruent with their values and the messages they send to employees and customers. Gaining this alignment may demand some hard choices, and exceptional leaders are not reluctant to fire executives who do not walk the talk.

▲ They know that their own behavior is highly symbolic and that employees and customers will consider their behavior to be the most accurate barometer of the alignment between the espoused values of the company and the values in practice. So these leaders tend to be models of the differentiating behaviors they want the company to manifest. George Zimmer of Men's Wearhouse insists that every corporate executive who visits a store serve customers. Herb Kelleher, who felt that flying should be fun, was renowned for his antics. Jeffrey Bleustein of Harley-Davidson rides a Harley and attends rallies wearing his leathers. Ritz-Carlton executives who visit a hotel property assume personal responsibility for resolving guest problems if they are the ones who become aware of the problems.

▲ They view managing the culture as their most important job responsibility. Herb Kelleher said, "Culture is your number one priority." As the champions of a culture that is capable of BD, these leaders typically devote a lot of time to teaching, coaching, and mentoring. It's not unusual to find them in the classroom at their corporate university or training facility. Like Sam Walton, they spend a lot of time in their company's facilities, talking to employees, answering questions, and spreading the word. They are evangelists for the values and beliefs about customers that lead to exceptional behavior.

▲ They understand that BD cannot be delegated. They may have a customer service director, but they know that to achieve consistent and sustainable BD, it must reach far and wide in the company. They cannot delegate the responsibility to someone else and expect that it will be taken care of. Behavioral differentiation is not like a property lease, a product design, or a marketing study. It cannot be handed off to others. BD begins at the top.

▲ They identify with their customers and employees and remain close to the experiences of both groups. The leaders who really excel at BD are driven by deep convictions about serving customers in ways they will find exceptional. Leaders like Jan Carlzon, Mike Ruettgers, George Zimmer, and Horst Schulze do not hide away in ivory towers. Rather, they are what Robert Greenleaf referred to as *servant leaders*.[3] They know the real action is at the interface between customers and front-line employees, so that's where they like to be. Mike Ruettgers of EMC said, "I want to know within eight hours of any customer problem that has not been resolved." At the Men's Wearhouse Web site, there is an "Ask George" feature with the following invitation: "Here's an opportunity to ask George Zimmer questions about most anything—retail business strategies, the Men's Wearhouse way of doing business, the challenges of being a servant leader, the Oakland A's, or political issues that impact individuals & businesses every day. You can find out his opinion about issues of interest to you or ask him questions about his personal philosophy."[4] Staying close to customers and employees is more than an article of faith for these leaders; it is a way of being that satisfies their personal needs.

▲ Finally, these leaders know that BD begins internally. When you create an exceptional environment, your employees will be more inspired to treat customers in exceptional ways, and you have a virtuous circle. What you sow inside the company, you will reap with your customers. It's not surprising, then, that companies that excel at BD are often cited in *Fortune's* annual survey of the best places to work. BD requires, first, an investment in the people who can make it happen, as Stanford University professor Jeffrey Pfeffer notes: "If you want a return on your investment in people, the first thing you've got to do is invest in them. You hire them and train them and develop them—you do all the things that will cause them to have the skills and abilities and motivation to do an effective job. You can't sit there and say, 'Gosh, I don't know why my people aren't doing a good job,' when you haven't put anything into it. Nothing in, nothing out."[5]

Employees who perceive that their company treats them exceptionally are more likely to treat customers exceptionally. This is true because of the nature of their social contract. When companies create environments where employees are listened to, feel valued and respected, feel appropriately rewarded for their contributions, and have a sense of ownership in the outcomes, they are more likely to remain loyal and committed and to behave in ways that reciprocate the value they feel coming from the institution. James Goodnight, founder of SAS Institute, a North Carolina-based software developer, said it more simply: "If you do right by people, they'll do right by you." It would be unreasonable to expect BD from employees whose self-talk includes, "It's just a job," "This is how I pay the rent," "I hate this place," or worse. Knowing this, exceptional leaders try to create environments where employees feel listened to, feel valued, have a sense of ownership, and believe that the company is doing some exceptional things for them.

St. Louis brokerage firm Edward Jones, for example, sends each of its professionals through 132 hours of training every year. Edward Jones was ranked number one on the 2002 *Fortune* list of "Best Companies to Work for."[6] That level of investment in professional development is not unusual among companies that excel at BD. The Container Store, number two on *Fortune's* 2002 list, has 162 professional training hours annually and ranks very high on "respect" (94% of employees surveyed feel they make a difference).[7] SAS Institute has a free onsite medical clinic. The Finova Group in Phoenix sponsors free on-site massages. Timberland provides pet insurance, and Autodesk, in San Rafael, California, allows dogs at work. Qualcomm has three fitness centers, tennis courts, a swimming pool, and a sand volleyball court. NIKE has an extensive running track around its Oregon campus and encourages employees to use its athletic facilities anytime.

Other perks among companies cited as "best places to work" include executive coaching and career counseling, mentoring programs, tuition reimbursement, paid and unpaid educational sabbaticals, work-life balance programs (such as flextime and telecommuting), paid community volunteering, onsite day care, contributions to education funds for newborns or adopted children, free trips, onsite manicures and haircuts, relaxed dress codes, college scholarships, free breakfast or snacks, free eye exams, personal computer discount purchase programs, company-owned vacation campsites, flu shots, wellness centers, health screenings or exams, stock options, bonus plans, 401k matching, profit sharing programs, earned family leave, and so on. AMGEN has an annual chili cook-off, which, as chili lovers, we think is especially appealing.[8]

In the late 1990s, at the height of what McKinsey & Company described as the War for Talent, a number of companies were compelled to offer more perks (including cars and signing bonuses) to attract and retain talented employees. However, Southwest Airlines has been able to attract and retain talented people for decades while paying them less than they could earn at rival airlines (for more on how they have done this, see Chapter 10). Exceptional companies do not use perks as bribes. Instead, they create environments that employees will find compelling, rewarding, and motivating. After all, if you behave like a mercenary and create a mercenary culture, you will have mercenaries working for you. If you treat employees generously and fairly, they will be more inclined to treat your customers very well. The perks we cited above may no longer exist in the form they did several years ago—or they may be more generous. Perks come and go as the economy permits and as employees' needs and desires change. What's important is the underlying philosophy of the company toward its employees and its customers, and that philosophy is shaped largely by the company's leaders and their observable behaviors, not just their pep talks. Enlightened leaders behave in ways that behaviorally differentiate them from other business leaders. Through their values, decisions, and actions, they shape the culture and create the processes that can result in BD.

> I believed then, and still do, that people are an organization's only sustainable competitive advantage. The leader should mind the interests of all stakeholders, of course, but he or she should also be an outspoken advocate for employees, making sure they are front and center in an organization.
> —Rich Teerlink, retired CEO, Harley-Davidson

The Culture Engine

Besides leadership, the other forces in companies that sustain behavior differentiation are culture and processes. Culture has a profound influence in shaping people's behavior, and its influence is ubiquitous. Leaders certainly shape culture, but the culture influences employees' decisions and treatment of customers even when the company's leaders are absent, which is what makes culture a powerful driver of BD. The effects of culture begin even before a new employee joins a company. In learning what they can about their potential employer, candidates discover what the company is about, what it prides itself on, and what it would mean for them personally to join the company. What they discover may be incomplete or even misleading, but the acculturation process begins with everything they learn about their potential employer and the decisions they make about how to present themselves during their employment interviews. Such simple issues as how to dress, how to talk about their education and experience, and what kind of impression to make are elements of acculturation because they shape candidates' behavior.

Once hired, new employees continue their acculturation process but now in a more committed way. They are no longer looking for the job, they are now employed, and this new phase of their life has begun. Like immigrants, sorority pledges, and army recruits, they now have to transform themselves from "who I was before I joined this company" to "who I am now." Acculturation, which the dictionary defines as "cultural modification of an individual, group, or people by adapting to or borrowing traits from another culture,"[9] is accomplished through the screening and hiring process; new-hire orientation sessions; policies and procedures manuals; introductory training programs; goal setting with managers; company newsletters and brochures; performance feedback; coaching and mentoring; and, of course, the powerful and informal channels of hall talk, gossip, and advice from peers.

Through these vehicles, new hires learn what the company says is important and what's *really* important, how things are supposed to work and how they *really* work, what gets rewarded and what doesn't, who is important and who's not, how to get what you need, how to do the right things, how to prioritize work, how to make the right decisions, and how to stay out of trouble. What they learn, beyond these simple survival skills, is how to navigate the company's emotional and spiritual landscape—how they should *feel* about the company itself and its products or services, what to *feel* about management and fellow employees, and how to *feel* about customers and various interactions with them. This is the heart and soul of the organization, and if a company is to behaviorally differentiate itself, then this emotional core must reflect the values, attitudes, and beliefs of exceptional behavior toward customers and exceptional treatment of employees and shareholders. The values underlying the culture are the key. In *Douglas MacGregor, Revisited: Managing the Human Side of Enterprise,* Gary Heil, Warren Bennis, and Deborah C. Stephens observe how values drive behavior: "A company's values are its code of ethics, its behavioral framework. Taken together, they form a statement of what the organization collectively deems important or valuable—what it stands for. When understood and adopted by employees, values provide a context for action. Values can provide a sense of order without rules, reduce ambiguity without a detailed plan, and bring focus and coherence while allowing individual expression and self-determination."[10]

The values that people in a company share form the foundation of the company's culture, which is why companies like Ritz-Carlton, Volvo, EMC, Men's Wearhouse, Hall Kinion, Heidrick & Struggles, and Southwest Airlines are so particular about the people they hire. Values persist over time and survive the comings and goings of individual employees. Consequently, company cultures tend to be self-perpetuating. John Kotter and James Heskett made this point in their 1992 study of the relationship between corporate cultures and performance: "Culture represents an interdependent set of values and ways of behaving that are common in a community and that tend to perpetuate themselves, sometimes over periods of time. This continuity is the product of a variety of social forces that are frequently subtle, bordering on invisible, through which people learn a group's norms and values, are rewarded when they accept them, and are ostracized when they do not."[11] Among the forces that build and perpetuate culture are the following:

▲ The image a company projects. The public image built through advertising, packaging, promotions, and other forms of market communication conveys how the company wants to be viewed in the marketplace. Invariably, these forms of marketing reveal elements of the company's culture, in particular its espoused values. If they are consistent over time, they help perpetuate the culture, and they teach employees and customers what the company stands for and what they can expect from it. George Zimmer's pledge in his advertisements—"You'll like the way you look. I guarantee it."—is a simple and effective message that communicates one of the central tenets of the Men's Wearhouse culture.

▲ Internal communications. Mission statements, operating principles, statements of values, newsletters, and other forms of internal communication reflect the culture's values and perpetuate the behavioral norms. If these communications are consistent with the way managers and employees *actually* behave, then these devices help perpetuate the culture. After a while, they may have an almost subliminal effect on employees, but the cultural messages are nonetheless reinforced. Exemplars of BD, like Ritz-Carlton, are often not so subtle. The Ritz-Carlton "Credo Card," which every employee is expected to carry, is a very explicit, continuous message about the company's culture and its behavioral expectations.

▲ What the leaders of the company communicate throughout the organization, as well as their external communications to Wall Street, customers, civic or special interest groups, and the government. What leaders emphasize in their messages is crucial, as is the alignment between their words and actions. Almost invariably, the companies that create positive behavioral differentiation have vocal leaders whose messages reinforce the importance of consistent, exceptional treatment of customers. Like Horst Schulze, Herb Kelleher, and George Zimmer, they also tend to be vocal about exceptional treatment of employees.

▲ Management's priorities as evidenced by what they attend to and what they ignore; what decisions they make; where they allocate resources; where they assign their high performers and high-potential young leaders; and how managers use their time. This last point is especially important because it reflects managers' values and priorities in action.

▲ The job qualifications and hiring criteria the company publishes, which include some cultural expectations and help the broad pool of job candidates self-select for that culture. The screening process that companies like Ritz-Carlton and Volvo use to select new employees further narrows the field of candidates to those who are likely fits with the culture. It's a form of natural selection and it tends to perpetuate the culture by ensuring that new hires are already temperamentally suited for the company. In Chapters 10 and 11 we will continue to explore how hiring processes are especially important to companies that excel at BD.

▲ Successes and failures in day-to-day interactions with customers, which influence how people behave in the future; the successes or failures of internal initiatives; what managers reward and what they punish. People in organizations are savvy at noticing what works and what doesn't. They take their cues from the events around them and modify their behavior accordingly. Particularly important is the system of *actual* rewards and penalties (as opposed to what the company says it rewards and discourages). Awards given to successful members of the company are especially powerful in reinforcing the culture's values and behavioral expectations.

▲ The working values of the organization—what people hold dear, what really matters, the *shadow* values underlying decisions. The working values are the values in practice, rather than the espoused values. A company may communicate that it holds certain values (such as, "We care most about our customers"), but the company's culture is based on the actual values in practice (such as, "Cut corners where you can"). People believe the values they see in practice and will become cynical if these deviate too far from the company's espoused values. If these are aligned, however, and if the system of rewards and penalties reinforces the values in action, then people will behave in ways that reflect the values.

The best starting point is recognizing that values count. Here, we're talking about the personal values of people in leadership positions. Leaders have to live the right message, day in and day out. When an organization picks up signals of ambivalence—or, worse, a gap between asserted belief and behavior—there is little chance of sustainable progress. Second, values have to be shared values, across the leadership of the organization. Values must be congruent to get the leaders over the inevitable bumps in the road. They must also be congruent to ensure that the efforts of employees won't be tugged and pulled in contradictory directions.
—Rich Teerlink and Lee Ozley, *More Than a Motorcycle: The Leadership Journey of Harley-Davidson*

▲ Environmental stresses on the organization. Strong growth or acquisitions will stress a company in one way, while downsizing will stress it in another. These stresses will influence values, decisions, and behavior. Environmental stresses can include severe market pressure, governmental action (such as the indictment against Arthur Andersen), or negative publicity (of the kind Exxon experienced after the *Exxon Valdez* oil spill in Alaska). In times of stress, the values underlying the culture may be sorely tested and abandoned, but often employees band together and rely on the culture to see them through hard times. After Arthur Andersen was indicted by the Justice Department, for instance, large groups of Andersen employees demonstrated publicly and proclaimed their pride in and loyalty toward the firm. As we write this, the outcome is uncertain, but if Andersen survives, this environmental stress could strengthen the culture rather than weaken it.

▲ Internal stresses on the organization, which could include employee morale, the quality of the work (Is it interesting and challenging or dull and bureaucratic?), belief in the work product (Are we doing something useful and valuable?), and the relationship between management and employees. Companies always have internal stresses, but when these are positive, challenging, and rewarding they reinforce and perpetuate the culture; when the stresses lead managers or employees to behave in ways that violate the core values or create conflict between groups, then the culture will begin to disintegrate.

▲ Corporate education and training. New hire orientation programs explicitly teach the cultural norms and values—"the way we do things around here." However, if they are designed and delivered thoughtfully, all education and training programs should reinforce the culture. The same could be said of department meetings, on-the-job tutorials, peer and manager coaching, and other forms of organizational learning.

▲ Coaching. Coaching and mentoring of employees reinforce the company's norms and raise the behavioral standards. Firms like McKinsey & Company and General Electric have an extraordinary dedication to coaching and mentoring. In McKinsey, a sizeable part of every partner's job is coaching and mentoring associates. Their coaching may include some technical aspects of management consulting, such as how to analyze a client's strategic alternatives, but one of the primary functions of this coaching is acculturation—how to be a good firm member, how to think correctly about client service, how to behave in a "one firm" environment. Companies that exemplify BD often have strong coaching and mentoring programs and practices.

▲ The company's systems, procedures, and processes. Whether or not companies publish their policies and procedures, there are always standard ways of doing things. These systems or processes define what is right and what is wrong. They establish the behavioral norms and thus reflect the company's values in action. As we noted in our discussion of operational BD, one of the best ways to institutionalize exceptional behaviors is to codify them in a process. So companies that behaviorally differentiate themselves usually do not leave very much to chance. They establish processes for managing customer interactions, sometimes, as we saw with Ritz-Carlton, to the point of identifying what employees should say. Scripting customer interactions may seem over-controlling, but if you want to create consistent and sustained BD you have to find ways to guide behavior at hundreds or thousands of touch points every day. These kinds of processes are among the most powerful ways in which companies perpetuate the culture.

▲ Finally, the mythos of the culture as told in stories and legends. The stories that get told at awards ceremonies, holiday parties, retreats, picnics, team dinners, divisional meetings, and other social gatherings of company people are powerful tools for building and sustaining the culture. Those stories often revolve around the culture's heroes and their good works and exploits—or, conversely, around the misfits or unfortunates who screwed up and are now gone. For the culture to perpetuate itself, it needs both heroes and goats. The stories that get told, in large public gatherings or around the water cooler, reinforce the culture's values and behavioral norms and serve both an inspirational and a cautionary purpose.

Our list of the forces that build and perpetuate a company's culture excludes some important elements, such as the company's physical environment (compare the facilities at Ritz-Carlton with those at Motel 6), the type of work the company does (contrast Disney with CH2M Hill, whose services include hazardous waste management), and the demographics of the average employee (the youthful Apple Computer vs. the more traditional State Farm Insurance). We have excluded these and other forces that influence culture not because they aren't important but because we wanted to focus on the forces leaders can influence in the short term. On a daily basis, a company's leaders can influence the image the company projects, the internal communications, what they communicate throughout the organization, their own priorities, the screening of new candidates, the system of rewards and penalties, and the organization's working values. They may not be able to control the environmental stresses on the organization, but they can control how the organization responds to those stresses, and they can manage the organization's internal stresses. They can take an active role in corporate education and training (as Jack Welch did at GE and Andy Grove did at Intel), and they can devote a significant portion of their time to coaching and mentoring. They can also design or influence the systems and processes that establish how things are done in the company. Finally, they should be among the company's most accomplished storytellers. One of a leader's primary functions is to be the culture's caretaker, the maker of myths and legends.

To one degree or another, the culture of a company is an extension of its leadership. The Herb Kellehers and Sam Waltons of the business world cannot be everywhere at once, so they shape their company's culture as a way to influence employee behaviors towards each other and toward customers at every touch point. Culture is the means through which leaders realize their vision, and in companies that excel at BD that vision invariably focuses on how people are treated, within the company and without. In their study of corporate culture and business performance, John Kotter and James Heskett discovered that the most successful companies were "driven by a value system that stresses meeting the legitimate needs of all the key constituencies whose cooperation is essential to business performance—especially customers, employees, and stockholders."[12] Leaders drive these values through their words and actions, their priorities and decisions, and through the cultures they create. If those cultures are powerful enough, they will shape behavior through the far-flung regions of a company's empire and will survive even when the leaders who created them are gone. As Mike Ruettgers, former CEO of EMC Corporation, observed: "High-performance organizations are not products of high-performance individuals. They are products of high-performance cultures. Why? Individuals come and go, but cultures pervade an organization and endure."[13]

The Process Engine

The real, tactical workhorses of BD are the policies, systems, and processes companies create to manage their interactions with customers at every touch point. EMC's process for escalating customer problems to the CEO if they are not resolved within 8 hours is one example of a policy that has a positive behavioral effect on customers. EMC's automatic monitoring of customer equipment, which enables them to identify and resolve potential equipment failures before customers become aware of them, is a system feature that customers perceive as a positively differentiated behavior on EMC's part. Ritz-Carlton's policy that all employees are responsible for resolving guest complaints—and have the spending authority to do so—is a management decision that can have a profound effect on how guests experience their stay at Ritz-Carlton.

Contrast these examples with a distributor's decision to keep inventory stocks low in order to save money. When customers need parts that are not in stock, those parts have to be ordered and may not arrive for days, even weeks. The distributor's business decision, which benefits the distributor by cutting its costs, has the collateral effect of frustrating customers who cannot operate their machinery without the replacement part. Customers experience this distributor's policy as a behavior—a negatively differentiated one if they don't experience the same delays when buying parts from other distributors. Consider the bank that proclaims its friendliness toward customers but has an elaborate automated answering system whenever a customer calls. "We're your friendly neighborhood bank," their TV spots assure. "We're here to help you with all your banking needs. Come see the friendly people at. . . ." Yet customers cannot reach a human being by telephone, and when they visit the bank they don't experience the people working there as any friendlier or more helpful than anyone else in other banks. The automated telephone answering system, in theory, should be a process that helps customers find the answers to their most common questions and direct them to the departments that can serve them. In practice, these systems and processes tend to negatively differentiate because they seem as cold and distant as, in fact, they are.

It would be fair to say that modern business is based on systems and processes that exist for a variety of reasons: to standardize and simplify work flows, to save time and money, to ensure compliance with policies, to improve interactions and coordination among divisions, to reduce cycle times, to facilitate communication, to comply with reporting and other requirements, to assure quality, to meet schedules, to ensure safety, and so on. Companies focus on these largely internal processes for good reason: They could not manage their operations efficiently and effectively if they did not have such processes in place. However, the danger is designing processes that benefit the company at a behavioral price to the customer. Cost-control or cost-cutting processes, for instance, frequently have an unintended negative consequence in terms of how customers experience the company or its products and services. Companies would be wiser to design systems and processes that achieve their efficiency goals while also having a positive effect on customers. Of course, in the real world trade-offs must be made. Too often, however, as business leaders cut costs to make their short-term numbers they sacrifice the behavioral advantages they might have had. In Sam Walton's days, for instance, Wal-Mart employees were consistent in following Sam's 10-foot rule (if you come within 10 feet of a customer, smile and offer to help). Now, a decade after Walton's death, the company is reducing the number of employees on the floor, and it's rare to shop at Wal-Mart these days and see an employee following the 10-foot rule. They are too busy. Wal-Mart's cost-cutting measures are negatively affecting a process that was once a behavioral differentiator for the giant retailer.

Too often, processes exist to satisfy management's need to run the business efficiently rather than to serve customers. For example, processes are designed to control employees, reduce employee theft, limit their decision-making authority, increase management oversight, or protect the business from unscrupulous customers. Are these processes necessary? In some businesses, they might be, to one degree or another, but they have a deleterious effect on employees and customers and often result in negative BD. Some retailers, for instance, have a policy prohibiting employees from returning items they have purchased to stores other than the one at which they work. Although this no doubt discourages pilfering, it also creates an atmosphere of distrust that reduces employee loyalty and increases turnover. In contrast, Men's Wearhouse has a policy of forgiving employees who have been caught pilfering and working with them to become better employees. The result? Men's Wearhouse has one of the lowest turnover rates in its industry, and customers returning to their stores are likely to encounter the same people who waited on them last time, which increases familiarity and builds customer loyalty. In the same vein, some retailers have a policy that prohibits customers from returning items for a refund, only for an exchange. This protects the company but customers often end up with something less than desired and resent it. The company's policy is basically, "Once we get your money, there's no way you'll get it back, even if it means losing you as a customer." In the long run, this negative behavioral differentiator is not worth the money it saves, but business leaders who are hell bent on protecting their tangible assets don't see that, and they wind up losing their most precious asset: those customers who won't return.

Smart companies create processes that enhance customers' experiences and motivate and empower employees. Often, these processes emerge from employees' solutions to problems they encounter or to the individual best practices they develop over time. Greg Elkins, formerly a sales manager for Gillette, offers an example:

> I was a district sales manager with Gillette in Philadelphia. I had one key account manager named Jay Overcash whose big account was Rite Aid Drug Stores. Our buyer at Rite Aid was Ed Kane. He was one of several buyers who were competing for ad space in Rite Aid's advertising circulars. These buyers had to present their recommendations to a buying committee, and the committee would choose which items would be promoted in upcoming ads. Jay's goal was to convince Ed Kane to recommend Gillette products.
>
> We found that our presentations to our buyer were not having the same impact with the committee as they did with the buyer. In other words, we were doing a good job of convincing Ed Kane, but he wasn't

conveying the same message, at least in a compelling way, to the committee, and our products weren't being selected as much as we wished. Jay and I decided to brainstorm what we could do to improve the transfer of information to the buying committee. We eventually came up with what we called a "committee board." The committee board was a poster with a six-to-eight page representation of our presentation to our buyer. These pages addressed Rite Aid's concerns and showed why the buying committee should choose Gillette products for promotion rather than our competitors' products. The first time we used this with our buyer, he was very impressed. He liked the idea and used the committee board as his presentation to the buying committee. He later told us that the presentation was very well received and that we gained the ad space we wanted.

We used this approach with all future presentations to the buyer. After two or three of these committee board presentations to Ed Kane, he started expecting them from us, and we were happy to comply. Needless to say, Rite Aid became one of Gillette's best strategic customers, and we turned the committee board concept into a standard way of helping buyers for other companies present recommendations to their advertising committees. From that point on, our process was to create the presentations our buyers needed to sell Gillette products inside their companies. We were successful because we did something our competitors didn't do that made the buyer's job easier. As far as I know, our competitors never caught on to what we were doing. They just knew Gillette was getting more ad space than they were.[14]

What makes this story interesting is the evolution of the concept from the result of brainstorming to solve a problem (How can we help our buyer be more successful at presenting our products to the buying committee?), to an individual best practice, to a process for working with all buyers. Further, like many processes that behaviorally differentiate, it served both an internal need (getting more ad space in Rite Aid's advertising circulars) and an external need (making the buyer's job easier and helping him be more effective in his presentations). The process added value to the customer and was something Gillette's competitors did not do; thus, it was a positive differentiator for them. The buyer experienced the "committee boards" as a behavior on the part of the salesman. If we could ask the buyer, he might say, "This is something Jay Overcash does for me that no one else does. He goes the extra mile." Remember that what to you is a *policy, best practice,* or *process,* your customers experience as your *behavior.* Furthermore, although individuals like Jay Overcash are doing the behaving, customers tend to attribute the behavior to the company. "This is what happens when I work with Gillette," the buyer will usually say. Buyers will individualize the behavior only when it deviates from the norm: "I don't generally receive this kind of treatment unless I'm working with Jay Overcash. Why don't all of your people do it this way?" Consequently, it's important to raise the behavioral bar throughout your company and to share behavioral differentiators as they are discovered. Individual best practices *should* become behavioral differentiators that *everyone* in your company does routinely. Then you can ensure that customers will see the positive behaviors as a characteristic of working with your company rather than as a pleasant anomaly they experience only when working with certain of your people. This is why processes can be powerful drivers of BD.

The Gillette story illustrates a *bottom-up* process in which an individual salesperson creates a behavioral differentiator at a particular touch point. BD is also driven by top-down processes in which leaders institute a process that behaviorally differentiates the company. One of the finest examples of this is Jack Welch at General Electric. Although much has been written about Welch and the Work-Outs he instituted, the story bears repeating as viewed through the BD lens. Welch originated Work-Outs as an internal process in the late 1980s. He was then focused on how to make each of GE's operating companies #1 or #2 in their industries. He accomplished that goal partly by divesting the units that would never be major players in their industries and in part by improving the units that remained. His watchwords for the business were "speed, simplicity, and self-confidence," and he felt that for the businesses to be more agile, they needed to have more candor and open communication. Many of the best ideas came from the front-line people who worked closest with customers, and Welch felt that these people were often stymied by middle managers who controlled the flow of ideas and slowed innovation.

So the original concept of Work-Out was to get the right people together, especially the front-line workers who experienced the problems daily; identify and sort through the problems; generate solutions; and then present the solutions to managers in a way that brought more speed and agility to problem resolution. At the end of each Work-Out was a "town meeting" in which the teams, their managers, and their managers' managers gathered to hear the teams' findings, and the managers were required to decide right then and there whether to implement the recommendations. Solutions could not get stuck in committees or lost in the stacks of paper on a manager's desk. Moreover, front-line workers were more motivated because they were listened to, their expertise was respected, and they bought into the solutions because they helped create them. That this process survived internally at GE for decades is a testament to the force of Welch's personality and to the fact that the process worked. It helped create the kind of boundaryless and agile organization

Welch envisioned, and GE's performance during the late 1980s and 1990s speaks for itself.

Lynette Demarest, a long-time GE manager and now an independent consultant, became involved in Work-Outs in 1989. She recalls how Welch explained the rationale for the process: "I'm going to give employees ownership for the way the work is done," she remembers him saying. "I'm going to get employee commitment based on their involvement. The people who can tell us how to do it better are the people who do it, not their bosses." In Work-Outs, everyone was equal. Anybody could be the champion. It didn't have to be the expert in the room or the supervisor. That equalitarianism helped strip away the boundaries in the hierarchy and between business units and make everyone part of the solution. At the time Welch introduced Work-Outs, he was also removing layers of middle management, which he felt were superfluous and were slowing down innovation and decision making. According to Demarest, "The first Work-Outs were geared at getting rid of the work of middle managers that no longer had to be done. Jack felt that you couldn't direct people to be engaged; you had to have a way for them to do it."[15] So he invented a process that gave employees a voice and thrust them into the heart of business problem solving on the front line. Do employees in other companies experience this degree of participation in the important business of solving front-line problems? Probably so, but perhaps not as consistently or to the extent GE achieved with this innovative process. Work-Outs behaviorally differentiated GE internally by making employee involvement systematic and raising the bar on employee engagement in problem solving and responsibility for finding and implementing solutions.

It wasn't long before GE applied the Work-Out process to customers. According to Demarest, they felt the process would help them understand their customer's needs better, and if they better understood the needs, they could develop better ways to meet those needs. Beyond this pragmatic rationale for customer Work-Outs was the sense that joint problem solving using this process would create partnerships with customers. Instead of "us" and "them," it would be "us together figuring out your needs."[16] The key early step in a customer Work-Out was determining the key issues or problems, painting a picture of what was working and what wasn't, and then getting the right people in both companies to participate. Who were the right people? They were those who were most impacted by the problem as well as those who could most impact it. GE would send a notice to those individuals, identify the issues, and assign them to teams to work on particular issues. The notice would include some questions, which were intended as thought starts, and a request for participants to come back with some initial ideas.

The Work-Out itself would usually begin with an offsite dinner with the primary goals of teeing up the problems being examined and breaking the ice.

Although relationship improvement was generally a secondary goal, it was important to break down the barriers. Some Work-Outs began with very hard feelings. It was "my company" versus "your company," and the leaders of the process knew that they wouldn't succeed until the dialogue got down to "John" and "Jane." The next day, a senior person would set the expectations and review the process. Then the group (consisting of 20 to 25 people from each company) would break into facilitator-led teams to clarify issues; analyze the problem; brainstorm solutions; examine the alternatives; and strive to reach consensus, which they defined as "something everyone could agree to support and not to sabotage once they left the group."

After the teams developed their recommendations, they would meet with the managers who were going to hear those recommendations so the managers were not surprised later. This departure from internal GE procedure helped make the process palatable to leaders who were not immersed in the GE culture and used to the mantra of "speed, simplicity, and self-confidence." At the end, the teams would present their recommendations to a GE-customer panel, and the panel would respond. If they agreed on a course of action, someone would sign up to be the change champion, and this person would be responsible for ensuring that the action plans were implemented. The follow-ups to the Work-Outs were as important as the Work-Out process itself. The point was to drive change, and GE went to extraordinary lengths to ensure that the champions fulfilled their roles, resolved problems, and communicated effectively with both organizations. According to Demarest, the dialogues with customers after a joint Work-Out were very different. "Our understanding of the customer's needs and issues was very different," she said. "And people from each company could literally pick up the phone and discuss issues with each other before problems escalated."[17] Other benefits of customer Work-Outs included:

▲ Developing a better understanding of each company's goals, expectations, and needs.
▲ Discovering ways to make it easier, more efficient, and more cost effective to work together.
▲ Improving the working relationship between the two companies and developing networks of professionals on both sides who could rely on each other for problem solving and issue resolution.
▲ Sharing and leveraging the best practices of both companies.
▲ Promoting diversity and cross-functional teamwork.
▲ Developing action plans that resolved real issues and problems, yielding lower costs, higher productivity, or other measurable business results.
▲ Creating a forum in which both companies could capitalize on joint business opportunities.

By now, GE's Work-Out process has been described in a number of books and emulated in one form or another by many companies, so how does it behaviorally differentiate GE? We need to remember that Work-Outs are now more than 15 years old—ancient by contemporary business innovation standards. When Jack Welch devised Work-Outs, very few companies were using such processes or using them with the rigor that GE was using them. Throughout the 1980s and 1990s, GE was the pioneer in new business processes. The company either invented or adopted and used a number of new and innovative processes during these two decades, including best practices, process mapping, benchmarking, Work-Outs, and Six Sigma (which GE learned from Motorola). Leading the pack and continually reinventing how business is done is a strong form of BD. Moreover, one of GE's strongest behavioral differentiators has been the fact that it shared its best practices and processes with customers to help them improve their businesses. As much as the business processes themselves, GE's willingness to reach out to customers in ways they hadn't seen before has been a powerful behavioral differentiator for the company that Thomas Edison built and Jack Welch led through some of its finest years.

The *leadership* in a company is the primary driver of BD. Leaders who understand the potential for BD and use it as a tool to create competitive advantage provide the energy and vision for BD in the company. Without that sustaining drive and direction, companies are unlikely to move to or remain in the upper 16 percent (one standard deviation above the mean) of the behavioral bell curve shown in Figure 3-1. Leadership is the spark that ignites the fire; it is the wind that feeds the flames. However, leaders cannot do it alone. The larger the company, the more they need *culture* and *process* to institutionalize and preserve the kinds of behaviors that will differentiate the company in the eyes of its customers.

The Drivers of Negative Behavioral Differentiation

As we have studied BD, it has become apparent to us that companies can also fall prey to some negative behavioral drivers. These are institutional attitudes and values, usually propagated and reflected by the companies' leaders, that result in behaviors toward customers that negatively differentiate the company from its competitors. The negative drivers we will describe are institutional narcissism, greed, insularity, schizophrenia, and scapegoating. The companies that manifest these syndromes have alienated customers, lost opportunities, and often been pilloried in the press.

Institutional Narcissism

The standard diagnostic manual for psychiatry is the *Diagnostic and Statistical Manual of Mental Disorders, Fourth Edition* (DSM-IV™). According to the DSM-IV, individuals with the narcissistic personality disorder "have a grandiose sense of self-importance," "believe they are superior, special, or unique and expect others to recognize them as such," and "generally have a lack of empathy and have difficulty recognizing the desires, subjective experiences, and feelings of others."[18] The term narcissism derives from Greek mythology and the story of Narcissus, the beautiful youth who fell in love with his own reflection in a pool of water and was turned into the narcissus flower. People who are narcissistic have a strong sense of entitlement (the world owes them much), believe that others are envious of them, and are arrogant or haughty. People who are said to be a "legend in their own mind" are likely to be narcissistic to some degree. Much of their speech is self-referential ("This is what *I* think." "If you were like *me*. . . ." "Here's how *I* see it."), they relate to the world mostly as it revolves around them, and they are the heroes of their own stories. To hear them tell it, they are always responsible for successes and never to blame for failures. Healthy, successful people may also be self-confident, proud of their accomplishments, and willing to accept responsibility for their successes, too, but they also acknowledge their shortcomings, share the credit with others, and have a realistic view of themselves as members of the human race. Narcissistic people typically have an abnormally high need for validation, which may mask subconscious fears that they are worthless, and they are often scornful of "the average person."

Institutions can be narcissistic, too. We met a consultant in a prestigious professional firm several years ago who told us that he didn't like any of his clients. We asked why and he said, "Because none of them is as smart as I am." When organizations attract and reward people with such attitudes, the institution itself can be infected with overweening pride and self-importance. The disease can spread to others in the organization who would not normally be arrogant and condescending and cause them to treat people who are not members of their elite club as though they were not worthy. This syndrome exists in sports teams, too. Successful teams can become so full of pride and so convinced of the accolades an adoring press heaps on them that they believe they are invincible. The inevitable loss to a "lesser team" is stunning. On a grander scale, armies have suffered the same fate. The Japanese military of World War II was spawned from the Bushido culture and believed itself to be superior and invincible, especially after a string of early victories throughout Asia. When its fortunes were later reversed, an army that had been arrogant and cruel became desperate and suicidal rather than face an unthinkable reconstruction of its self-image.

Narcissism is the sin of pride, and it can occur in any organization, or part of an organization, that prides itself on hiring the best and the brightest, or on having the world's finest products and services, or on being unbeatable in one way or another. Clearly, companies should strive to be best in class; they should attract and hire the smartest, most capable people they can find; and they should try to instill pride in their workforce. However, pride becomes narcissism when the people in the organization begin thinking that they are better than the people they serve. To attract the smartest people, organizations may promote themselves in ways that make them appear elite ("We're the most prestigious firm. We have the smartest people"), and this appeals to the vanity of the smart candidates they are trying to attract (as well as to the customers they serve). Then people in the firm start believing their own hype. They become inordinately proud of themselves and certain that no one knows more or is more capable than they are, and this institutional narcissism creates blind spots. If they are the smartest group of professionals, then what could they possibly learn from others, including their clients?

This fallacy of superiority is disastrous from a behavioral standpoint because it breeds arrogance, disdain for the people they are serving, and an inability to hear evidence or see perspectives that contradict their own. Arrogance can stifle listening (because no one else has anything useful to say) and learning (because they know it all already). It can make consultants blind to what they don't know and can't see. Besides being full of themselves, they don't know what they don't know. Their learning channels are shut off, so they misunderstand their clients' needs, make the facts fit their hypotheses, or propose solutions their clients can't adopt because of cultural or organizational barriers the consultants ignore. Moreover, they tend to treat all clients except the most senior executives as *resources*—necessary but inconsequential *means to an end.* The reputation for arrogance and insensitivity some consultants, accountants, lawyers, and bankers have stems from their callous treatment of people in client organizations they don't consider worthy.

We are not arguing that all professional firms are like this. On the contrary, most treat their clients well and some excel at positive BD. However, there is a tendency in organizations that take excessive pride in the brilliance of their professionals to assume an elite organizational persona that infects its members with arrogance and causes them to behave in ways that clients experience as insensitive, dismissive, and condescending. Several years ago, a senior project manager with a global engineering and construction company told us about the consulting firm they had hired to analyze their organization and recommend ways to improve its structure and performance. Throughout the project, the consultants were rude and condescending, he said, especially to anyone below the C-level (CEO, CFO, COO). They listened only to the people they thought were important, and they dismissed a number of the "soft issues" that most employees felt were a primary concern. When the project was completed, the senior project manager told us, "We all agreed that these consultants were real bright—and we'd like to get a couple of them in our headlights." He added that he would never agree to work with this firm again.

Institutional narcissism tends to afflict senior members of professional firms more than junior members (many of whom believe, at least for a while, that they were hiring mistakes), and it can pervade the organization. It can influence how firm members relate toward one another (creating a kind of Darwinian culture in which members compete with one another for the distinction of being *the* smartest) and how they relate toward the people they serve. It can cause the kind of ruthlessness seen in Enron before the collapse, depicted in the film *Wall Street,* and described by Tom Wolfe in *The Bonfire of the Vanities.* Further, it can cause the institution to value toughness (often disguised as "high standards") over compassion, which results in insensitivity and a callous disregard for human considerations the institution and its members deem trivial. Customers, like all human beings, don't like being trivialized or talked down to, so this behavior tends to negatively differentiate the narcissistic institution and its members.

The problem with narcissists is that they don't believe they have a problem. Their sense of superiority blinds them to the impact they are having on other people, and this is true of narcissistic institutions as well. They generally fail to see the impact of their negative behaviors on customers, and they don't hear it when outsiders try to tell them. Harvard's Chris Argyris believes that this stems from the fact that the smartest people are the ones who find it hardest to learn: "Those members of the organization that many assume to be the best at learning are, in fact, not very good at it. I am talking about the well-educated, high-powered, high-commitment professionals who occupy key leadership positions in the modern corporations."[19] Such professionals are usually very successful at what they do, so when they do fail, says Argyris, "They become defensive, screen out criticism, and put the 'blame' on anyone and everyone but themselves. In short, their ability to learn shuts down precisely at the moment they need it most."[20]

We identify with the institution in which we work, the god in which we believe, the football team for which we cheer. Institutional narcissism, with its narcissistic transference, can be even more powerful than individual narcissism, leading to mob rule, racism and persecution, to tribal and religious conflicts and wars of mass death and massive destruction. It can corrupt the institution and the purposes for which it was created.

—James Cumes, *The Human Mirror: Narcissistic Imperative in Human Behavior*

Institutional Greed

"Greed is good," proclaims Michael Douglas' character in the film *Wall Street*. However, this character, a ruthless Wall Street investment banker, is scorned, feared, and despised by all around him; is attacked by vengeful enemies; and winds up in prison, so audiences may well question the wisdom of his proclamation. The profit motive in and of itself is not the issue. Businesses exist to make money, and the markets reward those companies that excel at it. However, when making money becomes the sole or principal driver of a business and its leaders, greed can overshadow the core values of the people who work for the business and the people the business serves. When leaders are driven to maximize profits, which in turn fatten their paychecks and stock options, then the company's raison d'être is not to serve customers but to extract the maximum value from them. Greed distorts the reasons why most people join a profession and work for a company: to contribute to something they believe in, to meet interesting challenges, to add to society, and to help others through customer service. These more noble motives become perverted when the aims of an institution and its leaders are to enrich themselves at the expense of their customers, employees, and shareholders.

The problem for business leaders, particularly those in public companies, is the short-term pressure brought to bear by their boards, shareholders, and Wall Street to achieve results at any cost. When the primary goal is to make the numbers, leaders may try to hide losses and resort to the kinds of Ponzi schemes that Enron's leaders allegedly used to cover up years and years of bad deals. Short-term pressure aside, the fact is that some business leaders live for the deal and keep score by counting their victories and their opponents' losses. Making money becomes not just the ultimate goal but the *only* goal. That perspective soon permeates the organization, and it affects how employees treat customers. They serve customers only as a means to make money; they give customers only what they must to achieve their financial purpose; and they offer no loyalty except to those customers who represent the biggest paychecks. When greed rules, customers are nothing more than meal tickets, and it shows in how they are treated.

Institutional Insularity

When Lou Gerstner took over IBM, he found an organization so preoccupied with itself that it had become dysfunctional: "I have never seen a company that is so introspective, caught up in its own underwear, so preoccupied with internal processes," he said. "People in this company tell me it's easier doing business with people outside the company than inside. I would call that an indictment."[21] Institutional insularity occurs when an organization becomes so inwardly focused that it either neglects customers or begins treating them as a necessary evil. People are rewarded for running a tight ship, for making efficient use of their resources, and for meeting internal standards and schedules. It's hard to condemn these outcomes, and indeed we aren't, but when these outcomes become more important than meeting customers' needs, then the inmates have taken over the asylum. Companies often establish employee goals and reward systems that emphasize adhering to policies and meeting internal standards, even if that means inconveniencing a customer or being unresponsive to a customer's special request. Employees learn that satisfying the boss is far more important than satisfying a customer, and negative BD often results.

A corollary to this is the ivory tower syndrome among executives. Locked away in their ivory towers, far from the front lines where their employees are serving customers and learning what customers really want and need, these executives lose touch and begin making decisions that reflect their own need for information, organization, and control. Some senior executives refuse to get in the trenches. They seem to feel that they have done their time and paid their dues, and they've earned the right to provide their generalship from afar. Such navel gazing has brought down armies and companies. It's difficult to create positive BD when you are too far away from customers to know what behaviors they expect and what behaviors would be extraordinary. It's also difficult to lead positive BD when you conceive of leadership as "action at a distance." It doesn't work that way, and the best leaders know it.

Institutional Schizophrenia

In *Winning the Service Game,* Benjamin Schneider and David E. Bowen write, "The 'schizophrenic culture' is one in which management verbally declares it wants one kind of culture but creates routines and behaviors that send a message supporting a different kind of culture. The culture that employees believe exists will be the culture of the routines and behaviors they experience."[22] In institutional schizophrenia, the organization has multiple personalities—a *public persona* defined by the lofty goals and ideals expressed in the company's mission statement, operating principles, employee handbook, promises to customers, and marketing literature and a *private persona* (the evil twin) defined by the values, directions, and behaviors people actually practice.

The public face of the organization declares that it values and protects the environment; the evil twin orders toxic waste buried and covers up its actions. Publicly, the organization says that customers come first; privately, it tells store managers that their bonuses depend on hitting their profit goals. Nothing else matters as much. Publicly, the company proclaims that it has the fastest service and will fix any problems within four hours; privately, it controls costs by reducing its service staff and not buying the additional service trucks it needs to keep its promise.

Institutional schizophrenia is saying one thing but doing something else—it is the twisted, dark side of positive symbolic BD via alignment with core values and operating principles. It happens when a company's leaders have conflicting values (generally short-term profit pressure versus their historic value proposition to customers) that lead them to compromise one set of values to preserve another set. Gary Heil, Warren Bennis, and Deborah Stephens observe the consequence of this compromise: "Our failure to measure the extent to which we live up to our espoused values has made it easy for many to overlook how often we do not 'walk the talk.' The result has been lower levels of trust, greater confusion and frustration, and less sense of community among employees in many organizations . . . If we're not going to live our values, we would be better off not listing them. The only thing worse than not having a set of guidelines to provide order to behavior within the system is to have a visible set of values that are situationally enforced or largely ignored."[23]

Institutional Scapegoating

On March 24, 1989, the *Exxon Valdez* oil tanker, off course and apparently running without proper supervision, struck Bligh Reef in Prince William Sound, Alaska, spilling more than 11 million gallons of crude oil. It was the worst environmental disaster in American history. Initially, Exxon tried to limit its liability by denying that the captain had been drinking and by shifting culpability to anything other than itself. Many Alaskans and other Americans felt that Exxon dragged its feet in responding to the disaster and did not do enough in the days and weeks following to accept full responsibility for the spill or commit its considerable resources to mitigating the environmental consequences of all that crude pouring into a pristine bay. Exxon's initial response was a familiar pattern: the attorneys representing a company responsible for a crisis try to limit the company's liability by shifting the blame to someone or something else. "We are not responsible," is their refrain. Interestingly, "damage control," a naval term associated with efforts to keep a ship from sinking, has become a standard way to describe duplicity and cover-up. It's a song sung frequently when companies are in trouble. But even in good times some companies find scapegoats for problems their customers are having. Joanne Kincer relates this story:

I often get a good chuckle as I'm driving down the road and get a glimpse of a Time Warner Communications cable truck, with their slogan, "On Time. Every Time," in big, bright letters. Of course, everyone has a cable company story. It's understandable given that in most cities cable companies have no competition. After I closed on my new home in Houston, I had an appointment to meet the cable man at my home to install our cable television. I had not yet moved into the house, so the four-hour window they gave me caused some heartburn, as I knew I'd be spending those four hours sitting in an empty house. However, they wouldn't deviate from their policy, and I sat in the empty house for four hours. They never showed up.

To make a long story short, this same scenario happened four times! They didn't show up and they didn't call to let me know. Nothing. Because they were the only game in town, I still had to buy their service (in hindsight, I should have purchased a satellite system). After numerous irate calls, I finally got someone to show up and install my cable. To top it all off, it took additional screaming to get them to fulfill their promise of "On time or it's free." I did manage to get them to include several additional outlets and a premium channel for six months at no charge. By the way, they told me on several occasions that this was no fault of Time Warner because they subcontract to their installers and have "no control" over their operations.[24]

To consumers, the shifting of blame is a negative BD. It doesn't matter to them where the fault really lies. They experience scapegoating as an evasion of responsibility. Legal concerns notwithstanding, companies would be better off handling the problems themselves, as EMC does when equipment or software belonging to another provider fails. They remain engaged with a problem regardless of who is to blame for it. Customers know this, and it behaviorally differentiates EMC. Institutional scapegoating is rampant in bureaucracies, where departments send customers from one place to another because, "We don't handle that" or "It's not our problem. You have to get approval from so-and-so." Or they forward you to their automated customer service number, where you are either placed on eternal hold or are forced to endure an endless maze of automated options. We hate dealing with bureaucracies because the behavior manifested in their responsibility shifting is exasperating and seems designed to frustrate rather than serve.

Our brief discussion of these drivers of negative BD is intended to show how organizations can fall prey to attitudes and beliefs that result in behaviors that negatively differentiate the organization. Institutional narcissism, greed, insularity, schizophrenia, and scapegoating are not uncommon in the business world. They occur when leaders are themselves guilty of these syndromes, and the institutions come to reflect their personality.

Our Expectations of Managers

We will close this chapter by returning to our BD survey. In this case, we asked respondents what they expected of managers, what they experienced from managers at their best, and what they experienced from managers at their worst. At first glance, it may seem odd to think of managers as having customers, but this is consistent with the view of everyone in a company having internal customers. Managers have a constituency they serve, and their behavior can have a positive or negative effect on the members of that constituency. The finest managers behave in ways that positively differentiate them from other managers each person has had, and vice versa. Tables 9-1, 9-2, and 9-3 present our survey's findings. Not surprisingly, most of the factors people cited in their best- and worst-case examples of managers were behavioral.

(text continues on page 259)

Table 9-1. Customers' Expectations of Managers.

	Technical Expectations
	To be knowledgeable
	To be competent with the skills of the job
	To possess knowledge of all jobs underneath them
	To have subject matter expertise
	To have extensive knowledge of division/subject/ process
Competence, Knowledge, Expertise	To be intelligent and empowered to make the best decision to suit the situation
	To have good managerial skills
	To be someone who knows the department
	To be knowledgeable and competent
	To have a "Big Picture" awareness about the company vision/mission, client profile, and the departments role within the company
	To be an efficient planner, organizer and leader

Table 9-1. (continued)

	Behavioral Expectations
Creativity, Enthusiasm, Positivity	To find creative ways around obstacles To show confidence in their ability and the people they hired To be a mentor To motivate people in creative ways To have a vision for the future, be excited about it, and able to articulate it To be a real "go-getter" To show enthusiasm for whatever they are managing To have a fun and positive approach to the challenging world of business To show a positive attitude in negative situations
Communication and Responsiveness	To be an effective communicator—to employees, managers, and clients To be honest and frank To give clear answers on where we are going, what I need to do, and how he/she can help me get there To be a great listener To be able to articulate their expectations and be open to my ideas To give me a concise understanding of what is expected of me and how my performance will be measured To provide a clear objective To make his/her agendas explicit To be open and upfront with me on how the company and I stand To provide constructive feedback To clearly define the parameters of my decision-making limits To listen to my ideas and treat them as plausible contributions To provide an open and collaborative environment
Honesty, Integrity, and Courage	To have honesty and integrity To be able to trust all the words that come out of his or her mouth To trust that this individual will do what he or she says she will do To set a good example To be able to deliver tough messages well To be unafraid of confrontation

(continues)

Table 9-1. (continued)

Fairness, Tolerance, and Open-Mindedness	To be respectful and tolerant of individual differences To be fair to all the employees under him/her To be respectful to employer, co-workers, and employees To show respect for the workforce (the best idea in the room really can come from the janitor.) To listen to the problems that may arise and not judge the situation To show tolerance To not show or act on favoritism To be free from prejudice
Compassion and Support	To be understanding of pressures To support my efforts To be kind to employees To be caring and supportive To be concerned for the progress of those he manages To be compassionate about personal issues To be empathetic
Leadership	To be knowledgeable about and aware of the skills around him/her so they can help in any way they can To be a sound decision maker To be unafraid to make tough decisions To be willing to challenge authority if the need arises
Coaching and Interest in Others	To be attentive to development needs of staffing To have a true interest in my success and offer assistance if I need it To give advice on how I can improve To provide constructive feedback To be someone who cares about his/her people and their growth, both personal and professional To create a learning environment To coach for better performance To give the freedom to succeed and give guidance during crisis To help employees achieve success To have more concern for the people than for the tasks To have an almost altruistic view of their own position (the best managers see themselves as there to help their staff) To assist employees in setting goals by being a mentor and a coach

To motivate people to action
To have a genuine desire to help others grow
To be a teacher
To offer praise when it is warranted

Table 9-2. Negative Differentiating Behaviors of Managers.

	Poor Performance
Incompetence	He was professionally incompetent. He was unknowledgeable about the company's services and mission. She was a disorganized person who needed help to get through the day and saw the staff as servants to provide that help. He seemed to propagate chaos all around him. His low confidence caused him to overreact to things that didn't even matter in the long run. She was always making bad decisions. He wasn't interested in managing people, and tended to avoid us. She had a bad attitude and never seemed to expect or recognize success.
	Negative Behaviors
Autocratic, Close-Minded, and Inflexible	She was unwilling to listen to the team. He was a micromanager. She was unable to have any vision other then her own bottom line. She didn't listen well and wasn't open to anyone else's ideas. He dictated instead of working with the employees. He used the "it's my way or the highway" management theory. She gave me poor reviews for no reason other than that my style was different from hers. He never listened to anything we had to say. She was arrogant and tyrannical. He didn't listen, and that made it hard to respect him. She saw herself as wielding power instead of truly leading. He was a complete autocrat.

(continues)

Table 9-2. (continued)

	He purposefully withheld his knowledge when others needed it.
	She played favorites.
	He stole from the company.
	He was abusive to employees, yelling at them in public.
	He tried to make other staff members fail so that he would look better.
	She worried only about protecting herself.
	He continually passed the buck instead of taking personal responsibility.
	She was out to get ahead no matter the cost, which included trampling those she managed.
Dishonest, Unethical, and Self-Serving	He tries to cover up bad decisions or point the finger at someone else.
	She was dishonest with everyone: staff, clients, and board.
	He used threats and intimidation as his management tools.
	He was sexually harassing towards me.
	She was untrustworthy.
	She put an unfair letter in my file about a situation that was later proven to be no fault of mine. By then the damage was done.
	He didn't support the women in the department and was discriminatory.
	He used company resources for personal agendas.
	He never provided clear goals or expectations, and as a result my performance suffered.
	She seemed to change her expectations on a daily basis.
	His expectations were unrealistic.
Poor Communication and Unclear Expectations	He never explained what he needed very well.
	She provided no answers and no support.
	She was never interested in listening to what others had to say.
	He seemed to listen but we never saw any of our contributions implemented.
	She told me to do things without telling me why I was doing them.
	He only told me what I did wrong and never commented on what I did right.
	She seemed to enjoy keeping me in the dark about the organization and what was going on.

Incompassionate and Disrespectful	He was more concerned with tasks than people, and he wasn't much interested in tasks either. She was threatened by the growth of those she managed. She wasn't focused on developing my potential. He was disrespectful of anyone else's value or insight. He was rude and disrespectful to employees and customers. He didn't seem to realize he was working with people, not machines. She treated us condescendingly. He was full of negative criticism or didn't bother to say anything at all. She was completely uncaring and uncompassionate. He made it clear that we were all under him on the ladder. She was inaccessible and aloof.

Table 9-3. Positive Differentiating Behaviors of Managers.

	Excellent Performance
Competence	He was friendly, knowledgeable, enjoyed his work, and enjoyed managing. She embodies an agility in her position, being tough on problems and kind with people. She models her work and personal ethics at all times, and creates a cohesive team environment where others want to contribute. He demonstrates the importance of adding value to our clients. He never showed a lack of faith in our performance even when the situation seemed to be heading for a worst case type scenario, but kept us focused and we persevered. He was very open about himself, his goals, and his vision. I would have followed him into hell, and did. He knew how to manage an office of people from several different walks of life and to promote tolerance and understanding within the group.

(continues)

Table 9-3. (continued).

	Positive Behaviors
Communication and Responsiveness	She conducted a feedback session with me to determine my goals and aspirations, then developed an individual development plan to improve my opportunities in order to achieve my goals. He made me feel that my opinions were valid rather than just dismissing me and ordering me to get back to work. He provided frank feedback when he felt I needed it. She solicited my advice and recognized my contributions. He was able to communicate his overall view and had a plan to accomplish the goals. He was upfront about my performance so there was never any guesswork. She found opportunities to help me by walking me through my disappointments and discussing how I can overcome them or improve in the future.
Mentoring	He was a wonderful man, telling stories of his experiences in the business, and was always available if you needed him. She takes the time to see what would make my job more fulfilling, and follows up. He was a mentor and a friend, teaching me my job, leadership, management, and how to grow professionally and as a person. She includes me on important client calls so that I can learn how to interact with them and so that they can meet me and come to see me as a member of their team. He has a knack for acknowledging my frustrations but convincing me to set them aside for the good of the project. By challenging me, she taught me to trust myself and my capabilities. She showed concern for my development and wanted to help me achieve my goals, professionally and personally. He saw his role as a teacher and took the time to make sure I heard the lesson. He taught me to constantly raise my aspirations.

Taking a Personal Interest	He looks for ways to help us do our jobs. She went above and beyond a manager's responsibility, showing kindness that made the experience in my life more bearable. He made sure I had at least four months severance pay when our company shut down. She went out of her way to pick me up an drop me off every day for work when I had a leg injury that wouldn't allow me to drive. He treated me more like a daughter than an employee, taking me out to lunch when I was promoted and even buying my wedding dress for me when I got married. She spent time one-on-one talking about other things besides work.
Honesty, Integrity, and Consistency	He acts with candor. She is trustworthy, ethical, compassionate, honest and kind to people. He gives credit and takes blame. She is positive, encouraging, helpful, and very honest. He was always fair, intuitive, and gave credit when it was due. He never betrayed me or lied to make his case. When she was wrong, she admitted it. He made a mistake that negatively impacted my review and went out of his way to let our supervisors know that it was his mistake, not mine, thus clearing my record.

Challenges for Readers

1. To what extent do your organization's leaders behaviorally differentiate themselves? Are they in the upper one-sixth of all business leaders in terms of their behavior toward the three critical constituencies: customers, employees, and shareholders?
2. Do the leaders of your company consider behavior to be an element of strategy? Is behavior seen as a powerful source of competitive advantage? If not, why not?
3. Are your leaders evangelists for the values and beliefs about customers that lead to exceptional behavior? Is staying close to customers and em-

ployees more than an article of faith for your leaders? Is it a way of being that satisfies their personal needs?

4. How would you describe your company's culture? Is it a culture that supports and encourages positive behavioral differentiators?

5. What tools do you use to build and sustain your culture and ensure that it results in positive BD? How aligned are the elements of your culture that reflect your values in practice? Are there any gaps between your values in practice and your espoused values?

6. Processes are the workhorses of BD. What policies, systems, and processes does your company have in place to manage employees' interactions with customers at every touch point?

7. General Electric's Work-Out process became a mechanism for building customer relationships, solving problems, and leveraging the best practices of both companies. Do you have any equivalent processes in your organization? What other processes could you create to strengthen your customer relationships and behave in ways that customers would find positively differentiating?

8. Is your company guilty of any of the negative drivers of BD? Institutional narcissism? Greed? Insularity? Schizophrenia? Scapegoating? If so, what could you do about that?

9. Examine Tables 9-1, 9-2, and 9-3. Do your managers meet the expectations shown in Table 9-1? If you are a manager, reflect on your own behavior as a leader. To what extent do you exhibit the positive behaviors in Table 9-2 or the negative ones in Table 9-3? Your behavior is a reflection of your values, beliefs, and operating style. Are you differentiating yourself in the eyes of those you manage?

Endnotes

1. John Viney, *Drive: Leadership in Business and Beyond* (London: Bloomsbury Publishing, 1999), p. 50.

2. Ram Charan and Geoffrey Colvin, "Managing for the Slowdown," *Fortune* (February 5, 2001), p. 80.

3. For more information on this concept, see Robert K. Greenleaf, *Servant Leadership: A Journey into the Nature of Legitimate Power and Greatness* (New York: Paulist Press, 1977).

4. http://www.menswearhouse.com/home_page/our_company/co67_ask_george (March 31, 2002).

5. Jeffrey Pfeffer interviewed by Joel Kurtzamn, "An Interview with Jeffrey Pfeffer," *Strategy & Business,* Issue 12 (Third Quarter 1998), p. 90.

6. http://www.fortune.com/lists/bestcompanies/index.html (March 31, 2002).

7. Ibid.

8. This information comes from various sources, including *Fortune* magazine's discussions of the best companies to work for, 1998–2001.

9. *Merriam-Webster's Collegiate Dictionary, Tenth Edition* (Springfield, Mass.: Merriam-Webster, Incorporated, 1999), p. 8.

10. Gary Heil, Warren Bennis, and Deborah C. Stephens, *Douglas MacGregor, Revisited: Managing the Human Side of Enterprise* (New York: John Wiley & Sons, Inc., 2000), p. 122.

11. John P. Kotter and James L. Heskett, *Corporate Culture and Performance* (New York: The Free Press, 1992), p. 141.

12. Ibid., p. 142.

13. Michael C. Ruettgers, "I Pledge Allegiance to This Company: From Customer Satisfaction to Allegiance," *Chief Executive Magazine,* www.chiefexecutive.net/mag/147/article3.htm (December 7, 2001).

14. Greg Elkins e-mail message to Terry Bacon. Story used with permission.

15. Lynette Demarest interview with Terry Bacon (December 5, 2001). Quotations used with permission.

16. Ibid.

17. Ibid.

18. *Diagnostic and Statistical Manual of Mental Disorders, Fourth Edition* (Washington: American Psychiatric Association, 1994), pp. 658–659.

19. Chris Argyris, "Teaching Smart People How to Learn," in Rob Cross and Sam Israelit, ed., *Strategic Learning in a Knowledge Economy: Individual, Collective, and Organizational Learning Process* (Boston: Butterworth Heinemann, 2000), p. 279.

20. Ibid., p. 280.

21. Judith H. Dobrzynski, "Rethinking IBM," *Business Week*, http://www.businessweek.com/archives/1993/b333964.arc.html (October 4, 1993).

22. Benjamin Schneider and David E. Bowen, *Winning the Service Game* (Boston: Harvard Business School Press, 1995), p. 240.

23. Gary Heil, Warren Bennis, and Deborah C. Stephens, *Douglas MacGregor, Revisited: Managing the Human Side of Enterprise* (New York: John Wiley & Sons, Inc., 2000), pp. 122–123.

24. Joanne Kincer e-mail message to Terry Bacon (March 1, 2002).

10

WHY SOUTHWEST AIRLINES SOARS: B2C BEHAVIORAL DIFFERENTIATION

He who has a slight disadvantage plays more attentively, inventively and more boldly than his antagonist who either takes it easy or aspires after too much. Thus a slight disadvantage is very frequently seen to convert into a good, solid advantage.

—Emanuel Lasker

Everyone has a Customer, so if you are inclined to be a one-man show and not serve others, then you really don't want to be at Southwest. It's not a matter of right or wrong. It's just that we are so into team and so into positive attitudes and pride in how we deliver our services everyday to whomever we are interacting with, that if you don't really sign up to that theory, then you aren't going to be very happy here.

—Colleen Barrett, President and Chief Operating Officer, Southwest Airlines

Southwest Airlines is one of the most admired companies in the past twenty years. Few B2C (business to consumer) companies have been as consistently successful as this upstart air carrier, which in 2001 achieved its twenty-ninth consecutive year of profitability. Southwest is a darling of the business press because of its flamboyant cofounder, Herb Kelleher, who turned over the helm as president and CEO in 2001; its homey culture (Southwest's stock symbol is LUV); and its business model, which is a radical departure from other major airlines. A large part of Southwest's success can be attributed to the elements of its business model that have enabled it to put more planes in the air, at lower cost, with faster turnarounds, and less downtime than its larger competitors. As Jack Trout observes, "By using one kind of airplane they saved on training and maintenance costs. By offering no advanced seats they avoided expensive reservation systems. By offering no food they eliminated expense and time. By avoiding expensive hub airports and using less expensive smaller airports they avoided high gate charges."[1] Southwest's careful management of costs enabled it to be the low-fare, short-haul airline. However, it would be shortsighted to assume that the only reason for Southwest's success is its business model. As important, if not more so, are the unique culture Herb Kelleher created and the company's commitment to "positively outrageous service," which enabled it to create and sustain powerful behavioral differentiators, both internally and with the more than 64 million people who fly Southwest Airlines annually.

To understand how this unique company came to exemplify BD, we have to go back to 1966 at St. Anthony's Club in San Antonio. Legend has it that attorney Herb Kelleher met a client, Rollin King, over drinks at St. Anthony's to discuss King's idea for an intrastate airline serving San Antonio, Dallas, and Houston. They sketched the triangular route on a cocktail napkin, talked about how they could make money by doing it differently than the majors, and set a course that would later redefine the airline business. The core of their idea was simple: Get people to their destination when they want to go, get them there on time, and make it enjoyable. If you provide this kind of service, they reasoned, Customers* will choose your airline.

The plan was simple and as feasible as most cocktail napkin business ideas are, but getting into the air was not. Legal challenges grounded the fledgling carrier for more than three years. Texas International, Braniff, and Continental tried to eliminate the new competitor, and Herb Kelleher was forced to argue Southwest's case all the way to the U.S. Supreme Court, but he prevailed. On June 18, 1971, four years after its incorporation, Southwest initiated flights from Dallas' Love Field, and by 1973 the company was in the black and would remain there. The most important by-product of this prolonged battle to get into the air was that it galvanized the company as an underdog, and the Southwest "warrior spirit" was born. Colleen Barrett, now president

---

*Southwest Airlines' policy is to capitalize the words *Customer* and *Employee* to emphasize their importance to the company. To reflect the spirit of Southwest Airlines, in this chapter we will honor this convention except in direct quotes from people who are not part of Southwest Airlines. Throughout the rest of this book, we follow the normal rules of capitalization.

and COO of Southwest, believes that those early trials by fire were crucial in forming Southwest's culture: "I think the basics of our culture were created because of the warrior spirit that was dictated by those 'bad guys' out there who believed they could keep us out of the air. . . . I firmly believe in my whole heart and soul that if they had left us alone and basically ignored us we probably would have been out of business in two years."[2]

Southwest's first CEO was Lamar Muse. Recently retired from Universal Airlines at fifty, he had a wealth of airline experience and a tough, entrepreneurial attitude.[3] Muse raised money, began buying 737s (the only plane Southwest would fly), and hiring the right people. His senior staff initiated some of the fundamental and revolutionary operating procedures that set Southwest Airlines apart, even today. He also launched the "Now There's Somebody Up There Who Loves You" ad campaign, featuring a bit of 70s chic that today would not even qualify as nostalgia: flight attendants wearing hot pants and go-go boots. Herb Kelleher became president and CEO of Southwest in 1982 and later introduced a number of innovative programs, including a reduced fares program for leisure travelers (today's version is called Friends Fly Free) and a frequent flier program, Rapid Rewards, based on the number of flights taken instead of mileage. To attract passengers and improve tourism in Texas, Southwest joined forces with Sea World of Texas and made Southwest Airlines the official airline of Sea World. During this program, in yet another wacky move, Southwest created Shamu One, a Boeing 737 painted like Shamu the killer whale. More special theme planes were to follow. Herb also gained media attention by starring in Southwest's television commercials and by arm wrestling Kurt Herwald, chairman of Stevens Aviation, for the rights to the tag line, "Just Plane Smart" (Kelleher lost but the gimmick generated a lot of publicity).

> Greatness in marketing and customer service is a function of attitude, not resources.
> —Art Weinstein and William C. Johnson, *Designing and Delivering Superior Customer Value*

In 1990, Southwest hit the billion-dollar revenue mark and became, by anyone's definition, a major airline. During the nineties, the company continued to expand rapidly, adding destinations on the east coast and in California and Florida. Everywhere that Southwest went, it caused the dominant carriers to scramble to compete. In 1993, the U.S. Department of Transportation coined the expression "The Southwest Effect," which reflected the fact that average fares decreased and the number of passengers dramatically increased whenever Southwest Airlines began serving a new city. In its journey, Southwest is credited with a number of firsts:

▲ The first major airline to fly a single type of airplane (Boeing 737s).
▲ The first airline to use a no-seat-assignment boarding process.
▲ The first major airline to offer ticketless travel systemwide.
▲ The first airline to offer a profit-sharing program to its Employees (instituted in 1973).
▲ The first major airline to develop a Web site and offer online booking. In 2001, 40 percent ($2.1 billion) of its passenger revenue was generated through online bookings at southwest.com. Southwest's cost per booking via the Internet is about $1, compared to a cost per booking through travel agents of $6 to $8.

Another first is that although seven of the eight largest airlines in the U.S. continue to hemorrhage red ink, Southwest remains profitable year after year. In the first quarter of 2002, for instance, the majors (except for Southwest) lost nearly $2.5 billion; Southwest's profits dipped considerably in the first quarter of 2002 (part of the continuing fallout from the 9/11 tragedy), but it still managed to earn over $21 million.[4]

How does Southwest do it? The answer that comes to mind first is its unconventional business model, and indeed this is one reason why Southwest has soared. Although Southwest has grown to be one of the largest airlines in the United States, it has not significantly shifted from its initial focus: short-haul, point-to-point flights; low fares; high-frequency flights; a single type of airplane, which reduces maintenance and training costs; and conservative, fiscally responsible expansion. This operational game plan rests on speed, efficiency, and Customer service. Airlines such as the now-defunct People's Express had similar strategies and grew rapidly. However, People's then veered from its course with the acquisition of jumbo jets and competing with the major airlines on longer routes, with disastrous results.[5] Finding your niche, believing in your business strategy, and sticking to what you do well are highly differentiating strategies that have worked for Southwest. However, if we assumed that this is the only reason Southwest has soared, we would be missing the fundamental ingredient that has differentiated Southwest from its rivals in the airline industry and most companies in other industries: its behavior toward its Employees and its Customers.

The Behavioral Differences at Southwest Airlines

To say that much has been written about Southwest Airlines would be an understatement. Southwest has been a maverick in the airline industry and a company that has marched to a different drummer throughout its thirty-year history. It is one of the most admired and successful companies in America, so attention has readily come its way. In 1996, Kevin and Jackie Freiberg wrote *Nuts! Southwest Airlines' Crazy Recipe for Business and Personal Success* to tell Southwest's unconventional success story. The book was followed by hundreds of other written pieces—articles, book chapters and press releases—that elaborate upon Southwest Airlines' business model and behavior, yet no one has successfully copied them. In *Hidden Value: How Great Companies Achieve Extraordinary Results with Ordinary People,* Jeffrey Pfeffer and Charles A. O'Reilly raise two important questions about the mystery of Southwest Airlines: Why hasn't the competition been able to copy the Southwest model? and How has Southwest been able continue to grow and to be successful over such a long time? [6] Part of the answer to these questions is that unlike other product or service differentiators, positive BDs are much more difficult to imitate. In the B2B world, they are also much more difficult to observe, so what's stunning is that in this B2C world where the behaviors are as blatant as they are outrageous, the competition still can't imitate them regardless of how many memos management issues or training classes they put their people through. Southwest behaviorally differentiates itself in numerous ways. That has added greatly to the remarkable success of this company, and it provides a lens through which to better understand its sustained and largely unimitated model of success.

The Customer Service Business

Colleen Barrett, shown in Figure 10-1 with Herb Kelleher, likes to say, "We're in the Customer service business; we just happen to provide airline transportation." [7] Customer service takes top priority at Southwest Airlines, and they are dead serious about it. They call it "Positively Outrageous Service," which means that everyone regardless of rank or job position does whatever it takes to get the job done and please the Customer. Herb Kelleher, now Chairman of the Board, has been noted for helping out the baggage handlers on the Wednesday before Thanksgiving Day, one of the busiest flying times of the year. To emphasize the respect accorded to both Customers and Employees, Southwest always capitalizes the "C" in Customer and the "E" in Employee, a policy that underscores its alignment between behavior and op-

Figure 10-1. Herb Kelleher and Colleen Barrett. At Southwest Airlines, the spirit of fun starts at the top.

erating principles.[8] Barrett underscores the importance of the service difference: "Our behavior is certainly *a whole lot different.* It's certainly different than the airline industry in general, but I also think it's pretty easy to differentiate our Southwest Employees from almost any Customer service business, whether it's the airline industry or not."[9]

Operations as Internal Customer Service

All relationships at Southwest are considered part of the Customer service package. Passengers are not the only Customers. Everyone at Southwest has a Customer. The mechanics are told their number one Customer is the pilot; provisioning agents are told that their number one Customers are the flight attendants, and so on. All of these relationships are considered equally important, so the same servant leader mentality, Customer service orientation, and behaviors are expected of everyone. Colleen Barrett explains: "We are so culturally operational. The way we run our business is so involved in internal Customer service. As a nonoperational officer, I probably have the best understanding of our operations of any officer at Southwest. In order for me to provide internal Customer service, I have to work within the operational environment. I suppose that is unique for us versus some other airlines."[10]

The Southwest Spirit

Southwest has forged a unique culture inseparable from its brilliant, zany, celebrity CEO (now Chairman) Herb Kelleher, and a spirit synonymous with its underdog beginnings. From early on, Kelleher stood behind the idea that Employees came first. If Employees were happy and satisfied, then they would be able to provide the kind of experience to passengers that would keep them coming back for more. In order to keep costs low, Southwest had to maximize the productivity of both planes and people. In other words, Southwest Employees had to be willing to work harder. To handle that kind of stress, Kelleher knew they needed a sense of humor and a tight-knit family culture, which would create the warrior spirit of "doing whatever it takes." According to Joyce Rogge, Senior Vice President of Marketing, Herb instilled in the culture all the characteristics that went into making him a great person: being egalitarian, truly believing that people make the difference, and having a great love of people—talking to them and listening to their ideas.[11] It's the intangibles of vision, attitude, and core values that drive BD at Southwest Airlines, qualities that are hard to copy, as Herb Kelleher noted: "It's the intangibles that are the hardest thing for a competitor to imitate. You can get airplanes, you can get ticket counter space, you can get tugs, you can get baggage conveyors. But the spirit of Southwest is the most difficult thing to emulate."[12]

> In practice it is difficult in a service operation to distinguish clearly between the service, the process of providing service, and the system for delivering it. Since the service itself almost always consists of an act involving the customer, quality will be perceived by the customer in terms of this interaction. Similarly, the system producing the service will be judged from the behavior and style of the contact personnel and the physical tools and facilities on display. The very intangibility of a service automatically forces the customer to look for additional clues for evaluation.
> —Richard Normann, *Service Management: Strategy and Leadership in Service Business, 2d ed.*

We have argued throughout this book that behavioral differentiation is hard to copy because it is not simply a matter of observing how your competitors are behaving toward Customers and then sending out a memo asking your Employees to behave the same way. People are not robots, and their behavior is not like a broken part you can replace. Behavior is the outward manifestation of deeply rooted attitudes, values, and beliefs. Companies like Southwest Airlines know that they cannot fundamentally change what people bring to the organization, so they hire for those attitudes, values, and beliefs. Then they teach their new hires how to do the job. Furthermore, to sustain differentiating behaviors they create a culture that supports and rewards those behaviors and encourages people who are already disposed to treat Customers well to be themselves. As we were exploring BD at Southwest, we asked Joyce Rogge why Southwest has been able to sustain its BD while other companies that tried to copy Southwest were unable to do so. Here's what she said:

> I believe the sustaining part is the difficult part because we've had competitors try to copy us before. They've instructed their flight attendants to be friendlier or tell jokes, or they have copied some of our scripts and that will go along for a while, but the key is having Employees who will sustain that behavior. The difference is that for our Employees that kind of behavior is the norm. It's abnormal for us to trip up and give bad Customer service. Our norm is great Customer service (friendly and with a smile), extra effort, going the extra mile, that sort of thing. So sustaining that is just part of our life, whereas for somebody else it's easy to copy for a short period, but it's hard to keep it going.[13]

The Southwest Spirit is deeply embedded in the culture and is a source of pride for Southwest Employees. It creates a sense of uniqueness that comes from being part of a special organization, and it motivates people to try harder and do more for Customers than they would otherwise do. Airline analysts acknowledge that the effort Southwest Employees put forth makes a real difference. They also believe that short-haul clones designed to steal some of Southwest's business would have to reproduce Kelleher's operation with some precision and therefore face an uphill battle. According to veteran airline analysts, "No other carrier has demonstrated the operating skills and cultural cohesiveness needed to approach Southwest's standards of service and reliability on a broad scale."[14]

Hire for Attitude, Train for Skill

Recruiting and hiring the right people to fit the Southwest culture is a very high priority, as it is at Ritz-Carlton, Men's Wearhouse, and other exemplars of BD. According to Barrett, they are religious about it. Some companies may claim to hire for attitude, but Southwest backs up its claim with rigorous procedures to hire for positive attitudes and a straightforward dedication to weeding out anything different. Hiring is critical, Barrett says, because you cannot institutionalize behavior. Instead, you must identify those people who already practice the behaviors you are looking for. Then you can allow Employees to be themselves and make decisions about Customer service based on common sense and their natural inclinations.

Hiring at Southwest is a two-step process. The first step is a group interview, conducted by Employees, where candidates' interpersonal skills can be observed. Next are one-on-one interviews, where the questions are designed to uncover candidates' attitudes and orientation toward serving others. These hiring criteria apply regardless of the job function because all Employees play a Customer service role, internally or externally. *Every* job at Southwest is a Customer service position.

All new Employees at Southwest go to a new hire class at the University for People. There, they receive a Freedom Planner that describes benefit plans, people programs, services, and opportunities available to Employees of Southwest. The purpose of the Planner is to help new Employees understand how these programs can help them achieve their personal goals. Freedom is one of Southwest's themes. They talk about giving Customers the "freedom to fly" and their latest ad campaign is, "You're now free to move about the country." The Freedom Planner is intended to help Employees develop their own sense of personal freedom in eight ways:

▲ Freedom to Create Financial Security
▲ Freedom to Pursue Good Health
▲ Freedom to Work Hard and Have Fun
▲ Freedom to Make a Positive Difference
▲ Freedom to Learn and Grow
▲ Freedom to Create and Innovate
▲ Freedom to Travel
▲ Freedom to Stay Connected

Does this kind of Employee program work? Consider this. In 2001, the People Department at Southwest received nearly 200,000 resumes. They conducted more than 27,000 interviews, and hired 6,406 Employees. Since 1997, Southwest has been among the top five in *Fortune's* list of the Best Companies to Work For in America four times. In 2001, Southwest Employees received more than 30,000 Customer commendations and over 13,000 internal commendations for their "Positively Outrageous Service." This company is a superstar in Customer service, and it accomplishes it through hiring, development, and retention of outstanding people.

Donna Conover, Executive Vice President of Customers, says that Employees can be terminated for having bad attitudes, even if they are good at their job.[15] However, hiring for attitude makes life so much easier for everyone. She likens it to coaching teams. If a player is coachable—listens, has a good attitude, wants to work hard to achieve the team's goals—then you can teach them anything and they will work hard to learn. Under these conditions, it's easy to stick with Employees through the learning curve and support them through the mistakes that are an inevitable part of risk-taking and growth.

Leadership Bench Strength

In 2001 Southwest Airlines celebrated its thirtieth anniversary. To coincide with that event, Herb Kelleher stepped down from his role as President and CEO but stayed on as Chairman of the Board. Jim Parker was named CEO and Colleen Barrett became President and COO. Both are veteran leaders at Southwest, and their succession illustrates a longstanding policy at Southwest—to grow its leadership talent from within. Herb Kelleher has been an outstanding leader at Southwest, and whenever a strong, charismatic leader steps down people are apt to question whether the company and its culture can be sustained. In retrospect, there might have been more risk had Southwest sought a replacement CEO from outside the company who did not know the company's culture and was not as dedicated to preserving it.

Southwest emphasizes homegrown leadership and strives to move talented Employees up through the ranks—more so than most other companies. Leaders like Colleen Barrett, Jim Parker, and Donna Conover are just a few of the current leaders in the company who have grown with Southwest. For these longstanding representatives of Southwest's culture, Herb's change of role is a moot point. For them, it is business as usual with some shift in responsibilities. Colleen Barrett remembers telling an analyst who questioned whether the magic at Southwest could continue after Herb left, "You almost insult me! Do you think I've learned nothing from Herb in thirty years?"[16] Joyce Rogge echoes others in saying that Kelleher's major legacy at Southwest is the culture he created and people he attracted and nurtured. "Herb alone could not have brought the culture to bear," she says, "if he had not had people on his team, key top leaders who have been at Southwest for a long time, who also believed in it."[17] It is illuminating that *Fortune*, in its 2002 ranking of America's Most Admired Companies, cites Southwest's management bench strength as an important reason for its continued selection on this list.[18]

Places in the Heart

Southwest Airlines' courage to talk openly about love as a central emotional theme for the company is also unprecedented, and although that may sound hokey, it has created a degree of caring for Employees and Customers that has made both groups more loyal to the company. From the NYSE ticker symbol (LUV) to the hearts that abound in company visuals and communications, Southwest is not shy about the role of love in its success. The company began at Dallas' Love Field and for years used the tag line, "The airline that love built." One of the company's recognition programs for Employees who demonstrate the Southwest Spirit is called "Heroes of the Heart," and the monthly Employee newsletter is entitled *LUVLines*. This is not mere image making on Southwest's part; they live these values and believe deeply in them. It shows in the cards Colleen Barrett sends to Employees on their birthdays and other special occasions. It shows in the Employee Catastrophic Fund, in which Employees can donate a portion of their paychecks if they wish, and the money is distributed to Employees who have faced a devastating tragedy like a house fire or tornado. It even shows in Southwest's policy not to respond to Customer communications via email, which they consider too impersonal. Instead, when Customers send an inquiry or question, the company responds to each inquiry with an individually researched and prepared letter that responds to every one of the Customers' questions. Southwest Airlines never sends out form letters.

> People can copy our fares. They can copy how many flights we have between cities. And they can tell their people to tell jokes and read funny scripts. All those things can be programmatically put in place, but you can't force someone to be nice if they haven't had any modeling of that, or any training for it, or any rewards for doing it.
>
> —Joyce Rogge, Southwest Airlines

It shows, too, in the role fun plays at Southwest Airlines. People are hired in part because they enjoy life and don't take themselves too seriously. Herb Kelleher's antics are legendary (dressing as Elvis, for instance, or as an Arab sheik), but he's not alone. When he stepped down as CEO and his functions were taken over by Jim Parker and Colleen Barrett (see Figure 10-2), someone asked Jim how they were going to handle succeeding Herb, and he replied, "Well, Colleen's going to handle the smoking, and I'm going to handle the drinking."[19] Much of Southwest's lightheartedness centers on planned social events: annual chili cook-offs, spirit parties, Halloween celebrations,

Figure 10-2. Jim Parker, Herb Kelleher, and Colleen Barrett. When Kelleher stepped down as CEO in 2001, Parker became CEO and Barrett became president and COO. This experienced leadership team continues to drive behavioral differentiation at Southwest.

and deck parties. However, the spirit of fun is also casual and spontaneous: decorating work areas with family and Employee photos, creating games to entertain passengers at the gates and during flights, breaking into song, telling jokes, and holding impromptu birthday celebrations. Being wild and crazy is an art form at Southwest. People don't have to be comedians to work at Southwest, but it isn't discouraged either. The emphasis is on being yourself, being genuine, and being free to have a good time while you are working and serving others. More than most other companies we have seen, Southwest Airlines understands the value of fun and caring, and it encourages both organizational and individual behaviors that manifest those values. Clearly, this creates an environment in which interpersonal and exceptional BDs are more likely to occur.

Living The Golden Rule

The executive team at Southwest speaks regularly about the Golden Rule as the guiding principle behind all of their interpersonal interactions and relationships. The interpersonal skills that flow from this ethic are an integral part of the culture and Customer service orientation. The absence of this view and lack of skills that naturally flow from it is also a filter for employment.

The Golden Rule or the ethic of reciprocity is generally regarded as the most concise and general principle of ethics.[20] Simply put, it means to treat others as you want them to treat you. At Southwest, this means that management treats Employees with trust and respect because that's how they would like Employees to treat them. People are allowed to make mistakes and learn from them. In short, they are empowered to be themselves. According to the leaders at Southwest, people must join the company with a desire for service, and then the company can shape their behavior. The behavioral difference between Southwest Employees and other airlines' Employees is apparent, at least to Colleen Barrett. She believes that the kind of Customer interaction shown in Figure 10-3 is the norm at Southwest. She said, "I sit in gate lounges all the time and I can identify for you, even when they are not in uniform, who the Southwest Employees are versus other airline Employees, because they're talking to one another, they're animated, they're making eye contact. When they're walking down a corridor they're saying hello or at least acknowledging with their eyes the other people they are passing, whether they are our passengers or not. It's a human being thing!"[21]

Figure 10-3. At the Southwest Ticket Counter. The airline hires people who are comfortable with themselves and have a strong sense of service. Their values and attitudes help Southwest behaviorally differentiate itself from its rivals.

Barrett believes that the Golden Rule is a simple principle with a cumulative effect on Customer relationships and, ultimately, on the success of the business:

> If I try to teach anything to my front-line people, I teach them to deal with their passengers the way they would their grandmother, their next-door neighbor, or the person they sit next to in church. Because really and truly if you read our mission statement, which is posted all over, it is as simple as saying, "Practice the Golden Rule everyday." If you do that with your fellow workers as well as your passengers, you are going to have a happier day. Now it just stands to reason, and it's not really very complicated, if you have a better day, the people you are working with will probably have a better day. If our Employees are happy, some of that happiness will transmit to the passengers, if they are consistently happy when dealing with us, then they are more likely to come back, and then we probably are going to make a little money, and our shareholders are going to be happy. It's really pretty simple. We know people repeat Customer service stories all the time, so I would rather have them repeating good stories than bad.[22]

The Culture Committee

In Chapter 9, we discussed the important role culture plays in driving BD, and Southwest Airlines is virtually unique among large companies in having a standing committee dedicated to preserving the spirit and values of the company. In 1990, when she was still Executive Vice President—Customers, Barrett formed the Southwest Airlines Culture Committee. Its members represent all regions and departments across the system. Their purpose is expressed in the committee's mission statement:

> This group's goal is to help create the **SOUTHWEST SPIRIT** and culture where needed; to enrich it and make it better where it already exists; and to liven it up in places where it might be "floundering." In short, this group's goal is to do **"WHATEVER IT TAKES"** to create, enhance, and enrich the special **SOUTHWEST SPIRIT** and Culture that has made this such a wonderful Company/Family.[23]

Will Southwest Airlines be able to sustain its unique character after Herb Kelleher is gone? The answer lies in such tools as the Culture Committee, which will help sustain his legacy, and in the tiers of leaders he left behind to run the company. The Culture Committee is a powerful internal behavioral differentiator that helps sustain the external behavioral differentiators that affect Customers. Interestingly, this is one of the few standing committees in Southwest Airlines, and it's considered an honor to be a member.

From Customer Loyalty to Customer Advocacy

It should be clear from our discussion of Southwest Airlines that its "Positively Outrageous Service" is not the result of a department, or a program, or a mandate from management. It is not secondary to the product; it *is* the product. Southwest flies airplanes, but it *manages* behavior, and the behavioral differentiation that has made it the darling of the airline industry is based not on proprietary technologies, brilliant ideas, or clever financial dealings but rather on old-fashioned values and a strong sense of community. Is this unusual? According to Joyce Rogge, it is:

> "I've worked other places besides Southwest Airlines, and it isn't normal for a corporation of our size to have a culture that cares about its Employees. I've worked at a smaller company, and it had a family feel, but it was more of a 'daddy as dictator' family feel, as opposed to growing up and learning, being given opportunities, having a safety net—all those kinds of things. Although we are 34,000 people, it is a family. There is an incredible effort from upper management to continuing that feeling and that culture. We have a culture where being nice to one another has very high value. And it's internally first, even more than to our Customers."[24]

Southwest's behavior toward its Employees is a powerful behavioral differentiator. It creates the conditions in which those Employees are more likely to treat Customers in ways that behaviorally differentiate the company, and there are numerous stories of passengers who have received exceptional treatment from Southwest Airlines Employees who were willing to do more than was called for (and more than most other people would have done).

Imagine arriving at the airport gate to check your luggage with your husband and two small children in tow. You are on your way home from a visit to family in Florida. You arrive ninety minutes before departure only to discover that your wallet with every piece of identification is missing. You have your paperwork from your flight to Florida but nothing else. Luckily for you, the person behind the ticket counter was Amy, a Southwest Airlines Employee, because you have chosen to fly with Southwest. In this time of heightened security, was there anything Amy could do?

"Amy went over and above the call of duty to try to get us on the flight," this passenger recalls. "She called her supervisor to ask what she could do. The first attempt was to fill out a yellow form that was to allow us access to the concourse. However, when I attempted to pass through the security gate, the airport security would not allow me to pass without federally issued picture identification. They instructed me to return to the ticket counter. I then went back and talked to Amy again. Due to the enormous lines at both the ticket counter and the security gate, it was about 15 minutes before the flight was to depart. She then decided to personally escort us down through security and to the gate. When the security officer stopped us, Amy volunteered to personally take responsibility for us until we were able to get on the plane. Again, security would not allow even this. They said the only way they would allow me through was with a picture ID. I then decided to contact my employer and have them fax a copy of my work ID. Amy gladly gave me the local fax number for the airline and retrieved the fax when it arrived. In the meantime, she had to quickly get our luggage off the airplane. She helped us retrieve our luggage, then booked us on the next flight home without additional charges for the change in ticketing." Amy's efforts to solve this family's problems went well beyond what the family expected, and the Customer later wrote, "I have been a loyal Customer for several years before this incident, but now your company has not only a loyal Customer, but also a vocal advocate as well."[25]

On another occasion, an elated but weary mother-of-the-bride was on her way home from the wedding when security checked her briefcase and discovered an ornate cake knife. She was a frequent flyer and was normally careful to comply with the heightened security measures; however, in the commotion of the wedding the day before she had forgotten to put the knife in her checked luggage. Furthermore, this was a family heirloom, passed on to her from her mother, and she was not about to part with it. Security suggested that she go back through the long check-in line to check the serving piece. It was either that or lose it, she was told. But her Southwest flight was about to depart. As she accepted the inevitability of missing her flight, Greg, a Southwest agent who happened by, said he could help.

"I felt an immediate sense of relief," she later said. "There would be someone who could find an easier way to accomplish the same thing, without me having to miss my plane. He offered to personally take the cake piece to the baggage Customer service desk and to hand carry it to the plane to make sure it made it back home with me! I cannot tell you how relieved I was. The sentimental value of the piece was the most important part, of course. Greg understood my predicament and stepped right in and solved the problem. He even joked and smiled with me throughout the entire transaction. As he walked by me (I was waiting in line again, waiting for my boarding pass!), on the way to the plane, he smiled and said, 'We only do this for cake knives!'"[26]

The Golden Rule is of no use to you whatever unless you realize that it is your move.
—Frank Crane

Another passenger had a brief but memorable encounter with a Southwest agent named Kimberly at Austin's Bergstrom Airport. She had received a call from her twin sister in Lubbock, who told her that the caesarean delivery of her child, scheduled a few days later, had to be done that day for medical reasons. She had flight arrangements to get her to Lubbock for her twin's original delivery date, but getting there that day presented a serious challenge. Both twins had wanted to be together for this special occasion and were distraught that it might not happen. The seven-hour drive between Austin and Lubbock was out of the question because it would still get her there too late. But flying did not look feasible either. Southwest is the only carrier with direct flights to Lubbock, but the only flight with seats available that day would also get her there too late. The reservations agent she spoke to advised her to get to the airport as quickly as possible and try for standby. Once at the airport, however, she found that that was not easy either.

"I could not get through security without a ticket, and I could not buy a ticket due to the line," she recalls. "So I could not even attempt to get on standby. By then, I was a miserable mess. I approached the Customer service desk from the end and asked to see the supervisor, who turned out to be Kimberly. Barely able to speak by now, I told her a short version of my need to get to Lubbock. I can only imagine what she thought about this strange woman crying in front of her, but she looked me square in the eye and said, 'Let's see what we can do.'"

Kimberly was able to get her a ticket, the woman said. "She called the boarding gate and told them I was coming. Then, to top it off, she walked me through security and right to the boarding gate. I was bawling the whole time. I was only hoping to get on standby, and she got me on the plane. I hugged her and told her I would never forget what she had done." This story has a happy ending. The woman did make it to Lubbock in time to see her twin give birth to a baby girl.[27]

Is Southwest Airlines the only air carrier whose passengers would offer testimonials to exceptional treatment? That would be unlikely. People who are kind and empathetic, and who have a service mindset, can work anywhere, and given the opportunity they may go out of their way to help Customers in distress. However, such treatment is more likely to occur at Southwest because the company's policies and behavior toward its Employees encourage and reward them to go the extra mile for Customers—and to do it consistently.

The Behavioral Difference After September 11

The terrorist attacks on 9/11 had a devastating effect on the airline industry. Air travel ceased entirely for several days and then came back slowly as the government was able to institute more stringent security procedures. Jittery passengers were reluctant to fly, and it took months for the airline industry to recover. By October 17, just over a month after the attacks, more than 122,000 people in the airline industry had been laid off. The majors led the way: United and American laid off 20,000 each; Delta, 13,000; Continental, 12,000; U.S. Airways, 11,000; Northwest, 10,000; Air Canada, 9,000; British Airways, 7,000; and America West, 2,000.[28] As usual, Southwest took a different approach. Although demand was down, Southwest decided to keep flying a full schedule as soon as airports reopened—and they chose not to lay off a single Employee. Management did discuss whether to pay workers for the few days the planes were grounded during the crisis, but Colleen Barrett made it a short discussion. "Pay 'em. This isn't their fault. It's the right thing to do."[29] However, the board of Southwest Airlines, along with Kelleher, Parker, and Barrett, chose not to pay themselves. Following 9/11 and through December 31, 2001, the board declined to accept any board fees, and Southwest's top three leaders suspended their own salaries in order to preserve operating capital. *That* is an unprecedented example of leaders differentiating themselves through their behavior.

Southwest's cash-starved rivals may have had little choice but to cut back on flight schedules and Employees. Most were swimming in red ink already, and 9/11 dealt a severe blow. In contrast, Southwest decided to reduce fares and fly a full schedule, to get people back in the air as soon as they were ready to fly. They thought it was important to communicate confidence in the air traffic system and to help people return to what would pass for normalcy after the terrorist attacks. Geoffrey Colvin, writing in *Fortune,* noted how Southwest's bold decision to keep flying was paying off:

"I suspect Jim Parker is smiling. He's the new CEO of Southwest Airlines, having succeeded Herb Kelleher at the worst possible moment a few months ago. After September 11, I figured Southwest's profit streak, one of the most remarkable records in business—the company has made money every year for the past 28 years in a notoriously aw-ful industry—was finally toast. But maybe not. Alone among major airlines, Southwest has not cut back operations, and management actu-ally believes it could show a profit for the year. Just for the perspective, this year will probably be the worst in this business' pathetic financial history, with the industry losing $4 billion to $6 billion. Now imagine all those carriers going deeper in the hole every day, impairing their ability to invest, market, and hire for years to come, while Southwest stays in the black. That's why—you won't believe this, but it's true—Southwest is now worth more than all the other airlines in America combined."[30]

Southwest's response following 9/11 is indicative of the maverick way it has approached the airline industry and conducted its business all along. While the other airlines responded predictably and in mass, Southwest chose a different path that behaviorally differentiated it in the eyes of its Employ-ees and its Customers. Table 10-1 summarizes the behavioral differentiators and the impacts of those differentiators for this remarkable B2C company.

B2C Behavioral Differentiation

In business-to-consumer companies, much of the BD occurs during vari-ous interactions between Employees and Customers. However, as our dis-cussion of Southwest Airlines shows, the basis for differentiating behaviors with Customers is in how the company treats its Employees. Companies like Southwest Airlines pay an extraordinary amount of attention to their culture and to the way Employees are treated internally. Exceptional behavior toward Employees is almost a prerequisite for exceptional behavior toward Cus-tomers. Indeed, in businesses that treat Employees as second-class citizens, it's difficult to imagine how or why Customers would be treated any differ-ently. You reap what you sow, and if you hire Employees for their service ori-entation and friendly attitudes, if you treat them well and give them the lati-tude and responsibility to treat Customers well, and if you establish policies and procedures that enable exceptional Customer treatment, then you have the right conditions for systematic and consistent behavioral differentiation.

In our research on BD, we examined a number of professions to determine what Customers expected and what happened when they received exception-ally positive treatment and exceptionally poor treatment. We included one profession—new car salesperson—that most of us like to complain about and that represents one of the purest forms of a business-to-consumer transaction.

(text continues on page 285)

Table 10-1. Southwest Airlines' Behavioral Differentiators.

BD Driver	Behavioral Differentiator	Impact
Leadership	Leaders like Jim Parker and Colleen Barrett, who are grown from within	Strengthens commitment to the culture; ensures that transitions in leadership are not jarring to the culture; communicates commitment to employees; offers opportunity internally, which increases retention
Leadership	Herb Kelleher's antics (such as arm wrestling for the right to use a slogan)	Differentiates from the stony seriousness of rival business executives and airlines; creates a lightheartedness and sense of fun that encourages other employees not to take themselves too seriously
Leadership	Not furloughing employees after 9/11 despite the required grounding of flights immediately after the attacks	Sends a strong message to employees, customers, and the market; builds employee loyalty; reinforces the "people first" values
Leadership	Deciding to pay employees after 9/11 for the days they did not work	Stands by employees through an event that was not their fault; builds employee loyalty and retention; enhances employees' willingness to stand by and help customers
Leadership	Herb Kelleher, Jim Parker, and Colleen Barrett suspending their own salaries after 9/11 and through the end of 2001; the Board declining to accept board fees for the same period	Sends a strong message that they are willing to sacrifice first and most; builds employee admiration and loyalty through their willingness to bear the pain themselves
Leadership and Culture	A deep commitment to "Positively Outrageous Service"	Communicates a high service standard; sets the expectation of the extraordinary

(continues)

Table 10-1. (continued)

BD Driver	Behavioral Differentiator	Impact
Leadership and Culture	Employees come first; believing and behaving as though people make the difference	Makes employees feel valued; creates conditions in which employees will value and support each other; encourages already service-minded people to treat customers exceptionally well
Leadership and Culture	Viewing themselves as being in the customer service business (they just happen to fly airplanes)	Focuses the business in the right ways; encourages service behaviors that differentiate; helps everyone prioritize efforts to achieve the primary goal
Leadership and Culture	The "love" theme manifest in many ways: slogans, campaigns, messages internally and to customers	Communicates a strong sense of caring, both internally and externally; appeals to customers' family values; conveys the people first attitude of the company; makes people feel better about working at Southwest
Leadership and Culture	Numerous rewards programs, such as "Heroes of the Heart"	Reinforces the right behaviors, as well as the culture; helps create cultural myths, legends, and heroes; makes people feel good about themselves and the company
Leadership, Culture, and Process	Having a culture committee that looks after and builds the culture	Emphasizes the importance of culture and the determination to sustain it; delegates responsibility for cultural preservation to employees; sustains the founders' momentum; makes Southwest unique
Culture	A "warrior spirit" that has helped the company face numerous challenges and continues to make it more competitive today	Imbues the company and its employees with a sense of uniqueness; increases the willingness to work harder and do more to "prove" to

		those who sought to crush the company and who still criticize its unconventional approach
Culture	Everyone at Southwest has a customer; all relationships are considered equally important	Reinforces the service mindset; creates a set of mutual dependencies; guides behavior
Culture and Process	Regardless of rank or position, everyone helps get the planes in the air.	Reinforces the egalitarianism of the culture; is a strong behavioral differentiator for employees, who see that managers are willing to load baggage, too
Culture and Process	Routinely going the extra mile for customers, such as escorting them to the departure gate when they are running late	Encourages exceptional BD; helps customers solve problems; builds customer loyalty; makes employees feel good through helping others
Culture and Process	The words "Customer" and "Employee" are always capitalized in Southwest communications.	Distinguishes the culture from others; sends a strong message about the importance of these two constituent groups
Culture	The spirit of fun; many lighthearted events and celebrations; numerous occasions where people dress in costumes	Creates a warmer, friendlier environment; encourages people to make work enjoyable; helps people bond internally and thus be more supportive and helpful with each other
Culture	The lighthearted spirit on airplanes; jokes and games from pilots and flight attendants	Can take some tension out of flying for passengers who are anxious; makes the experience more enjoyable; brightens the day
Culture	Living the Golden Rule as a matter of principle and using it as a behavioral guide	Sets a high behavioral standard; gives a simple rule for guiding behavior; establishes the primacy of

(continues)

Table 10-1. (continued)

BD Driver	Behavioral Differentiator	Impact
		treating others well; brings a sense of humanity to the work; reinforces the culture and values
Culture	A tight-knit "family" culture	Helps employees feel supported; creates a stronger sense of belonging; encourages people to look out for one another; breaks down barriers between functions and ranks; encourages employees to be themselves and feel accepted
Culture and Process	Friendliness and good humor are the norm; people are hired for attitude and values and then encouraged to be themselves	Creates a more pleasant working experience for employees and a more pleasant flying experience for passengers; builds a sense of liking for Southwest's employees, which builds a stronger sense of liking and loyalty for Southwest Airlines
Process	Rapid Rewards program, which is based on number of flights rather than miles	Rewards frequent travelers on Southwest's city-to-city routes and does not penalize them because the distances are not cumulatively large; is a more generous program and customers know it.
Process	A group interviewing process during hiring that focuses on attitudes and service orientation	Helps ensure cultural fit of new hires; makes employees feel part of the process, which increases their ownership; reinforces the tight-knit family culture

Process	Southwest's University for People	The name itself communicates an important distinction between this educational group and other corporate universities.
Culture and Process	The Freedom Planner new hires receive while attending the University for People	Establishes a unique, participatory contract with employees; reinforces the culture; encourages employees to take responsibility for themselves and others
Process	Sending cards to employees on their birthday and other special occasions	Communicates caring; enhances the feeling of family
Process	Responding to customer communications via letter instead of email	Is a more personal form of communication; conveys the message that Southwest is different; increases customer loyalty

The results of our surveys are shown in Tables 10-2, 10-3, and 10-4. First, we will look at what Customers expect when they encounter someone selling new cars.

We suspect that these expectations apply to every situation in which a consumer buys something from a company. Whether the company is selling new cars, life insurance, groceries, lumber, wrapping paper, watch bands, computer software, or transportation to Phoenix, consumers expect the seller to know the product, to provide accurate information that helps them make informed choices, and to be a capable and honest advisor. What we as consumers further expect, though we are often suspicious of this, is that the sellers will act in our best interests, that they will steer us in a direction that is primarily right for us (and perhaps coincidentally right for them). Sellers whose behaviors create positive BD will sometimes advise us not to buy a particular product (even though they lose the sale) because they want to see us make the right buying decision. Sellers on the other end of the BD spectrum will let or even encourage us to buy something that is not right for us if it is profitable to them. Often, we later discover that this has occurred, and we

(text continues on page 291)

Table 10-2. Behavioral Expectations of New Car Salespeople.

	Technical Expectations
Knowledge, Information, and Answers	To provide clear answers on technical questions To be able to compare different models and makes To know their product well enough to explain the benefits as they relate to my needs To be knowledgeable about the automobiles in inventory to help me make a buying decision To have knowledge about the services available To educate me on the different options available for each automobile and its functionality To be aware of new and upcoming technologies that will be on the market, like hybrid cars, etc. To know about the features and quality of cars To be aware of the quality and safety ratings assigned to each car To have extensive knowledge in their field
	Behavioral Expectations
Honesty, Candor, and Straightforward Communication	To be upfront and honest with me To provide "just the facts" with no embellishment To be honest To not pull the, "Well, I'll have to check with my manager." To answer all questions in plain English To have the ability to be straightforward To not take years negotiating a price To be honest about the weaknesses of the product as well as the strengths To be fair on the price
Respect	To treat customers like intelligent people To show me only what I ask to see and nothing more To be sensitive of my time by not wasting it To treat me with respect To let me look the cars over at my convenience To not hover over me but still be accessible if I have a question or wish to take the car for a test drive To not be pushy To not shove what they know down my throat To be a good listener To know when to back off

Responsive	To meet reasonable needs and requests To bend over backwards to please me To go above and beyond to find the color/style I want To give quick, courteous service To give good follow up service To be helpful
Customer-First Attitude	To listen to my needs and help me to obtain the car that will fit my needs To understand my limits and expectations without butting in To ask me questions about my needs To focus more on fulfilling my needs than on making a sale To be a consultant in matching the car, features, and price with my needs To show me ways to better help me; e.g., with financing, servicing, and convenience To help me find the car that is right for me To fully represent my needs To tailor their sales efforts to my needs, not theirs To ask me questions about my family and lifestyle in order to help find the appropriate choice To identify my needs and explain the benefits to the features that address my issues To provide me with solutions that reflect my needs To ask a lot of questions To take pride in giving the customer the best deal possible

Table 10-3. Positive Differentiating Behaviors of New Car Salesmen.

	Excellent Performance
Competence	He didn't pressure but gave me all the information I needed about the car. She was very informative and extremely helpful. He knew everything about cars! He even knew all the features of competing brands, and he was right. I checked. The time spent with him was like getting an education on automobiles. I've never met someone who loved his work as much as this guy did. He didn't make me feel stupid for wanting what I wanted but began an extensive search to find the vehicle I was looking for.

(continues)

Table 10-3. (continued)

	Positive Behaviors
Good, Open Communication	She worked with me over the phone for three months before I was ready to buy the car and kept me informed of the promotions/deals that they were having.
	She listened to what I wanted and answered my questions.
	He would give me information and usually attached a very thoughtful question that helped me decide what I did need and what I didn't.
	She was forthright and upfront during the purchasing transaction.
	He didn't try to hide anything under the table.
	She did not pressure me but followed up every week for the next three weeks.
Nonintrusive and Responsive	He wasn't pushy but was very low-key and sincere.
	He didn't try to push the "fluff" that the car had to offer, but explained the benefits of the features that I seemed to have issues with.
	He listened carefully and worked on my behalf, negotiating fairly and patiently.
Customer-Satisfaction Oriented	He didn't try to push an in-stock car on me when they didn't have the car I was looking for on the lot, but searched until he found the one I wanted.
	She called twice after the sale to see if things were going well.
	He arranged a great deal on the car I wanted and made me feel like a winner when I drove it home.
	He didn't try to sell me more than I wanted.
	She listened to me and understood my needs and my budget and respected them.
	He wanted to know what was important to me before trying to put me behind the wheel.
Showing Caring and Taking a Personal Interest	He had a sense of humor and treated me like we were friends, which we later became.
	He was interesting and interested, and when I did ask a question about the vehicle, he knew the answer without having to go ask someone else or look it up.
	She knew I didn't have much money and so she did her best to get me the best financing possible, even going so far as to suggest I wait to buy because she knew of a great deal that was coming up.

Exceeding Expectations	He gave me some of his classical CDs that he was finished with because he knew my daughter was a classical musician. He went out of his way to do little extra acts of service, like setting my radio stations for me and programming my door opener. He offered to let me take the car for the weekend and even gave me gas vouchers.

Table 10-4. Negative Differentiating Behaviors of New Car Salespeople.

	Poor Performance
Incompetent or Unprofessional	He did a horrible job of explaining the lease terms. I learned more on the Internet than this guy could tell me about the car. He was truly worthless, but he expected to make a big commission on the sale. She didn't show up for an appointment that we made with her. She didn't know anything about the car's performance. Every time we asked her a question about the safety record or the gas mileage or scheduled maintenance she had to go ask someone else. He did not deliver the car on the day promised and had a lot of lame excuses about why it wasn't ready when I needed it.
	Negative Behaviors
Condescending or Patronizing Attitude	He went out of his way to make me feel stupid. He spoke down to me as if I wouldn't know the steering wheel from the brake pedal. She assumed I had not done the requisite research. He had a condescending attitude.
Chauvinistic or Prejudiced	He had to go with us on a test drive and when we wanted to switch drivers so that I could see how the car handled he wouldn't let me drive because I am a woman. He assumed that because I was female I had no clue about the product. He ignored me (I was actually the one buying the car) and instead tried to sell the car to my boyfriend.

(continues)

Table 10-4. (continued)

	He didn't bother answering my questions and only answered the questions of my male friend who was accompanying me.
Intrusive	He kept butting in with his own opinion as my husband and I were trying to discuss the car among ourselves. He wanted to sell what he had, not what I wanted. He used "salesy" language, which completely turned me off. She was entirely too pushy. He seemed to be willing to say anything to get a sale.
Unconcerned with Client Needs	She showed me cars other than what I was looking for. He made assumptions instead of asking and listening to what I wanted and why. He only wanted to talk about monthly payments. He focused on selling me a luxury car when what I needed was an economy car for my daughter. She tried to push a truck on me that didn't meet my needs. He didn't listen to me and was only concerned with making the sale. He was impatient and demanding. He tried to talk me into a car that was way above my price range. He did not listen and so we went to a different lot.
Manipulative and Dishonest	He lied to me about the financing rates I was getting. He told me those were the best he could offer and when I told him that I could get lower rates from the bank he suddenly decided he could offer lower rates. He didn't point out major flaws in a used car that he should have been aware of. He wouldn't be straight with us about the price. Every time he showed us the latest "offer" from his "sales manager" something new had been added that we hadn't asked for and they didn't bother to explain. When hell freezes over and they are the last car dealership on earth, I may go back to them. Or I may just travel by bus. He tried to talk me into add-ons that were totally ridiculous. She lied about the product, the price and the maintenance. He was unwilling to negotiate in good faith.

> He took the keys to the car I was going to trade in, if I found a car I wanted, and wouldn't give them back when I didn't decide on anything.
> He seemed slick and manipulative. He had one of those "game face" smiles that he wore when he talked to customers. I didn't trust anything he told me.

vow not to return to that seller. Smart companies never try to cheat the Customer, even inadvertently, and that leads us to consumers' behavioral expectations of new car salespeople (and, by extension, all salespeople).

In a nutshell, consumers expect sellers to be honest and candid with them. This is really a bedrock expectation, because nothing else matters if this is not true. They also want to be treated with respect. They want to be listened to and understood, and then they expect sellers to help them get what they want, which may not be what's sitting on the shelves, what's being discounted that day (because of overstocking), or what the seller gets the biggest commission on. Consumers don't want to be pressured into making the buying decision, but when they are ready they expect sellers to be fair and reasonable in negotiating the terms. This is not earthshakingly new, but it is remarkable how many companies and salespeople don't seem to know this or don't care about it.

Behavior matters. If you or your Employees treat Customers badly, or even carelessly, it will affect your business. Sooner or later, poor behavior will cripple you because consumers will prefer to shop elsewhere. They don't need you; they need what you are selling. If they can buy it from someone else who treats them better, who is honest and forthright, who has a light-hearted attitude and makes them laugh, who looks out for their interests and occasionally goes the extra mile to help them, then that is where they will shop. It's very simple, and a lot of businesses, including major airlines that compete with Southwest, don't get it. Southwest does get it, and it has had a record three decades of profitability in a troubled industry that has seen every other major carrier lose money repeatedly. Enough said.

Tables 10-3 and 10-4 report what Customers experienced from new car salespeople when they had remarkably positive experiences and remarkably negative ones. As we have shown in other chapters, what Customers remember, what sticks in their mind as they reflect on their buying experiences, are positive and negative *behaviors*. Technical competence accounts for very little of their impression. First and foremost in their minds is how the sellers *behaved* toward them.

We are going to close this chapter with another quotation from Colleen Barrett. We said in Chapter 6 how important it was for behavior to be genuine. Most people have finely-tuned BS detectors. They know a forced smile when they see one, they can tell when someone's just going through the motions, and they can spot insincerity the moment the faker assures them how sincere he is. That's why hiring right is a prerequisite to building a workforce that will behaviorally differentiate you with Customers. Then they have to be themselves, as Barrett describes here:

> When I go to new hire classes and there are a hundred and seventy people in the room, I tell them, "This is an incredible offer I am making you, one that doesn't get offered very often in corporate America. I want you to take your ingredient, whatever it is, and I want you to think about it before you go out for the first flight. Something about you turned the recruitment team on, and I can't figure that out in ten minutes for each of you. I'll bet, though, if you dig around in your soul, you can figure out what it was. And that is what I want you to take with you every day to work. It might be a warm smile. It could be that simple. It might be a clearly altruistic spirit that people just can't miss. It might be an incredible sense of humor. It might be that you want to sing every single PA that you ever make! It might be that you are the best joke teller they ever met. Whatever it is, if you'll share that everyday just with your fellow workers, to me that's half the key. It isn't just with the passengers. We are giving you the freedom to be individualistic. Most companies, especially in the airline business, don't want that. They want the exact opposite.[31]

Challenges for Readers

1. Part of Southwest Airlines' success can be attributed to its business model, which is a radical departure from the business model most other airlines follow. How different is your business model from the one your rivals use? Map the business model used by most players in your industry. Then challenge each element and assumption. Does it have to be this way? Do the same with the behavioral paradigm in your industry. How could you treat Customers differently? In ways that would behaviorally differentiate your company?

2. Southwest is known for its innovative programs, such as a frequent flyer program that rewards passengers for the number of trips rather than accumulated miles. How innovative are your programs? What could you do differently that would delight your Customers and differentiate you from your rivals?

3. Southwest Airlines' BD stems from its attitude toward its Employees and the differentiated way the company treats its Employees. Southwest has a family spirit and encourages people to be themselves and have fun. How does that compare with the way your Employees are treated? Do you have a family atmosphere? Do people encourage and support one another? Do your top managers step in and perform front-line jobs now and then? (Or do they remain in the ivory tower?) Is your workplace a fun place? The point isn't that you have to be like Southwest Airlines but that you create a working environment that people enjoy, that motivates them to work hard for you even if you are not paying top dollar in wages and benefits. How well are you doing in this area?

4. There's an old saying in Texas that you can't light a fire with a wet match. If you want fire, you have to have some spark in you. Southwest got a lot of publicity based on Herb Kelleher's jokes, costumes, and irreverent attitude. Again, the point is not to emulate Herb Kelleher, but do your leaders light people's fires? Is there some energy and excitement in your company that prompts others to be as carefree and committed as Southwest Airlines' Employees are?

5. Southwest Airlines preaches and practices the Golden Rule. What do you preach and practice?

6. Herb Kelleher and other senior leaders at Southwest believe that culture is their number one priority. They formed a culture committee to preserve, protect, and extend their unique culture. Have you done anything similar? How do you manage your culture? What more could you do to ensure that this important driver of BD is a powerful and sustaining force in your organization?

7. Tables 10-2 through 10-4 present what Customers expect from new car salespeople, as well as their best and worst experiences with them. Consider conducting a similar survey of your Customers or people in the marketplace who purchase your types of products or services. What do they expect of you? In their best experiences, what have they received? In their worst experiences, what has happened? How do your own company's behaviors stack up?

Endnotes

1. Jack Trout, *Differentiate or Die: Survival in Our Era of Killer Competition* (New York: John Wiley & Sons, 2000), pp. 46–47.

2. Colleen Barrett quoted in Margaret Allen, "GROUND Controller," *Dallas Business Journal* (August 2001).

3. Kevin Freiberg and Jackie Freiberg, *Nuts! Southwest Airlines' Crazy Recipe for Business and Personal Success* (Austin, Tex.: Bard Press, 1996).

4. "SWA in a Nutshell," Southwest Public Relations, Revised (January 18, 2002), p. 2.

5. Freiberg and Freiberg, op cit., p. 62.

6. Jeffrey Pfeffer and Charles A. O'Reilly III, *Hidden Value: How Great Companies Achieve Extraordinary Results with Ordinary People* (Boston: Harvard Business School Press, 2000), p. 21.

7. Colleen Barrett interview with Pamela Wise (March 1, 2002).

8. "SWA in a Nutshell," Southwest Public Relations, Revised (January 18, 2002).

9. Barrett, op cit.

10. Ibid.

11. Joyce Rogge interview with Pamela Wise (March 1, 2002).

12. Herb Kelleher quoted in "The Jack and Herb Show," *Fortune* (January 1999), p. 166.

13. Rogge, op cit.

14. Kenneth Labich, "Is Herb Kelleher America's Best CEO?" *Fortune* (May 1994), p. 129.

15. Donna Conover interview with Pamela Wise (March 1, 2002).

16. Barrett, op cit.

17. Rogge, op cit.

18. Matthew Boyle, "America's Most Admired Companies: The Right Stuff," *Fortune* 145, 5 (March 2002), p. 86.

19. Herb Kelleher quoted in Katrina Brooker, "The Chairman of the Board Looks Back," *Fortune* (May 2001), p. 76.

20. "Shared Belief in the Golden Rule," www.religioustolerance.org/reciproc.htm (April 1, 2002).

21. Barrett, op cit.

22. Ibid.

23. Southwest Airlines Culture Committee Mission Statement. Used with permission.

24. Rogge, op cit.

25. Stories adapted from selected Customer letters sent to Southwest Airlines, November-December, 2001. Reprinted with permission.

26. Ibid.

27. Ibid.

28. *LUVLines,* Special Issue (October 2001).

29. Colleen Barrett quoted in "Nothing but the plain truth," *U.S. News & World Report* (January 2002), p. 58.

30. Geoffrey Colvin, "Smile! It's Recession Time!," *Fortune* (October 29, 2001); www.fortune.com/indext.jhtml?channel=print_article.jhtml& doc_id=204725 (December 19, 2000).
31. Colleen Barrett interview with Pamela Wise (March 1, 2002).

11

SEARCHING FOR STARS: B2B BEHAVIORAL DIFFERENTIATION

It was a huge lesson to me that supporting people was ultimately better for my pocketbook than managing people, and it fit my personality, a more feminine way of management. A lot of people saw this shift during the late 80s, a shift from male management structures to a softer side of management. The more people-reliant your business is, the more a feminine side of management becomes important. Nurturing and developing people become bigger deals. And the truth is, it pays better.

—Brenda Rhodes, CEO, Hall Kinion

I'd rather jump out of the window here on the 31st floor than have one of our assignments go bad.

—Wes Richards, Heidrick & Struggles

Throughout the early parts of this book, we have been exploring how B2C companies behaviorally differentiate, and, as we've seen, it often occurs through frontline sales and service people. In these types of firms, the sales cycle can be short and simple: a customer walks into a store, hotel, or restaurant, or boards an airplane, or has an appliance delivered, and is served by people whose purpose is to facilitate the customer's experience and complete the transaction. Later, the customer may need help from customer service people, whose roles are relatively straightforward. But the situation is murkier in B2B companies, where potential customers may interact with a number of people whose normal roles do not include selling or servicing—executives, financial analysts, administrators, estimators, engineers, technologists, programmers, architects, chemists, surveyors, technicians, scientists, auditors, and so on.

Of course, *everyone* is a salesperson, but the reality behind this old saw is that most people in B2B firms don't think of themselves as salespeople, are not trained to sell, don't like to sell, and may even be repulsed by the idea of selling. It's easy to see how frontline sales and customer service reps in B2C firms can and should differentiate themselves behaviorally, but how do engineers do it when they are conferring with the customer's engineers? Isn't that just a technical discussion? A conversation between experts? Is it possible for technicians installing computer equipment at a customer site to behaviorally differentiate themselves? To create an experience for the customer that is differentially better than the experience they've had with competitors' technicians? In our discussion of EMC in Chapter 5 we saw that it clearly is possible for behavioral differentiation to occur during technical service calls. What about in nontechnical B2B transactions? Is it possible for staffing or executive search consultants to behaviorally differentiate themselves from similar consultants? Can a firm of management consultants, lawyers, or accounts *outbehave* rival firms? Can the employees of a commercial bank, a steel fabricator, or an oil field service company *outbehave* the employees in competing companies? Clearly, we believe they can, and in this chapter we'll begin to explore how B2B firms do that. We're going to examine two professional services firms—Hall Kinion and Heidrick & Struggles—whose work on two ends of the recruiting industry illustrates how B2B firms can create and sustain behavioral differentiation.

Going the Extra Mile at Hall Kinion

She grew up on a sugar beet farm, which taught her that life is unpredictable and all you can expect is uncertainty. She watched her parents strategize when to plant their seeds, when to try new crops, and when to harvest. Her upbringing taught her to be industrious and resourceful, and if it didn't turn her into a gambler it at least gave her an appetite for risk. She later followed her parents into real estate and worked in her father's real estate agent training firm. In her twenties, she finished one year of college, and she married and had two daughters. When her marriage later ended, the small income she had was important because she received no child support. But the most serious obstacle Brenda Hall faced came in 1981 when her father died. She was 28, unemployed, unmarried, and financially—but not emotionally—bankrupt. The indomitable spirit she developed as a child drove her away from self-pity and into enterprise.

She joined Snelling and Snelling, the nationwide staffing firm, and discovered that she had a natural talent for business. She soon remarried, bought a house, had a third daughter, and was earning what, for her, was a phenomenal income. After six years at Snelling and Snelling, her life took another sharp turn when her boss fired her. She had not expected it, and like most people in her position she felt betrayed, but Brenda was confident that she could make her own way. She now knew this business heart and soul. Two months after being fired, and with three children to raise, she borrowed against her house and purchased a Snelling and Snelling permanent placement franchise in San Jose. Her confidence was immediately rewarded. Within two months of opening the office she was out of the red, and by the end of the year she had won the company's "Fast Start" award by outperforming twenty-four other new franchise offices. In the second year of owning her business, she hired Todd Kinion and several other key employees. Their sales reached nearly $1.4 million, and they earned the top award (Office of the Year, Permanent Division) by outperforming more than 550 other Snelling and Snelling offices. For five consecutive years (1988 through 1992) her San Jose office won Office of the Year. By 1991, she had given birth to a fourth daughter and was working a four-day week. When asked what she did for a living, Brenda replied, "I'm raising four daughters—plus I get to be a CEO."[1]

In 1990, when the closest Snelling and Snelling temporary placement office closed, she was given the opportunity to open a new division for temporary placements. Though her family cautioned against it, she and Todd Kinion put up the money for the franchise. By the end of the year, they had billed $2.9 million in permanent placements and $465,000 in temporary. The turning point in the young company's history came in 1993 when they reached nearly $10 million in sales, opened two new offices, and renamed their company Hall Kinion. Their remarkable growth rate continued through the technology boom of the 1990s, and Brenda's odyssey continued as well. Again divorced, in 1995 she married Jesse Rhodes, owner of BayPac Racing, who had two daughters of his own, so together they were raising six daughters. By 2000, Hall Kinion had begun expanding internationally and had reached nearly $300 million in sales. As a Silicon Valley–based staffing firm, the company had focused on placing high-level, skilled professionals in the IT industry, so it was hit hard by the dot.com crash but has since begun recovering, along with other firms in the tech sector.

Hall Kinion (HK) is on our list of exemplars of behavioral differentiation because the company has achieved extraordinary growth and financial returns through the quality of its leadership, the youthful nature of its culture and values, and the strength of its processes (Figure 11-1). Together, these drivers of BD have created a unique experience for HK's employees, candidates, consultants, and customers. In HK, as in so many companies, behavioral differentiation begins at the top. It begins with Brenda Rhodes' resilience and indomitable spirit. Like the mythical Phoenix rising from the ashes, she has weathered every storm in her life and has imbued her company with two qualities that set it apart: the value of nurturing and developing people and the determination to prevail. In her own words:

> We have "How can we?" attitude, not "We don't want to." How can we? This attitude has to start internally. If our people don't think they can get anything done internally, then it doesn't work. When employees are empowered, they go out and do the same thing for our customers, and we make heroes and legends out of their stories. My favorite example is one of failure. Early on in the company, we'd been open for eight months, and we were breaking records. Then one month (February 1988) we couldn't close a single deal. We couldn't close a deal for the life of us. By the third week of February, our sales team was drooping, and no deals were closing, and we thought we had lost our magic.
>
> So the last week of the month, when it was clear nothing was happening, I said, "Let's have a funeral on Friday afternoon to bury the month." I told everybody to dress in black and bring any issues they wanted to bury. People want to celebrate, and sometimes that means celebrating failure. So one guy wrote a eulogy. Another guy brought a small 2-ft coffin, and they ripped up stories and buried them. One guy brought a

Figure 11-1. Hall Kinion's Theme. The company is based on the idea of going the extra mile—internally and with customers.

resume from a candidate who turned down a job. We all listened to each other's stories, and we marched to the *Requiem*. Then we went upstairs and had pizza and laughed. On Monday morning, March began, and it was a bang-up month. We stopped. We listened to what happened. We honored it, gave it a voice, then buried it and moved forward.[2]

Stories of leaders who have "failed forward" are legendary, but it's unusual to celebrate disaster and use the experience to buoy employees' spirits. Brenda's use of ritual to signal the transformation from bad times to better times is a behavioral differentiator for her. Most leaders would have imposed cost-cutting measures and a few would have ranted and raved at the staff for not delivering the sales. Brenda's behavior built employee loyalty.

Hall Kinion's Differentiation Strategies

From the outset, the focus at HK has been technology staffing. Their goal was to be the staffing firm of choice for companies that relied heavily on technological expertise (although recently they have added a second focus: finance and accounting). HK chose to focus exclusively on technology because there is high demand for IT experts. They also decided to be what Peter Senge and others have termed a learning organization, which they felt would benefit their customers and their recruits. They accomplish this by continually inspecting their processes and those of their competitors, listening to their internal and external customers, researching and reporting on customer needs and trends, and providing a high level of education. They differentiate themselves not merely by developing new processes and fine-tuning old ones but by embedding very important behavioral expectations within them (Figure 11-2). All processes—ranging from recruiting their own employees, to training them, to recruiting contractors and job candidates, to placing them—include behavioral expectations of HK employees, behaviors that enable them to create rewarding and memorable experiences.

Many staffing firms are much larger and generate more sales than HK, but this is partly by design. According to Jeffrey Neal, senior vice president, they have created a niche for themselves in a small but significant market: research and development technology firms (Figure 11-3). "We are in the space of human capital management. In our sector, knowing the simplicity of our business creates differentiation. Our business is not rocket science, and this is a source of competitive advantage because it keeps us focused. We built a footprint in the industry that was organized around research and development. We focused on R&D technology companies, rather than being the staffing firm for any customer."[3] Their timing could not have been better, catching, as

Figure 11-2. Brenda Rhodes and Rita Hazell. Rhodes (left) and Hazell (right) celebrate Troy Isom's sales record at the 2001 Hall Kinion Awards Gala.

they did, the technology boom from 1980 to 2000. But their success was not entirely serendipitous. They were determined to do business in a new and different manner from their competitors. The staffing industry has traditionally been very transactional, according to Neal. When customers have needs, they call. The staffing company checks its files of available people and sends someone. Then they wait for more calls. The average fill ratio in the industry is 35 percent.

We guarantee both perm and contract placements. We guarantee from one day to two weeks for contractors. If they're not succeeding, the customer doesn't have to pay, or we can try to find someone new. If it's a permanent placement, our guarantee goes up to a year. If not successful, we can find a new person, or the customer can pay a fee on a prorated basis. We guarantee our delivery because we are totally confident in our processes.

—Jeffrey Neal

Figure 11-3. Jeffrey Neal.
One of the executives who
drives BD at Hall Kinion,
Neal founded Hall Kinion
University.

To get away from the transactional game, HK knew they needed to deliver more value and to build stronger relationships with their customers and with the technologists they place. They believe in the adage that it is easier to do the hundredth job with the first customer than the first job with the hundredth customer. To build repeat business, they created procedures and a mindset for developing relationships that would bring their job candidates and customers back to the table again and again. For example, they created a strategic internal marketing group to gather information about their customers' staffing needs. From the surveys, they generate a report, deliver it to their internal account managers and technical recruiters, and discuss the results with customers. The report allows them to play back their customers' needs in ways that help customers understand what's happening more globally in their industry. Furthermore, the report demonstrates that HK is listening, that they are major players in the industry, and that they care about the long-term health of their customer relationships. They continue to differentiate themselves through these processes and through the commitment to establish relationships rather than settle for one-time transactions. Their goal is to achieve a fill ratio of 80 percent—and they are currently hitting 55 percent, well above the industry average. The behavioral differences we describe in this chapter are what enable them to achieve this level of performance.

Their focus on technology helped them build internal expertise because each recruiter had time and was expected to learn their customers' language and "talk shop." Developing expertise in technology built their credibility and thus their sales. Once companies learned that HK was a reliable provider of technology talent because they understood their business, they returned with more job orders and referred HK to other companies. Neal believes that their expertise continues to be a strong differentiator because general staffing firms don't have this comfort level with technology. Throughout the technology boom, HK grew at the same phenomenal rate as its technology customers because they were working alongside them, and their recruiters had the time and the interest to keep up with the technology changes as the industry evolved. In contrast, general staffing firms could not keep the same pace because they had a diverse clientele pulling them in different directions. HK was fortunate to catch the same wind that blew their customers' sails. According to Neal, "This 'keep it simple' strategy has worked well in differentiating us from other staffing firms. As technologies have changed and technology staffing needs have changed, the technology companies have brought us along."[4]

Hiring Employees

Whether HK is recruiting employees for their own business or for customers, they follow the same seven-step recruiting methodology. Serious candidates jobs at HK are asked to participate in a group interview. Like the Ritz-Carlton, HK wants all levels of the organization to make the decision and live with the consequences. No one can blame Human Resources for hiring mistakes. These interviews are scheduled during their routine Monday morning meetings where recruiters, account managers, and office managers can ask candidates questions. In this group interview process, which employees affectionately refer to as "the gauntlet," prospects introduce themselves, talk about their background and experience, and explain what they are looking for in their new job. Then they must entertain questions from the group. Successful candidates are those who can withstand the pressure and perform with grace and clarity. Unsuccessful candidates usually fall apart, becoming nervous, disoriented, inarticulate, and even defensive. Successful candidates are invited to become HK employees and work side by side with their former "interrogators." The gauntlet is not without high purpose: the candidate's performance is indicative of future customer interactions where HK employees must remain calm, focused, articulate, and positive. Collectively, the group decides who fits in HK and who does not. Once they decide to hire a prospect, it is everyone's job to bring new people up to speed on their jobs and assimilate them into the company.

Because HK is in the human capital business, it is not surprising that they devote so much time to their own hiring process. What may be surprising, especially for a company focused on technology staffing, is that they care much less about the technical backgrounds of their own prospective employees than they do about their attitudes and behavior. HK serves customers in a dynamic, energetic, youthful industry—so those are the types of people they need. You can educate people about technology, but you can't change a person's age, attitudes, or the habits of a lifetime. So they look for dynamic, energetic, youthful, and eager individuals, people who naturally exhibit the behaviors that make HK so successful. Their recruiters are vital to their mission because each of them is the marketing department. If they are bright, dynamic, and enthusiastic, they will be walking, talking billboards for the company. Jeffrey Neal elaborates:

> At the core of what we do, we make sure that when we hire people they have a real commitment to come to the recruiting industry. They must have the skill set to be a recruiter as well as a seller. We make sure that the people we hire fit the Hall Kinion profile: they are high energy and are articulate; they have an overachieving background. We start with their success track record (girl scouts or boy scouts) and explore their earliest experiences with success. We want to know about their character. We go after them. We recruit very hard. We want competitive, aggressive, intelligent, and successful people. We spend a tremendous amount of time doing this. Consequently, you can walk into any office at Hall Kinion, and you'll meet a high-energy person.[5]

HK strives to create a special "Hall Kinion experience" for candidates, consultants, and customers. They want the people who experience HK to be aware that this is something different. The HK experience begins with HK's leaders and their own commitment to building and providing something special. It extends through the culture Brenda Rhodes, Todd Kinion, Rita Hazell, Jeffrey Neal, and others have created, but it is embodied, day by day, in how HK's front-line employees think of themselves and how they behave toward recruits and customers.

Recruiting Consultants and Candidates

HK recruits both contractors (called *consultants*) and permanent hires (*candidates*). Consultants are highly skilled professionals who, according to Neal, "like to move around, execute a project, immerse themselves in new technologies, and then move on. They are happy to work ten months of the year or work time-and-a-half and just gobble up technology." Their methodology for working with both consultants and candidates is to create a highly personal experience that benefits the job seekers as well as customers they might be placed with. Jeffrey Neal explains:

> When someone interacts with us, we want them to have a good experience, so we sit down and help them build a career plan, assess their background and capabilities, and help them find the right opportunities. This platform goes well beyond just putting them into a database where we say, 'We'll call you if something comes up.' We differentiate ourselves by the types of people we represent. We require face-to-face interactions with candidates, we do reference checks, and we do technical screening—proof of a candidate's technical skills. We remain in contact with companies before and after placements. We try to mutually agree with candidates that we will work together. We want them to feel value in working with us.[6]

Once they find the right recruits, they lavish them with attention, and these are the behaviors that most differentiate HK from its staffing rivals. For instance, HK recruiters devote a significant portion of every Friday to hand-delivering paychecks to consultants at customer locations. Along with the paychecks, they often bring bagels or donuts, so these visits have been dubbed "bagel drops" or "donut drops (see Figure 11-4)." The trip has a dual purpose. The recruiters want to check in with the consultants, make sure they are doing well, and show that HK cares about them and their success. But these trips also give recruiters a chance to walk the customers' hallways, to be present at their customers' sites regularly, and to keep their ears to the ground. It's the best way to maintain their relationships with consultants and customers and to keep abreast of customers' developments and evolving needs. Jeffrey Neal elaborates:

> When our people bring out the checks for contractors, they are walking the halls and talking to customers at the same time. And they're bringing things like HK mints and stress balls and handing those out. Occasionally, we'll sponsor a lunch and exchange business cards with customer people we don't know. We try to be very visible in our customers' communities. Our bagel and donut drops are incredibly successful. People go nuts over this. In this business, a lot has to do with timing. We stay in contact. We actively talk with people we have recruited, whether or not they are employed with us. We try to maintain a "high touch" environment. Some of our competitors do some of the things, but we do

Figure 11-4. The Hall Kinion Bug. Symbolizing the youthful spirit at Hall Kinion, the Bug is often used for bagel and donut drops and Friday deliveries of contractor checks.

these things *consistently*. In our business, everything is about delivery, delivery, delivery. So you have to differentiate yourself consistently. There are a lot of good firms out there, but we emphasize the consistency of the experience, and we train and manage the processes to ensure that consistency.[7]

Another innovative behavior is HK's Star Contractor program, which was developed in the early 1990s. HK wanted to be the agent of choice for technology professionals who wanted contract work. To make their vision a reality, HK studied the acting and modeling industry for clues about how to behave as the agents to the stars do. Their goal was to become the "Ford Modeling Agency of the staffing world" and to treat their technology consultants like stars the way Ford treats Cindy Crawford. When they discover a candidate of star status, they create postcards from professional photos and highlight their most significant accomplishments and credentials. The recruiting "agent" delivers the "portfolio" to prospective customers. Furthermore, HK treats consultants exceptionally well. They offer them "Cool

Perks" such as stock options, dinners, and hotel and airline discounts, "just to make sure you know you're a star."[8] HK also has its own contests (like the Oscars) to reward the contractor of the year. For the 2001 recipient, Jeff Glickman, this meant special guest status at the 2002 Network Leadership Conference as well as national exposure. HK nominated him for *Contract Professional* (a premier publication in the technology industry) All-Star of the Year, and he won it. Now his name is being circulated around the globe. That's not only special attention, that's a *Hall Kinion experience,* one consultants like Glickman won't find working with other staffing agencies. Glickman identified the differentiated behavior long before his national award:

> It was hard to get work in Hood River, Oregon. I needed some help with marketing so I contacted twelve to fifteen firms. One of them was Hall Kinion. What I discovered is that they treated me differently. The folks at Hall Kinion just seemed to be different, and I couldn't put my finger on it at first. I wasn't a commodity to them. I wasn't something to buy and sell. Instead of being just a client, I became part of the company, part of their family, really. It wasn't just what they could get out of it for better profit but what we could all get out of it. They were judicious about sending me to the right places, not just a dozen places like out of a shotgun. They were more like a marriage broker. They were being smart and trying to hook up people with like attitudes. They say what I'm good at and what I'm bad at because I'm not everything to everyone. I think that's what most contracting firms do—sell people. HK approaches the problem very differently. I respect intelligent people, and they were being very smart about the way they were doing business.[9]

The stock options mentioned above were part of Brenda Rhodes' vision early in the history of the company. She sought a way to make HK attractive to employees and contractors in an industry not known for company loyalty. Technologists who thrive on solving technical problems and don't want long-term employment with the same company are among the world's modern nomads. They happily migrate from place to place and job to job, seeking greater technical challenges and satisfactions. How do you make them loyal to your company? Brenda knew she couldn't do it alone, that it meant creating a company culture where *everyone* would behave in ways that built loyalty. She explains:

> I found that the way we treated ourselves was the way our salespeople treated their contractors and their customers. In our contractor days, the

first thing we did when we set our five-year strategy was to put stock in the hands of our employees. We started giving stocks to our recruiters and salespeople, something not widely practiced among private companies. This was when we were pre-public. We were able to get great people to work with us. Then, when we wanted to differentiate ourselves with contractors, we formed a technical advisory board where they got to spend time with me. I didn't always like what they were saying because they told me that it doesn't matter who you're working for so long as the gig is good. They had no preference for hiring firms. So we came up with a unique way to give contractors stock options, and we're still the only one I know of that does this. They get the same stock options as employees do. It's a reason for them to call us when they're ready to work again. What I needed was *one reason* for them to make their first call to HK. As soon as contractors return to work with us, they start vesting again. This encouraged them to make that first call to us. And this comes from an attitude of plenty, not scarcity. As long as we always treated everyone like there's plenty to go around, they worked hard and came back to HK again and again.[10]

HK's behavior toward consultants is their way of saying, "Thanks for working with us. We'd like to do it again." Consequently, consultants act as a mouthpiece for HK when they talk to other technology contractors about the way HK treats them. Beyond the short-term jobs they get, they have a vested interest in HK's success, and the stock option program enables them to build an equity stake and to plan for the future even though their principal short-term focus is on the technology challenges that drive them. HK's success in building consultant loyalty and seeing consultants return after each completed engagement can be attributed primarily to their differentiated behavior toward the people they place.

> Only the player with the initiative has the right to attack.
> —William Steinitz

Differentiating HK with Customers

One important differentiator for HK is that they are as particular about the companies they work with as they are about their employees, consultants, and candidates. "We carefully screen our customers," says Neal. "We train our people that it isn't a job order unless it meets specific criteria; otherwise, our people know not to take them as a customer. We have to agree with customers on the process we both will follow, and then they'll get exactly what they're looking for. We fill over 90 percent of the jobs this way. We begin with a real simple question: 'Have you used staffing companies before?' From there, our recruiters follow a qualification process that has a script about how to conduct the interview." HK is rigorous in following this process, and they know that some company job orders won't meet their criteria. Neal explains: "The number one thing our customers tell us is this: 'I have to have the right people in place.' Getting in and understanding their resource planning or hiring strategies and asking the questions that are specific to their objectives is key. We get in there and use our model to understand exactly what the customer expects from our delivery. And we are not afraid to walk away from business if it's not right. We have very high standards, and let customers know that up front. We try to ensure that we are aligned with our customers, and then we deliver to keep the promise: the right talent in the right place the first time."[11]

Once HK and the customer have agreed to mutual terms, HK goes out of its way to fill the job order. HK's process for filling orders is flexible and has evolved as customers have given HK feedback on what works best for them. HK's goal is to fill job orders as rapidly as possible, and they do it through a proprietary process called PowerMatch. Although we cannot describe that process in depth, we can provide an overview. PowerMatch is a recruiting methodology *and* a delivery methodology that allows HK to explain to customers how HK will recruit and deliver the right candidates and consultants. In its delivery form, PowerMatch has three approaches customers can choose based on the approach that best meets their needs. The intention is to make hiring as easy as possible, as Jeffrey Neal explains: "The bottom line is that we make sure they achieve their recruiting goals."[12]

The goal is not merely to help both parties meet their objectives quickly and easily. It's more to redefine the process and the means of reaching those objectives. HK hires only energetic and competent recruiters, and they train them to follow a reliable hiring method. They do both of these things in order to redefine what is otherwise a stressful, slow, even painful process. HK wants its customers and candidates to be delighted, both with the outcomes and the *experience* along the way, and without the differentiating behaviors they have created and consistently implemented those two results would be impossible to achieve.

In customers surveys, more than 70 percent of HK customers rate "candidate screening and matching for technical skills and culture" as the biggest challenges in hiring technical people. So the recruiting form of PowerMatch includes HK's processes for taking precision job orders, screening candidates, and collecting performance evaluations. Many customers want to customize this process, and HK distinguishes itself behaviorally by being willing to meet customers halfway. HK recruiters are expected to go the extra mile when customers request it so they are delighted both with the process and the outcome. Again, Jeffrey Neal explains:

> A big push in HK is "how can we?" Every customer has different expectations for delivery, and we want to understand their desires. "How can we?" is all about the customer, and it's a strong cultural differentiator. We have a clearly defined process for successful recruiting, but we know we'll have better success if we see eye to eye with our customers. We convince them that they can gain a competitive advantage if they arm us with informational tools to entice people to join their organization. We sell their needs, technology, culture, and business initiatives to our recruits so we can excite people about their company. This is a competitive advantage because we go to great lengths up front to learn about the customer. If a prospective customer still doesn't understand the benefits of our approach, we'll say, "Even if you give us the ugliest order ever, as long as we have the proper information, we will go away and return with something our competitors won't." Sometimes, if a company is being pursued by fifty recruiting firms, we ask, "Do you have an ugly order that you want to give us, one that's been sitting there for six months? Will you talk to us about that?" We want the ugliest order so we can get our foot in the door. We grab the ugliest order and find the needle-in-the-haystack skill set. We want those orders because our recruiting processes are so succinct and successful that we know we'll find the people. Once we do, we have a customer for life.[13]

Hall Kinion University

As with other exemplars of behavioral differentiation, HK places an extraordinary amount of emphasis on professional development and education. Jeffrey Neal founded Hall Kinion University (HKU) in 1994. As the company began expanding rapidly, HK management felt that they needed a centralized and professional training process that all HK employees would go through, partly to build a "one-firm" spirit and partly to perpetuate the HK experience through education. HK's passion to drive the process was fueled by its belief that HK could differentiate itself from competitors only if HK people could march to the same beat. HK envisioned an educational system that would help all employees learn the recruiting, delivery, and customer relationship processes that HK had developed and would encourage continuous

learning through sharing of best practices. A decade later, all HK employees are required to participate in HKU programs every year.

In their first year of employment, beyond their initial orientation, new hires receive a minimum of two weeks of training, which might include learning the sales process or learning to speak the language of different industries. They also learn the recruiting methodology. All the training materials are available online, and new employees are expected to read them before their training begins. Before they can move to later programs, they have to pass tests to show that they have mastered their current program. Although these aspects of HKU may not be unique, a number of aspects of the program are. First, the recruiting training is "live," which means the new hires pursue actual leads during the course. Second, when they return to their offices, they are expected to conduct a "teach-back"—to share what they have learned by teaching others. Teach-backs help new hires practice their skills, and it keeps other office members up to date on changing issues. "We know this is a proven cycle," says Neal. "If they do these things, they will be successful. And the program ensures that everyone is speaking the same language."[14]

HKU has a comprehensive approach to training people in the field that includes on-the-job training (OJT); online, self-directed learning; and formal instructor-led, classroom programs. These modes of learning are commonplace today among Fortune 100 companies, but few of HK's rivals in the staffing industry sponsor employee education that is as thorough and diverse. According to Catie Fitzgerald, training manager for HKU, "Most of our competitors rely heavily on online learning and on-the-job training conducted by tenured sales staff. These programs usually vary from office to office, lacking a definitive structure. In addition, our competitors usually do not offer a formal classroom experience designed and facilitated by professional sales trainers. If they do conduct classroom-based programs, it is often more on a spur-of-the-moment basis with more of a presentation style."[15]

Branch managers at HK are primarily responsible for training their staff. New hires start with three online courses customized for each division of the company. These courses help new hires integrate into the company, learn the fundamentals of HK's approach to recruiting and selling HK services, and become skilled in using HK's WebPAS database system. Branch managers and fellow team members reinforce the learnings through teach-backs, coaching, and guest speakers. Classroom education includes programs in sales skills, strategic account management, advanced WebPAS use, improving sales performance, and new manager skills. All these programs incorporate best practices HK recruiters have developed through the years and have a distinct HK flavor. Finally, HKU sponsors an annual "Network Sales Conference," which includes training components. In these network conferences, which began in 1992, HK invites employees from around the globe to meet, socialize, learn, share experiences, and agree on the annual strategic goals. Beyond their educational value, these conferences reinforce the company's culture and embody employees' sense of the HK experience.

As we have seen throughout this book, companies that behaviorally differentiate themselves from their competitors generally invest more in education than their rivals do. That investment not only helps employees learn and embrace the culture and develop the skills they need, it also reinforces the behaviors that companies want to see at all customer touch points. Moreover, for employees themselves, a company that provides a significant amount of education and skill development behaviorally differentiates itself from other companies that the employees might work for. Beyond the BD benefits, is a higher investment in education correlated with stronger financial performance? In March 2002, *The New York Times* reported on a recently completed study indicating that education does indeed pay off. According to the report, "Companies that ranked in the top 20 percent or so in spending on training and development would have earned an average of 16.2 percent, annualized, in the five years through 2001, or 6.5 percentage points a year more than the Wilshire 5000 index. Better yet, that market-beating performance was produced with about 10 percent less risk, as measured by the volatility of returns. . . . Over those same five years, companies at the bottom of the training-expense rankings had significantly lower returns. And the researchers obviously couldn't include companies that did not report training expenses and presumably performed even worse."[16]

What we have not captured in this profile of HK so far is the dynamism of the culture. Brenda Rhodes founded the company on the strong values of honesty, respect, open communication, active listening, learning, high performance, customer service, and leadership. But most obviously, Brenda and her management team have a strong people orientation. HK employees are "recruited based on their performance in life. Brenda's story is a reflection of that. Our awards presentations are full of stories about the person who went from rags to riches and the person who realized their biggest significant career leap at Hall Kinion because the opportunity exists for those willing to excel—we provide equal opportunity for women, men, young, old, disabled, and all diverse backgrounds."[17]

They capture their energetic and people-oriented culture in the youthful look and feel of their business cards and marketing collateral materials; offices that look like they were designed by The Gap; national conferences where people dress in costume (at the 2002 national conference, the theme was "the 40s"); recognition of people's birthdays and anniversaries with cards, gifts, and songs; and in their sponsorship of a race car (see Figure 11-5). The race car symbolizes the pace at which they work and the speed with which they complete placements. The spirit of their culture is captured in the gong people bang whenever a placement is made. It's captured in the hand-written notes and "thank you" cards they send to customers and candidates; in the web casts of their awards ceremonies; in the theme park excursions they take with employees and their families; in the program of "Cool Perks" they offer to consultants; and in the unusual promotional items they give to customers, candidates, and consultants (such as HK Doh—the HK version of Play Doh). Normal staffing companies give people coffee mugs. HK gives them big travel mugs and water glasses in colors like mandarin orange, lime green, and wild grape. Through self-conscious impression management, HK creates a feeling, an aura, and an experience that is as powerful and unique in its niche as the feelings created, just as self-consciously, by Harley-Davidson and Ritz-Carlton and Southwest Airlines. That feeling of youthful energy and excitement, of caring for people, and of commitment to the craft is what be-haviorally differentiates Hall Kinion and makes it unique among staffing firms. Jeff Glickman, their star contractor for 2001, summarized this when he said, "People naturally gravitate towards places where there are good people and people are treated well. I think that's the case with Hall Kinion. I think it

Figure 11-5. NASCAR Featherlight Racer No. 03. Hall Kinon's sponsor-ship of this race car reflects its emphasis on speed and talent.

starts with Brenda. She has a strong value system, and people gravitate to her because of this."[18]

Table 11-1 summarizes HK's behavioral differentiators and the impacts they have.

Building the World's Finest Leadership Teams

At the high end of the recruiting industry is Heidrick & Struggles (H&S), one of the finest professional service firms in the world. Founded in 1953 by Gardner Heidrick and John Struggles, H&S was one of the first executive search firms in the U.S. It has since expanded globally (more than fifteen hundred H&S professionals now operate in over sixty offices throughout North and South America, Europe, the Middle East, Africa, and Asia) and has become the world's premier leadership consulting firm. A *Wall Street Journal* market survey ranked H&S as the top search firm among thirty competitors for quality of candidates, value of services, and overall reputation.[19] We have chosen to include H&S in this book because of the professionalism and quality of its consultants and the extraordinary ways in which those consultants treat clients.

We have noted throughout this book that many people know how to behave in ways that clients find remarkable, but few of them do it consistently. There is often a gap between *knowing* and *doing*. In professional service firms, the only way to close the gap and achieve consistent BD is to attract and hire people who understand how to treat clients well and are motivated to do so. The most sustaining motivators are intrinsic: a deep sense of professionalism, the desire to serve others, a passion for the work, an abiding sense of integrity, and a commitment to doing what it takes to do it well. People who are driven more by extrinsic motivators, such as money, tend to be more transactional and unpartnerlike and eventually leave firms like H&S (if, indeed, they have been invited to join them in the first place). This is not to say that extrinsic motivators are not important to H&S consultants. Like all professionals, they want to make a good living. But it became clear to us as we researched H&S that what distinguishes this firm from its competitors is the quality of its people and the intrinsic satisfaction they receive from serving clients exceptionally well.

The Moment-by-Moment Differences

"You absolutely must establish yourself as an intellectual and business peer to your client," says John Gardner, vice chairman of H&S' Board Ser-

(text continues on page 318)

Table 11-1. Hall Kinion's Behavioral Differentiators.

BD Driver	Behavioral Differentiator	Impact
Leadership and Culture	A "how can we?" attitude that begins with Brenda Rhodes and permeates the company.	Imbues employees with a "can do" spirit that enhances flexibility and resolve to meet customers' needs.
Process	Continuous reflection on internal processes, coupled with an environmental scan that identifies and bench-marks competitors' processes and identifies and responds to emerging customer needs.	These continuous learning processes show HK's commitment to being the best. Moreover, they communicate to customers that HK is listening, is flexible and responsive to customer needs, and is continually evolving to provide the best and quickest solutions for customers.
Culture and Process	All internal and external processes include behavioral expectations that are intended to create a unique "Hall Kinion experience" for employees, candidates, consultants, and customers.	The "HK experience" creates a sense of pride in being part of something unique and hip—a specialness not available elsewhere. HK's cultivation of this unique experience is its *quid pro quo* in return for employee, candidate, and consultant loyalty.
Culture	HK strives to build strong relationships with customers. Account managers are responsible for devoting time to building relationships, getting to know the customers'company and industry, and going out of their way to meet customers' needs. HK's relationship focus is unusual in an	Although HK's relationship focus is not unusual in business, it is unusual in the staffing industry, and it behaviorally differentiates by signaling a stronger commitment to customers and more caring about them, their industry, and their success. HK's technology niche enables it

(continues)

Table 11-1. (continued)

BD Driver	Behavioral Differentiator	Impact
	industry that has traditionally been very transactional.	to devote the resources necessary to develop stronger relationships and deeper industry and customer knowledge.
Process	HK's strategic internal marketing group gathers information on customers' needs and sends reports to customers that help them benchmark themselves in their industries.	This value-added service helps HK adapt to evolving customer needs and helps customers improve their resource planning and human capital management.
Culture	HK focuses on a limited set of human resource needs (primarily IT technologists) and expects its recruiters to learn the customers' language and be able to talk shop with them. HK attends industry conferences and participates in special interest groups.	Their knowledge of their customers' industries helps them find and recruit the right candidates and consultants. Further, their willingness to learn the lingo shows their commitment to understanding customers beyond the transactional level.
Process	HK follows its own recruiting methodology when screening and hiring new employees.	HK walks the talk, and it continually tests and refines its recruiting process and can apply lessons learned to recruiting for customers.
Culture	HK employee candidates participate in a group interview process and must complete what HK employees affectionately call "the gauntlet."	This screens employee candidates for cultural fit and gives them a sense of belonging through a "trial by fire," much as success in boot camp gives new Marines a sense of identity and pride.
Culture	HK hires people for their attitudes and behavior rather than their technical backgrounds. HK wants bright, youthful, energetic employ-	Like Southwest Airlines, Ritz-Carlton, and other exemplars of BD, they are more concerned with how people behave than what

	ees. They educate employees on the technology.	they know. Because they emphasize behavioral traits and outcomes in their hiring process, they get employees who are more likely to behave in ways that positively differentiate the company.
Culture	HK helps job seekers assess their skills, develop career plans, and find the right opportunities. They remain in touch after placements and behave as though they are the agents to the stars.	Rivals have tried to copy HK's "star agent" approach, but few show the long-term interest in placements that HK does. HK provides value-added career counseling and guidance on skill development that distinguishes HK in the eyes of candidates.
Culture and Process	HK hand-delivers paychecks to consultants every Friday, sometimes with bagels, donuts, or other goodies like HK mints or stress balls. Some rivals copy this behavior, but HK does it consistently.	Keeps recruiters in touch with consultants, gives consultants personal attention, enables recruiters to solve problems or reassess needs, and keeps HK close to customers. It shows a degree of caring unusual in the staffing industry and reflects the HK experience.
Culture and Process	HK offers a stock option plan for consultants. Consultants are temporary placements, not HK employees, so HK's stock option plan is unusual and unique in the industry.	Communicates a greater commitment to consultants/temporary placements and builds loyalty by demonstrating loyalty.
Culture and Process	HK screens its customers through a rigorous qualification process; it ensures that the customers it serves are the right fit for HK and its pool of candidates and consultants.	Seeking alignment in expectations and values shows that HK cares about the fit. It sets a higher standard, which all stakeholders value, and puts a greater premium on the HK experience.

(continues)

Table 11-1. (continued)

BD Driver	Behavioral Differentiator	Impact
Process	Through its proprietary PowerMatch™ process, HK offers customers flexible ways to recruit and deliver the right candidates and consultants as rapidly as possible.	Helps customers meet their staffing needs through an approach they prefer, rather than "one size fits all." Also, HK makes it as convenient as possible for customers, which communicates that HK cares more about customers' convenience than its own.
Leadership, Culture, and Process	HK invests heavily in training and education. Hall Kinion University offers a robust curriculum including online, self-study, classroom, and manager-delivered programs. New hires are expected to "teach back" what they have learned in their introductory programs when they return to their units.	Demonstrates a strong commitment to employees, reflects a learning culture and the HK experience, and communicates to customers that HK is staying sharp and keeping pace as the industry and customers' needs evolve. In the fast-paced technology arena, this is a strong behavioral message.
Leadership and Culture	HK cultivates a dynamic and youthful culture that is aligned with the dynamic and youthful technology industries it serves.	Reflects the values and interests of HK's employees; creates a sense of energy and excitement; engages the youthful techies who are drawn to technology companies, and creates a spirit of fun and adventure that is very different from traditional staffing companies.

vices group and managing partner of the firm's Office of the Chairmen. "If you are subservient, you're nothing but a vendor." Lee Hanson, a partner in the San Francisco office, elaborates: "Clients have to view you as their peer and partner, as opposed to somebody who only takes orders to fill a search. The transactional relationship is short lived. You have to follow their industry, really understand the dynamics of their business, and help them think

through their strategic decisions, especially regarding leadership talent. Sometimes, you have to push back and advocate the person or solution you know is right for them. Those are the long-term relationships you seek." From time to time, argues partner Emeric Lepoutre of the Paris office, you even have to turn down an assignment the client is trying to give you. "I try to give good advice," he says. "And the good advice may be, 'No, you don't need to find someone. You have the right person internally.' That has happened to me a few times, and the clients are astonished, but it really helps to build a confident relationship between us."[20] Moment by moment in client relationships, these are the kinds of attitudes and behaviors that distinguish H&S and its consultants.

> At Heidrick & Struggles, we have a simple vision inspiring everything we do. It is this: We help our clients build the best leadership teams in the world.
> —Piers Marmion, CEO, Heidrick & Struggles

It comes down to this: to behaviorally differentiate yourself, you must behave exceptionally well during *every* moment with clients. There are no time-outs or allowable lapses. You must wear your professionalism on your sleeve at *every* touch point and during *every* interaction. This is as fundamental as keeping your promises, which is another of those basic behaviors exceptional professionals do consistently: "When I have had the last interview," says Thord Thorstensson, a partner in Stockholm, "I discuss it with the client and the candidate and say when I will get back to them. And if I say Monday, then I call them on Monday. If I promise to call back on Tuesday at three o'clock, then I do that. This is extremely important. It very much helps build my relationships." The importance of this professional courtesy, really a commitment, seems self-evident, but it fails to happen a remarkable number of times with some consultants. Ignacio Perez, a partner in the Mexico City office, says that 80 percent of the candidates he encounters who have met with other search firms are not kept informed afterward: "Ignacio," they tell him, "Nobody informs me when I'm out after the offer closes. So you are making a difference. It really is a service you provide us."[21]

For Caroline Ballantine, making a moment-by-moment difference means always having your client top of mind. Based in Chicago, this senior partner never stops working for clients. "Whenever I meet someone in business or socially who I think would be a terrific fit for one of our clients," she said, "I make a mental note of them. Later, I will call the client and say, 'I met someone the other day who you should meet!' You always think about your clients, always have them top-of-mind and be tuned in to their needs, whether or not you are currently engaged in a search assignment for them." Bonnie Gwin, managing partner of H&S' Cleveland office, makes a difference by being available anytime her clients or candidates need her: "I have a special phone in my home that is a duplicate of my office phone. I will take calls at all hours of the night because, in some ways, my role is a bit like a doctor. In a sense, we're on call, and it's important for the health and well being of our clients and candidates. They have to know that they can reach me twenty-four/seven. Sometimes I'll pick up the phone at two o'clock on Saturday afternoon and spend an hour or two with a client. It can be hard to take time from my personal life, but my clients really appreciate it. They are paying us to do wonderful and long-lasting things for their organization and to be there when they need us, and I'm not going to let them down."[22]

In *The Trusted Advisor*, David Maister, Charles Green, and Robert Galford argue that professionals who become trusted advisors focus on clients rather than themselves; continually try to find new ways to be of greater service to clients; are motivated by doing the right things; and, among other things, are dedicated to helping clients with their issues.[23] Maister also likes to invoke the Golden Rule in describing the fundamental professional ethic: Serve others as you would like to be served. We encountered this simple principle at Southwest Airlines, too. And we heard it from a number of H&S partners. Thord Thorstensson said it simply: "Behave as you would like to be treated." Andy Talkington, the firm's global practice leader in chemicals and natural resources, said, "I serve clients as I would like myself served. If I were a client, how would I want to be treated? How would I want the other person to work for me? You become a good advocate and consultant for clients by jumping into their shoes as quickly as possible."[24] Fundamentally, then, the Golden Rule is a behavioral dictum, not just a homily about being a nice person.

> I know it sounds simple, but I keep saying follow the golden rule of service. Serve others as you yourself would like to be served.
>
> —Herb Kelleher

The attitudes and behaviors we have been describing are not rocket science. Most BD isn't. The difference at Heidrick & Struggles is that these attitudes and behaviors are part of the fabric of the organization. It's "how we do business around here. It's as ingrained as our partnership culture." New principals claim to sense these behaviors and partnership culture as early as during the interviewing process, when the tables are turned and their first experience with the firm is from a candidate's perspective. Once on board, they learn these fundamentals during an apprenticeship with seasoned veterans such as John Gardner and Gerry Roche, the latter of whom joined the firm in

1964. Nearly forty years later, this senior chairman is recognized by peers and clients as the "Recruiter of the Century," and is very active with global Fortune 100 boards and CEOs, simultaneously as search consultant, trusted advisor, and talent scout. Gardner is a frequent speaker on the issues of leadership and corporate governance and was recognized and profiled, for the third time, as one of the country's top executive recruiters in HarperCollins' *The New Career Makers*. He has also been featured as one of the search industry's top global search consultants in *The Global 200 Executive Recruiters,* a ranking compiled by executive search industry expert Nancy Garrison-Jenn.

Piers Marmion, chairman and chief executive of the global consultancy, attributes much of the firm's success to its partnership culture. "In any firm, the senior partners are responsible for sustaining the professionalism so critical to the firm's credibility and for modeling how to best serve clients by building lasting, trust-based relationships. Our firm is fortunate to have some of the most accomplished people in the industry who are extraordinarily generous in working with our junior consultants. Without that transfer of behaviors and learned code of conduct, our next generation of talent would be our last."[25]

Just Fire Me Today

One of the behaviors clients value most from professionals is their willingness to be candid, to speak the truth no matter how uncomfortable it might be. The senior executives who work with H&S especially value candor because many of them suffer from the captain-of-the-ship syndrome. Everyone else on the ship can go talk to the captain or some other officer if they have a problem or need some advice, but the captain has no one to talk to. That's why, as the old saying goes, it's lonely at the top. Many senior executives find it immensely valuable to have trusted advisors they can confide in—people who will challenge them, speak candidly, and warn them when they are about to make the wrong decision. It takes a lot of courage to confront CEOs and other senior executives. They did not reach their positions by being wilting lilies. Many are headstrong, confident, opinionated, and powerful. The smartest executives encourage dissent and are receptive to perspectives other than their own, but some directly or indirectly punish dissenters and send the signal that disagreeing with them can be, well, disagreeable. Yet even the toughest of these executives generally welcomes counsel from someone they trust and respect if that someone is willing to stand up to them and deliver even bad news candidly.

Although we met many partners in H&S who met these criteria, the person who most impressed us as candid with clients was Joie Gregor, a vice chairman of the firm and considered one of the top executive recruiters in the world. She told us:

> I think of myself as a problem solver, not as a search consultant. I look at everything I do as a business opportunity for my clients. Either they come to us or we go to them because of a perceived need, but it is never just about finding good candidates. That would be too transactional and short term. Instead, you should think of yourself as a partner in solving your client's problem. You are focusing on their strategic and tactical needs, you are thinking about how certain people will help them reposition and grow their company, and you feel compelled to help them achieve their overall business goals. Some days you have to be empathetic; other days you have to be tough as nails and say, "Look, if you persist in this direction, you're going to fail." Similarly, you have to be intellectually and emotionally honest with both clients and candidates about what is in their best interest.
>
> In this kind of trust-based relationship, you start by getting up every day with one mission: to solve your client's problems. You never lose sight of that goal. You have to genuinely care about them and their business. You have to be adamant about creating value and about shareholder value, and my clients know that I am. If you called my clients today, they would tell you that I get up every day genuinely caring about them as people, and that I care about the success of their organization. They damn well better get results because my credibility as a consultant is on the line every day. It is a dogged quest for excellence. As a result, I will tell clients if I think their business model or human capital strategy is off base. I will question them and re-question them and I'll continue to push really hard if I think they need it. At the end of the day, it is a collaborative process that strengthens their strategy and position. A client once remarked, "When you work with Joie on a particular issue or search, it can be a rather arduous experience. The process is not always comfortable because she is on you and on you and on you, guiding you to make the right decisions. However, in the final hurrah, when Joie says a person is good, that person is good. You can absolutely trust and respect the result."[26]

Michael Flagg, managing partner of H&S' Global Communications practice, also tells an interesting story about pushing back. "We had a client who gave us two weeks to solve a problem," he told us. "They said if we didn't solve it in two weeks they'd never work with us again. Our vice chairman asked me to handle it, so I dropped what I was doing, called the client's head of Human Resources and said, 'I'm ready to come out tomorrow and meet with the CEO and figure this out." He said I didn't need to come out and waste my time because we only had two weeks, and if I spent the next three or four days going back and forth to gather more data, I'd never make enough progress in two weeks not to get fired. So I said, 'Great. In that case, we'd prefer to get fired today." And he said, 'What do you mean, get fired today?' I said, 'Because there's absolutely no chance that I can make any progress in two weeks without talking to your executives, so why pretend? I'll just tell our vice chairman that this is over, and it's too bad. On the other hand, I'm willing to meet with your CEO anywhere. I want to meet with him and your entire management team one-on-one so that I can understand what you're looking for. Then I'll know if we can actually solve this problem in short order.' The guy was so frustrated he practically came through the phone to throw me out the window. Eventually, he said, 'Fine. You've got your two weeks. If you want to spend it that way, then spend it that way.' The good news is that, begrudgingly, everybody took the meetings. The problem was not solved in two weeks (it never could be), but we made significant progress, which gave the client the confidence that we could solve it and gave us the time to do it right. We later did resolve the issue to their delight. It's turned out to be a phenomenal relationship for us and them—but only because we insisted on *really* understanding what the CEO and the management team wanted."[27]

Visionaries of Total Human Capital Management

Historically, executive search firms have focused on helping clients acquire the leadership talent they need. If the client's question was, "How can we find the right top-caliber person to fill a key executive vacancy?" then firms like H&S could provide the answer. However, if clients needed to fill a *temporary* rather than permanent vacancy, benchmark their leadership team against other leaders in their industry, assess their team's strengths and weaknesses, or develop their executives through coaching and education, then traditional search firms had only ad hoc solutions at best. H&S set out to redefine itself and its relationship with clients by developing the capability to meet all these human capital needs. The message H&S is sending to clients is that the firm is committed to helping them build the finest leadership teams in the world and doing it not only through search but also through interim placement, assessment, coaching, team building, and education. H&S' view of its extended mission is shown in Figure 11-6.

One of the people who helped craft this vision is senior managing partner Wes Richards, who is as much at home behind a guitar and a microphone as he is in front of clients. Richards is responsible for the firm's growing lead-

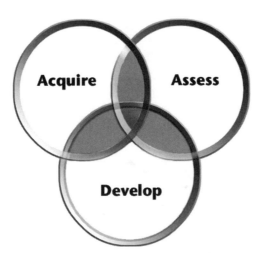

Figure 11-6. Heidrick & Struggles' Suite of Services. Viewing itself as a visionary of total human capital management, H&S helps clients acquire, assess, and develop their leadership talent.

ership services practice, and he feels as passionate about that as he does playing bass guitar with The Staff, H&S' own rock-and-roll band. Richards told us:

> Competitive advantage comes primarily from the people a company has. The difference between leading an industry or lagging it has much more to do with the quality of your leadership talent than any other factor. So we are finding that companies are increasingly thinking about their leadership pipeline. They're thinking about their succession planning and how they're developing leadership talent. They're thinking about executive education, which normally stops once executives pass the managerial level. But when you are fighting a war for talent, developing your senior people is not optional; it's mandatory. Companies are thinking about their talent gaps, and they're asking themselves whether they need a top-notch person to come in for a couple of years to help them with a problem or whether they need a permanent solution. They're asking whether they have the right people on their leadership teams and what they can do to ensure that their leaders across the board are high performing.
>
> Though executive search is and always will be the foundation of our service to clients, we have redefined ourselves in much the same way IBM did when they said, "We're not in the typewriter business; we're

in the office automation business." We are telling clients now that the answer to their leadership talent problem *may* be to search for the finest person available to take a critical position. Or it may be to coach and develop someone in place. Or to do a systematic assessment of the entire leadership team so they know where they have strengths to leverage and weaknesses to overcome. We are looking very broadly at how we can help clients maximize their leadership talent, not just through search but through a full spectrum of solutions including coaching, education, team building, assessment, and interim placement. We have always been asked to do some coaching and consulting, and like any good search firm we stepped up and helped clients when we could, but we weren't always best qualified to provide the kind of help they needed. Now we are.[28]

No other executive search firm now offers the comprehensive array of leadership services H&S offers. Of course, these are product differentiators, not behavioral differentiators. But it is easy to see how they translate into behavioral differences. As CEO Piers Marmion observes, "For much of its history, executive search has been transactional in nature. Relationship building and key account management were primarily the purview of management consulting firms and advertising agencies. But that has been changing in recent years. And we are eager to lead the way as we move toward offering advisory services rather than transactional assignments. The benefits that accrue to our clients—and to us—by evolving into a relationship-focused culture are increasingly apparent."[29] When consultants are trying to help clients build their leadership teams using a variety of capabilities, rather than focusing on selling and executing individual searches, they behave quite differently:

▲ They are focused not just on search needs but on the broad spectrum of ways clients can acquire, assess, and develop their leadership talent.
▲ They are more inclined to think of themselves as partners and consultants to clients than as transactors seeking to close a deal.
▲ They take a longer and deeper review of the client's challenges and opportunities.
▲ They have more ways to help clients so they don't view every problem as a search need or every solution as the acquisition of talent. Search firms without H&S' broad capabilities in human capital management are likely to wield search as a hammer and perceive every client need as a nail. (Here, we are borrowing psychologist Abraham Maslow's famous pronouncement: "To the man who only has a hammer in the toolkit, every problem looks like a nail.")

▲ They can engage in more robust dialogues with clients about talent development and thus help clients think through human capital needs from diverse perspectives.

Clients perceive these behaviors as far less transactional and more consultative. It helps H&S consultants truly put their clients' interests first because they offer far more than search alone, and this client-facing behavior is an enormous differentiator.

Caring as a Way of Being

We began this section by arguing that what differentiates Heidrick & Struggles from its rivals is the professionalism and quality of its consultants and the extraordinary ways in which they treat clients. Underlying their differentiating behaviors is caring: They genuinely care about meeting and exceeding clients' expectations; they genuinely care about providing the best, long-term solution for clients; and they genuinely care about their clients' businesses. For Gerry Roche, caring is a very personal commitment: "I will not allow you to be unhappy with us," he tells clients. "And I'll see that you are not." For Roche, it is this resolute attitude that differentiates H&S from other search firms. "It's not a policy; it's an attitude. Our consultants are essentially very caring people. They follow through. They persevere, and they put the client first always. When clients call, we're there, and when clients bleed, we bleed with them. We are in the human capital business, and that business is about human beings. Our people understand that they have obligations and responsibilities to be there when clients need them and to use their good judgment to help."[30]

Bonnie Gwin is one of those consultants who feel a strong sense of responsibility: "In every assignment, one of the things I think about is that I'm changing somebody's life. This isn't just about understanding a client's needs and finding qualified candidates. This is a very complex process involving people, and when all is said and done, I will have played a major role in changing somebody's life, always hopefully for the better." Emeric Lepoutre calls it "a permanent client-care focus." After candidates accept a job offer, they often call to thank him, and Lepoutre says, "Please don't thank me. But call me in a year or two and tell me you're still happy." His hope, he says, is that they will say, "Thanks to Heidrick, I'm a different man or woman, and I have grown professionally." For Michael Flagg, caring means overdelivering: "We want to make sure we give the client both advice and candidates that are better than they deserve. This may sound odd, but it's the truth. Your goal is not to get the person they could have gotten on their own. Your goal is to find someone who truly is far better than the opportunity or situation warrants."[31]

This kind of passion for the work and caring for the client is not manufactured every morning when these consultants get out of bed. It is deeply engrained and is one reason they were attracted to H&S in the first place. We asked them what it took to be successful in this profession. Daan de Roos, a partner in the Amsterdam office, said, "You have to have a genuine interest in the people you work with, and that's something you can't fake. It makes a big difference in how you treat clients when you are enthusiastic, excited, and genuinely interested in them and their business." Denise Studi, a partner in the Zurich office, agreed: "You have to love your job, but you must have a greater love for people to be successful as a recruiter."[32] That seemed to be the universal sentiment among H&S consultants. The intrinsic rewards that come from serving clients exceptionally well make the job worthwhile, and now and then unexpected things happen with clients that form memorable experiences for them and the consultant. Caroline Ballantine told us this story about having the right solution for a client and persisting because it was the right solution—and later discovering an unexpected outcome from the assignment:

> Our client's organization was launching a new line of business that would require hiring a number of experienced people from outside their company's core industry. We helped them hire the first executive. Then the first executive was in charge of hiring the next. So our "new" client (formerly a candidate) called me to do the search, which was difficult for a variety of reasons. During the search, I met the perfect person. She was bright and had everything it takes to be successful, but she was a little "off."
>
> I called my client and said, "Let me use a wild card, because she's different but perfect for the role." He agreed to see her so I wrote an e-mail to him and said, "Jane Jones is a diamond in the rough, but she's fabulous." I didn't want him to meet this woman with weird hair and wacky clothes and say, "Caroline, are you crazy?" The phone rang right away, and he didn't even say who he was. The first words out of his mouth were, "How rough?" I said, "Although she first appears as somewhat unsophisticated, she's got a lot of substance. She gets what you are trying to do with your business. She's absolutely wonderful, and you are going to love her." He agreed to see her and wound up hiring her.

Several weeks later he called me and said, "Tell her how to dress. She can't dress this way." I said, "Give her two more weeks because she's smart. She will figure it out. If necessary, I'll do a little coaching." I called him back two weeks later and asked, "How is it going?" He replied, "You know, she cut her hair and got a more appropriate wardrobe. Now she fits in. And you were right, she is perfect for the job." Despite his initial misgivings, Jane was hugely successful in the position, and, as fate would have it, they later married each other.[33]

While our client relationships frequently start at the top, it is by building broader and deeper client relationships that we can fully leverage our access and influence. True client partnerships begin as we develop intimate knowledge of their business and culture over a period of time. Then, we can tailor our counsel and services to their specific needs, creating value for them and a more dependable revenue stream for us.
—Piers Marmion, CEO, Heidrick & Struggles

In the executive search business, where there is an intense focus on people, it is perhaps no surprise that H&S would attract consultants who are outgoing, sociable, and people oriented. But there is more to it than having employees with good interpersonal skills and a natural interest in people. As we noted in Chapter 9, creating and sustaining BD requires inspired leadership, a supportive culture, and processes that institutionalize exceptional behavior. H&S' culture is shaped by the collective behavior of senior partners who exemplify the kind of caring, client commitment, and willingness to go the extra mile that developing consultants learn to adopt. They reinforce exceptional behavior in the coaching and mentoring they do, the wisdom they share when they work with other consultants on assignments, and the stories they tell in office meetings and social gatherings. One such story concerns Bill Paley, the legendary former head of CBS. Over a 20-year period, Gerry Roche did nearly ninety searches for CBS and got to know Bill Paley and his wife, Babe, very well.

Babe was a beautiful and fine person, and a famous Boston socialite. If you got Babe Paley to your party, it was automatically a big success. Anyway, Babe died. Months later, Bill came to me with tears in his eyes and said, "I don't know what I'm going to do." She was really the cen-

ter of his life, and he was still grieving over her loss. But he also had a practical problem. In his position, he still had to do a lot of entertaining, and Babe had always been the hostess of the parties at their Long Island home. He asked me if I could find him a hostess. So I went back to my staff and said, "I've never been asked to search for a hostess before. I don't know if this is the kind of business we're in, but CBS is a valued client. Bill is one of the most important men in the world, and he has a need. We went to work and got him the head of the American Airlines Admiral's Club. She loved the job, and he thought she was terrific. Everything went swimmingly. I still look back on that and believe it was one of the most important searches I ever did for Bill Paley.[34]

Challenges for Readers

1. Fundamental to Hall Kinion's culture is a "How can we?" attitude. That attitude helps drive BD by encouraging employees to be creative and to think of solutions instead of barriers and reasons why something can't be done. What are the underlying behavior attitudes in your company?
2. Hall Kinion strives to create a "Hall Kinion experience" for candidates, consultants, and customers. They are self-conscious about their behaviors and the effects of their behaviors on customers. What kind of experience do your customers have when they work with you? Is that experience uniquely positive in any way? Does that experience differentiate you from your competitors? If not, how could you recraft your customers' experiences so they do differentiate you?
3. At Heidrick & Struggles, behavioral differentiation occurs in the moment-by-moment differences their consultants make. We cited a number of the things H&S consultants do to make a difference. Reflect on your own company. What do your people do, moment by moment, to make a difference with customers?
4. H&S has a number of senior partners like Gerry Roche and John Gardner who model exceptional behaviors for younger consultants. Their collective behavior forms the culture of H&S, and that culture helps ensure that BD is consistent and sustainable across the world. How do your senior people coach and mentor young people and help reinforce and sustain superior behaviors toward customers?
5. Ultimately, BD is about caring. If you don't care, you won't go out of your way to treat customers exceptionally well. When you don't care, it's just a job. Do your employees care? How does your culture reinforce caring? How do your leaders model caring and inspire others to care?

Endnotes

1. Judy Semas, "Hall Kinion's Brenda Hall: Success for her seems more than temporary," *The Business Journal* (November 8, 1993).
2. Brenda Rhodes interview with Laurie Voss (March 14, 2002).
3. Jeffrey Neal interview with Laurie Voss (2001/2002).
4. Ibid.
5. Ibid.
6. Ibid.
7. Ibid.
8. www.hallkinion.com/ctalent/ctalent.html (December 13, 2001).
9. Jeff Glickman interview with Laurie Voss (May 1, 2002).
10. Rhodes, op cit.
11. Neal, op cit.
12. Ibid.
13. Ibid.
14. Ibid.
15. Catie Fitzgerald memo to Terry Bacon (March 29, 2002).
16. Mark Hulbert, "Within Companies, Too, Education Proves Its Value," *The New York Times on the Web,* http://www. nytimes.com/2002/03/31/ business/yourmoney/31STRA. html (March 31, 2002).
17. Rita Hazell personal communication with Laurie Voss (May 1, 2002).
18. Glickman, op cit.
19. Heidrick & Struggles Web site, http://www.heidrick.com/ about_us.htm (June 9, 2002).
20. John Gardner, Lee Hanson, and Emeric Lepoutre interviews with Meredith Ashby and Stephen Miles (April 2002).
21. Thord Thorstensson and Ignacio Perez interviews with Meredith Ashby and Stephen Miles (April 2002).
22. Caroline Ballantine and Bonnie Gwin interviews with Meredith Ashby and Stephen Miles (April 2002).
23. David H. Maister, Charles H. Green, and Robert M. Galford, *The Trusted Advisor* (New York: The Free Press, 2000), pp. 13–14.
24. Thorstensson and Talkington interviews with Meredith Ashby and Stephen Miles, op cit.
25. Piers Marmion interview with Meredith Ashby (June 2002).
26. Joie Gregor interview with Meredith Ashby and Stephen Miles (April 2002).
27. Michael Flagg interview with Meredith Ashby and Stephen Miles (April 2002).

28. Wes Richards interview with Meredith Ashby and Stephen Miles (April 2002).
29. Piers Marmion presentation at Lehman Brothers Global Services Conference (May 9, 2002).
30. Roche, op cit.
31. Gwin, Lepoutre, and Flagg, op cit.
32. Daan de Roos and Denise Studi interviews with Meredith Ashby and Stephen Miles (April 2002).
33. Gwin, op cit.
34. Roche, op cit.

CREATING AND SUSTAINING BEHAVIORAL DIFFERENTIATION

Will is the master of the world. Those who want something, those who know what they want, even those who want nothing, but want it badly, govern the world.

—Ferdinand Brunetière

Rhetoric is frequently an essential first step toward taking action. But just talking about what to do isn't enough. Nor is planning for the future enough to produce the future. Something has to get done, and someone has to do it.

—Jeffrey Pfeffer and Robert I. Sutton, *The Knowing-Doing Gap*

One of the dangers of business books that discuss real companies is that the exemplary companies cited may later falter, which can appear to disprove the authors' theses. As many pundits have pointed out, this occurred most famously following the 1984 publication of *In Search of Excellence* by Thomas J. Peters and Robert H. Waterman, Jr., when some of the excellent companies they wrote about later turned in less-than-excellent results. Another book, *Lessons from the Top: The Search for America's Best Business Leaders,* published in 1999 by Thomas J. Neff and James M. Citrin, included a section on Ken Lay and Enron in which the authors praised how Lay "aggressively moved Enron into nonregulated businesses."[1] We can imagine how the authors must have felt when Enron collapsed in 2001 because of its questionable moves into nonregulated businesses.

This book could suffer the same fate. One of our exemplars of BD is Ritz-Carlton. However, a story published on April 8, 2002, in the *Wall Street Journal* suggested that the Ritz-Carlton's legendary service may be declining at some properties as the luxury hotel chain expands, perhaps too rapidly (although a first-person perspective by Paul Hemp in the June 2002 *Harvard Business Review* suggests otherwise). Even in the best of companies, service may sometimes fall below the exceptional standard the companies have set. No doubt there are customers who have had a bad experience with Southwest Airlines or were not well treated (at least in their view) by Men's Wearhouse—two of our other exemplars of BD. But let's be fair. It is impossible to *satisfy* everyone all the time, much less *delight* them all the time. Behavioral differentiation is not easy to establish in the first place, and it's much more difficult to sustain. Why? Because, as the 1988 David Mamet film *Things Change* so humorously illustrated, things change.

As we write this book, Ritz-Carlton, Volvo, Men's Wearhouse, Southwest Airlines, EMC, Harley Davidson, and the other companies we profiled do exemplify the concept of behavioral differentiation. However, in the future, under different business conditions, with different leaders, even these stalwarts of behavioral differentiation may become merely average. It is not easy to sustain BD. The tendency is to regress toward the middle of the behavioral spectrum because that's where most people naturally behave. Companies are collections of individuals, each of whom will *normally* treat customers in ways that reflect his or her *normal* behavior. Some of those individuals will excel at customer handling because they are naturally inclined to treat people well, and some won't. Consequently, sustaining BD throughout a large organization of people requires inspired leadership, a strong culture that reinforces differentiating behavior internally and externally, and processes that maintain and reward exceptional behavior. There must be an *organizing principle* at work in a company that motivates exceptional behavior toward customers and an infrastructure that normalizes those behaviors, and this is not easy to create, much less maintain over a long period under changing leadership. Yet Harley-Davidson has sustained its symbolic BD for nearly a century; Heidrick & Struggles has done it for half that. Southwest Airlines, Ritz-Carlton, and Men's Wearhouse have sustained it since the 1970s. What do these companies teach us?

Lessons Learned from Companies That Exemplify BD

The most important lesson we learn from companies like Men's Wearhouse, SAS, Volvo, and Southwest Airlines is that in exemplary companies

BD is not a passing fancy but a deeply rooted idea. It's one of the governing principles of the organization, and it's driven by the leaders' or founders' convictions about how to treat employees, customers, and other stakeholders. In these exemplary companies, BD is not a program imposed by a new CEO or the head of customer service; it's a set of core beliefs about how to behave. Those beliefs are embraced at all levels of the organization: They are used to screen candidate employees; they are taught in introductory training programs and corporate universities; they are reinforced in regular meetings of employees; and they are modeled by the organization's leaders.

We must become the change we want to see.

—Ghandi

Moreover, in a remarkable number of our exemplary companies, the leaders act like servant leaders. It's George Zimmer's favored philosophy, and you can still find him waiting on customers and mentoring the next generations of leaders at Men's Wearhouse. Herb Kelleher still loads baggage at Southwest Airlines. Go to a Harley-Davidson rally, and you are likely to run into Jeffrey Bleustein (the CEO) or Willie G. Davidson. If you had flown SAS while Jan Carlzon was still there, he might have checked you in for your flight or welcomed you on board the airplane. These are not ivory tower leaders. They understand that they can't mandate BD; they have to live it themselves, and that means rolling up their sleeves and working alongside employees to serve customers. In an article for *Fast Company*, Alan M. Webber sums it up well: "Where do you start? You start with a philosophy, and the rest follows from that. If you believe in training and developing people, you don't necessarily need a huge training budget. You begin by imparting knowledge in various ways—by holding meetings, by talking to people, by coaching them, by mentoring them. If you believe in reciprocal commitments, you start by building those commitments with the people you work with. If you believe in information sharing, you share information with the people you have the most contact with. In other words, you begin in your immediate sphere of influence. You start with your own behavior."[2]

For Horst Schulze, the deeply rooted idea was that Ritz-Carlton is distinguished by ladies and gentlemen serving ladies and gentlemen. A consummate gentleman, he embodied that philosophy himself and modeled it for others. For Herb Kelleher, the core idea was getting people to their destination when they want to go, getting them there on time, and making it enjoyable. He drove that concept with persistence and a class clown's appreciation of the value of levity. For George Zimmer the core idea was selling suits with soul. An iconoclast from birth, he turned the business model of his chosen indus-

try on its head and treated his employees as though they were the most important people in his business. Each of these leaders had not only a behavioral principle that would distinguish them from their rivals but also the *will* to drive that principle through the fabric of the organizations they led. The leaders' will *in action* is the fundamental difference between companies that know what to do and do it and those who know what to do but don't. Here are some other lessons learned from companies that exemplify BD:

▲ You have to be thoughtful about your behavior. It becomes an important element of corporate strategy as well as the basis for decisions you make about the people you hire, the jobs you create, the training and education you provide, the goals and expectations you set, the responsibilities and authorities you delegate, the rewards and recognition you give, and the processes you create for running the business on a day-to-day and moment-by-moment basis. For example, SAS and Ritz-Carlton identified every customer touch point and thought about how to behave at those touch points to serve customers exceptionally well and build a behavioral advantage. Ritz-Carlton specified those behaviors in its Gold Standards (shown in Figure 5-1) and reinforces them in daily lineups of employees. Men's Wearhouse promoted a clinical psychologist and specialist in human behavior to one of its most important executive positions: Executive Vice President for Store Operations.

▲ You have to invest more in employee education and development than your competitors do. The exemplars of BD spend an extraordinary amount of time and money training, educating, and coaching employees on their behavior toward customers. As we have observed throughout this book, companies like Southwest Airlines, Ritz-Carlton, Hall Kinion, and Men's Wearhouse invariably spend more to develop their people than their rivals do. The corporate universities at Ritz-Carlton, Southwest Airlines, Hall Kinion, and Men's Wearhouse are among the finest in corporate America.

▲ Along with a strong commitment to education, you have to build systems and processes that make the exceptional treatment of customers routine. These systems include policies for interacting with customers, decision rules (such as how to handle returns) that enable employees to make decisions that will delight customers, and performance expectations that result in exceptional treatment of customers. EMC's rapid-escalation protocols, for instance, minimize downtime for customers' systems and behaviorally differentiate EMC.

▲ You have to enable people who are on the front line with customers to make the decisions that will result in extraordinary behavior, which means that you have to trust frontline employees. Clearly, this level of trust does not come automatically. To build high trust in their employees, exemplary companies like Heidrick & Struggles, Hall Kinion, and Southwest Airlines screen job candidates carefully, generally with teams of employees doing the screening. Then they give new hires a comprehensive program of orientation and education. They set very high expectations, provide ongoing coaching and reinforcement of core behavioral principles, and then monitor customer satisfaction closely. Obviously, other companies also screen candidates, train new hires, and monitor customer satisfaction. However, in the exemplary companies these functions are carried out with an almost religious conviction. Companies on the negative end of the behavioral spectrum often do not trust employees or customers. They offer less training, have punitive policies (designed to keep employees in line and minimize customer misbehavior), and use managers and supervisors as police. It is important to bear in mind what Benjamin Schneider and David E. Bowen observed: "Workers are the service organization to the customers they serve."[3] When they feel trusted and empowered, positive BD is possible; when they feel distrusted and powerless, the only BD you may get is negative.

▲ You have to create a culture that dignifies and respects the individual. We found it remarkable, although not surprising, that the companies that behaviorally differentiate themselves with customers also behaviorally differentiate themselves as employers. They have lower turnover and higher employee satisfaction scores than their competitors. They are consistently ranked among the best places to work. Since 1997, for instance, Southwest has been among the top five in *Fortune's* list of the "Best Companies to Work For in America" four times. Men's Wearhouse has made *Fortune's* list three times in the last three years. *Forbes* also named it one of the "Best Big Companies in America" three times in a row. BD begins at home. You differentiate yourself as an employer first. You create a workplace that elevates employees' self-esteem and makes it a rewarding place to work. That becomes the foundation for expecting and getting extraordinary behaviors from your employees.

▲ You create reinforcing mythologies around differentiated behaviors toward customers. You turn your behavioral superstars into heroes and tell stories about them in company e-mails, newsletters, meetings, awards ceremonies, and other forms of communication and social interaction. We felt that of all the companies we studied, Ritz-Carlton and EMC did the best job of this, but all of them found ways to tell stories about exceptional treatment customers received and the people who treated them that way.

▲ You have to think like the customer and then craft the kinds of customer experiences you would want if you were the customer. In many of our interviews with people in exemplary companies, we heard a similar version of the Golden Rule: *Serve customers as you would like to be served.* Maybe it is as simple as this simple rule, yet we have noted throughout this book that knowing what to do is not the same as doing it, and that most companies never realize the full potential of this principle. Herb Kelleher understood both the simplicity of the concept and the fact that most companies fail to do it. "You want them to get off the plane," he said, "with the feeling that they were welcome, that they enjoyed great hospitality, that they were, perhaps, entertained. You want it to be a warm event in their lives, so that they will come back. And that's the hardest thing for a competitor to emulate."

Good players are always looking for ways to make their pieces as active as possible. Knights need to find advanced support points, Bishops need open diagonals, and open files must be created for your Rooks.
—Jeremy Silman, *The Complete Book of Chess Mastery*

The Secret to Creating and Sustaining Behavioral Differentiation

What is the secret to creating and sustaining behavioral differentiation? It's just this: *You have to manage your customers' experiences from start to finish. You have to think about what they are experiencing at every touch point and then design interactions that surpass what they experience when they interact with your competitors.* For your company to achieve this, you may need the operational discipline of an EMC or the strong service-oriented culture of a Ritz-Carlton. You may need the creativity and willingness to take risks that Kim Hansen showed at General American Telecom, and the commitment to employee training and education we saw at Southwest Airlines, Hall Kinion, and Men's Wearhouse—or the professionalism and disciplined mentoring of a Heidrick & Struggles.

It takes *skill* and *will* to create and sustain BD. Both are important, but without the will, the skill won't matter. So, although training and education are crucial, simply training people to behave well won't make a lasting difference in how they treat customers. Behavioral differentiation does not happen serendipitously. It must be led. It won't happen if leaders pay only lip service to it, and it won't happen if leaders don't walk the talk themselves. It won't happen with signs and slogans alone. It requires a constant infusion of energy, focus, and direction from the leadership of the organization. In Chapter 9 we wrote about the three engines that drive BD: leadership, culture, and processes. To behaviorally differentiate yourself from your competitors, you need all three of these engines running smoothly.

We suspect that many leaders understand this but are unable to overcome the inertia of a culture in which people just do what it takes to get the job done or to surmount the resistance of entrenched managers who are too focused on internal matters to grasp and commit to behavioral differentiation as a way of being. We also suspect that many leaders themselves don't get it. What makes most companies common and undistinguished is that it's easy to become distracted by the day-to-day problems, the immediacy of the telephone ringing, and the urgency of yet another meeting to attend. Gustav Metzman, who was once president of the New York Central Railroad, observed how the tyranny of the here and now prevents us from doing what we really should be doing to build the future: "Most business men generally are so busy coping with immediate and piecemeal matters that there is a lamentable tendency to let the long run or future take care of itself. We often are so busy putting out fires, so to speak, that we find it difficult to do the planning that would prevent those fires from occurring in the first place. As a prominent educator has expressed it, Americans generally spend so much time on things that are urgent that we have none left to spend on those that are important."[4]

To create or increase BD in your company, then, you need to avoid being sidetracked by the minutiae and distractions of the day-to-day business life. If you do not behaviorally differentiate yourself now, then a change program to develop BD is likely to require a significant effort, in part because behavioral changes are difficult and in part because the behaviors you may need to change are ubiquitous, involving not only direct interactions between your employees and your customers but also every indirect touch point. In *At America's Service,* Karl Albrecht observed: "When the customer sees an advertisement for your business, that's a moment of truth; it creates an impression. Driving by your facility is, for the customer, a moment of truth. Entering a parking lot, walking into a lobby and getting an impression of the place, receiving a bill or a statement in the mail, listening to a recorded voice on the telephone, getting a package home and opening it, all of these are events that lead to an impression of your service. The sum total of all of the possible moments of truth your customers experience, both human and nonhuman, becomes your service image."[5] Albrecht is focusing on customer service, but it should be clear that his argument extends to the overall behavioral impression your company creates.

It's important to keep in mind that you cannot avoid giving behavioral impressions to customers. You are always signifying by your behavior that you are either distinctly better than your competitors, or no different from your competitors, or distinctly worse than your competitors. Whether you like it or not, customers are always coming to one of those three conclusions about you. If you choose to ignore behavior as a potential source of competitive advantage, then at best you are likely to fall into the bland, undifferentiated middle hump of the behavioral bell curve (see Figure 3-1), and you will be outdistanced by your competitors who do differentiate themselves behaviorally. At worst, you will lose customers by falling into the negatively differentiated left side of Figure 3-1. Or you can be thoughtful and strategic about your behavior toward employees, customers, and other stakeholder groups and use behavior to differentiate yourself and gain competitive advantage. The choice is yours.

Why You Should Care About Behavioral Differentiation

If we take the most uncomplicated look at business, we see that business leaders can really manage only three things: the products or services they produce; what they charge for those products or services, which is a function of the ability to control costs; and how they behave toward customers. Everything else in business management is a function of these three things: *products, price,* and *behavior.*

Products

Businesses devote considerable time and attention to *what* they produce and *how* they produce and distribute it. Companies normally strive to differentiate themselves on one or more of these functions of business management: innovation, product/ service design, production, distribution, marketing & sales, or the design of after-sales service systems. Although these are reasonable avenues for differentiation, competitors with the resources and will to copy them can easily do so. In the highly competitive and entropic markets most companies face today, product and service differentiation has a short half-life. You can perhaps gain some temporary advantages through innovation, but your competitors will be motivated to eliminate those advantages as quickly as possible.

Price

Price can differentiate you if your products cannot. However, to sustain price as a competitive advantage you must have the internal systems and external controls necessary to remain the low-price leader. Your competitors will envy your cost controls and will try to emulate them, so you may have to beat down costs relentlessly. Wal-Mart has succeeded thus far, but there are signs that their strategy is weakening. To keep costs down, they have had to reduce the number of employees in their stores, and some employees have filed lawsuits contending that Wal-Mart is forcing them to work off the clock.[6] Already, customers are feeling the effects of these issues. It's harder to get service in a Wal-Mart these days. Employees no longer abide by Sam's 10-foot rule. If Wal-Mart persists in a low-price strategy as its primary means of differentiation, the company will lose the behavioral advantages it enjoyed in the past.

Behavior

Finally, behavior can be a powerful differentiator if product and price are undifferentiating. In other words, if your products are similar to your competitors' products and you charge about the same amount, then superior behavior can be a powerful differentiator. However, if a competitor offers a superior product on the market, then the effect of behavior will be diminished. If price is not a barrier, customers will prefer to buy the superior product. If the superior product costs considerably more, then customers will weigh the benefits of the superior product and determine whether the price tradeoff is worth it. However, when product and price are relatively equal in the customer's mind, then behavior becomes the strongest differentiator.

Today, especially in mature industries and markets, the competing products are very similar and the prices being charged are usually close to the mean. Any imbalances in the function or quality of competing products tend to be eliminated quickly, and differences in price tend to evaporate as competitors learn what their rivals are charging and adjust their pricing accordingly. Consequently, behavior is playing a greater and greater role in how customers make decisions. When they can get essentially the same products or services at essentially the same prices, then they will choose to work with the suppliers whose behavior toward them is most positive.

You should care about behavioral differentiation because it is an aspect of your business that you can manage. You *can* behave in ways that enable you to build competitive advantage. You should care about behavioral differentiation because if your competitors are outbehaving you, then you are losing business you should not be losing. You should care about it because it is an excellent source of sustainable advantage and because it can help you build greater customer loyalty and market share. In this era of hypercompetitive markets and increasing competition, behavioral differentiation may be the best opportunity you have to win more business.

> The chessboard is the world; the pieces are the phenomenon of the universe; the rules of the game are what we call the laws of nature. The player on the other side is hidden from us. We know that his play is always fair, just, and patient. But also we know, to our cost, that he never overlooks a mistake, or makes the smallest allowance for ignorance.
>
> —Thomas Henry Huxley

Challenges for Readers

1. To what extent does your organization think about behavior as an element of competitive strategy? Are you self-conscious about your behavior toward customers, employees, suppliers, partners, and other stakeholders? Are you using behavior as a competitive tool now? What more could you do to make behavior a source of competitive advantage?
2. The "C" level executives in a company normally include the CEO (chief executive officer), COO (chief operating officer), and CFO (chief financial officer). Many companies today also have a CIO (chief information officer), CTO (chief technology officer), or CLO (chief learning officer). What about a chief behavior officer (CBO)? Although we don't want to be accused of proliferating the C's, behavior is an increasingly important source of competitive advantage. Who in an organization should have oversight for behavior?
3. Review our list of lessons learned from the companies that exemplify BD. How does your organization compare to them? Do you have a governing principle that drives BD? Are you thoughtful about your behavior? Do you invest more in education and training than your rivals do? Do you have systems and processes that promote and support exceptional behavior? Do you give your frontline people the authority and responsibility to behave exceptionally? Do you have a culture that dignifies and respects employees? Do you tell stories about your behavioral heroes? Do you explicitly follow the Golden Rule? If your answers to any of these questions is no, then what can you do about it?

4. We have argued that you should care about behavioral differentiation because it can have a profound effect on your business and is a great source of competitive advantage. Do you care?

Endnotes

1. Thomas J. Neff and James M. Citrin, *Lessons from the Top: The Search for America's Best Business Leaders* (New York: Currency Doubleday, 1999), p. 217.
2. Alan M. Webber, "Danger: Toxic Company," *Fast Company,* www.fastcompany.com/online/19/toxic.html (May 20, 2002).
3. Benjamin Schneider and David E. Bowen, *Winning the Service Game* (Boston: Harvard Business School Press, 1995), p. 237.
4. Gustav Metzman, quoted in Ted Goodman, ed., *The Forbes Book of Business Quotations: Thoughts on the Business of Life* (New York: Black Dog & Leventhal Publishers, 1997), p. 652.
5. Karl Albrecht, *At America's Service* (Homewood, Ill.: Dow Jones-Irwin, 1988), p. 27.
6. Steven Greenhouse, "Suits Say Wal-Mart Forces Workers to Toil Off the Clock," *The New York Times,* www.nytimes.com/2002/06/25/national/25WALM.html?todaysheadlines (June 25, 2002).

Index